Chevelle

USED PARTS BUYERS GUIDE

1964-1972

Paul Herd

PAH PUBLISHING

All rights reserved. With the exception of quoting brief passages for the purposes of review, no part of this publication may reproduced without the prior permission from the publisher.

The information in this book is true and complete to the best of our knowledge. All recommendations and procedures are made without any guarantee on part of the author or publisher who also disclaims any liability incurred in connection with the use of this data or any specific details.

We recognize that words, model names and designations, for example, mentioned herein are the property of the trademark holder. We use them for identification purposes only. This is not an official GM publication.

All drawings and illustrations in this book are the copyrighted property of General Motors and they are reproduced under license for General Motors Corp.

PAH Publishing 711 Hillcrest St. Monett, MO 65708

Printed and bounded in the United States of America

© Paul Herd 2020

First published by MBI in 1999 under title of Chevrolet Part Interchange Manual 1959-1970

Second publishing Used Parts Buyers Guide 1964-1977 Chevelle Parts Interchange. By PAH Publishing

Chevelle Used Parts Buyers Guide, 1964-1972/

Paul Herd

p. cm.

Includes index

ISBN: 978-17350743-8-2

1. Chevrolet Car Parts Catalogs. 2.Chevelle-Parts Catalog. 1 Title 2020

Cover: Emblems form Chevelles

Contents

Acknowledgments..4
Preface...4
Introduction..5
Chapter 1 Engines..11
Chapter 2 Fuel Systems...30
Chapter 3 Oiling and Cooling Systems....................................55
Chapter 4 Exhaust Systems...65
Chapter 5 Transmissions...69
Chapter 6 Frame, Suspension and Steerin.............................85
Chapter 7 Drive Shafts and Rear Axles.................................112
Chapter 8 Brakes...121
Chapter 9 Electrical Systems..132
Chapter 10 Wheels, and Trim Rings.....................................179
Chapter 11 Sheet Metal...189
Chapter 12 Grilles and Bumpers...209
Chapter 13 Trim and Mouldings...216
Chapter 14 Glass and Mirrors...224
Chapter 15 Emblems and Nameplate..................................236
Chapter 16 Interior..256
Index..280

Acknowledgments

This book would not have been possible without the assistance of the following individuals: Melissa Carman and Nancy Finey of Chevrolet Public Relations who gracefully provided the original model photos; very special thanks to Barbara Hillick and all those at YEAR ONE, who went out of their way to provide additional photos of reproduction parts. And to Classic Industries who supplied some of the replacement and reproduction parts that were used in this book Also thanks to Ed Witte for digging out parts to allow me to photograph them. A special thank you to those that gave me press passes to get into the many car show, and the owners who allowed me to photograph their cars and the many dealers that allowed me to photograph the parts at swap meets. And finally, but certainly not least Daniel B. Dryke and others at STG for giving me license to use GM illustrations.

Preface

The Chevelle SS Super Sport may not take the honors of being the first muscle car it does, however, take the honor of America's favorite muscle car. More Chevelle SS were sold than GTO's or any model in its class.

Chevelle was a true winner right from the start, with a total of **370,834** sold in its first year. Of that total 76,860 were Malibu Super Sport's. Number that could compete with the "Pontiac Tiger"-the GTO-zero. A 327-ci V-8 just was not going to compete with the 'goat's' 389-ci V-8. Taking a cue from their sister's corporation, Chevrolet looked to a motor from their full-size line. Not the aging 409-ci but a new powerhouse that was just making its debut in 1965 the-Turbo-Jet 396-ci big block.

The 396-ci was just the pill the doctor the ordered for the Super Sport packing 425-hp (yes it was advertised as less but that was what it was packing) and stuffed like a jelly doughnut into the engine bay for the light weight Chevelle, it became a favorite with racers all over the nation. It would also be the birth of a model that was best known by SS 396.

Becoming a full blown model the next year with the SS 396 selling 74,272 and with Chevelle total sales totaling over a half-million in 1969 and the SS 396 surpassing the *founding father* of muscle car in sales it never looked back even topping the legendary Hemi in horsepower in 1970 with the big block 454-ci pumping out 450-hp. It was the same powerplant that was used in the Corvette that was rated at 465-hp, and that was still below what it really could pump out.

In later years the horsepower would fade away like the dawn over taking the night and in two short years later the letters would remain, but it was really nothing more than just a shadow of the great ones.

When your classic Chevelle was brand new it had both specialty and line, or interchangeable, parts. Specialty parts are those designed specifically for a certain model. Line, or interchangeable, parts are those used in several different model types and model years. These interchangeable parts allowed the manufacturer to keep production costs down and gave you an affordable method of transportation.

Now, several years later, you most likely view your Chevelle in a different light. You-and legions of other collectors-consider it a piece of automotive history. Fortunately, the ability to use interchangeable parts still exists.

That brings us to the purpose for writing this book. By referring to the book before you go looking for used parts at the salvage yard or swap meet you will be able to find the correct part that will fit your car, even though the part may or may not have come from the same model as yours. The book can also be a guide to buying a reproduction part.

Many times, a part from a Chevelle may be higher than say a part from a Nova or full-size Chevrolet, even though they are the same part!

In most cases the interchange in this manual is based on the part number, meaning that the same part number was used for all models listed. However, there are cases where a different part number will fit while appearing and performing the same as the original unit. Also, when different colors are offered (for example, in seatbelts) there is no color interchange. Instead, interchange is based the premise that the same part was used for all of the models and that either you find the correct color or charge it to fit your needs.

Introduction

How to Use This Book

The book is divided into sixteen chapters, which are further organized into sections covering specific components. For example, chapter 1 (engines) is broken down into eleven sections, or categories. These sections cover everything related to the engine, from cylinder blocks to crankshafts to valve covers. Each section is on a particular part and includes a model identification chart that give, you interchange numbers.

The chart will look similar to this:

Door, Front

Model Identification   *Interchange Number*
Chevelle
1964-1965
Two door sedan..1
Two door hardtop..2
Convertible...2
El Camino...3
1966-1967
Two door sedan..4
Two door hardtop..5
Convertible...5
El Camino...6
1968
Two door sedan..7
Two door hardtop..8
Convertible...8
El Camino...9

Look for your model and year of car. That will give you the interchange number for the model(s) on which that particular part can be found. Then skim through the following pages, still in the same section, to find the interchange chart, which gives interchange numbers and any other information you are looking for. The interchanges are listed in numerical order. The chart will look something like this:

Interchange
Interchange Number: 1
Part Number(s): RH, 4492500; LH, 4492501
Usage: 1964-1865 Chevelle 2 –door sedan
Interchange Number: 2
Part Number(s): RH, 4492506; LH, 4492507
Usage: 1964-1965 Chevelle two door hardtop or convertible
Interchange Number: 3
Part Number(s): RH, 4492504; LH, 4402505
Usage: 1964-1965 El Camino
Interchange Number: 4
Part Number(s): RH, 4492502; LH, 4492503
Usage: 1964-1965 Chevelle four door sedan

Part numbers, if listed, are either the original or original replacement numbers. Also listed are the models that the part was used on (under "Usage"). "Notes" include things to watch for during interchange, such as body style restrictions or modifications that can be done to make other parts fit. And it may cross-reference another interchange that will also fit.

Let's say you are looking for a door for your 1965 Chevelle SS convertible. Go down the list and as see that body style under her year heading. You see the interchange number 2 will fit your car. You find interchange 2 and see that those from a 1964-1965 two door hardtop will also fit widening your chances in finding a door.

Typical 1964 style e of VIN to would translate to a 1964 Malibu Super Sport two door hardtop with a V-8 and was the 77,776th car built at the Kansas, City assembly plant.

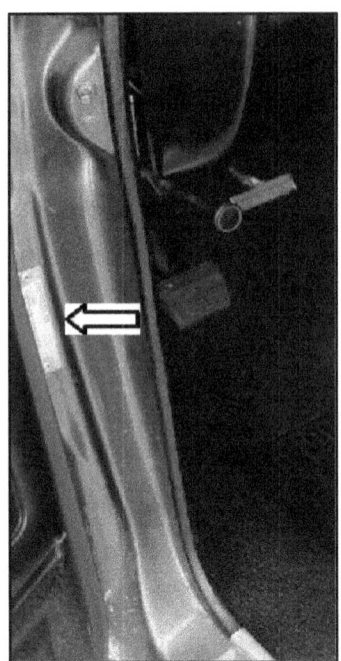

VIN plate location for 1964-1967 models.

Decoding VIN Tag

The various letters and numbers that make up a car or truck Vehicle Identification Number, or VIN, help to identify such things as engine type, place and year of manufacture, and other factors all are which is important in the interchange of parts.

1964

For the first year of the Chevelle, the VIN tag was located riveted to the left-hand front door hinge pillar, and is a number stamped on a stainless-steel plate.

The ID number began with the last digit of the model year: 4-1964. This was followed by a four digit-digit code indicating the model. A single letter next indicates the assembly plant and the last digits are the serial number where plant began each year with the number 100001.

1964 Chevelle Models			
Code	Model	Code	Model
5311	Chevelle 300 2-door sedan-6cyld.	5411	Chevelle 300 2-door sedan-V-8.
5315	Chevelle 300 2-door wagon 6cyld.	5415	Chevelle 300 2-door wagon V-8
5335	Chevelle 300 4 door wagon 6cyld.	5435	Chevelle 300 4 door wagon V-8
5369	Chevelle 300 4 door sedan 6 cyld.	5469	Chevelle 300 4 door sedan V-8
5380	Chevelle 300 El Camino 6 cyld.	5480	Chevelle 300 El Camino V-8
5511	Malibu 2-door sedan-6cyld.	5611	Malibu 2-door sedan-V-8.
5515	Malibu 2-door wagon 6cyld.	5615	Malibu 2-door wagon V-8
5535	Malibu 4 door wagon 6cyld.	5635	Malibu 4 door wagon V-8
5569	Malibu 4 door sedan 6 cyld.	5669	Malibu 4 door sedan V-8
5580	Malibu El Camino 6 cyld.	5680	Malibu El Camino V-8
5537	Malibu 2 door hardtop 6 cyld	5637	Malibu 2 door hardtop V-8
5545	4 door wagon 3 seat 6 cyld.	5645	Malibu 4 dr wagon 3 seat V-8
5567	Malibu convertible 6 cyld.	5667	Malibu convertible V-8
5737	Malibu Super Sport 2 door hardtop 6 cyld.	5837	Malibu Super Sport 2 door hardtop V-8
5767	Malibu Super Sport convertible 6 cyld.	5867	Malibu Super Sport convertible V-8

1964 Chevelle Assembly Plants	
A ~	Atlanta, GA
B ~	Baltimore, MD
H ~	Fremont, CA
K ~	Kansas City, MO
L ~	Van Nuys, CA

1965-1967

Location of the VIN tag was still riveted to the front left door hinge pillar. However, the format was changed in 1965. This was done to streamline assembly of various GM models. All those build by Chevrolet will begin with the number 1, which indicate Chevrolet.

This is followed by the four-digit model code, next is the model year 5-1965, 6, 1967, 7-1967 Next is the assembly plant code, and the last six digits are the serial number. Each plant began each model year with 100001.

Typical 1965-1967 VIN plate. This one would be for a 1967 Super Sport 2-door hardtop and was the 500th car built at the Atlanta, Georgia plant.

1965-1967 Assembly Plants			
A	Atlanta, Georgia	B	Baltimore, MD
F	Flint, MI	G	Framingham, MASS
K	Kansas City, MO		
F	Flint, Michigan		
G	Framingham, Massachusetts		

1965 Chevelle Models			
Code	Model	Code	Model
3111	Chevelle 300 2-door sedan-6cyld.	3211	Chevelle 300 2-door sedan-V-8.
3169	Chevelle 300 4 door sedan 6 cyld.	3269	Chevelle 300 4 door sedan V-8
3180	Chevelle 300 El Camino 6 cyld.	3280	Chevelle 300 El Camino V-8
3167	Chevelle 300 convertible 6cyld	3267	Chevelle 300 convertible V-8
3311	Chevelle 300 Deluxe 2-door sedan-6cyld.	3411	Chevelle 300 Deluxe 2-door sedan-V-8.
3369	Chevelle 300 Deluxe 4 door sedan 6 cyld.	3469	Chevelle 300 Deluxe 4 door sedan V-8
3380	Chevelle 300 Deluxe El Camino 6 cyld.	3480	Chevelle 300 Deluxe El Camino V-8
3367	Chevelle 300 Deluxe convertible 6cyld	3267	Chevelle 300 Deluxe convertible V-8
3535	Malibu wagon 6cyld	3635	Malibu wagon V-8
3537	Malibu 2 door hardtop 6 cyld.	3637	Malibu 2 dr. hardtop V-8
3539	Malibu 4 door hardtop 6 cyld.	3639	Malibu 4 dr. hardtop V-8
3567	Malibu convertible 6 cyld.	3667	Malibu convertible V-8
3580	Malibu El Camino 6cyld	3680	Malibu El Camino V-8
3737	Super Sport 2 hardtop 6cyd.	3837	Super Sport 2 door hardtop V-8
3767	Super Sport convertible 6 cyld.	3867	Super Sport convertible V-8

1966-1967 Chevelle Models			
Code	Model	Code	Model
3111	Chevelle 300 2-door sedan-6cyld.	3211	Chevelle 300 2-door sedan-V-8.
3169	Chevelle 300 4 door sedan 6 cyld.	3269	Chevelle 300 4 door sedan V-8
3180	Chevelle 300 El Camino 6 cyld.	3280	Chevelle 300 El Camino V-8
3167	Chevelle 300 convertible 6cyld	3267	Chevelle 300 convertible V-8
3311	Chevelle 300 Deluxe 2-door sedan-6cyld.	3411	Chevelle 300 Deluxe 2-door sedan-V-8.
3369	Chevelle 300 Deluxe 4 door sedan 6 cyld.	3469	Chevelle 300 Deluxe 4 door sedan V-8
3380	Chevelle 300 Deluxe El Camino 6 cyld.	3480	Chevelle 300 Deluxe El Camino V-8
3367	Chevelle 300 Deluxe convertible 6cyld	3267	Chevelle 300 Deluxe convertible V-8
3535	Malibu wagon 6cyld	3635	Malibu wagon V-8
3517	Malibu 2 door hardtop 6 cyld.	3617	Malibu 2 dr. hardtop V-8
3539	Malibu 4 door hardtop 6 cyld.	3639	Malibu 4 dr. hardtop V-8
3567	Malibu convertible 6 cyld.	3667	Malibu convertible V-8
3580	Malibu El Camino 6cyld	3680	Malibu El Camino V-8
3735	Concours wagon * 6yld.	3817	Super Sport 2 door hardtop V-8
3835	Concours wagon * V-8	3867	Super sport convertible V-8
*-1967 only			

1968-1972 VIN location is on the instrument panel readable through the windshield

1968-1971

Location of the VIN tag was changed in 1968 it was now riveted to the instrument panel and was visible through the windshield on the driver's side. The formula for decoding the plate was the same as in 1965-1967. It will begin with the number 1 which indicates Chevrolet.

This is followed by the four-digit model code, next is the model year 8-1968, 9, 1969, 0-1970 and 1-1971. Next is the assembly plant code, and the last six digits are the serial number. Each plant began each model year with 100001. Except 1969 which began at 300001, and 1970 where it depended on the assembly plant and date. All but the Arlington, TX and the Oshawa, Canada plants stated the year at 100001 in 1969. Chevelle was added to the Texas plant in January in 1970 and the y began at 200001 while the plant in Canada began at 500001. This happen again in 1971 where all plants but the Oshawa began at 100001, while the Canada plant again began at 500001.

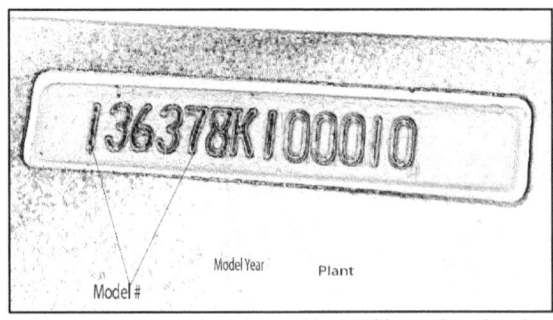

Typical 1968-1971 VIN it is a 1968 Malibu 2-door hardtop and was the 10th car built at the Kansas City, MO plant that year.

1968 Chevelle Models	
Code	Model
3111	Chevelle 300 Deluxe 2-door sedan-6cyld.
3169	Chevelle 300 Deluxe 4 door sedan 6 cyld.
3180	Chevelle 300 Deluxe El Camino 6 cyld.
3167	Chevelle 300 Deluxe convertible 6cyld
3211	Chevelle 300 Deluxe 2-door sedan-V-8.
3269	Chevelle 300 Deluxe 4 door sedan V-8
3280	Chevelle 300 Deluxe El Camino V-8
3267	Chevelle 300 Deluxe convertible V-8
3535	Malibu wagon 6cyld
3537	Malibu 2 door hardtop 6 cyld.
3539	Malibu 4 door hardtop 6 cyld.
3567	Malibu convertible 6 cyld.
3580	Malibu El Camino 6cyld
3635	Malibu wagon V-8
3637	Malibu 2 dr. hardtop V-8
3639	Malibu 4 dr. hardtop V-8
3667	Malibu convertible V-8
3680	Malibu El Camino V-8
3837	SS396 2 door hardtop
3867	SS 396 convertible
3880	SS396 El Camino
3735	Concours wagon 6 cyld.
3835	Concours wagon V-8
1969-1971 Chevelle Models	
Code	Model
3111	Chevelle 2-door sedan-6cyld.
3169	Chevelle 4 door sedan 6 cyld.
3180	Chevelle El Camino 6 cyld.
3167	Chevelle convertible 6cyld
3211	Chevelle 2-door sedan-V-8.
3269	Chevelle door sedan V-8
3280	Chevelle El Camino V-8
3267	Chevelle convertible V-8
3535	Malibu wagon 6cyld
3537	Malibu 2 door hardtop 6 cyld.
3539	Malibu 4 door hardtop 6 cyld.
3567	Malibu convertible 6 cyld.
3580	Malibu El Camino 6 cyld
3635	Malibu wagon V-8
3637	Malibu 2 dr. hardtop V-8*
3639	Malibu 4 dr. hardtop V-8
3667	Malibu convertible V-8*
3680	Malibu El Camino V-8*
3735	Concours wagon 6yld.
3835	Concours wagon V-8
*-Super Sport now an option on these models	

1968-1970 Assembly Plants			
A	Atlanta, Georgia	B	Baltimore, MD
F	Flint, MI	G	Framingham, MASS
K	Kansas City, MO		
F	Flint, Michigan		
1	Oshawa, Ontario, Canada		

1971 Assembly Plants			
A	Atlanta, Georgia	B	Baltimore, MD
F	Flint, MI	G	Framingham, MASS
K	Kansas City, MO		
1	Oshawa, Ontario, Canada		

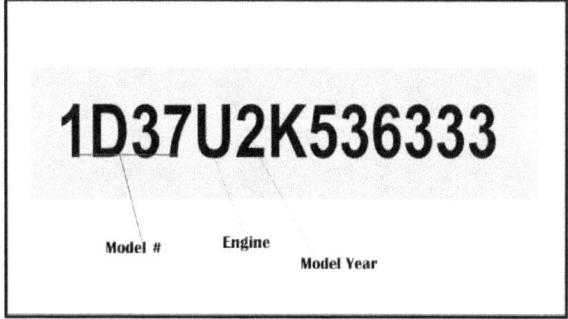

Typical 1972 VIN. This is for a 1972 Malibu with a 396 (402-ci) V-8 and was the 36,333rd car built that the Kansas City, MO plant that year.

1972

For 1972 the VIN plate was till found on the LH side of the instrument panel, however the format was again changed. It still began with the number 1 for the Chevrolet division but the second character was now a single letter that indicated the models, "C" for Base Chevelle/ El Camino models and "D" for Malibu line- which also includes Custom El Camino. this was followed by a two-digit code for body style. The fifth character was a letter or number that indicates the original engine that was installed in the vehicle. While this may not show what engine is in the model now, it is a great indicator of suspension type that could be on the vehicle. Sixth digit is the last digit of the model year 2-1972, Seventh character indicates the assembly plant and the eighth through Thirteenth characters: Sequential Production Number, which began at 500001 at each plant.

1972 Model Codes

Code	Models
C	Chevelle
D	Malibu

1972 Body Styles

37	2 dr. Notch Back Hardtop Coupe
80	El Camino
67	Convertible

1972 Engine ID VIN CODES

Code	Engine	Code	Engine	Code	Engine
			1972		
D	6-250-ci	F	307 V-8	H	350 V-8 2-bbl
J	350 v-8 4bbl	U	396-ci (402-ci)	W	454-ci

Chapter 1 Engines

Engine

As explained in the introductory pages, this chapter is divided into sections of parts that make up the engine as a whole, as complete engines are pretty much interchangeable.

If your car was available from the factory with a particular engine, that engine will probably fit in your car. For example, your 1970 Chevelle came with a 307ci. That car was also available from the factory with a 454ci engine, so it is likely that a big block will fit (in some cases, you will have to change the motor mounts).

When making such drastic changes, such as a big block from a six cylinder; components like transmission, suspension, and rear end may have to be changed to accommodate the heavier and more powerful engine.

Cylinder blocks can be identified by a casting number this casting number signifies the 1967 high performance 327

Cylinder Block

Cylinder block are identified by their casting number. On small blocks, this number is located at the back of the block on the passenger's side of the flywheel flange. On big block, it is located on boss near the top of the bell housing on the driver's side. (Note that this interchange is limited to a bare block only. Short-blocks can use the same block on a low-powered passenger car and a special high-performance, the internal part was what made the high-performance engine special.

When it comes to early (1964-1967) Chevy II V-8-cylinder blocks, remember that they are unique to this model only. Due to clearance problems, the oil filter mount was moved forward about 2.5in, thus, these blocks ore not interchangeable with other models or later than 1968 Chevy II models.

Model Identification   *Interchange Number*

1964
283-ci..1
327-ci..2

1965
283-ci..1
327-ci
Except Special High Performance................2
Special High Performance..............................9
396-ci..3

1966-1967
283-ci..1
327-ci
Except Special High Performance................2
Special High Performance..............................9
396-ci
Except 375 hp..4
375 hp...3

1968
307-ci..8
327-ci..10
396-ci
Except 375 hp..4
375 hp...3

1969
307-ci..8
350-ci..11
396-ci
Early
Except 375 hp...4
375 hp..3
Late (402-ci)
Except 375 hp...5
375 hp..6
1970
307-ci..15
350-ci..11
396/402-ci
Except 375 hp...5
375 hp..6
454-ci
Except 450 hp...12
450 hp..13
1971-1972
307-ci..15
350-ci..14
400(402-ci)…. 5
454-ci
Except 425 hp...12
450 hp..13

Interchanges

Interchange Number: 1
CID: 283
Casting Number'(s): 3864812, 3896948, 3789935
Usage: 1964-1967 Chevelle; 1964-1967 full-size Chevrolet; 1964-1967 C10-C30 Chevrolet truck; 1865-1967 GMC truck.

Interchange Number: 2
CID: 327-ci
Casting Number'(s): 3782870, 3789817
Usage: 1964-1967 Chevelle; 1964-1967 full-size Chevrolet; 1967 Camaro.

Interchange Number: 3
CID: 396
Casting Number'(s): 3855962, 3873858, 3902406, 3902466, and 3935440
Usage: 1965-1968 Chevelle; 1965-1968 full-size Chevrolet; 1968 Nova; 1967-1968 Camaro
Note(s): All with 375-hp Special high performance. 4-bolt-mains.

Interchange Number: 4
CID: 396
Casting Number'(s): 3902406, 3916323, 3935440
Usage: 1965-early 1969 Chevelle; 1965-early 1969 full-size Chevrolet; 1968-early 1969 Nova.
Note(s): All except with 375-hp Special high performance. 2-bolt-mains.

Interchange Number: 5
CID: 402
Casting Number'(s): 3969854, 3955272,
Usage: Late 1969-1972 Chevelle; Late 1969-1972 full-size Chevrolet; Late 1969-1972 Nova.
Note(s): All except with 375-hp Special high performance. 2-bolt-mains. Has 4-1/8 inch bore.

Interchange Number: 6
CID: 402
Casting Number'(s): 3969854, 3955272,
Usage: Late 1969-1970 Chevelle; Late 1969-1970 full-size Chevrolet; Late 1969-1970 Nova.
Note(s): With 375-hp Special high performance. 4-bolt-mains. Has 4-1/8 inch bore.

Interchange Number: 7
CID: 402
Casting Number'(s):,
Usage: 1971-1972 Chevelle; 1971-1972 full-size Chevrolet; Late 1971-1972 Nova; 1971-1972 Camaro; 1971-1972 C1-C30 truck; 1500-35000 GMC truck; 1971-1972 Monte Carlo
Note(s): with all outputs.

Interchange Number: 8
CID: 307
Casting Number'(s): 3914653
Usage: 1968-1969 Chevelle; 1968-1969 full-size Chevrolet; 1968-1969 Nova; 1969 Camaro; 1968-1969 C10-C30; 1500-3500 GMC truck

Interchange Number: 9
CID: 327
Casting Number'(s): 3892657
Usage: 1965-1967 Chevelle with 327-ci 360 hp V-8; 1967 Camaro Z-28.

Interchange Number: 10
CID: 327
Casting Number'(s): 3794460
Usage: 1968-1969 Chevelle, Camaro, full-size Chevrolet, Corvette, with 327-ci
Notes: All outputs. Large journal

Interchange Number: 11
CID: 350
Casting Number'(s): 3855961,3932388
Usage: 1969-1970 Chevelle, Camaro, full-size Chevrolet, Corvette, with 350-ci V-8 except high performance and 1970 Z-28
Notes: 2-bolt

Interchange Number: 12
CID: 454
Casting Number'(s): 3969854
Usage: 1970-1972 Chevelle, full size Chevrolet, C10-C30 truck, 1500-3500 GMC truck all with 454-ci V8 except 450-hp or 425-hp
Notes: 2-bolt

Interchange Number: 13
CID: 454
Casting Number'(s): 3969854
Usage: 1970-1972 Chevelle with 454-ci 450/425-hp; 1970 Corvette with 454-ci 460 hp V-8
Notes: 4-bolt

Interchange Number: 14
CID: 350
Casting Number'(s): 3858618, 3914678, 3956618, 3970014
Usage: 1971-1974 Chevelle; 1971-1974 full-size Chevrolet; 1971-1974 Nova; 1971-1974 Camaro; 1971-1974 C10-C30; 1500-3500 GMC truck
Notes: All outputs

Interchange Number: 15
CID: 307
Casting Number'(s): 3970641,3932371
Usage: 1970-1972 Chevelle, full-size Chevrolet Nova Camaro; 1970-1973 C10-C30; 1500-3500 GMC truck; 1970-1973 Monte Carlo; 1971-1972 Ventura II
Notes: All outputs

Engine ID code is found on a pad at the front of the cylinder block just below the passenger cylinder head, these can be hidden by items like the alternator. On big blocks the stamp may be behind the timing chain cover. The ET in this photo indicates a 1968 396-ci 325-hp with automatic transmission built on May 22 at the Tonawanda plant.

Short Block

A short block is a complete engine without the induction system, cylinder head, exhaust system and oil pan. To be interchangeable the block must have the same inner components, note engine code may differ between models.

The engine identification code is a system of letters and numbers that indicate where the engine was build the date it was built, the model(s) it will fit, and the horsepower it will generate. The code can be found on the passenger's side cylinder head. A typical code will look like this: T 10 10 MQ. This particular engine was manufactured at the Tonawanda engine plant (T), on October 10 (1 0 10), and the MQ indicates that it was originally installed in a 1967 Camaro with a 396ci 375hp V-8. Engine identification codes are included in the Interchange chart for short-block. The letter F or V indicates the Flint (F) engine plant. You may also see the M- if it was assembled in Mexico or 'K' for St. Catherine's, Ontario.

Model Identification	Interchange Number
1964-1965	

283-ci..1
327-ci
Except Special High Performance............................4
Special High Performance...3

1966
283-ci..1
327-ci
Except Special High Performance............................4
Special High Performance...3
396ci
Except High Performance or Special High performance 10
High Performance..12
Special High Performance.....................................11

1967
283-ci..1
327-ci..4
396ci
Except High Performance or Special High performance 10
High Performance..12
Special High Performance.....................................11

1968
307-ci..5
327-ci..6
350-ci..7
396-ci
Except High Performance or Special High performance 10
High Performance..12
Special High Performance.....................................11

1969
307-ci..5
350-ci..8
396-ci
Except High Performance or Special High performance 10
High Performance..12
Special High Performance.....................................11

1970
307-ci..5
350-ci..8
396-ci
High Performance..13
Special High Performance.....................................11
454-ci
Except 450 hp..14
450 hp...15

1971
307-ci..5
350-ci..9
396/402-ci...15
454-ci
Except 425 hp...16
425 hp...17

1972
307-ci..5
350-ci..9
396/402-ci...15
454-ci...16

Interchanges

Interchange Number: 1
CID: 283
Part Number: 3970164
Usage: 1964-1968 Chevelle; 1964-1968 Full-size Chevrolet; 1967 Camaro all with 283-ci V-8.
Manual: MD, MD, HA, HB,HI,, HI, HL, HL, GA, GC, GK, GS, GU, DA, DB, DI, CQ, DN
Automatic: MJ, MU, HC, HF, HG,HH, HK, HJ, HM, HN, GF,GO, CT, DJ DE

Interchange Number: 2
CID: 307
Part Number: 3970651
Usage: 1968-1972 Chevelle; 1968-1972 Camaro; 1968-1972 Full size Chevrolet; 1969-1972 Chevrolet truck; 1969-1972 GMC truck all with 307-ci V-8; 1968-1972 Nova with 307-ci V-8
Manual: DA, DB, DO, DP,DQ,DE, CNC, CND, CCA, CKG,CAY
Automatic: DE,DH, DK,DS,DR,DD,DC, CNE, CNF,CNE, CNF, CCC, CKH CAZ,CTK, CMA

Interchange Number: 3
CID: 327
Part Number: 3970189
Usage: 1964-1968 Chevelle, 1968 Nova; 1968 Camaro , all with 327-ci Special high performance.
Manual: EP,ES,JS,EC

Interchange Number: 4
CID: 327
Part Number: 3970134
Usage: 1964-1967 Chevelle; 1964-1967 full-size Chevrolet; 1967 Camaro; 1964-1967 C10-C30 Chevy truck; 1964-1967 GMC truck. All with 327-ci V-8 except high performance and Special High Performance
Manual: JQ,JT, HA, EA, ED, HB, KE, EB,EQ
Automatic: SR, HC, EE, HF, KM, KL CR, CS, CT, CQ

Interchange Number: 5
CID: 327
Part Number: 3970654
Usage: 1968-1969 Chevelle Nova with 327-ci V-8; 1968-1969 full-size Chevrolet; 1968-1969 Nova. Except Special High Performance
Manual: EA,MK,MA,FA,FJ,FY
Automatic: EE,MM,ME, FB,FC,FH,FG,FK, FL,FZ,GA,GB

Interchange Number: 6
CID: 327
Part Number: 3933044
Usage: 1968 Chevelle ;1968 Nova with 327-ci and Special High Performance
Manual: ML,EP,ES
Automatic:

Interchange Number: 7
CID: 350
Part Number: 3933043
Usage: 1968 Chevelle or Nova ;1968 full-size Chevrolet; 1968 Camaro with 350-ci V-8
Manual: MS
Automatic: MU

Interchange Number: 8
CID: 350
Part Number: 3970655
Usage: 1969-1970 Chevelle;1969-1970 full-size Chevrolet ; 1969-1970 Nova; 1969-1970 C10-C30; 1969-1970 GMC truck; 1969-1970 Corvette All with 350-ci V-8 except 1970 Special high performance
Manual: HG, HI, HD, HP,HT, IQ,IR, IW, HA, HC, HQ
Automatic: GE, HD, HF, HH, HJ, HK, HL, HM, HN, HU, HY, IA, IL IN, IP, IS, IT, IV, IX, IY, IZ, HB, HE, HR, HS

Interchange Number: 9
CID: 350
Part Number: 3997466
Usage: 1971-1972 Chevelle ;1971-1972 full-size Chevrolet ; 1971-1972 Nova; 1971-1972 C10-C30; 1971-1972 GMC truck; 1971-1972 Corvette All with 350-ci V-8 except 1970 Special high Performance.
Manual: CKK,CKA, CDA,CDG, CRG
Automatic: CTL,CKD, CSH, CMD,CDD, CAR,CKB,CDB , CRD

Interchange Number: 10
CID: 396
Part Number: 3981817
Usage: 1968-1969 Chevelle ;1965-1969 full-size Chevrolet ; 1966-1969 Nova; 1968-1969 C10-C30; 1968-1969 GMC truck. All with 396-ci V-8 except high performance and Special high performance
Manual: MX,MQ.MW,MY, JN,JT, JR, JA, KG, JV KI, KE
Automatic: MR, MW, JO, JP,JQ, JK, KH JU, JM

Interchange Number: 11
CID: 396
Part Number: 3981822
Usage: 1968-1970 Chevelle ;1965-1970 full-size Chevrolet ; 1966-1970 Nova; 1968-1970 C10-C30; 1968-1970 GMC truck. All with 396-ci V-8 Special high performance 375 HP.
Manual: MQ, JD, KD, JH, KE,MR,CTY,CKQ,CKQ, CKT, CKU
Automatic: KF, JL, JM, KA,KC, CKP

Interchange Number: 12
CID: 396
Part Number: 3981821
Usage: 1968-1970 Chevelle ;1965-1970 full-size Chevrolet ; 1966-1970 Nova; 1968- 1970 C10-C30; 1968- early 1969 GMC truck. All with 396-ci V-8 high performance 360 HP.
Manual: EF, MX,EJ, CTZ CTX
Automatic: EL, MR, EN,JI, CTW

Interchange Number: 13
CID: 396 (402)-ci
Part Number: 3981817
Usage: 1970 Chevelle ;1970 full-size Chevrolet ; 1970 Nova; 1970 C10-C30; 1970 GMC truck. All with 402-ci 4bbl (big block)
Manual: CTX,CKO, CLC
Automatic: CTW, CTY,CLD

Interchange Number: 14
CID: 454-ci
Part Number: 3981818
Usage: 1970 Chevelle, full-size Chevrolet, Corvette with 454-ci except special high performance.
Manual: CRN, CRT
Automatic: CRQ

Interchange Number: 15
CID: 454-ci
Part Number: 3981820
Usage: 1970 Chevelle, Monte Carlo, Corvette with 454-ci LS6 454-ci V-8 450/460 hp
Manual: CRT,CRV
Automatic: CRR, CRS

Interchange Number: 16
CID: 454
Part Number: 6272185
Usage: 1971-1972 Chevelle, Monte Carlo, Full-size Chevrolet, C10-c30, 1500-3500 GMC truck 1971-1972 Corvette all with 454-ci except 425 hp Special High horsepower.
Manual: CPA, CPG,CPD, CLA, CLS, CTA
Automatic: CLB, CTB,CTJ,CPD,CPG,CRW,CRY

Interchange Number: 17
CID: 454
Part Number: 3997548
Usage: 1971 Chevelle, Monte Carlo, Corvette all with 454-ci 425/430 hp Special High horsepower.
Manual: CPP, CPS
Automatic: CPR,CPT

Things can really get confusing in 1970-1972 with the big block 396-ci. Its displacement was actually 402-ci, but it was decked out with the 396 decals, but in some manuals it is referred to as a 400-ci. At the same time there was a small block 400-ci V-8. The thing to remember is if it has a 4-bbl it is the 402/396-ci

Short Block Testing

It is best to run tests on a running engine. That way you can perform a series of tests, which include compression, leak down and vacuum, and you can listen for mechanical noises and look for signs of wear like smoke. However, in most cases finding a running engine is impractical. Yet there are tests that you can still run that will help you evaluate the engines condition.

First, you should give the block and its components an overall inspection. Look for signs of damage such as cracks and breaks; take extra time inspecting the area around mating areas. If possible, remove the cylinder heads, intake and exhaust manifolds. Take extra care in looking at these areas as cracks tend to occur here. A cracked block is not worth the trouble.

Next, check to see if the engine is frozen. Pour a small amount of oil down each of the bores to prevent cylinder ring scoring. Then use a large break over wrench, not under ½-inch drive, and a socket to attach to the front of the crankshaft and check to see if the engine is free moving. An engine that will not move indicates a frozen block, which can mean rusted parts and require a complete rebuild. The engine should offer some resistance, as a free moving engine means the rings are worn. An engine that moves, and then suddenly stops can indicate broken engine parts. Pulling the spark plugs and inspecting them can give you an indication of the engine's condition.

Wet black deposits on the plugs indicate that oil is blowing past the rings, or the intake-valves. Black dry fluffy deposits on the plugs indicate a rich mixture and are not much of a consideration in determining an engine's overall condition. If you find damage to a plug's electrode tip, be wary of misaligned engine parts. Another simple test is to pull the oil dipstick and look for signs of water, which will show up as droplets. This can indicate a cracked block.

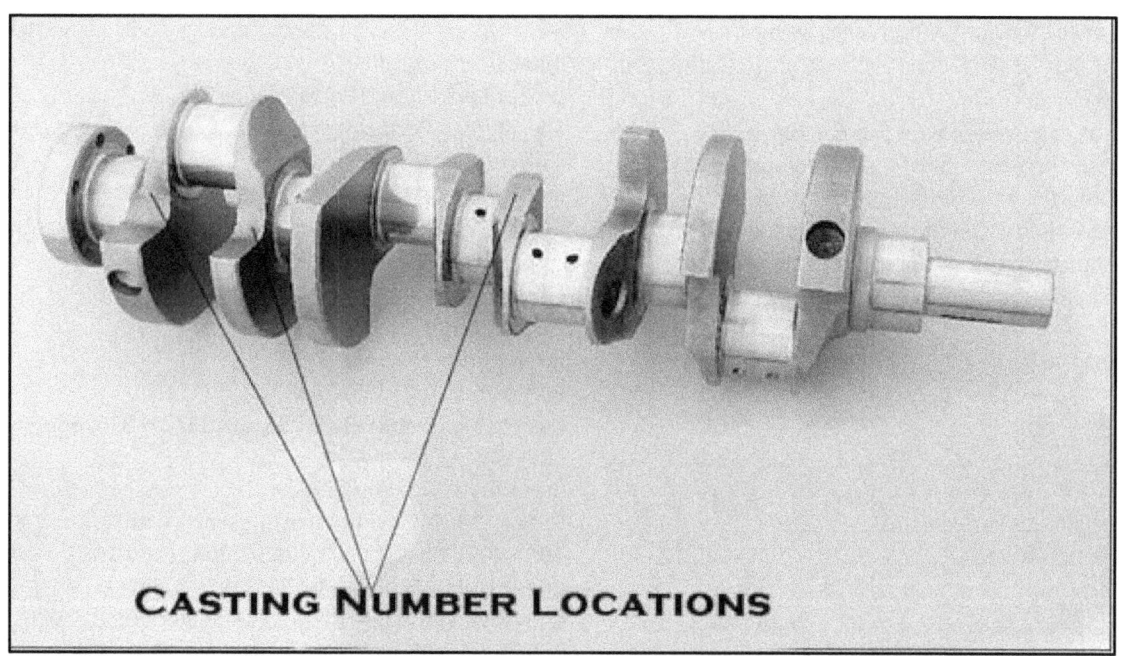
CASTING NUMBER LOCATIONS

Crankshaft

Chevrolet crankshafts available in two different materials: cast nodular iron and forges steel. The first type came standard in most engines, and therefore are the most common. The forged crankshafts are mostly used in high performance applications. For this reason, you can use a forged crankshaft in place of a cast crankshaft, but a cast crankshaft must *never* be used in place of a forged unit. A forged crankshaft can be quickly identified to the way it sounds when lightly tapped with a metal wrench or hammer, a forged steel crankshaft will ring out like a bell, while the cast iron shaft will have a dull sound. When interchanging from a manual transmission to an automatic, be sure to remove the pilot bushing.

First, check the crankshaft for signs of damage. Check the counterweights for cracks and chips which could fail under load conditions. Next check the condition of the ends of the shaft, making sure all mating areas are solid and free from cracks and are not worn out around bolt holes. Next, check crankshaft alignment, this is best done with dial indicator and the crankshaft setting a set of oil V-blocks.

This task is nearly impossible in salvage yards or at a swap meet. Another method is to stand the crankshaft on its end and place a straight edge along its side, or to lay it on its side and -note floor will have to be perfectly flat for this work- lightly roll the shaft back and forth to see if the shaft lays flat. If it appears that one end wants to stick up this could indicate an out of alignment shaft. Note: if the alignment is not too bad it can be straightened by several different methods. However, this procedure is best left done by a professional machine shop.

Next, check the conditions of the journals. Be cautious of rusted over journals, rust indicates that the shaft has been weathered and rust can hide flaws. All journals should be absolutely *smooth*. Any roughness, ridging or scoring will require the journals to be reground. Note- a dark line around the journal is normal; it is caused by the oil groove in the insert and is not a concern unless it is more than .0004 inch above the surface of the journal. This line can be removed with *crocus cloth* (an extremely fine abrasive), which is pulled around the journal in a shoeshine method. If the journals are in good condition, check for out-of-roundness with a dial micrometer.

Measure at each end of each journal, but avoid measuring on the fillet radius, the raised portion that graduates into the counterweights. Write down each measurement. Out of roundness is the difference between the two points and should not exceed .001 inch.

Model Identification	Interchange Number
Chevelle	
1964	
283-ci	1
327-ci	
Except Special High Performance	3
Special High Performance	12
1965-1967	
283-ci	1
327-ci	
Except Special High Performance	3
Special High Performance	12
396-ci	
Except Special High Performance	5
Special High Performance	18
1968	
307-ci	8
327-ci	
Except Special High Performance	8
Special High performance	13
396-ci	
Except Special High Performance	5
Special High Performance	18
1969	
307-ci	9
350-ci	10
396-ci	
Except Special High Performance	5
Special High Performance	18
1970	
307-ci	9
350-ci	10
396-ci	
Except Special High Performance	5
Special High Performance	18
454-ci	
Except Special High Performance	
Manual Transmission	14
Automatic Transmission	15
Special High Performance (LS6)	16
1971-1972	
307-ci	9
350-ci	10
396-ci	
Except Special High Performance	5
Special High Performance	18
454-ci	
Except Special High Performance	17
Special High Performance (LS6)	16

Interchange

Interchange Number: 1
Part Number(s): 3889303
Casting Number(s): 3735236, 3815822, 3836266, 3849847
Crankshaft Type: forged
Usage: 1957-1967 full size Chevrolet with 283-ci V-8; 1964-1967 Chevelle with 283-ci V-8; 1964-1967 Chevy II with 283-ci V-8; 1955-1956 full-size Chevrolet with 265-ci V-8; 1955-1956 Corvette with 265-ci V-8; 1967-1961 Corvette with 283-ci V-8.

Interchange Number: 2
Part Number(s): 3828836
Casting Number(s): 3733223, 3824553
Crankshaft Type: forged
Usage: 1961 full size Chevrolet with 348-ci V-8; 1962-1965 Chevrolet truck with 348-ci V-8

Interchange Number: 3
Part Number(s): 3888304
Casting Number(s): 3782680, 4577
Crankshaft Type: Forged
Usage: 1962-1967 full size Chevrolet with 327-ci V-8; 1964-1967 Chevelle; 1964-1967 Chevy II; 1967 Camaro; 192-1967 Corvette. All with 327-ci V-8 except Special high performance.

Interchange Number: 4
Part Number(s): 3833147
Casting Number(s): 3795589, 3829027, 383416
Crankshaft Type: Forged
Usage: 1961-1965 full size Chevrolet with 409-ci V-8.

Interchange Number: 5
Part Number(s): 3882841
Casting Number(s): 6223
Crankshaft Type: Forged
Usage: 1965-1972 full size Chevrolet; 1965-1972 Chevelle SS 396,; 1967-1972 Camaro; 1968-1972 Nova all with 396-ci V-8; 1971 Chevelle, Nova, Camaro, C10-C30 1500-3500 GMC with 402-ci big block; 1972 Chevelle, Nova, Camaro, C10-C30 1500-3500 GMC with 402-ci big block except high performance

Crankshafts are identified by a casting number This is for a 396-ci 325 hp powerplant

Interchange Number: 6
Part Number(s): 3882849
Casting Number(s): 6223
Crankshaft Type: Forged
Usage: 1966-1969 full size Chevrolet; 1966-1969 Corvette with 427-ci except special high performance.

Interchange Number: 7
Part Number(s): 3882842
Casting Number(s):
Crankshaft Type: Forged
Usage: 1966-1969 full size Chevrolet; 1966-1969 Corvette with 427-ci except special high performance.

Interchange Number: 8
Part Number(s): 3930809
Casting Number(s): 3911001
Crankshaft Type: Nodular
Usage: 1968 full size Chevrolet; 1968 Chevelle; 1968 Camaro; 1968 Chevrolet truck; 1968 Corvette; 1968 Nova with 307-ci or 327-ci V-8 except special high performance. .

Interchange Number: 9
Part Number(s): 3941172
Casting Number(s): 3941174
Crankshaft Type: Nodular
Usage: 1969-1973 full-size Chevrolet; 1969-1973 Camaro; 1969-1973 Nova; 1969-1973 Chevelle; 1969-1973 C10- C30 truck; 1500-3500 GMC truck all with 307-ci V-8

Interchange Number: 10
Part Number(s): 3932444
Casting Number(s): 3932442
Crankshaft Type: nodular
Usage: 1969-1985 full-size Chevrolet; 1969-1985 Camaro; 1969-1979 Nova; 1969-1977 Chevelle; 1970-1977 Monte Carlo; 1969-1979 C10- C30 truck; 1969-1979 1500-3500 ; 1969-1981 Corvette with 350-ci V-8 except high performance; 1978-1985 Malibu, Skylark, Century, Monte Carlo; 1969-1985 C10-c30, 1500-3500 GMC trucks all with 350-ci V-8

Interchange Number: 11
Part Number(s): 3937739
Casting Number(s):
Crankshaft Type: Nodular
Usage: 1969 full-size Chevrolet with 427-ci 335 hp. V-8

Interchange Number: 12
Part Number(s): 3838495
Casting Number(s): 2680
Crankshaft Type: Forged
Usage: 1965-1967 Chevelle 1966-1967 Nova; 1965-1967 Corvette with 327-ci 325/350/365-hp p. V-8

Interchange Number: 13
Part Number(s): 3914681
Casting Number(s): 1130
Crankshaft Type: Forged
Usage: 1968 Chevelle 1968 Nova; 1968 Corvette with 327-ci 325/350 V-8

Interchange Number: 14
Part Number(s): 3975945
Casting Number(s):
Crankshaft Type: Forged
Usage: 1970 Chevelle, Monte Carlo, full-size Chevrolet with 454-ci with manual transmission except Special high performance; 1970 Corvette with 454-ci except 460 hp.

Interchange Number: 15
Part Number(s): 3967463
Casting Number(s): 353039
Crankshaft Type: Nodular
Usage: 1970 Chevelle, Monte Carlo, full-size Chevrolet with automatic 454-ci except Special high performance; 1973-1974 C10-C30 and 1500-3500 GMC truck with 454-ci.

Interchange Number: 16
Part Number(s): 3963523
Casting Number(s): 3521
Crankshaft Type: Forged
Usage: 1970-1971 Chevelle, Monte Carlo, with 454-ci Special high performance LS6; 1970-1971 Corvette with 454-ci 465 hp.

Interchange Number: 17
Part Number(s): 3993878
Casting Number(s): 353039
Crankshaft Type: Nodular
Usage: 1971-1972 Chevelle, Monte Carlo, full-size Chevrolet with 454-ci;1971-1972 Corvette with 454-ci V-8.

Interchange Number: 18
Part Number(s): 3882848
Casting Number(s): 6223
Crankshaft Type: Forged
Usage: 1965-1966 full size Chevrolet; 1966-1970 Chevelle SS 396,; 1967-1970 Camaro; 1968-1970 Nova all with 396-ci 350-hp V-8
ci V-8.

Connecting Rods

1964-1967
283-ci V-8..2
327-ci...4
1965
283-ci V-8..2
327-ci...4
396-ci...7
1966-1967
283-ci V-8..2
327-ci...4
396-ci
Except 375-hp..6
375 hp..7
1968
327-ci...5
350 ci...5
396-ci
Except 375-hp..6
375 hp..7
1969
307-ci...3
350-ci...8
396-ci
Except 375-hp..6
375 hp..7

1970
307-ci...7
350-ci...11
396-ci
Except 375-hp..6
375 hp..7
454-ci
Except 450 hp..6
450 hp..8
1971
307-ci...3
350-ci...5
402-ci...6
454-ci
Except 425 hp..6
425 hp..8
1972
307-ci...3
350-ci...5
402-ci...6
454-ci...6

Interchanges

Interchange Number: 1
Part Number(s): 3788435
Casting Number(s): 3788437 (cap)
Usage: 1962-1970 Nova; 1963-1965 Chevrolet or GMC truck with 4 cylinder; 1962-1972 Nova; 1962-1969 full-size Chevrolet; 1964-1969 Chevelle; 1967-1969 Camaro; 1962-1969 C10-C30 Chevrolet or 1500-3500 truck. All with six cylinder.

Interchange Number: 2
Part Number(s): 3864881
Casting Number(s):
Usage: 1964-1967 Nova, full-size Chevrolet, C10-C30 or 1500-3500 GMC truck with 283-ci V-8; 1964-1967Corvette with 283-ci V-8; 1967 Camaro with 283-ci V-8.

Interchange Number: 3
Part Number(s): 3916396
Casting Number(s):
Usage: 1968-1973 Nova, full-size Chevrolet, C10-C30 or 1500-3500 GMC truck; 1968-1973 Chevelle; 1968-1973 Camaro all with 307-ci V-8

Interchange Number: 4
Part Number(s): 3864881
Casting Number(s):
Usage: 1964-1967 Nova, full-size Chevrolet, C10-C30 or 1500-3500 GMC truck;1964-1967 Chevelle; 1967 Camaro. All with 327-ci V-8

Interchange Number: 5
Part Number(s): 3916396
Casting Number(s):
Usage: 1968-1969 Nova, full-size Chevrolet, C10-C30 or 1500-3500 GMC truck; Chevelle; Camaro. All with 327-ci V-8; 1968-1979 Nova with 350-ci; 1968-1977 Chevelle with 350-ci V-8; 1968-1981 Camaro with 350-ci; 1968-1981 Full-size Chevrolet, C10-C30 or 1500-3500 GMC truck with 350-ci; 1968-1981 Corvette with 350-ci; 1970-1981 Monte Carlo with 350-ci; 1978-1980 Cutlass with 350-ci V-8; 1977-1981 Firebird with 350-ci V-8. 1976-1977 Chevelle; 1978-85 Malibu; 1977-1985 full-size Chevrolet; 1976-1985 Camaro; 1976-1985 C10-C30 truck; 1976-1985 1500-3500 GMC truck; 1977-1980 Regal-1977-1985 full-size Pontiac; 1977-1985 full-size Oldsmobile; 1977-1985 full-size Buick; 1977-1980 LeMans; 1976-80 Corvette; 1976-1979 Nova; 1978-1979 Sunbird; 1978-1980 Grand Prix; 1977-1979 Omega; 1977-1985 Firebird; 1976-1985 Cutlass. All with 305-ci V-8
Note: Some early 1968 327-ci models used 1967 rods.

Interchange Number: 6
Part Number(s): 473388
Casting Number(s):
Usage: 1968-1970 Nova with 396-ci; 1967-1970 Camaro; 1966-1970 Chevelle with 396-ci V-8; 1965-1970 Full-size Chevrolet; 1967-1970 C10 to C30 Chevrolet truck or 1500-3500 GMC truck with 396-ci V-8; 1965-1966 Corvette with 396-ci Except special high performance (375-hp); 1970-1971 Nova, Chevelle, full size Chevrolet, Monte Carlo, C10- C30 or 1500-3500 GMC truck with 402-ci (big Block 4-bbl); 1972 Nova, Chevelle, full size Chevrolet, Monte Carlo, C10- C30 or 1500-3500 GMC truck with 402-ci; 1970-1975 Chevelle, Full-size Chevrolet, Corvette, C10-C30 or 1500- 3500 GMC truck with 454-ci V-8 except with Special high performance.
Notes: Orange stripe

Interchange Number: 7
Part Number(s): 3856240
Casting Number(s):
Usage: 1968-1970 Nova with 396-ci; 1967-1970 Camaro; 1966-1970 Chevelle with 396-ci V-8; 1965-1970 Full-size Chevrolet; 1967-1970 C10 to C30 Chevrolet truck or 1500-3500 GMC truck with 396-ci V-8; 1965-1966 Corvette with 396-ci Except special high performance (375-hp)
Notes: Blue stripe and rib on cap

Interchange Number: 8
Part Number(s): 3963552
Casting Number(s):
Usage: 1970-1971 Chevelle or Corvette with 454-ci 450/460 hp LS6.

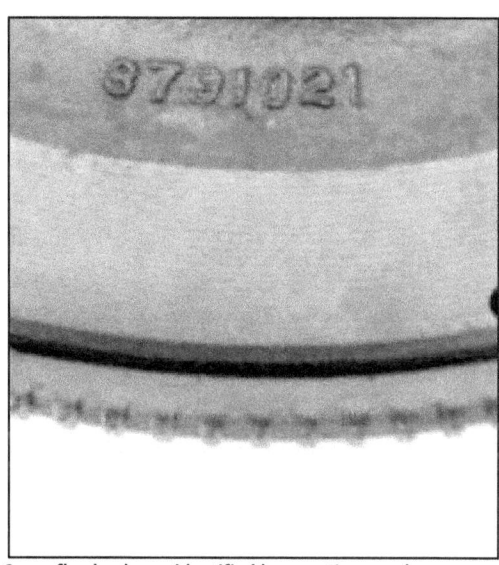
Some flywheels are identified by a casting number.

Flywheels

Chevrolet used two different types of flywheels those with a small block, a 153 tooth 12-3/4 inch in diameter that was used with the small blocks and the 14-inch diameter wheel that has 168 teeth. However, there is difference between one with an automatic and a manual transmission.

Small block fly wheels will have a counterweight on them as the internally balanced and have a 3.58 bolt patterns. Bolt pattern is measured by the distance between l bolt patterns.

Model Identification	*Interchange Number*
Chevelle	
1964	
283-ci V-8	
Manual Transmission	
With 10-inch clutch..........................1	
With 11-inch clutch..........................2	

Automatic Transmission..................................4

327-ci
Manual Transmission....................................1
Automatic Transmission..................................4

1965
283-ci V-8
Manual Transmission
With 10 inch clutch.....................................1
With 11-inch clutch.....................................2
Automatic Transmission..................................4
327-ci
Manual Transmission....................................1
Automatic Transmission..................................4
396-ci V-8
Manual Transmission....................................3
Automatic..5

1966-1967
283-ci V-8
Manual Transmission
With 10-inch clutch.....................................1
With 11-inch clutch.....................................2
Automatic Transmission..................................4
327-ci
Manual Transmission....................................1
Automatic Transmission..................................4
396-ci V-8
Manual Transmission....................................3
Automatic
Powerglide...5
T.H. 400..6

1968
307-ci/ 327-ci V-8
Manual Transmission....................................1
Automatic Transmission..................................4
327-ci
Manual Transmission....................................1
Automatic Transmission..................................4
350-ci or 396-ci V-8
Manual Transmission....................................3
Automatic
Early...6
Late..7

1969
307-ci V-8
Manual Transmission....................................1
Automatic Transmission..................................4
350-ci
255-HP
Manual Transmission....................................1
Automatic Transmission..................................5
300-HP
Manual Transmission....................................2

Automatic Transmission..................................7
396-ci V-8
Manual Transmission....................................3
Automatic..6

1970-1972
307-ci V-8
Manual Transmission....................................1
Automatic Transmission..................................4
350-ci
2-bbl
Manual Transmission....................................1
Automatic Transmission..................................5
4-bbl
Manual Transmission....................................2
Automatic Transmission..................................6
396-ci V-8
Manual Transmission....................................3
Automatic..6
454-ci
Manual Transmission....................................8
Automatic..9

Interchanges

Interchange Number: 1
Part Number(s): 3973452
Casting Number(s): 3791021
Transmission: Manual
Usage: 1963-1967 full-size Chevrolet with cylinder, 283 ci; 1962-1968 full-size Chevrolet with 327-ci V-8; 1968-1973 Full size Chevrolet, Camaro, Chevelle, Nova with 307-ci V-8 or 350-ci V-8, except special high performance; 1962-1970 Chevy II/Nova with 4 cylinder, or six cylinder; 1967-1969 Camano with 302-ci V-8. All models with manual transmission
Notes: with 10 inch or 10-1/2 inch clutch.

Interchange Number: 2
Part Number(s): 3986390
Casting Number(s): 3729004 or 3703870
Transmission: Manual
Usage: 1959-1962 full-size Chevrolet with 283-ci V-8; 1958-1961 full-size Chevrolet with 348-ci 1962-1964 full-size Chevrolet with 409-ci V-8; 1970-1971 full-size Chevrolet with 350-ci 2 bbl V-8; 1973-1974 C10-C30 with 250-ci six cylinder without H.D. clutch; 1970-1974 Monte Carlo with 350-ci 300 hp 1970-1974 Nova with 350-ci V-8; 1956-1962 Corvette; 1970-1974 Camaro with 350-ci, except Z-28; 1975-1979 Camaro with manual transmission except Z-28 or Warner transmission; 1980 Camaro with 305-ci V-8; 1981 Camaro with V-8 and manual transmission, except Z-28; 1976-1981 Corvette; 1977-1979 Firebird with 305-ci or 350-ci and manual transmission; 1975-1979 Nova with 305-ci or 350-ci and manual transmission. All models with manual transmission
Notes: with 10 inch or 10-1/2 inch clutch.

Interchange Number: 3
Part Number(s): 3998281
Casting Number(s): 3856579
Transmission: Manual
Usage: 1965 full-size Chevrolet with 409-ci V-8; 1966-1970 full-size Chevrolet, Chevelle with 396-ci V-8; 1967-1970 Camaro with 396-ci V-8; 1968-1970 Nova with 396-ci V-8; 1966-1969 Impala with 427-ci V-8; 1966-1969 Corvette with 427-ci V-8; 1970-1974 Monte Carlo with 350-ci 2 bbl; 1970-1974 Nova with 350-ci 2 bbl V-8; 1956-1962 Corvette; 1970-1974 Camaro with 350-ci, 4-bbl except Z-28; 1971 Chevelle, Monte Carlo with 400 ci 4bbl big block; 1977-1981 Camaro Z-28 with manual transmission. All models with manual transmission.
Notes: 11 inch clutch

Interchange Number: 4
Part Number(s): 3789821
Casting Number(s):
Transmission: Automatic
Usage: 1962-1967 full size Chevrolet with 327-ci V-8; 1963-1967 full-size Chevrolet with 283-ci V-8; 1968-1969 full-size-Chevrolet with 307-ci V-8; 1967-1970 Camaro with 250-ci six cylinder; 1967 Camaro with 283-ci V-8; 1969-1970 Camaro with 307-ci V-8; 1969 Camaro with 350-ci V-8 (255 HP) ; 1962-1970 Nova with automatic transmission, except 350-ci or 396-ci V-8's ; 1964-1969 Chevelle except 396-ci V-8

Interchange Number: 5
Part Number(s): 3868806
Casting Number(s):
Transmission: Automatic
Usage: 1965-1966 full-size Chevrolet; 1966 Chevelle or Corvette with 396-ci and Powerglide; 1969-1970 full-size Chevrolet with 350-ci and Powerglide

Interchange Number: 6
Part Number(s): 3991401
Casting Number(s):
Transmission: Automatic
Usage: 1965-1970 full-size Chevrolet; 1966-1969 Chevelle; 1967-1969 Camaro; 1968-1969 Nova; 1970 Camaro, Chevelle, Nova with 396-ci 375-hp V-8. All with 396-ci V-8 an T.H. automatic transmission.
Notes: Two designs in 1968 interchange number 7 also used. This fly wheel has a single bolt pattern.

Interchange Number: 7
Part Number(s): 3937736
Casting Number(s):
Transmission: Automatic
Usage: Late 1968-1970 full-size Chevrolet Late 1968-1969 Chevelle; Late 1968-1969 Camaro; Late 1968-1969 Nova; 1970 Camaro, Chevelle, Nova with 396-ci except 375-hp V-8. All with 396-ci V-8 an T.H. automatic transmission; 1975-1977 Chevelle with 305-ci or 350-ci V-8; 1975 Apollo with automatic transmission; 1969-1978 Blazer with 350-ci V-8; 1976-1978 Blazer, Chevelle, Monte Carlo, Camaro with 305-ci V-8 or 350-ci V-8; 1977-1978 Firebird with automatic transmission; 1969-1978 C10-C30 or 1500-3500 GMC truck with automatic transmission; 1976-1978 LeMans with 305-ci V-8; 1976-1979 Nova with automatic transmission; 1976-1978 Phoenix with automatic transmission; 1975-1977 Buick Regal with automatic transmission; 1977 full-size Buick, Oldsmobile, Pontiac with 305-ci or 350-ci V-8 and automatic transmission.
Notes: Two designs in 1968 interchange number 6 also used. This fly wheel has two staggered bolt holes. The inner pattern is 10-3/4 inch diameter, and the outer 11-1/2 in diameter pattern.

Interchange Number: 8
Part Number(s): 3993827
Casting Number(s):
Transmission: Manual
Usage: 1970-1975 Chevelle with 454-ci V-8; 1970 full-size Chevrolet; 1970-1975 Corvette; 1970-1975 C10-C30 Chevrolet or 1500-3500 GMC truck. All models with 454-ci and manual transmission.

Interchange Number: 10
Part Number(s): 3992069
Casting Number(s):
Transmission: Manual
Usage: 1970-1975 Chevelle with 454-ci V-8; 1970 full-size Chevrolet; 1970-1975 Corvette; 1970-1975 C10-C30 Chevrolet or 1500-3500 GMC truck. All models with 454-ci and automatic transmission.

Cylinder Heads

Chevrolet used two different types of cylinder heads, the more common version made of cast iron, and the other that was used in certain special high-performance applications that were made of aluminum. The interchange here is the bare head stripped of the valve and rocker arms.

Cylinder heads are identified by a casting number, this number when it is known is given.

Cylinder heads are identified by a casting number. This number is are for the very rare aluminum 1968 L89 heads.

Model Identification	Interchange Number
Chevelle	
1964	
283-ci V-8	1
327-ci V-8	
Except High Performance	1
High performance	5
1965	
283-ci V-8	1
327-ci V-8	
Except Special High Performance	1
Special High Performance	6
396-ci	11
1966-1967	
283-ci V-8	1
327-ci V-8	
Except Special High Performance	1
Special High Performance	6
396-ci	
Except 375 hp	12
375 hp	14
1968	
307-ci V-8	2
327-ci / 350-ciV-8	
Except Special High Performance	1
Special High Performance	6
396-ci	
Except 375 hp	16
375 hp	17
1969	
307-ci V-8	2
327-ci	
Special High Performance	8
350-ci V-8	
Except Regular Fuel	6
Regular Fuel	9
396-ci	
Except 375 hp	18
375 hp	
Cast Iron Heads	16
Aluminum Heads	15
1970	
307-ci V-8	2
350-ci V-8	6
396-ci/454-ci	
Except 375 hp or 450-hp	19
375 hp/ 450-hp	20
1971	
307-ci V-8	3
350-ci V-8	6

402-ci/454-ci
Except 425-hp..21
425 hp..22
1972
307-ci V-8
Early..3
Late...4
350-ci V-8...6
402-ci..21
454-ci..23

Interchanges

Interchange Number: 1
Part Number(s): 3817680
Casting Number(s): 3795896
Type: Cast iron
Usage: 1964-1967 Chevelle; 1958-1967, full –size Chevrolet, Nova all with 283-ci V-8; 1967 Camaro; 1955-1961 Corvette with 283-ci V-8, except with fuel injection, or special high performance.; 1962-1964 full-size Chevrolet with 327-ci V-8; 1964 Chevelle with 327-ci V-8; 1964 Chevy II with 327-ci V-8; 1964 Corvette with 327-ci V-8. Except high performance.

Interchange Number: 2
Part Number(s): 3958602
Casting Number(s): 3917290
Type: Cast iron
Usage: 1968-1970 Chevelle, Camaro, full-size Chevrolet, Nova, C10-C30 or 1500-3500 GMC with 307-ci V-8; 1970 Monte Carlo with 307-ci V-8

Interchange Number: 3
Part Number(s): 3997417
Casting Number(s):
Type: Cast iron
Usage: 1971- early 1972 Chevelle, Camaro, full-size Chevrolet, Nova, Monte Carlo, C10-C30 or 1500-3500 GMC with 307-ci V-8
Notes: Has 69 cc chambers.

Interchange Number: 4
Part Number(s): 6272069
Casting Number(s): 3998991
Type: Cast iron
Usage: Late 1972 -1973 Chevelle, Camaro, full-size Chevrolet, Nova, Monte Carlo, C10-C30 or 1500-3500 GMC with 307-ci V-8
Notes: Has 75 cc chambers.

Interchange Number: 5
Part Number(s): 3958603
Casting Number(s): 3782461
Type: Cast iron
Usage: 1964 Chevelle with 327-ci high performance; 1965-1968 Chevelle, Chevy II/Nova with 327-ci V-8, except special high performance; 1967-1968, Camaro with 327-ci V-8; 1965-1968 full-size Chevrolet with 327-ci V-8; 1965-1968 C10-30 or 1500-3500 GMC with 327-ci V-8; 1964 Corvette with 327-ci V-8 with high performance; 1967-1969 Chevelle, Camaro, full-size Chevrolet, Corvette, C10-C30 or GMC 1500-3500 truck with 350-ci V-8, expect regular fuel 1969; 1970 Chevelle, Camaro (except Z-28), , full-size Chevrolet, Corvette, C10-C30 or GMC 1500-3500 truck with 350-ci 4-bbl V-8.

Interchange Number: 6
Part Number(s): 3987376
Casting Number(s): 3890462
Type: Cast iron
Usage: 1965-1968 Chevelle, Nova, and Corvette with 327-ci special high performance.

Interchange Number: 7
Part Number(s): 3958607
Casting Number(s):
Type: Cast iron
Usage: 1967-1968 Chevelle, Nova, Corvette, full-size Chevrolet, C10-c30 or 1500-3500 GMC truck with 327-ci except special high performance.

Interchange Number: 8
Part Number(s): 3958602
Casting Number(s) 3912291
Type: Cast iron
Usage: 1969 Chevelle, Nova, full-size Chevrolet, C10-C30 or 1500-3500 GMC truck with 327-ci except special high performance.

Interchange Number: 9
Part Number(s): 3958606
Casting Number(s)
Type: Cast iron
Usage: 1969 Chevelle, Nova, full-size Chevrolet, C10-C30 or 1500-3500 GMC truck with 350-ci with regular fuel; 1970 Chevelle, Nova, full-size Chevrolet, C10-C30 or 1500-3500 GMC truck with 350-ci 2 bbl V-8.

Interchange Number: 10
Part Number(s): 14034808
Casting Number(s) 464036, 3990941, 6260856, 6272070, 14019821, 14034808
Type: Cast iron
Usage: 1971-1977 Chevelle; 1971-1979 Nova, 1971-1979 full-size Chevrolet, 1971-1986 C10-C30 or 1500-3500 GMC truck; 1971-1981 Camaro, except Z-28; 1971-1985 Corvette, except high performance; 1978-1986 Malibu; 1978-1986 Cutlass, Regal, Skylark, Cutlass, LeMans. All models with 350-ci V-8 except special high performance models

Interchange Number: 11
Part Number(s): 3931062
Casting Number(s): 3856206
Type: Cast iron
Usage: 1965 Chevelle, full-size Chevrolet, Corvette with 396-ci V-8.

Interchange Number: 12
Part Number(s): 3931062
Casting Number(s): 3904390, 3872702
Type: Cast iron
Usage: 1966-1967 Chevelle, full-size Chevrolet, Corvette with 396-ci 325/350 hp V-8; 1966-1967 full-size Chevrolet with 427-ci V-8 except special high performance

Interchange Number: 14
Part Number(s): 3919839
Casting Number(s): 3919840,
Type: Cast iron
Usage: 1966-1967 Chevelle, full-size Chevrolet, Corvette with 396-ci 375 hp V-8; 1966-1967 full-size Chevrolet or Corvette with 427-ci Special high performance 425/430 hp

Interchange Number: 15
Part Number(s): 3919838
Casting Number(s): 3919842
Type: Aluminum
Usage: 1968-1969 Chevelle, 396-ci 375 hp V-8 aluminum heads; 1968-1969 Corvette 427-ci with aluminum heds.

Interchange Number: 16
Part Number(s):
Casting Number(s): 3917215, 3856260
Type: Cast iron
Usage: 1968- Chevelle, full-size Chevrolet, Camaro, Nova with 396-ci except 375 hp V-8; 1968 full-size Chevrolet or Corvette with 427-ci except special horsepower.

Interchange Number: 17
Part Number(s):
Casting Number(s): 3919840
Type: Cast iron
Usage: 1968-1969 Chevelle, Camaro, Nova with 396-ci 375 hp V-8; 1968-1969 full-size Chevrolet or Corvette with 427-ci special horsepower (425/430/435 hp)

Interchange Number: 18
Part Number(s):
Casting Number(s): 3931063
Type: Cast iron
Usage: 1969 Chevelle, full-size Chevrolet, Camaro, Nova with 396-ci except 375 hp V-8; 1969 full-size Chevrolet or Corvette with 427-ci except special horsepower.

Interchange Number: 19
Part Number(s): 3964286
Casting Number(s): 3946074, 3964290
Type: Cast iron
Usage: 1970 Chevelle, full-size Chevrolet, Camaro, Nova with 396-ci except 375 hp V-8; 1970 Chevelle, full-size Chevrolet, Monte Carlo Corvette with 454-ci V8 except special high performance.

Interchange Number: 20
Part Number(s): 3964287
Casting Number(s): 3964292
Type: Cast iron
Usage: 1970 Chevelle or Corvette with 454-ci LS^ 450/460 hp; 1970 Chevelle, Monte Carlo with 396-ci 375 hp

The 1964-1967 283-ci and 327-ci used the same valve covers

Rocker Arm

Model Identification   *Interchange Number*

Chevelle

1964

283-ci/ 327 ci V-8..1
327-ci

1965-1967

283-ci/ 327 ci V-8..1
396-ci...2

1968-1969

307-ci/ 327/350-ci V-8..1
396-ci V-8..2

1970-1972

307-ci/350-ci V-8..1
396-ci/ 454-ci V-8...2

Interchanges

Interchange Number: 1
Part Number(s):
Type: Inlet and exhaust
Usage: 1955-1964 full-size Chevrolet, Corvette with 265-ci or 283-ci V-8; 1968-1973 full-size Chevrolet, Camaro, Chevelle, Nova, C10-C30 or 1500-3500 GMC truck all with 307-ci V-8; 1967-1981 Camaro with 350-ci V-8; 1968-1977 Chevelle with 350-ci V-8; 1968-1979 Nova with 350-ci V-8 1968-1981 full-size Chevrolet, C10-C30 or 1500-3500 GMC truck, Corvette with 350-ci V-8; 1978-1981 Malibu with 350-ci V-8; 19701-981 Monte Carlo with 350-ci V-8; 1967-1969 Camaro Z-28 302-ci V-8; 1962-1969 full size Chevrolet with 327-ci V-8; 1967-1969 Camaro with 327-ci V-8; 1963-1969 Nova with 327-ci V-8; 1962-1969 C10-C30 or 1500-3500 GMC truck with 327-ci; 1962-1968 Corvette with 327-ci V-8; 1970-1975 Monte Carlo, full-size Chevrolet with 400-ci 2-bbl SMALL BLOCK; ; 1976-1978 LeMans with 305-ci V-8; 1976-1979 Nova with automatic transmission; 1976-1978 Phoenix with automatic transmission; 1975-1977 Buick Regal with automatic transmission; 1977 full-size Buick, Oldsmobile, Pontiac with 305-ci or 350-ci V-8 and automatic transmission.
Notes: Stamped with letter "O" on inside of pad end.

Interchange Number: 21
Part Number(s): 3993818
Casting Number(s): 3993820
Type: Cast iron
Usage: 1971-1972 Chevelle, full-size Chevrolet, Camaro, Nova with 396-ci except 375 hp V-8; 1971 Chevelle, full-size Chevrolet, Monte Carlo Corvette with 454-ci V8 except special high performance; 1971-1972 C10-C30 with 402-ci V-8.

Interchange Number: 22
Part Number(s): 3994025
Casting Number: 3994026
Type: Cast iron
Usage: 1971 Chevelle or Corvette with 454-ci LS6 425/450hp.

Interchange Number: 23
Part Number(s): 3999240
Casting Number: 3999241
Type: Cast iron
Usage: 1972 Chevelle, full-size Chevrolet, Corvette, Monte Carlo or C10-C30 and 1500-3500 GMC truck with 454-ci V-8

Interchange Number: 2
Part Number(s): 6258611
Type: Inlet and exhaust
Usage: 1965-1970 full-size Chevrolet, Chevelle; 1967-1970 Camaro; 1971 Chevelle, Camaro, Monte Carlo, C-10 to C-30 or 1500-3500 GMC truck with 400-ci 4-bbl BIG BLOCK; 1972 Chevelle, Camaro, Nova, full-size Chevrolet, C10-C30 or 1500-3500 GMC truck with 402-ci V-8; 1965-1966 Corvette with 396-ci; 1966-1969 full-size Chevrolet or Corvette with 427 V-8; 1970-1975 full-size Chevrolet, Chevelle, Monte Carlo, Corvette with 454-ci V-8

Valve Covers

Model Identification   Interchange Number
Chevelle
1964
283-ci/ 327-ci V-8...1
1965
283-ci V-8..1
327-ci
Except Special Horsepower...............................1
Special Horsepower...2
396-ci...4
1966-1967
283-ci V-8..1
327-ci
Except Special Horsepower...............................1
Special Horsepower...2
396-ci
Except Special or High Performance. 4
High Performance or Special High Performance........5
1968
307 ci V-8..10
327-ci
Except Special Horsepower...............................3
Special Horsepower...11
350-ci...10
396-ci
Except Special or High Performance.............4
High Performance or Special High Performance........5
1969
307 ci/ 350-ci V-8..10
396-ci
Except Special Horsepower...............................4
Special Horsepower
Without Aluminum Heads..................................5
With Aluminum Heads..6

1970-1972
307 ci/ 350-ci V-8..10
396-ci/ 454-ci
LH Hand..7
RH Hand..4

Interchanges

Interchange Number: 1
Part Number(s): 3910298
Side: fits either side.
Usage: 1964-1967 Chevelle, full-size Chevrolet Nova; 1967 Camaro with 283-ci; 1964-1967 Chevelle, full-size Chevrolet Nova; 1967 Camaro with 327-ci, except special high performance.
Notes: Painted steel

Interchange Number: 2
Part Number(s): 3910297
Side: fits either side.
Usage: 1966-1967 Chevelle, Nova with 327-ci Special High Performance; 1967 Camaro Z-28 302-ci V-8; 1964-1967 Corvette with 327-ci V-8 with Special High Performance; 1967 Camaro with 350-ci V-8
Note: Chrome cover

Interchange Number: 3
Part Number(s): 3973392 RH 3973393 LH
Side: Passenger side/driver's side
Usage: 1968-1969 Full-size Chevrolet, Chevelle. Camaro, Nova, Corvette with 327-ci V-8 without Special High Performance.
Notes: Painted cover

Interchange Number: 4
Part Number(s): 338262 RH 338261 LH
Side: Passenger's/Driver's
Usage: 1965-1969 Chevelle, full-size Chevrolet, C10-30 truck, 1500-3500 truck with 396-ci without special horsepower; 1967-1969 Camaro with 396-ci V-8 expert with special horsepower; 1968-1969 Nova with 396-ci V-8 except with special horsepower; 1970 Chevelle, Camaro, Nova, full-size Chevrolet, C10-30 or 1500 -3500 GMC truck all with 396-ci passenger side only; 1971 Chevelle, Camaro, Nova, full-size Chevrolet, C10-30 or 1500 -3500 GMC truck all with 400-ci BIG BLOCK passenger side only; 1970-1972 Chevelle, Monte Carlo, full-size Chevrolet, with 454-ci V-8 passenger side only; 1972 Chevelle, Monte Carlo, full-size Chevrolet with 402-ci or 454-ci drivers and passenger side.
Note: Painted cover

Interchange Number: 5
Part Number(s): 325174 RH 325169 LH
Side: Passenger's/Driver's
Usage: 1965-1969 Chevelle; 1967-1970 Camaro; 1968-1970 Nova with 396-ci with high performance or special horsepower; 1966-1969 SS 427-ci 425 hp.
Note: Chrome cover

Interchange Number: 6
Part Number(s): 3902390 RH 3908923 LH
Side: Passenger's/Driver's
Usage: 1968-1969 Chevelle, Camaro, Nova, full-size Chevrolet, or Corvette with 396-ci or 427-ci with aluminum heads.
Notes: Chrome covers

Interchange Number: 7
Part Number(s): 3993841 LH
Side: Passenger's/Driver's
Usage: 1970 Chevelle, Camaro, Nova, full-size Chevrolet, C10-30 or 1500 -3500 GMC truck all with 396-ci passenger side only; 1971 Chevelle, Camaro, Nova, full-size Chevrolet, C10-30 or 1500 -3500 GMC truck all with 400-ci BIG BLOCK passenger side only; 1970-1971 Chevelle, Monte Carlo, full-size Chevrolet with 454-ci.
Notes: Painted steel

Interchange Number: 8
Part Number(s): 330892 RH 330891 LH
Side: Passenger's/Driver's
Usage: 1973-1974 Chevelle, Monte Carlo full-size Chevrolet, Corvette with 454-ci V-8
Notes: Painted steel

Interchange Number: 9
Part Number(s): 346286 RH 346285 LH
Side: Passenger's/Driver's
Usage: 1975 Chevelle, Monte Carlo full-size Chevrolet, Corvette with 454-ci V-8
Notes: Painted steel

Interchange Number: 10
Part Number(s) 6272227LH/ RH
Side: Passenger's/Driver's
Usage: 1968-1973 Chevelle, Camaro, Nova, full-size Chevrolet, Corvette, C10-C30 Chevrolet or 1500-3500 GMC truck all with 307-ci 350-ci V-8 except Special high performance or Z-28; 1970-1973 Monte Carlo with 350-ci V-8 1970-1973 Chevelle, Monte Carlo, full-size Chevrolet with 400-ci SMALL BLOCK
Notes: Painted steel

Interchange Number: 11
Part Number(s): 3923226 RH/LH
Side: Passenger side/driver's side
Usage: 1968, Chevelle, Nova with 327-ci V-8 with special performance; 1968 Camaro Z-28 302-ci V-8.
Notes: Chrome cover

1967-1968 327-ci Special high performance used chrome plated valve covers

1969 models with aluminum heads required special chrome valve covers they can also be found on Corvettes.

Chapter 2 Fuel Systems

Fuel Tank

Model Identification *Interchange Number*

Chevelle

1964-1967
All models except El Camino..1
El Camino...2

1968-1969
All models except El Camino..3
El Camino...4

1970
Without E.E.C.
All models except El Camino..5
El Camino...4

With E.E.C.
All models except El Camino..6
El Camino...7

1971-1972
All models except El Camino..6
El Camino...7

Interchanges

Interchange Number: 1
Part Number(s): 3867745
Capacity: 20 gallons
Usage: 1964-1967 Chevelle all body styles except El Camino and station wagon; 1965-66 full-size Chevrolet all but station wagon

Interchange Number: 2
Part Number(s): 385 7231
Usage: 1964-1967 El Camino; 1965-67 Chevelle station wagon ; 1964 Chevelle station wagon with two seats only
Notes: 1964 Chevelle station wagon with three seats will not interchange.

Interchange Number: 3
Part Number(s): 3940133
Usage: 1968-1969 Chevelle all body styles except El Camino and station wagon

Interchange Number: 4
Part Number(s): 393080
Capacity: 18 gallons
Usage: 1968-1969 El Camino; 1970 El Camino without E.E.C

Interchange Number: 5
Part Number(s): 3998309
Capacity: 18 gallons
Usage: 1970 Chevelle, all body styles except Ela Camino or station wagon. All without E.E.C

Fuel pumps are sometimes stamped with an ID number

Interchange Number: 6
Part Number(s): 3977534
Capacity: 18 gallons
Usage: 1970 Chevelle, all body styles except El Camino or station wagon. All with E.E.C; 1971-1972 Chevelle all body styles except El Camino or station wagon; 1970 Monte Carlo with E.E.C. 1971-1972 Monte Carlo.

Interchange Number: 7
Part Number(s): 3995767
Capacity: 18 gallons
Usage: 1970 El Camino, with E.E.C; 1971-1972 El Camino.

Fuel Pump

Model Identification *Interchange Number*

Chevelle

1964
283-ci V-8
2-bbl..2
4-bbl..1
327-ci V-8..1

1965-1966
283-ci V-8
2-bbl..2
4-bbl..1

327-ci V-8
Except Special High Performance............................1
Special High Performance..7
396-ci V-8..12
1966
283-ci V-8
2-bbl...2
4-bbl...1
327-ci V-8...1
396-ci V-8
Except Special High Performance..........................11
Special High Performance..13
1967
283-ci V-8..3
327-ci V-8
Early..3
Late...5
396-ci V-8..14
1968
307-ci V-8..3
350-ci V-8..6
396-ci V-8..14
1969
307-ci V-8..3
350-ci V-8..6
396-ci V-8..14
1970
307-ci V-8..3
350-ci V-8..6
396-ci V-8
325 hp...15
360 or 375 hp..14
454-ci V-8
Except 450 hp..15
450-hp...14
1971
307-ci V-8..3
350-ci V-8..6
402-ci/ 454-ci V-8 16
1972
307-ci V-8..3
350-ci V-8..6
402-ci V-8 14
454-ci..14

Intake manifold casting number location

Interchange
Interchange Number: 1
Part Number(s): 6415616
Stamped: 4432, 4657 4662
Usage: 1964-1966 Chevelle with 283-ci 4-bbl or 327-ci V-81964-1966 full-size Chevrolet 283ci 4-bbl V-8 or 327-ci V-8

Interchange Number: 2
Part Number(s): 6415824
Stamped: 6942 or 40510
Usage: 1964-1966, all models with 283ci 2bbl
Interchange Number: 3
Part Number(s): 641671 2
Stamped: 40503, 40433, 40232, 6858
Usage: early 1967 full-size Chevrolet, Chevelle, Nova, Camaro, C10-C30 or 1500-3500 GMC truck with 327ci; early 1968-1972 Camaro, Chevelle, full-size Chevrolet, Nova, C10-C30 or 1500-3500 GMC truck with 307-ci V-8; 1967 Camaro, Chevelle, full-size Chevrolet, C10-C30 with 283-ci V-8
Interchange Number: 4
Part Number(s): 6415616
Stamped: 4432, 4656, 4657, 4662
Usage: 1959-1962 348ci 4bbl (except high-performance or special high-performance); 1959-1966 283ci 4bbl; 1962-1966 327ci 4bbl (except Special horsepower 350 or 360hp); 1962-1965 full-size Chevrolet with 409ci (all outputs)

Interchange Number: 5
Part Number(s): 6470422 (AC 40524 or 40725)
Stamped: 40524 or 40725
Usage: 1967-1968 302ci; late 1967-1968 Camaro, Chevelle, full-size Chevrolet, C10-C30 or 1500-3500 GMC truck with 327ci V-8; 1967-1968 Camaro, Nova, Chevelle, full-size Chevrolet 350ci V-8

Interchange Number: 6
Part Number(s): 6470779
Stamped: 40669-69 40726 1970-1972 40987 1973-1980
Usage: 1969 Camaro Z-28 302ci; 1969 Camaro, Chevelle, full-size Chevrolet, Nova 350ci; 1969 Camaro, Nova, full-size Chevrolet with 327ci; 1970-1975 full-size Chevrolet, Camaro, Chevelle, Monte Carlo, Nova, C10-C30 or 1500-3500 GMC truck with 350-ci V-8; 1970-1975 Monte Carlo with 400-ci SMALL BLOCK 2-bbl
1976-1977 Chevelle; 1976-1980 Malibu, Monte Carlo, Nova C10-30 or 1500-3500 GMC truck, full-size Chevrolet, Camaro; 1978-1980 Cutlass. LeMans, Skylark, Nova, Omega, Apollo, Phoenix; 1978-1980 full-size Oldsmobile, Buick, Pontiac. ALL Models with 305-ci V-8.; 1977-1981 Camaro with manual transmission with air conditioning or without air conditioning.

Interchange Number: 7
Part Number(s): 6415563
Stamped: 40148
Usage: 1965 327ci Special horsepower 350hp

Interchange Number: 8
Part Number(s): 5621887
Stamped:
Usage: 1962-1965 409-ci with two four barrel carburetors.

Interchange Number: 9
Part Number(s): 6470310
Stamped: 40777
Usage: 1970-1972 Camaro with 350-ci V-8 except Z-28; 1973-1975 Camaro, Chevelle, Nova, Impala with 350ci 4bbl V-8; 1976 Camaro with 350-ci; 1977-80 Camaro or firebird with 350-ci V-8 and air conditioning and automatic transmission
; 1981 Camaro or Firebird with 305-ci and air conditioning; 1981 Camaro Z-28; 1983 Monte Carlo with "7" in VIN; 1984-1986 Monte Carlo with "G" in VIN

Interchange Number: 10
Part Number(s): 6470779
Stamped: 40726
Usage: 1970-1972 Camaro, Chevelle, full-size Chevrolet, Nova, Monte Carlo with 350ci, except 300hp in 1970; 1971-1972 Monte Carlo, full-size Chevrolet with 400ci small-block

Interchange Number: 11
Part Number(s): 6415961
Stamped: 40193
Usage: 1965-1966 Chevelle, full-size Chevrolet with 396-ci V-8, except 360 or 375hp; 1966 full-size Chevrolet with 427-ci V-8 except 425hp

Interchange Number: 12
Part Number(s): 6416245
Stamped: 6415325
Usage: 1965 Chevelle SS 396 (Z-16); 1965 Impala 425 hp

Interchange Number: 13
Part Number(s): 6416459
Stamped: 40358
Usage: 1966 Chevelle 396ci 375hp; 1966 Impala With 427-ci 425 hp

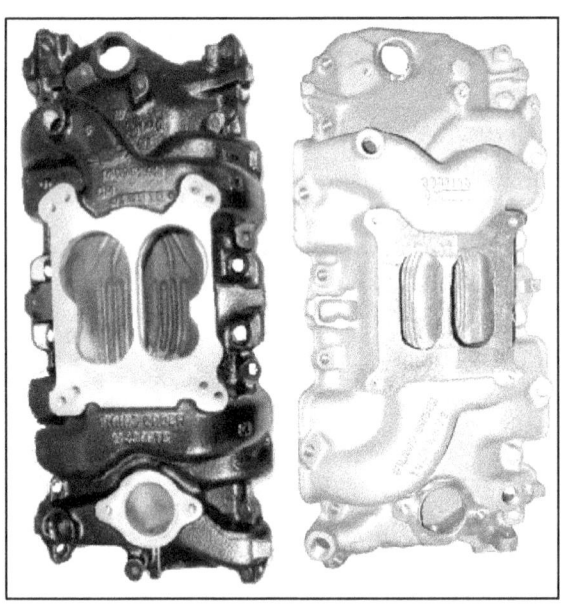

Factory intakes came in both cast iron, right and aluminum, left.

1965 327 special high performance used a chrome air cleaner

Interchange Number: 14
Part Number(s): 6470424
Stamped: 40468 for 1967-1968; 40470 for 1967-1969; 40727 for 1970-1972
Usage: 1967-1969 full-size Chevrolet, Corvette with 427ci; 1967-1972 Camaro with 396/400-ci BIG BLOCK or 402-ci V-8; 1967-1970-1971 Chevelle with 396-ci V-8 360 or 375 hp; 1970 Chevelle, Monte Carlo, Corvette with 454-ci V-8 450/460 hp

Interchange Number: 15
Part Number(s): 6470307
Stamped: 40768
Usage: 1970 Chevelle, Monte Carlo, Nova C10-30 or 1500-3500 GMC truck with 402ci 330hp; 1970 Chevelle, Monte Carlo, Corvette, full-size Chevrolet with 454ci 360hp

Interchange Number: 16
Part Number(s): 6470570
Stamped:
Usage: 1971-1972 Chevelle, Monte Carlo, full size Chevrolet, C10-C30 or 1500-3500 GMC truck with 400-ci BIG BLOCK, 402-ci or 454-ci V-8

Intake Manifold

Model Identification *Interchange Number*
Chevelle

1964
283-ci V-8
2bbl..1
4bbl..2
327-ci V-8
Except High performance..................................2
High Performance...10

1965
283-ci V-8
2bbl..1
4bbl..3
327-ci V-8
Except High performance/ special high Performance..3
High Performance...11
Special High Performance................................12
396-ci V-8..14

1966
283-ci V-8
2bbl..15
4bbl..4
327-ci V-8
Except Rochester carburetor............................4
With Rochester carburetor..............................16
396-ci V-8
With Holley..17
With Rochester..18
High Performance...16
Special High Performance................................14

1967
283-ci V-8
2bbl..15
327-ci V-8
With Rochester carburetor..............................16
With Holley...5
396-ci V-8
325 HP
With Holley..17
With Rochester..18
High Performance...16
Special High Performance................................14

1968
307-ci V-8
2bbl..20
327-ci V-8..16
396-ci V-8
325 HP
With Rochester..18
High Performance...17
Special High Performance................................14

1969
307-ci V-8
2bbl 20
350-ci V-8
2bbl 21
4bbl 8
396-ci V-8
325 HP
With Rochester 18
360-hp 18
375 hp 14

1970
307-ci V-8
2bbl 20
350-ci V-8
2bbl 21
4bbl
Except Special High Performance 8
Special High Performance 9
396-ci V-8
325 HP
With Rochester 22
High Performance 22
Special High Performance 23
454-ci V-8
Except 450-hp. 22
450 hp 23

1971
307-ci V-8
2bbl 24
350-ci V-8
2bbl 25
4bbl 26
402-ci 22
454-ci V-8
Except 425-hp. 22
450 hp 23

1972
307-ci V-8
2bbl 27
350-ci V-8
2bbl 28
4bbl 26
402-ci V-8 29
454-ci V-8 29

Interchanges

Interchange Number: 1
Part Number(s): 3382585
Casting Number(s): 3840905
Usage: 1964-1965 Full-size Chevrolet, Chevelle, Nova, C10-C30 1500-3500 GMC truck with 283-ci 2bbl V-8.

Interchange Number: 2
Part Number(s): 3852568
Casting Number(s): 3746829
Usage: 1958-1964 Full-size Chevrolet; 1964 Chevelle; 1964 Chevy II/Nova all with 283ci 4-bbl; 1962-1964 full-size Chevrolet; 1964 Chevelle, Chevy II/Nova with 327ci, 4-bbl except special high-performance

Interchange Number: 3
Part Number(s): 3870394
Casting Number: 3866922
Usage: 1965 Chevelle, full-size Chevrolet, Chevy II/Nova with 283 and 327ci 4bbl, except high-performance or special high-performance
Note: Cast iron.

Interchange Number: 4
Part Number(s): 3888885
Casting Number: 3872783
Usage: 1966-1967 Chevelle, full-size Chevrolet, Nova with 327-ci Holley or Carter Carburetor.

Interchange Number: 5
Part Number(s): 3893594
Casting Number: 3890490
Usage: 1967 Chevelle with 327-c Holley 4-bbl; 1966-1967 Nova with 327-ci Holley 4bbl. 1866-1967 Corvette with 327ci/350 hp
Notes: Aluminum intake.

Interchange Number: 6
Part Number(s): 3958627
Usage: 1968-1969 302ci V-8 with aluminum intake

Interchange Number: 7
Part Number(s): 393157 5
Casting Number:
Usage: 1967-1968 Camaro, Nova, Chevelle, full-size Chevrolet, C10-C30 or 1500-3500 GMC truck with 327ci 4bbl, except special high-performance; 1967-1968 full-size Chevrolet, Camaro, Chevelle, Nova C10- C30 or 1500-3500 GMC truck with 350ci 4bbl

Interchange Number: 8
Part Number(s): 3987361
Casting Number: 3927184
Usage: 1969-1970 Camaro, except Z-28; 1969-1970 Chevelle, Nova, full-size Chevrolet, C10-C30 1500-3500 GMC truck all with 350ci 4-bbl except special high performance.

Interchange Number: 9
Part Number(s): 3972114
Casting Number: 3972114
Usage: 1970 Z-28; 1970 Chevelle 330hp; 1970 Corvette 370hp

Interchange Number: 10
Part Number(s): 3852569
Casting number: 3794129
Usage: 1962-1963 Nova, full size Chevy with 327ci 300hp

Interchange Number: 11
Part Number(s): 3852569
Casting Number: 3844459
Usage: 1964-1965 Nova , Chevelle with 327ci with high-performance, except Special high-performance versions

Interchange Number: 12
Part Number(s): 3852570
Casting Number(s): 3795397
Usage: 1965 Chevelle, Nova with 327ci 360hp Notes: aluminum intake

Interchange Number: 13
Part Number(s): 3760436

Interchange Number: 14
Part Number(s): 3947084
Casting Number(s): 3866963
Usage: 1965 Chevelle SS 396; 1965 full-size Chevrolet with 396-ci 425-hp; 1966-1969 full-size Chevrolet with 427-ci 425-hp; 1966-1969 Chevelle SS396 with 375 hp; 1968-`1969 Nova with 396-ci 375 hp; 1965 corvette with 396-ci; 1966- Corvette with 427-ci V-8; 1967-1968 Camaro wit 396-ci V-8 375 hp
Notes: Aluminum intake

Interchange Number: 15
Part Number(s): 388899
Casting Number(s): 3877652
Usage: 1966-1967 Full-size Chevrolet, Chevelle, Nova, C10-C30 1500-3500 GMC truck; 1967 Camaro all models with 283-ci 2bbl V-8.
Notes: with hole for water temperature

Interchange Number: 16
Part Number(s): 3931575
Casting Number(s): 3905393
Usage: 1966-1967 , Chevelle, Nova 327-ci with Rochester carburetor; 1967-1968 Camaro with 327-ci V-8; 1966-1968 full-size Chevrolet with 327-ci V-8 and Rochester carburetor; , Nova, C10-C30 1500-3500 GMC truck; 1967 Camaro all models with 283-ci 2bbl V-8; 1968 Nova with 327-ci or 350-ci 4bbl V-8; 1968 Corvette with 327-ci 4 bbl V-8; 1967-1968 C10-C30 1500-3500 GMC 327-ci 4-bbl V-8.
Notes; Cast iron

Interchange Number: 17
Part Number(s): 3876818
Casting Number(s): 3856289
Usage: 1966, Chevelle 396-ci 325 hp with Holley carburetor; 1967 Chevelle, Camaro with 396-ci 350-hp V-8 with Holley; 1966 full-size Chevrolet with 396-ci or 427-ci and Holley 4-bbl

Interchange Number: 18
Part Number(s): 3957996
Casting Number(s): 3883948
Usage: 1966, Chevelle 396-ci 325 hp with Rochester carburetor; 1967-1969 Chevelle, Camaro with 396-ci with Rochester carburetor ; 1966-1969 full-size Chevrolet with 396-ci or 427-ci and Rochester 4-bbl

Interchange Number: 19
Part Number(s): 3888899
Casting Number(s): 3919801
Usage: 1968 Camaro with 327-ci 2-bbl V-8; 1968 Camaro, Chevelle, Nova full-size Chevrolet, C10-C30, 1500-3500 GMC truck with 307-ci 2 bbl V-8

Interchange Number: 20
Part Number(s): 3958622
Casting Number(s): 3927183
Usage: 1969-1970 Camaro Chevelle, full-size Chevrolet, Nova, C10-C30, 1500-3500 GMC truck with 307-ci 2 bbl V-8
Notes: Cast iron with Rochester 2-bbl. Oil fill tube and water by-pass boss eliminated. Heater nipple boss drilled and tapped on right thermostat passage.

Interchange Number: 21
Part Number(s): 3958626
Casting Number(s): 3916313
Usage: 1969-1970 Camaro Chevelle, full-size Chevrolet, Nova, C10-C30, 1500-3500 GMC truck with 350-ci 2 bbl V-8

Interchange Number: 22
Part Number(s): 3977609
Casting Number(s): 3955287
Usage: 1970-1971 Camaro Chevelle, Nova, with 396-ci 4 bbl V-8 or 400-ci BIG BLOCK 4-bbl V-8, except 375-hp; 1970-1971 Monte Carlo Chevelle, full-size Chevrolet with 454-ci V-8 except 450/425/hp; 1970-1971 Corvette with 454-ci V-8 except 460/430 hp.
Notes Cast iron with Rochester 4-bbl. Low rise intake. No oil splash shield.

Interchange Number: 23
Part Number(s): 3977608
Casting Number(s): 3963569,
Usage: 1970 Camaro Chevelle, full-size Chevrolet, Nova, with 396-c 4 bbl 375-hp V-8 or 1970-1971 Monte Carlo, Chevelle, full-size Chevrolet with 454-ci V-8 450/425/hp; 1970-1971 Corvette with 454-ci V-8 460/430 hp.
Notes: Aluminum intake

Interchange Number: 24
Part Number(s): 3991005
Casting Number(s): 3973465
Usage: 1971 Camaro Chevelle, full-size Chevrolet, Nova, C10-C30, 1500-3500 GMC truck with 307-ci 2 bbl V-8
Notes: Cast iron with Rochester 2-bbl. Heater outlet boss on upper right thermostat passage. Oil splash shield.

Interchange Number: 25
Part Number(s): 3990948
Casting Number(s): 3973467
Usage: 1971 Camaro Chevelle, full-size Chevrolet, Nova, C10-C30, 1500-3500 GMC truck with 350-ci 2 bbl V-8
Notes: Cast iron with Rochester 2-bbl. Heater outlet boss on upper right thermostat passage. No oil tube boss . With oil splash shield.

Interchange Number: 26
Part Number(s): 6262932
Casting Number(s): 3973469
Usage: 1971 Camaro Chevelle, full-size Chevrolet, Nova, C10-C30, 1500-3500 GMC truck with 350-ci 4 bbl V-8
Notes: Cast iron with Rochester 4-bbl. Heater outlet boss on upper right thermostat passage. With oil splash shield.

Interchange Number: 27
Part Number(s): 6262928
Casting Number(s): 6262936
Usage: 1972 Camaro Chevelle, full-size Chevrolet, Nova, C10-C30, 1500-3500 GMC truck with 307-ci 2 bbl V-8
Notes: Cast iron with Rochester 2-bbl. Heater outlet boss on upper right thermostat passage. Oil tube boss eliminated. With oil splash shield. Intake runners have cylinder cast in them.

Interchange Number: 28
Part Number(s): 6262930
Casting Number(s): 6263752
Usage: 1972 Camaro Chevelle, full-size Chevrolet, Nova, C10-C30, 1500-3500 GMC truck with 350-ci 2 bbl V-8
Notes: Cast iron with Rochester 2-bbl. Heater outlet boss on upper right thermostat passage. Oil tube boss eliminated. With oil splash shield. Two accessory bosses between runners.

Interchange Number: 29
Part Number(s): 6262901
Casting Number(s): 6263753
Usage: 1972 Camaro Chevelle, full-size Chevrolet, Nova, C10-C30, 1500-3500 GMC truck with 402-ci 2 bbl V-8; 1972 Chevelle, Monte Carlo, Corvette, full-size Chevrolet with 454-ci V-8
Notes: Cast iron with Rochester 4-bbl. Intake runners have numbers cast for their port. No oil splash shield.

Some parts like intake manifolds and cylinder heads are stamped 'HI PERF' for high performance but this is not always the case.

Carburetor

Carburetors differ in a number of ways: engine size, engine output, type of transmission, emission controls, and in some cases, options installed on the car.

Three different brands of carburetors were used on Chevrolet models. The most popular was the Rochester, next was the Holley and then the Carter. Interchange is based on the same part number and or model number.

Rochester Carburetor

Typically, the Rochester ID number is found stamped on a metal tag. Location of this tag varies with carburetor model. For example, on 4CG models the tag is triangular in shape and attached to the top of the air horn. For 4MV models (Quadrajet) the tag is fixed to the lower

The ID for Rochester 2-bbl carburetor is located here. By this ID we know this carb is for a 1960 Chevrolet with a manual transmission.

body assembly of the carburetor, usually just in front of the throttle control. Some have the number stamped into the body itself.

The Rochester part number breaks down to decode what the carburetor was designed for. The first three digits reveal the model era the carb was designed for: 702- 1960's (703 if with AIR emissions); 704 1970-1975. Beginning in 1976 a "1" was added and 1976-1979 used the code "1705" while 1980's models used "1708".

The next digit indicates the production year, so the code 7021 would be for 1961 while the code 7041 would be for 1971.

Next digit is the type of carburetor: 0-Fedearal 1 barrel; 1-Federal 2-barrel 2- Federal 4-barrel; 6- 2-bbl vari-jet; 3- California 1-barrel; 4- California 2-barrel; 5- California 4-barrel.

GM division is indicated next, 0,1 or 2 is used for Chevrolet, while 4- Buick, 5-Oldsmobile and 6 and 7 are for Pontiac.

Seventh digit indicates transmission type odd numbers 1,3,5,7,9 are for manual transmission while those with 0,2,4,6,8 are for automatics.

Sometimes the ID number for the Q-jet carburetor is stamped here

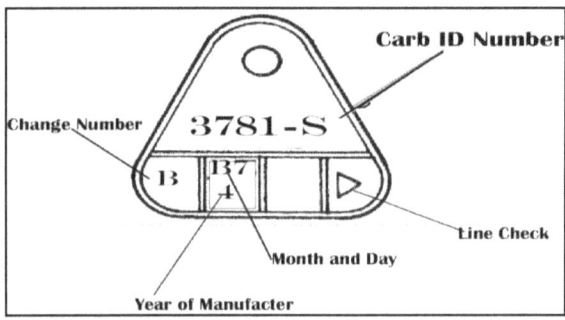
Cater carburetor ID tag

Carter Carburetor

The ID number is found stamped on a brass metal tag that is attached to the top of the bowl or is stamped into the base of the carburetor. This tag is easily broken off, so they are a re find on an original carburetor.

Holley Carburetor

Holley's, be it a two-barrel or a four-barrel have an identification number that is stamped into the side of the air horn.

Model Identification   Interchange Number
1964
283-ci V-8
2bbl
Manual transmission..1
Powerglide...2
4-bbl
Manual transmission..3
Powerglide...4
327-ci
Except High Performance
Manual Transmission..3
Automatic Transmission...4
300 Hp High Performance..5
1965
283-ci V-8
2bbl
Manual transmission..1
Powerglide...2
4bbl
Manual Transmission...12
Automatic Transmission...4

Holley carburetors are identified by a number stamped on the air horn.

327-ci
Except High Performance
Manual Transmission...12
Automatic Transmission...4
High Performance..5
396-ci V-8...17
1966
WITHOUT AIR
283-ci V-8
2bbl
Manual transmission..1
Powerglide...2
4bbl
Manual Transmission...12
Automatic Transmission...4
327-ci V-8 4-bbl
Carter
Manual Transmission..6
Automatic Transmission...7
Holley
Manual Transmission..8
Automatic Transmission...9
Rochester
Manual Transmission...19
Automatic Transmission...20
396-ci V-8
325-hp
Manual..25
Automatic..26

Holley
Manual Transmission..15
Automatic Transmission..16
360 –hp..10
375-hp..11
WITH AIR
283-ci
2bbl
Manual transmission..1
Powerglide...2
4bbl
Manual Transmission..12
Automatic Transmission..4
327-ci V-8 4-bbl
Manual Transmission..19
Automatic Transmission..20
396-ci V-8
325-hp
Rochester
Manual...25
Automatic..26
360-hp
Manual transmission..13
Automatic transmission..14

1967
WITHOUT AIR
283-ci V-8
 2bbl
Manual transmission..29
Automatic transmission..30
327-ci
Manual transmission..21
Automatic transmission..22
325-hp..18
396-ci V-8
325-hp
Manual...34
Automatic..35
350-hp
Manual...10
Automatic..49
375-hp..47
WITH AIR
283-ci V-8
 2bbl
Manual transmission..29

Automatic transmission..31
327-ci
Manual transmission..32
Automatic transmission..33
325-hp..48
396-ci V-8
325-hp
Rochester
Manual...36
Automatic..37
350-hp
Manual transmission..13
Automatic transmission..14
375-hp..47

1968
307-ci V-8
2bbl
Manual transmission..40
Automatic Transmission
Powerglide...41
Turbo-Hydra-Matic..42
327-ci
Manual transmission..43
Automatic Transmission...44
325-hp..38
396-ci V-8
325-hp
Manual transmission..45
Automatic Transmission...46
350-hp
Manual transmission..45
Automatic Transmission...55
375-hp..47

1969
307-ci V-8
2bbl
Manual transmission..54
Automatic Transmission...42
350-ci
2bbl
Manual transmission..50
Automatic Transmission...51
4bbl
Manual transmission..52
Automatic Transmission...53

396-ci V-8 4bbl
325-hp
Manual transmission..45
Automatic Transmission...46
350-hp
Manual transmission..13
Automatic transmission..14
375-hp..47

1970
307-ci V-8
2bbl
Manual transmission..56
Automatic Transmission...57
350-ci V-8
2bbl
Manual transmission..58
Automatic Transmission...59
4bbl...60
396-ci V-8
330-hp..61
350- hp..62
375-hp
Without E.E.C
Manual transmission..64
Automatic transmission..66
With E.EC.
Manual transmission..63
Automatic transmission..65
454-ci V-8
Except 450-hp..61
450-hp
Without E.E.C
Manual transmission..64
Automatic transmission..66
With E.EC.
Manual transmission..63
Automatic transmission..65

1971
307-ci V-8
2bbl
Manual transmission..67
Automatic Transmission...68
350-ci V-8
2bbl
Manual transmission..69
Automatic Transmission...70

4bbl...71
402-ci..72
454-ci
Except 425-hp..72
425-hp..73

1972
307-ci V-8
2bbl
Manual transmission..74
Automatic Transmission...75
350-ci V-8
2bbl
Manual transmission
Without California Emissions.....................................77
With California Emissions..76
Automatic Transmission
Without California Emissions.....................................79
With California Emissions..78
4bbl...80
402-ci..81
454-ci..81

Interchanges

Interchange Number: 1
Part Number(s): 7025103
ID Number(s): 7024101, 7025103
Type: Rochester
Usage: 1964-1966 full-size Chevrolet, Chevelle, with 283-ci 2bbl V-8 with manual transmission.

Interchange Number: 2
Part Number(s): 7024112
ID Number(s): 7024100, 7024102, 7024106, 7024108, 7024110, 7024112
Type: Rochester
Usage: 1964-1966 full-size Chevrolet, Chevelle Nova with 283-ci 2bbl V-8 with Powerglide automatic.

Interchange Number: 3
Part Number(s): 7024225
ID Number(s): 7024125, 7024225
Type: Rochester 4GC
Usage: 1964 Chevelle, Nova with 283-ci or 327-ci 4-bbl and manual transmission except high performance

Interchange Number: 4
Part Number(s): 7025128
Type: Rochester
ID Number(s): 7011108, 7012126, 7012128, 7013004, 7013006, 7013010, 7013012, 7015004, 7015006, 7015010, 7015012, 7019004, 7019006, 7019010, 7019014, 7020006, 7020012, 7020022, 7023006, 7023012, 7024122, 7024126, 7024220, 7024226, 7025121, 7025122, 7025126, 7025128
Usage: 1956-1961 full-size Chevrolet with 283 or 348-ci 4-bbl V-8; 1962-1965 full-size Chevrolet 327-ci 250-hp V-8 with Rochester; 1965-1966 full size Chevrolet with 283 -ci 4bbl V-8 with automatic transmission; 1964-1966 Nova with 283-ci 4bbl V-8 and automatic transmission; 1964-1965 Chevelle with 283-ci 4bbl V-8 with automatic transmission; 1966 full size Chevrolet, Chevelle with 283-ci V-8 with automatic transmission without AIR

Interchange Number: 5
Part Number(s): 3851762
Type: Carter AFB
ID Number(s): 3721
Usage: 1962-1965 full-size Chevrolet with 327-ci 4bbl 300-hp V-8; 1964-1965 Chevelle with 327-ci 4-bbl with high performance; 1965 Nova with 327-ci 4-bbl high performance; 1963-1965 Corvette with 327-ci high performance.

Interchange Number: 6
Part Number(s):
Type: Carter
ID Number(s): 4027
Usage: 1966 Chevelle, nova with 327-ci V-8 4-bbl with manual transmission

Interchange Number: 7
Part Number(s):
Type: Carter
ID Number(s): 4028
Usage: 1966 Chevelle, nova with 327-ci V-8 4-bbl with an automatic transmission

Interchange Number: 8
Part Number(s): 3876747
Type: Holley 4160
ID Number(s): 3123
Usage: 1966 Chevelle, Nova with 327-ci with Holley carburetor and manual transmission. High performance

1964 283-ci standard air cleaner part number 6420903

Interchange Number: 9
Part Number(s): 3876747
Type: Holley 4160
ID Number(s): 3230
Usage: 1966 Chevelle, Nova with 327-ci with Holley carburetor and automatic transmission. High performance

Interchange Number: 10
Part Number(s):
Type: Holley 4160
ID Number(s): 3419, 3420, 3837
Usage: 1966 Chevelle SS396 with 360-hp without AIR emissions; 1967 Camaro, Chevelle with 396-ci 360-hp V-8. All have manual transmissions.

Interchange Number: 11
Part Number(s):
Type: Holley 4150
ID Number(s): 3246
Usage: 1966 Chevelle SS 396 with 375 hp V-8.

Interchange Number: 12
Part Number(s): 7026121
ID Number(s): 7025127, 7026121
Type: Rochester
Usage: 1965-1966 full-size Chevrolet, Chevelle Nova with 283-ci 4 bbl V-8 with manual transmission; 1965 full-size Chevrolet, Chevelle, Nova with 327-ci 4-bbl V-8 except special high performance or high performance.

Interchange Number: 13
Part Number(s):
ID Number(s): 3839
Type: Holley 4160
Usage: 1966-1967 Chevelle, 1967 Camaro with 396-ci 4-bbl 360/350-hp with manual transmission and with AIR emissions

Interchange Number: 14
Part Number(s):
ID Number(s): 3838
Type: Holley 4160
Usage: 1966-1967 Chevelle, Camaro with 396-ci 4-bbl 360/350-hp with automatic transmission and with AIR emissions

Interchange Number: 15
Part Number(s):
ID Number(s): 3139
Type: Holley 4160
Usage: 1965-1966 full-size Chevrolet with 396-ci 4-bbl 325-hp with manual transmission; 1966 Chevelle 396-ci 325-hp with Holley carb, without AIR emissions.
Notes: Interchange number 16 will fit.

Interchange Number: 16
Part Number(s):
ID Number(s): 3140
Type: Holley 4160
Usage: 1965-1966 full-size Chevrolet with 396-ci 4-bbl 325-hp with automatic transmission; 1966 Chevelle 396-ci 325-hp with Holley carb, with automatic transmission without AIR emissions.

Interchange Number: 17
Part Number(s):
ID Number(s): 3124, 3130
Type: Holley 4160
Usage: 1965 full-size Chevrolet with 396-ci 425-hp V-8; 1965 Chevelle SS 396 Z-11; 1965 Corvette with 396-ci

Interchange Number: 18
Part Number(s):
Type: Holley 4150
ID Number(s): 3245
Usage: 1967 Chevelle, Camaro, Nova with 327-ci 4-bbl 325-hp with manual transmission.; 1966 Nova with 327-ci 350-hp V-8. Without AIR emissions

Interchange Number: 19
Part Number(s): 7026203
Type: Rochester
ID Number(s): 7026203
Usage: 1966 full-size Chevrolet, Chevelle, Nova with 327-ci 4 bbl with manual transmission. All without AIR emissions.

Interchange Number: 20
Part Number(s): 7026210
Type: Rochester
ID Number(s): 7026202, 7026210
Usage: 1966 full-size Chevrolet, Chevelle, Nova with 327-ci 4 bbl with automatic transmission. All without AIR emissions.

Interchange Number: 21
Part Number(s): 7027213
Type: Rochester
ID Number(s): 7027203, 7027213
Usage: 1967 full-size Chevrolet, Chevelle, Nova with 327-ci 4 bbl with manual transmission; 1967 Camaro with 327-ci or 350-ci 4-bbl V-8 with manual transmission. All without AIR emissions.

Interchange Number: 22
Part Number(s): 7027218
Type: Rochester
ID Number(s): 7027212, 7027218
Usage: 1967 full-size Chevrolet, Chevelle, Nova, Camaro, with 327-ci 4 bbl with automatic transmission; 1967 Camaro with 350-ci 4-bbl V-8 with automatic transmission. All without AIR emissions.

The 1966 L79 327-ci air cleaner was chrome plated.

There were only 201 Z-16 SS 396 built however the air cleaner was also used on the 1965 Impala with the 396-ci 425-hp which was the true rating of the Z-16

Interchange Number: 23
Part Number(s): 7036203
Type: Rochester
ID Number(s): 70362003
Usage: 1966 full-size Chevrolet, Chevelle, Nova with 327-ci 4 bbl with manual transmission. All with AIR emissions.

Interchange Number: 24
Part Number(s): 7036210
Type: Rochester
ID Number(s): 7036202, 7036210
Usage: 1966 full-size Chevrolet, Chevelle, Nova with 327-ci 4 bbl with automatic transmission. All with AIR emissions.

Interchange Number: 25
Part Number(s): 7026201
Type: Rochester
ID Number(s): 7026201
Usage: 1966 full-size Chevrolet, Chevelle, with 396-ci 4 bbl with manual transmission. All without AIR emissions.; 1966 full-size Chevrolet with 427-ci 390-hp V-8. All without AIR emissions

Interchange Number: 26
Part Number(s): 7026200
Type: Rochester
ID Number(s): 7026200
Usage: 1966 full-size Chevrolet, Chevelle, with 396-ci 4 bbl with automatic transmission. All without AIR emissions; 1966 full-size Chevrolet with 427-ci 390-hp V-8 with automatic transmission. All without AIR emissions

Interchange Number: 27
Part Number(s): 7036201
Type: Rochester
ID Number(s): 7036201
Usage: 1966 full-size Chevrolet, Chevelle, with 396-ci 4 bbl with manual transmission. All with AIR emissions.; 1966 full-size Chevrolet with 427-ci 390-hp V-8. All with AIR emissions

Interchange Number: 28
Part Number(s): 7036200
Type: Rochester
ID Number(s): 7036200, 7036204
Usage: 1966 full-size Chevrolet, Chevelle, with 396-ci 4 bbl with automatic transmission. All with AIR emissions; 1966 full-size Chevrolet with 427-ci 390-hp V-8 with automatic transmission. All with AIR emissions

Interchange Number: 29
Part Number(s): 7027103
Type: Rochester
ID Number(s): 7027101, 7027103
Usage: 1967 full-size Chevrolet, Chevelle, Nova with 283-ci 2 bbl with manual transmission. All without AIR emissions.

Interchange Number: 30
Part Number(s): 7027116
Type: Rochester
ID Number(s): 7027110, 7027112, 7027114, 7027116
Usage: 1967 full-size Chevrolet, Chevelle, Nova with 283-ci 2 bbl with automatic transmission. All without AIR emissions.

Interchange Number: 31
Part Number(s): 7037116
Type: Rochester
ID Number(s): 7037116
Usage: 1967 full-size Chevrolet, Chevelle, Nova; 1967 Camaro with 283-ci 2 bbl with automatic transmission. All with AIR emissions.

Interchange Number: 32
Part Number(s): 7037213
Type: Rochester
ID Number(s): 7037203, 7037213
Usage: 1967 full-size Chevrolet, Chevelle, Nova with 327-ci 4 bbl with manual transmission; 1967 Camaro with 327-ci or 350-ci 4-bbl V-8 with manual transmission. All with AIR emissions.

Interchange Number: 33
Part Number(s): 7037218
Type: Rochester
ID Number(s): 7037212, 7037218
Usage: 1967 full-size Chevrolet, Chevelle, Nova, Camaro, with 327-ci 4 bbl with automatic transmission; 1967 Camaro with 350-ci 4-bbl V-8 with automatic transmission. All with AIR emissions.

Interchange Number: 34
Part Number(s): 7027211
Type: Rochester
ID Number(s): 7027201, 7027211
Usage: 1967 full-size Chevrolet, Chevelle, Camaro with 396-ci 4 bbl with manual transmission. All without AIR emissions.; 1967 full-size Chevrolet with 427-ci 390-hp V-8. All without AIR emissions

Interchange Number: 35
Part Number(s): 7027216
Type: Rochester
ID Number(s): 7027200, 7027216
Usage: 1967 full-size Chevrolet, Chevelle, Camaro with 396-ci 4 bbl with automatic transmission. All without AIR emissions; 1967 full-size Chevrolet with 427-ci 390-hp V-8 with automatic transmission. All without AIR emissions

Interchange Number: 36
Part Number(s): 7037211
Type: Rochester
ID Number(s): 7037201, 703711
Usage: 1967 full-size Chevrolet, Chevelle, Camaro with 396-ci 4 bbl with manual transmission. All with AIR emissions.; 1967 full-size Chevrolet with 427-ci 390-hp V-8. All with AIR emissions

Interchange Number: 37
Part Number(s): 7037216
Type: Rochester
ID Number(s): 7037200, 7037216
Usage: 1967 full-size Chevrolet, Chevelle, Camaro with 396-ci 4 bbl with automatic transmission. All without AIR emissions; 1967 full-size Chevrolet with 427-ci 390-hp V-8 with automatic transmission. All with AIR emissions

Interchange Number: 38
Part Number(s): 7028229
Type: Rochester
ID Number(s): 7028219, 7028229
Usage: 1968 Nova, Chevelle with 327-ci 325-hp V-8; 1968-1969 Corvette with 327-ci 350-hp V-8.

Interchange Number: 39
Part Number(s):
Type: Holley 4160
ID Number(s): 3911
Usage: 1967 full-size Chevrolet, with 427-ci 425 hp V-8; 1967 Camaro Z-28 with 302-ci V-8 ; 1967 Chevelle, Camaro with 396-ci 375-hp V-8 with manual transmission All without AIR emissions

Interchange Number: 40
Part Number(s): 7028103
Type: Rochester
ID Number(s): 7028101, 7028103
Usage: 1968 full-size Chevrolet, Chevelle, Nova, Camaro with 307-ci 2bbl V-8 with manual transmission.

Interchange Number: 41
Part Number(s): 7028112
Type: Rochester
ID Number(s): 7028110, 7028112, 7038110, 7038112
Usage: 1968 full-size Chevrolet, Chevelle, Nova, Camaro with 307-ci 2bbl V-8 with Powerglide transmission.

Interchange Number: 42
Part Number(s): 7029112
Type: Rochester
ID Number(s): 7029110, 7029112
Usage: 1968-1969 full-size Chevrolet, Chevelle, Nova, Camaro with 307-ci 2bbl V-8 with Turbo Hydromantic transmission.

Interchange Number: 43
Part Number(s): 7029203
Type: Rochester
ID Number(s): 7028213, 7029203
Usage: 1968-1969 full-size Chevrolet, Chevelle, Nova, Camaro, C10-C30, 1500-3500 GMC truck with 327-ci 4bbl or 350-ci 4bbl with manual transmission.

Interchange Number: 44
Part Number(s): 7029233
Type: Rochester 4MV
ID Number(s): 7028213, 7029233
Usage: 1968-1969 full-size Chevrolet, Chevelle, Nova, Camaro, C10-C30, 1500-3500 GMC truck Corvette with 327-ci 4bbl or 350-ci 4bbl with automatic transmission. Except Special high performance.

Interchange Number: 45
Part Number(s): 7029215
Type: Rochester 4MV
ID Number(s): 7028217, 7029201, 7029215
Usage: 1968-1969 full-size Chevrolet, Chevelle, Nova, Camaro, with 396-ci V-8 except high performance or special high performance; 1968-1969 full-size Chevrolet or Corvette with 427-ci V-8 All with manual transmission. Except Special high performance.

Interchange Number: 46
Part Number(s): 7028210
Type: Rochester 4MV
ID Number(s): 7028210
Usage: 1968 full-size Chevrolet, Chevelle, Nova, Camaro, with 396-ci V-8 except high performance or special high performance; 1968 full-size Chevrolet with 427-ci V-8 all with automatic transmission. Except Special high performance.

Interchange Number: 47
Part Number(s):
Type: Holley 4150
ID Number(s): 4053
Usage: 1968--1969 full-size Chevrolet, with 427-ci 425 hp V-8; 1968-1969 Camaro Z-28 with 302-ci V-8 ; 1968-1969 Chevelle, Camaro, Nova with 396-ci 375-hp V-8; 1969 corvette with 350-ci 370-hp. with manual transmission All without AIR emissions

Interchange Number: 48
Part Number(s):
Type: Holley 4150
ID Number(s): 3607
Usage: 1966-1967 Nova with 327-ci 335/350 hp; 1967 Chevelle with 327-ci 325 hp V-8 with AIR emissions. All have manual transmission.

Interchange Number: 49
Part Number(s):
Type: Holley 4160
ID Number(s):
Usage: 1967 Chevelle, Camaro SS396 350-hp with automatic transmission without AIR emissions

Interchange Number: 50
Part Number(s): 7029115
Type: Rochester
ID Number(s): 7029113, 7029115
Usage: 1969 full-size Chevrolet, Camaro, Chevelle, Nova with 350-ci 2bbl V-8 with manual transmission.

Interchange Number: 51
Part Number(s): 7029116
Type: Rochester
ID Number(s): 7029114, 7029116
Usage: 1969 full-size Chevrolet, Camaro, Chevelle, Nova with 350-ci 2bbl V-8 with automatic transmission.

Interchange Number: 52
Part Number(s): 7029203
Type: Rochester
ID Number(s): 7029203
Usage: 1969 full-size Chevrolet, Camaro, Chevelle, Nova, Corvette with 350-ci 4 bbl V-8 with manual transmission. Except Z-28 or special high performance.

Interchange Number: 53
Part Number(s): 7029202
Type: Rochester
ID Number(s): 7029202
Usage: 1969 full-size Chevrolet, Camaro, Chevelle, Nova, Corvette with 327-c V-8 4-bbl or 350-ci 4 bbl V-8 with automatic transmission. Except Z-28 or special high performance.

Interchange Number: 54
Part Number(s): 7029103
Type: Rochester 2GV
ID Number(s): 7029101, 729103
Usage: 1969 Chevelle, Camaro, Nova with 307-ci V-8 with manual transmission. 1969 Camaro 327-ci V-8 2-bbl with manual transmission.

Interchange Number: 55
Part Number(s):
Type: Rochester 4MV
ID Number(s): 7928216, 7028218
Usage: 1968-1969 Chevelle, Camaro; 1969 Nova with 396-ci 350-hp with automatic transmission; 1968-1969 corvette with 427-ci 390-hp V-8 with automatic transmission.

1966-1967 air cleaner with base 396-ci V-8

Interchange Number: 56
Part Number(s): 7040103
Type: Rochester 2GV
ID Number(s): 7040101, 7040103
Usage: 1970 Chevelle, Camaro, Nova with 307-ci 2-bbl V-8 manual transmission,

Interchange Number: 57
Part Number(s): 7040112
Type: Rochester 2GV
ID Number(s): 7040110, 7040112
Usage: 1970 Chevelle, Camaro, Nova with 307-ci 2-bbl V-8 automatic transmission,

Interchange Number: 58
Part Number(s): 7040115
Type: Rochester 2GV
ID Number(s): 7040113, 7040115
Usage: 1970 Chevelle, Nova , full-size Chevrolet , Monte Carlo with 350-ci 2-bbl V-8 manual transmissions.

Interchange Number: 59
Part Number(s):7040136
Type: Rochester 2 GV
ID Number(s): 7040134, 7040136
Usage: 1970 Chevelle, Nova , full-size Chevrolet , Monte Carlo with 350-ci 2-bbl V-8 automatic transmissions.

Interchange Number: 60
Part Number(s): 7040213
Type: Rochester 4 MV
ID Number(s): 7040202, 7040203, 7040212, 7040213
Usage: 1970 Chevelle, Camaro (except Z-28), full-size Chevrolet, Nova, Monte Carlo, Corvette (except high performance) with 350-c 4-bbl V-8

Interchange Number: 61
Part Number(s): 7040221
Type: Rochester 4MV
ID Number(s):7040200, 7040201,7040221
Usage: 1970 Chevelle, Monte Carlo with 396-ci 330-hp; 1970 Chevelle, Monte Carlo, full-size Chevrolet with 454-ci V-8, except 450-hp.

Interchange Number: 62
Part Number(s): 7040205
Type: Rochester 4MV
ID Number(s):7040204, 7040205
Usage: 1970 Chevelle, Monte Carlo, Nova, Camaro with 396-ci 350-hp; 1970 Corvette with 454-ci V-8 390-hp.

Interchange Number: 63
Part Number(s):
Type: Holley 4150
ID Number(s): 4491A, 4493A
Usage: 1970 Chevelle, Monte Carlo, Nova, Camaro with 396-ci 375-hp; 1970 Chevelle, Monte Carlo, Corvette with 454-c 450/465 hp V-8. All have manual transmission and with E.E.C.

Interchange Number: 64
Part Number(s):
Type: Holley 4150
ID Number(s): 4557A 4559A
Usage: 1970 Chevelle, Monte Carlo, Nova, Camaro with 396-ci 375-hp; 1970 Chevelle, Monte Carlo, Corvette with 454-c 450/465 hp V-8. All have manual transmission and without E.E.C.

Interchange Number: 65
Part Number(s):
Type: Holley 4150
ID Number(s): R4556A
Usage: 1970 Chevelle, Monte Carlo, Nova, Camaro with 396-ci 375-hp; 1970 Chevelle, Monte Carlo, Corvette with 454-c 450/465 hp V-8. All have automatic transmission and with E.E.C.

Interchange Number: 66
Part Number(s):
Type: Holley 4150
ID Number(s): R4429AA
Usage: 1970 Chevelle, Monte Carlo, Nova, Camaro with 396-ci 375-hp; 1970 Chevelle, Monte Carlo, Corvette with 454-c 450/465 hp V-8. All have automatic transmission and without E.E.C.

Interchange Number: 67
Part Number(s): 7041101
Type: Rochester 2GV
ID Number(s): 7041101
Usage: 1971 Chevelle, Camaro, Nova, Ventura II with 307-ci 2-bbl V-8 manual transmission,

Interchange Number: 68
Part Number(s): 704110
Type: Rochester 2GV
ID Number(s): 7040110
Usage: 1971 Chevelle, Camaro, Nova Ventura II with 307-ci 2-bbl V-8 automatic transmission,

Interchange Number: 69
Part Number(s): 7041113
Type: Rochester 2GV
ID Number(s): 7041113
Usage: 1971 Chevelle, Nova, full-size Chevrolet , Monte Carlo with 350-ci 2-bbl V-8 manual transmissions.

Interchange Number: 70
Part Number(s):7041114
Type: Rochester 2 GV
ID Number(s): 7041110, 7041114
Usage: 1971 Chevelle, Nova, full-size Chevrolet, Monte Carlo with 350-ci 2-bbl V-8 automatic transmissions.

Interchange Number: 71
Part Number(s): 7041213
Type: Rochester 4 MV
ID Number(s): 7041212, 7041213
Usage: 1971 Chevelle, Camaro (except Z-28), full-size Chevrolet, Nova, Monte Carlo, Corvette (except high performance) with 350-c 4-bbl V-8

Interchange Number: 72
Part Number(s): 7041205
Type: Rochester 4MV
ID Number(s):7041200, 7041201, 7042204, 7041205
Usage: 1971 Chevelle, Monte Carlo, Nova, Camaro with 396-ci ;1970 Corvette with 454-ci V-8 390-hp except 425/430 hp.

Interchange Number: 73
Part Number(s):
Type: Holley 4150
ID Number(s): 4803-1AAS
Usage: 1971 Chevelle, Monte Carlo with 454-ci V-8; 1971 Corvette with 454-ci 425-hp

Interchange Number: 74
Part Number(s): 7042101
Type: Rochester 2GV
ID Number(s): 7042101
Usage: 1972 Chevelle, Camaro, Nova, Ventura II with 307-ci 2-bbl V-8 manual transmission,

Interchange Number: 75
Part Number(s): 7042100
Type: Rochester 2GV
ID Number(s): 7042100
Usage: 1972 Chevelle, Camaro, Nova, Ventura II with 307-ci 2-bbl V-8 automatic transmission,

Interchange Number: 76
Part Number(s): 7042833
Type: Rochester 2GV
ID Number(s): 7042833
Usage: 1972 Chevelle, Nova , full-size Chevrolet , Monte Carlo with 350-ci 2-bbl V-8 manual transmissions.
Notes: California Emissions

Interchange Number: 77
Part Number(s): 7042113
Type: Rochester 2GV
ID Number(s): 7042113
Usage: 1972 Chevelle, Nova, full-size Chevrolet , Monte Carlo with 350-ci 2-bbl V-8 manual transmissions.
Notes: Without California Emissions

Interchange Number: 78
Part Number(s):7042834
Type: Rochester 2 GV
ID Number(s): 7042834
Usage: 1972 Chevelle, Nova, full-size Chevrolet, Monte Carlo with 350-ci 2-bbl V-8 automatic transmissions.
Notes: With California Emissions'

Interchange Number: 79
Part Number(s):7042114
Type: Rochester 2 GV
ID Number(s): 7042114
Usage: 1972 Chevelle, Nova, full-size Chevrolet, Monte Carlo with 350-ci 2-bbl V-8 automatic transmissions.
Notes: Without California Emissions'

Interchange Number: 80
Part Number(s): 7042203
Type: Rochester 4 MV
ID Number(s): 7042202,7042203
Usage: 1972 Chevelle, Camaro (except Z-28), full-size Chevrolet, Nova, Monte Carlo, Corvette (except high performance) with 350-c 4-bbl V-8

Interchange Number: 81
Part Number(s): 7042220
Type: Rochester 4MV
ID Number(s): 7042220
Usage: 1972 Chevelle, Monte Carlo, full-size Chevrolet, Corvette with 454-ci V-8

1969 L35 base air cleaner

Air Cleaner

Air cleaners can cross over some models, and some engine sizes. But basically, engine size and carburetor type affects the interchange.

Model Identification   Interchange Number
Chevelle
1964
283 -ci V-8
2bbl..1
4bbl..3
327-ci
4bbl 3
1965
283 -ci V-8
2bbl..1
4bbl..3
327-ci
Except Special High Performance.................3
Special High Performance............................4
396-ci..14

1966
283 -ci V-8
2bbl..1
4bbl..3
327-ci
275-hp
Without AIR Emissions.................................25
With AIR Emissions......................................16
With Level Ride..17
350-hp
Without AIR Emissions.................................14
With AIR Emissions......................................15
396-ci
325-hp 5
360-hp
Without AIR emissions.................................13
With AIR Emissions..6
375-hp
Without AIR emissions.................................20
With AIR Emissions..6

1967
283 -ci V-8
With Level Ride..21
Without AIR
Early..22
Late..23
With AIR..24
327-ci
Except Special High Performance
With Level Ride..21
Without AIR
Early..22
Late..23
With AIR..26
Special High Performance
Without AIR emissions..7
With AIR Emissions..8
396-ci
325-hp..5
350-hp/ 375 hp
Without AIR emissions......................................31
With AIR emissions..6

1968
307 -ci V-8
Except Malibu or Concours
Manual Transmission..32
Automatic transmission....................................33
Malibu
Manual Transmission..34
Automatic transmission....................................35
327-CI 4-BBL
Except Special High performance
Manual transmission...36
Automatic transmission....................................37
Special High Performance..................................9
396-ci V-8
325-hp
Manual transmission...10
Automatic transmission....................................11
350 hp..31
375-hp..31

1969
307 -ci V-8
Manual transmission...12
Automatic transmission....................................15

350 -ci V-8
2-bbl
Manual transmission...40
Automatic transmission....................................46
396-ci
325-hp
Manual transmission...18
Automatic transmission....................................19
350 hp..31
375-hp..31

1970
307 -ci V-8
Except Malibu..48
Malibu..15
350 -ci V-8
2-bbl...40
4-bbl...41
396-ci
Except 375-hp
Without ducted hood...42
With Ducted hood..47
375-hp
Without ducted hood...45
With Ducted hood..47
400-ci 4-bbl BIG BLOCK...................................49
454-ci
Except 450-hp
Without ducted hood...42
With Ducted hood..47
450-hp
Without ducted hood...45
With Ducted hood..47

1971
307 -ci V-8
Except Malibu..48
Malibu..15
350 -ci V-8
2-bbl...40
4-bbl...41
402-ci...49
454-ci
Except 425-hp
Without ducted hood...50
With Ducted hood..51

450-hp
Without ducted hood..43
With Ducted hood..52

1972
307-ci V-8
Except Malibu..48
Malibu...15
350-ci V-8
2-bbl...40
4-bbl...41
402-ci..49
454-ci
Except 425-hp
Without ducted hood..53
With Ducted hood..51

Interchanges
Interchange Number: 1
Part Number(s): 6484445
Type: Single snorkel
Usage: 1964-1966 full-size Chevrolet, Chevelle, Nova with 283-ci 2-bbl V-8.
Note: Close vent system

Interchange Number: 2
Part Number(s): 6420903
Type: Single snorkel
Usage: 1959-1966 full-size Chevrolet with 283-ci 4-bbl V-8; 1959-1961 full-size Chevrolet with 348-ci V-8 except 3x2-bbl; 1962-1965 full-size Chevrolet with 327-ci 4-bbl V-8; 1964 Chevelle, Nova with 327-ci 4-bbl V-8
Notes: Does not have vent tube for closed ventilation. Interchange number 3 will fit, but closed vent tube must be pinched shut.

Interchange Number: 3
Part Number(s): 6484455
Type: Single snorkel
Usage: 1964 full-size Chevrolet with 283-ci 4-bbl V-8; 1964 full-size Chevrolet with 327-ci 4-bbl V-8; 1964 Chevelle, Nova with 327-ci 4-bbl except special high performance
Note: with closed vent system

Interchange Number: 4
Part Number(s): 6484420
Type: Dual snorkel
Usage: 1965 Chevelle with 327-ci Special High performance
Notes: Chrome plated

Interchange Number: 5
Part Number(s): 6484411
Type: Single snorkel
Usage: 1966-1967 Chevelle SS 396 with 325-hp.

Interchange Number: 6
Part Number(s): 6423269
Type: Open element
Usage: 1966-1967 Chevelle 396-ci 360-hp or 375-hp with AIR emissions

Interchange Number: 7
Part Number(s): 6423506
Type: Dual snorkel
Usage: 1967 Chevelle with 327-ci Special high performance without AIR emissions

Interchange Number: 8
Part Number(s): 6423507
Type: Dual snorkel
Usage: 1967 Chevelle with 327-ci Special high performance with AIR emissions

Interchange Number: 9
Part Number(s): 6423272
Type: Open element
Usage: 1968 Chevelle, Nova with 327-ci special high performance

Interchange Number: 10
Part Number(s): 6484226
Type: Single Snorkel
Usage: 1968 Chevelle SS 396 325-hp with manual transmission

Interchange Number: 11
Part Number(s): 6484227
Type: Single Snorkel
Usage: 1968 Chevelle SS 396 325-hp with automatic transmission

Interchange Number: 12
Part Number(s): 6484597
Type: Single snorkel
Usage: 1969 Chevelle, Nova, Camaro with 307-ci 2-bbl with manual transmission; 1969 Camaro with 327-ci 2-bbl with manual transmission
Notes: Those from a Malibu will not fit, not will this fit Malibu.

The 1968 307-ci air cleaner differed between Chevelle and Malibu models.

1970 air cleaner used with cowl duct hood

Interchange Number: 13
Part Number(s): 6484409
Type: Open Element
Usage: 1965-1967 full-size Chevrolet with 396-ci except 425-hp; 1966 full-size Chevrolet with 427-ci except with 425-hp or level ride; 1967 full-size Chevrolet with 427-ci 390-hp with AIR emissions except Impala SS 427
Notes: Open vent system.

Interchange Number: 14
Part Number(s): 6421214
Type: Dual snorkel
Usage: 1965 full-size Chevrolet with 396-ci 425-hp.; 1965 Chevelle SS396 Z16.
Notes: Close vent system.

Interchange Number: 15
Part Number(s): 6487430
Type: Single snorkel
Usage: 1969-1972 Camaro, 1970-1972 Chevelle, Nova with 307-ci 2-bbl V-8 and automatic transmission; 1969 Camaro with 327-ci 2-bbl V-8 with automatic transmission
Notes: Note for Malibu, Concours, or El Camino custom

Interchange Number: 16
Part Number(s): 6484410
Type: Single snorkel
Usage: 1966 full-size Chevrolet, Nova, Chevelle with 327-ci V-8 with AIR emissions or with level ride Except special high performance
Notes: Closed vent system

Interchange Number: 17
Part Number(s): 6422191
Type: Single snorkel
Usage: 1966 full-size Chevrolet, Nova, Chevelle with 327-ci V-8 with level ride. Except special high performance
Notes: Closed vent system

Interchange Number: 18
Part Number(s): 6484589
Type: Single snorkel
Usage: 1969 Chevelle SS 396 325-hp with manual transmission.

Interchange Number: 19
Part Number(s): 6484589
Type: Single snorkel
Usage: 1969 Chevelle SS 396 325-hp with automatic transmission.

Interchange Number: 20
Part Number(s): 6484415
Type: Open element
Usage: 1966-1967 full-size Chevrolet with 427-ci Special high performance 425-hp Without AIR emissions; 1966 Chevelle SS 396 375-hp without AIR emissions
Notes:

Interchange Number: 21
Part Number(s): 6423927
Type: Single snorkel
Usage: 1967 full-size Chevrolet, Chevelle with 283-ci V-8 with level ride.
Notes: Closed vent system

Interchange Number: 22
Part Number(s): 6424491
Type: Dual snorkel
Usage: Early 1967 full-size Chevrolet, Chevelle, Nova without AIR emissions 283-ci or 327-ci V-8
Notes: Closed vent system. Two tubes

Interchange Number: 23
Part Number(s): 6484489
Type: Single snorkel
Usage: Late 1967 full-size Chevrolet, Chevelle, Nova without AIR emissions 283-ci or 327-ci V-8
Notes: Closed vent system. One tube

Interchange Number: 24
Part Number(s): 6424803
Type: Single snorkel
Usage: 1967 full-size Chevrolet, Chevelle, Nova with AIR emissions 283-ci V-8
Notes: Closed vent system. One tube

An open element air cleaner was used on most high-performance models up to 1970

Interchange Number: 25
Part Number(s): 6421966
Type: Single snorkel
Usage: 1967 full-size Chevrolet, Chevelle, 327-ci V-8
Notes: Open vent system.

Interchange Number: 26
Part Number(s): 6484410
Type: Single snorkel
Usage: 1967 full-size Chevrolet, Chevelle, 327-ci V-8 with AIR Emissions
Notes: Open vent system.

Interchange Number: 27
Part Number(s): 6484580
Type: Single snorkel
Usage: 1969 Malibu, Concours with 307-ci automatic transmission
Notes: Plain Chevelle, used a different air cleaner.

Interchange Number: 28
Part Number(s): 6484579
Type: Single snorkel
Usage: 1969 Malibu, Concours with 307-ci manual transmission
Notes: Plain Chevelle used a different air cleaner.

Interchange Number: 29
Part Number(s): 6485902
Type: Single snorkel
Usage: 1969 plain Chevelle with 307-ci with automatic transmission
Notes: Malibu will not interchange.

Interchange Number: 30
Part Number(s): 64
Type: Single snorkel
Usage: 1970 plain Chevelle with automatic transmission
Notes: Malibu will not interchange.

Interchange Number: 31
Part Number(s): 6423907
Type: Open element design
Usage: 1967-1969 full-size 427-ci 425-hp without AIR emissions; 1966-1969 Chevelle SS 396 with 350-hp or 375 hp without AIR emission
Notes:

350-ci Air cleaner used from 1970-1972

Interchange Number: 32
Part Number(s): 6483655
Type: Single snorkel
Usage: 1968 Biscayne or Bel Air, Nova, Chevelle (except Malibu or Concours) with 307-ci V-8 a manual transmission
Notes: lid has a higher center dome than those sued with Impala or Caprice, or Malibu or Concourse models. Requires a different carburetor stud.

Interchange Number: 33
Part Number(s): 6424425
Type: Single snorkel
Usage: 1968 Biscayne or Bel Air, Nova, Chevelle (except Malibu or Concours) with 307-ci V-8 an automatic transmission
Notes: lid has a higher center dome than those sued with Impala or Caprice, or Malibu or Concours models. Requires a different carburetor stud.

Interchange Number: 34
Part Number(s): 6484219
Type: Single snorkel
Usage: 1968 Impala, Caprice, Malibu, Concours with 307-ci V-8 a manual transmission
Notes: Lid has a lower center dome than those sued with Biscayne, Be Air or regular Chevelle models. Requires a different carburetor stud.

Interchange Number: 35
Part Number(s): 6484218
Type: Single snorkel
Usage: 1968 Impala, Caprice, Malibu, Concours with 307-ci V-8 an automatic transmission
Notes: Lid has a lower center dome than those sued with Biscayne, Be Air or regular Chevelle models. Requires a different carburetor stud.

Interchange Number: 36
Part Number(s): 6484220
Type: Single snorkel
Usage: 1968 full-size Chevrolet, Nova, Chevelle, Camaro with 327-ci 4 bbl V-8 and manual transmission, except special high performance.

Interchange Number: 37
Part Number(s): 6484221
Type: Single snorkel
Usage: 1968 full-size Chevrolet, Nova, Chevelle, Camaro with 327-ci 4 bbl V-8 and an automatic transmission, except special high performance.

Interchange Number: 38
Part Number(s): 6484225
Type: Single snorkel
Usage: 1968 full-size Chevrolet, Nova, Chevelle, Camaro with 327-ci 4 bbl V-8 and an automatic transmission.

Interchange Number: 40
Part Number(s): 6484668
Type: Single snorkel
Usage: 1969-1972 Chevelle, full-size Chevrolet with 350-ci 2-bbl V-8; 1971 Monte Carlo with 400-ci SMALL BLOCK 2-bbl V-8; 1972 full-size Chevrolet with 400-ci 2-bbl SMALL BLOCK

Interchange Number: 41
Part Number(s): 6485240
Type:
Usage: 1970-1972 Chevelle, full-size Chevrolet with 350-ci 4-bbl

Interchange Number: 42
Part Number(s): 6485239
Type: Single snorkel
Usage: 1970 Chevelle, Camaro, Nova without out Special high performance or ducted hood.
Notes: Chrome cover

Interchange Number: 43
Part Number(s): 6485257
Type: Open Element
Usage: 1970-1971 Chevelle with 396-ci 375-hp or 454-ci 450-hp without ducted hood; 1970 Nova with 396-ci 375 hp.

Interchange Number: 44
Part Number(s): 6484668
Type: Single snorkel
Usage: 1969 full-size Chevrolet, Chevelle with 327-ci or 350-ci 2-bbl with an automatic transmission
Notes: those unit s from a 1969 Camaro or Nova will not fit.

Interchange Number: 45
Part Number(s): 6485257
Type: open element
Usage: 1970 Chevelle, Nova with 396-ci 375-hp V-8 without ducted hood; 1970 Chevelle with 454-ci 450-hp without ducted hood.

Interchange Number: 46
Part Number(s): 6484667
Type: Single snorkel
Usage: 1969 full-size Chevrolet, Chevelle with 350ci 2-bbl with manual transmission

Interchange Number: 47
Part Number(s): 6485235
Type: Single snorkel with seal
Usage: 1970 Chevelle with 396-ci or 454-ci with ducted hood; 1971 Chevelle with 454-ci with ducted hood.

Interchange Number: 48
Part Number(s): 6487428
Type: Single snorkel
Usage: 1970-1972 Malibu, Concours and El Camino Custom
Note: Plain Chevelle will not fit.

Interchange Number: 49
Part Number(s): 6485252
Type: Single snorkel
Usage: 1970 Chevelle with 400-ci BIG BLOCK V-8; 1971-1972 Chevelle with 402-ci V-8

Interchange Number: 50
Part Number(s): 6485254
Type: Single snorkel
Usage: 1971 Chevelle with 454-ci without ducted hood, or special high performance.

Interchange Number: 51
Part Number(s): 6485236
Type: Single snorkel
Usage: 1971-1972 Chevelle with 454-ci with ducted hood, or except special high performance.

Interchange Number: 52
Part Number(s): 6485257
Type: Single snorkel
Usage: 1971 Chevelle with 454-ci with ducted hood, with special high performance.

Interchange Number: 53
Part Number(s): 6487394
Type: Single snorkel
Usage: 1971 Chevelle with 454-ci without ducted hood

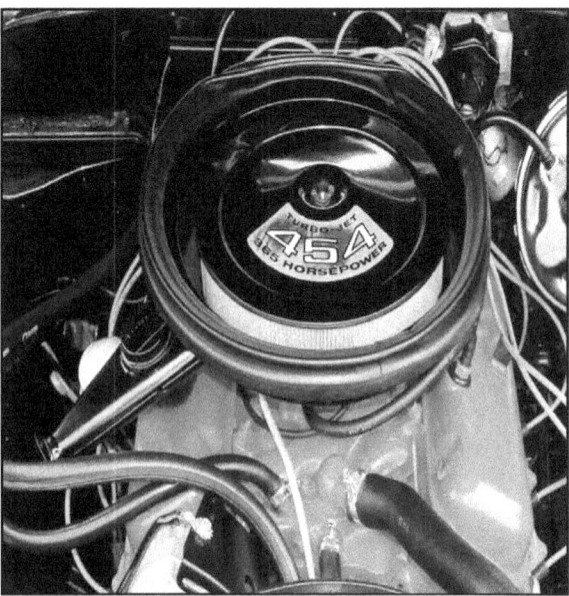
1971-1972 air cleaner used with cowl induction hood.

Chapter 3 Oiling and Cooling Systems

Oil Pump

Model Identification   *Interchange Number*

Chevelle

1964
283-ci/ 327-ci V-8..1

1965
283-ci/ 327-ci V-8..1
396-ci V-8...3

1966-1967
283-ci/ 327-ci V-8..1
396-ci V-8
Except Special High Performance.......................2
Special High Performance....................................3

1968-1969
307/327/350-ci V-8..1
396-ci V-8
Except Special High Performance.......................2
Special High Performance....................................3

1970-1972
307/327/350-ci V-8..1
396-ci/ 454-ci V-8
Except Special High Performance.......................2
Special High Performance....................................3

Interchanges

Interchange Number: 1
Part Number(s): 3821979
Usage: 1964-1977 Chevelle; 1967-1981 Camaro; (EXCEPT 1969-1972 Z-28) or 1968-1979 Nova with 283-ci, 305-ci, 307-ci V-8, 327-ci, 350-ci V-8,; 1959-1981 Corvette with 283-ci, 327-ci or 350-ci, except 1965 special high performance with mechanical lifters or fuel injection; 1959-1981 full-size Chevrolet with 283-ci, 305-ci, 327-ci or 350-ci, 1966-1981 C10-C30 with 283-ci, 305-ci, 307-ci, 327-ci, or 350-ci V-8; 1966-1974 GMC 1500-3500 with 283-ci, 305-ci 307-ci, 327-ci, or 350-ci V-8; 1970-1981 Monte Carlo with 305-ci, 350-ci or 400 SMALL-BLOCK; 1962-1965 full-size Chevrolet with 409-ci except special high performance or 2x4 bbl; 1978-1980 Malibu with 305-ci or 350-ci V-8 or 200-ci six cylinder;1975-1979 Monza with 305-ci or 350-ci V-8; 1971-1972 Ventura II with 307-ci; 1977 Ventura II with 305-ci;1977-1981 Firebird with 305-ci V-8; 1977-1978 Firebird 350-ci V-8; 1978-1981 Grand Prix with 305-ci V-8; 1977-1981 Lemans with 305-ci V-8; 1978 Lemans 350-ci (L-VIN code only); 1977-1980 Phoenix with 305-ci V-8 or 350-ci (L Code only); 1978-1979 Sunbird with 305-ci V-8; 1977-1980 Century with 305-ci V-8; 1977-1979 Skylark with 305-ci or 350-ci (L-code only) ;1978-1980 Cutlass with 305-ci V-8; 1978-1979 Cutlass with 350-ci V-8)L-code only); 1977 full-size Oldsmobile (L-code or 2-bbl only); 1977-1979 Omega with 305-ci V-8 or 350-ci (L-code only); 1970-1981 GMC with 305-ci, 307-ci, 350-ci.

Interchange Number: 2
Part Number(s): 3904827
Usage: 1966-1972 Chevelle; 1967-1972 Camaro; 1968-1970 Nova with 396-ci V-8 except 375-hp;; 1965-1972 full-size Chevrolet with 396 ci or 402-ci; 1966-1969 full-size Chevrolet, Corvette with 427-ci except with special high performance; 1970-1975 Chevelle, Corvette with 454-ci except special high performance (450, 465, 430, 425-hp); 1968-`1972 C10-C30 with 396-ci, 402-ci V-8; 1973-1975 C10-C30 with 454-ci; 1969-1972 GMC 1500-3500 with 396-ci or 402-ci or 400-ci BIG BLOCK; 1973-1975 GMC 1500-3500 with 454-ci V-8; 1970-1975 Monte Carlo with 454-ci V-8, except special high performance (450 or 425 hp); 1962-1965 full-size Chevrolet with 409-ci except high performance or 2x4bbl;

Interchange Number: 3
Part Number(s): 3904826
Usage: 1965-1972 Chevelle; 1967-1972 Camaro; 1968-1970 Nova with 396-ci 375- hp V-8; 1965-1972 full-size Chevrolet with 396 ci 375-h or 425-ci 425-hp; 1966-1969 full-size Chevrolet with a 427-ci 425-hp V-8; 1967-1969 Corvette with 427-ci with special high performance (400, 430 or 435-hp)1970-1971 Chevelle or Monte Carlo with 454-ci with special high performance (450-hp or 425-hp); 1970-1971 Corvette with 454-ci with special high performance 425 or 460-hp); 1964-1965 full-size Chevrolet with 409-ci special high performance or 2x4bbl; 1967-1969 Camaro Z-28 with 302-ci; 1970-1972 Camaro Z-28 with special high performance LT-1 350-ci V-8; 1970-1972 Corvette with LT-1 350-ci V-8

Oil Pan

Model Identification   Interchange Number

Chevelle

1964
283-ci V-8..1
327-ci
Except High performance..1
High Performance..2

1965-1967
283-ci/ 327-ci V-8..1
396-ci..4

1968-1969
307-ci/327-ci/350-ci V-8...3
396-ci..4

1970-1972
307-ci/ 350-ci V-8..3
396-ci/ 454-ci V-8..4

Interchanges

Interchange Number: 1
Part Number(s): 3788816
Usage: 1958-1964 full-size Chevrolet with 283-ci V-8; 1962-1964 full-size Chevrolet with 327-ci V-8; 1958-1964 Chevrolet truck or GMC truck with 283-ci V-8; 1964-1967 Chevelle, except 1964 327-ci high performance
Note: has one baffle

Interchange Number: 2
Part Number(s): 3830090
Usage: 1964 Chevelle with 327-ci high performance V-8.
Note: has two baffles, used with forged crankshaft.
Notes (2): Interchange Number 1 will fit.

Interchange Number: 3
Part Number(s): 3974252
Usage: 1968-1979 Nova with 283-ci, 327-ci V-8; 1967-1979 Camaro, except 307-ci, 327-ci or 350-ci except Z-28; 1968-1977 Chevelle with 283-ci , 307-ci, 327-ci or 350-ci V-8; 1965-1979 full-size Chevrolet with 283-ci, 307-ci ,327-ci or 350-ci V-8; 1970-1979 Monte Carlo with 350-ci V-8; 1971-1972 Ventura II 307-ci V-8l;1971-1973 C10-C30 with 350-ci V-8- except 4 wheel drive.; 1976-1979 Corvette with 350-c V-8; 1976-1979 Camaro, Nova, full-size Chevrolet with 305-ci V-8; 1974-1979 C10-C30 1500 to 3500 GMC with 305-ci or 350-ci V-8; 1977-979 Firebird with 305-ci V-8; 1978-1979 Firebird with 350-ci V-8; 1977-1978 Firebird with 350-ci V-8; 1978 Malibu with 350-ci V-8 ; 1971-1972 Ventura II with 307-ci; 1977 Ventura II with 305-ci;1977-1978 Lemans with 305-ci V-8; 1978 Lemans 350-ci (L-VIN code only); 1977-1980 Phoenix with 305-ci V-8 or 350-ci (L Code only); 1977-1980 Century with 305-ci V-8; 1977-1979 Skylark with 305-ci or 350-ci (L-code only) ;1978 Cutlass with 350-ci V-8; 1977 full-size Oldsmobile (L-code or 2-bbl only); 1977-1979 Omega with 305-ci V-8 or 350-ci (L-code only); 1970-1981 GMC with 305-ci, 307-ci, 350-ci.

Interchange Number: 4
Part Number(s): 3985999
Usage: 1968-1970 Nova with 396-ci; 1965-1972 Chevelle with 396-ci V-8; 1970-1972 Monte Carlo with 396/402-ci V-8; 1971-1975 full-size Chevrolet with 454-ci; 1970-1975 Chevelle with 454-ci V-8; 1970-1975 C10-C30, 1500-3500 GMC with 402-ci or 454-ci V-8; 1967-1972 Camaro with 396/402-ci V-8

Radiator

The radiator core interchange is heavily influence on the model itself and engine size and output. Other factors that may affect it are certain options transmission type, as those with automatic transmissions require a transmission cooler, those models with Heavy-Duty cooling or air conditioning can also affect the interchange.

  The core is identified by its overall length, width and thickness. It can be identified by the Harrison ID number that can be found stamped into a metal tag that is clipped to the core itself. It is usually found attached the right-hand side, but some are found on the left and even at the top.

  This is usually a two-letter code that is found in the bigger font on the right hand side of the tag. These codes when know are given, however these tags are easily lost and can be switched so always use other methods besides this to identify your core.

  Note that those from a car with automatic transmission with the same engine and if equipped options (i.e. Heavy –duty cooling or air conditioning) will fit a car with manual transmission if the cooler line inlet is blocked off. This was what was usually done in later years as replacement cores put out, it was the unit for automatics. A unit for a car with manual transmission does not contain an inner cooler and will not fit cars with automatic transmissions.

Model Identification   **Interchange Number**

Chevelle

1964

283-ci
Without Air conditioning or Heavy-Duty Cooling
Manual transmission..1
Automatic transmission...3
With Air conditioning or Heavy-Duty Cooling
Manual transmission..2
Automatic transmission...4

327-ci
Without Air conditioning or Heavy-Duty Cooling
Manual transmission..1
Automatic transmission...3
With Air conditioning or Heavy-Duty Cooling
Manual transmission..2
Automatic transmission...4

1965

283-ci
Without Air conditioning or Heavy-Duty Cooling
Manual transmission..1
Automatic transmission...5
With Air conditioning or Heavy-Duty Cooling
Manual transmission..2
Automatic transmission...6

327-ci
Except 360-hp Special High Performance
Without Air conditioning or Heavy-Duty Cooling
Manual transmission..1
Automatic transmission...5
With Air conditioning or Heavy-Duty Cooling
Manual transmission..2
Automatic transmission...6
360-hp...7
396-ci...10

1966

283-ci
Without Air conditioning or Heavy-Duty Cooling
Manual transmission..8
Automatic transmission...9
With Air conditioning or Heavy-Duty Cooling
Manual transmission...12
Automatic transmission...13

327-ci
Without Air conditioning or Heavy-Duty Cooling
Manual transmission...28
Automatic transmission...29
With Air conditioning or Heavy-Duty Cooling
Manual transmission...12
Automatic transmission...13

396-ci
Manual transmission...10
Automatic transmission...11

1967

283-ci
Without Air conditioning or Heavy-Duty Cooling
Manual transmission..8
Automatic transmission...9
With Air conditioning or Heavy-Duty Cooling
Manual transmission...12
Automatic transmission...13

327-ci
Without Air conditioning or Heavy-Duty Cooling
Manual transmission...14
Automatic transmission...15
With Air conditioning or Heavy-Duty Cooling
Manual transmission...12
Automatic transmission...13

396-ci
325-hp or 350-hp
Manual transmission...16
Automatic transmission
Powerglide
Without Air Conditioning...18
With Air Conditioning or
Heavy-Duty Cooling..17
Turbo-Hydromantic...20
375-hp...21

1968

307-ci
Without Air conditioning or Heavy-Duty Cooling
Manual transmission...21
Automatic transmission...29
With Air conditioning or Heavy-Duty Cooling
Manual transmission...22
Automatic transmission...31

350-ci
Without Air conditioning or Heavy-Duty Cooling
Manual transmission..21
Automatic transmission...30
With Air conditioning or Heavy-Duty Cooling
Manual transmission..22
Automatic transmission...31
396-ci
Without Air Conditioning or Heavy-Duty Cooling
Manual transmission..22
Automatic transmission...23
Heavy-Duty cooling or Air Conditioning....................23

1969
307-ci
Without Air conditioning or Heavy-Duty Cooling
Manual transmission..21
Automatic transmission...30
With Air conditioning or Heavy-Duty Cooling
Manual transmission..22
Automatic transmission...31
350-ci
Without Air conditioning or Heavy-Duty Cooling
Manual transmission..21
Automatic transmission...30
With Air conditioning or Heavy-Duty Cooling
Manual transmission..22
Automatic transmission...31
396-ci
Except 375-hp
Without Air conditioning or Heavy-Duty Cooling
Manual transmission..25
Automatic transmission...24
With Air conditioning or Heavy-Duty Cooling
Manual transmission..24
Automatic transmission...24
375-hp...24

1970-1972
307-ci
Without Air conditioning or Heavy-Duty Cooling
Manual transmission..21
Automatic transmission.......................................30, 33
With Air conditioning or Heavy-Duty Cooling
All..22, 34
350-ci
Without Air conditioning or Heavy-Duty Cooling
Manual transmission..21
Automatic transmission...30
With Air conditioning or Heavy-Duty Cooling
Manual transmission..22
Automatic transmission.......................................31, 34
396-ci/ 454-ci
Except 375-hp, 425 or 450 hp
Without Air Conditioning or Heavy-Duty Cooling
Manual transmission..22
Automatic transmission...31
With Air Conditioning or Heavy-Duty Cooling
Manual transmission..26
Automatic transmission...32
375hp/ 425-hp/450-hp...24

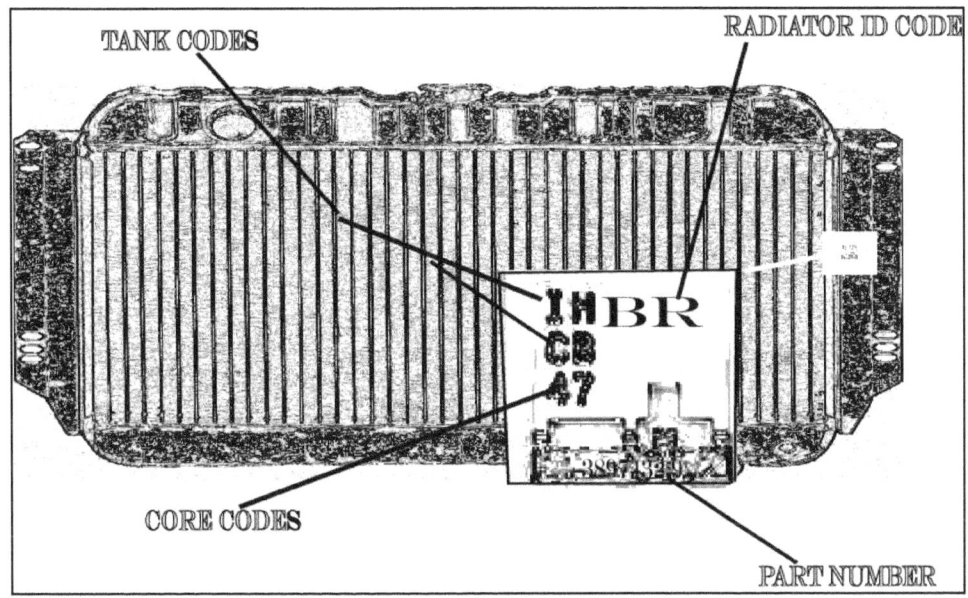

Harrison radiators are identified by a code letters or numbers that are on tag on the core. Location of this tag varies but it is usually found her on the right hand side of the core.

Interchange Number: 1
Part Number(s): 3159110
ID Number(s): 619A
Dimensions: 15 ½ x 23.02 x 1 .26 inches
Usage: 1964-1965 Chevelle with 283-ci manual transmission; 1964 Chevelle with 327-ci with manual transmission
Notes: Interchange Number 4 is the replacement core and will fit.

Interchange Number: 2
Part Number(s): 3002011
ID Number(s): 611A
Dimensions: 15 ½ x 25.22 x1.985 inches
Usage: 1964-1965 Chevelle 283 ci or 327-ci V-8 with manual transmission with air conditioning or heavy-duty cooling
Notes: Interchange Number 4 is the replacement core and will fit.

Interchange Number: 3
Part Number(s): 3159118
ID Number(s): 619A
Dimensions: 15 ½ x25.22 x1.26 inches
Usage: 1964 Chevelle 283 ci or 327-ci with automatic transmission
Notes: Interchange Number 4 is the replacement core and will fit.

Interchange Number: 4
Part Number(s): 3002019
ID Number(s): 619A
Dimensions: 15 ½ x25.22 x1.985 inches
Usage: 1964 Chevelle with 283ci and automatic transmission with air conditioning; 1964 Chevelle with 327-ci with automatic transmission and air conditioning or Heavy-Duty cooling
Notes: This unit was used as a service part and will fit 1964-1965 283ci Chevelles with any type of transmission

Interchange Number: 5
Part Number(s): 3004518
ID Number(s): 10
Dimensions: 15 ½ x23.02x 1 .26 inches
Usage: 1965 Chevelle with 283 ci V-8 with automatic transmission without air conditioning or Heavy-Duty cooling;1965 Chevelle with 327ci except special high-performance
Notes: Interchange Number 6 is the replacement core and will fit.

Interchange Number: 6
Part Number(s): 3004519
ID Number(s):
Dimensions: 15 ½ x25.22x 1.985 inches
Usage: 1965 Chevelle with 283 or 327ci with automatic transmission with air conditioning; Late 1967 Nova with 327ci Powerglide with air conditioning or heavy-duty cooling. Except special high performance.
Notes: Service part will fit 1964-1965 Chevelle, all applications.

Interchange Number: 7
Part Number(s): 3003616
Dimensions: 15 ½ x23.02 x 1 .75 inches
Usage: 1965 Chevelle with 327ci 360hp V-8 (special high performance)
Notes: No other interchange.

Interchange Number: 8
Part Number(s): 3007610
Dimensions: 15 ½ x23 x1 1/4 inches
Usage: 1966-1967 Chevelle with 283-ci or 327-ci V-8 and manual transmission without AIR emissions, air conditioning, or heavy-duty cooling

Interchange Number: 9
Part Number(s): 3007618
Dimensions: 15 ½ x 23.02 x 1.26 inches
Usage: 1966-1967 Chevelle with 283 ci with automatic transmission; 1967 Chevelle with 327-ci and automatic transmission with AIR emissions, but without air conditioning.

Interchange Number: 10
Part Number(s): 3007620
Dimensions: 15 ½ x25.25 x 2.00 inches
Usage: 1965-1966 Chevelle SS 396 with manual transmission with or without
heavy-duty cooling and or air conditioning

Interchange Number: 11
Part Number(s): 3007621
Dimensions: 15 ½ x25 ¼ x 2.00 inches
Usage: 1966 Chevelle SS 396 with automatic transmission

Interchange Number: 12
Part Number(s): 3012212
Dimensions: 15 ½ x23 x1 1/4 inches
Usage: 1966-1967 Chevelle 283 ci or 327-ci V-8 with manual transmission with Heavy-Duty cooling or air conditioning. Except special high performance

Interchange Number: 13
Part Number(s): 3012519
Dimensions: 16x 25.1 /4 x 1.314 inches
Usage: 1966-1967 Chevelle 283 ci or 327 ci V-8 with automatic transmission with air conditioning

Interchange Number: 14
Part Number(s): 3012213
Dimensions: 15 ½ x23 x1-1/4 inches
Usage: 1967 Chevelle with 327 ci 275hp V-8 and manual transmission.

Interchange Number: 15
Part Number(s): 3012241
Dimensions: 15 ½ x23 x 1-1/4 inches
Usage: 1967 Chevelle with 327ci V-8 with automatic transmission

Interchange Number: 16
Part Number(s): 3012137
Dimensions: 15 1 12x25.1 l4x1 3/4 inches
Usage: 1967 Chevelle SS 396 except 375hp with manual transmission

Interchange Number: 17
Part Number(s): 3010209
Dimensions: 15 ½ x 25-1/4 x 2 5/8 inches
Usage: 1967 Chevelle SS 396ci with Powerglide automatic transmission with heavy-duty cooling or air conditioning

Interchange Number: 18
Part Number(s): 3013424
Dimensions: 15 ½ x25-1/4 x 1-3/4 inches
Usage: 1967 Chevelle SS 396 with Powerglide without air conditioning or heavy-duty cooling

Interchange Number: 19
Part Number(s): 3007620
Dimensions: 15-1/2 x25-1/4 x 2.00 inches
Usage: 1966-1967 Chevelle with 327-ci V-8 325-hp with manual transmission with heavy-duty cooling or air conditioning; 1966-1967 Chevelle SS 396 375-hp
Notes: Interchange number 20 will fit.

Interchange Number: 20
Part Number(s): 3007621
Dimensions: 15-1/2 x 25-1/4 x 2.00 inches
Usage: 1967 Chevelle SS 396ci with Turbo Hydra-Matic 400

Interchange Number: 21
Part Number(s): 3022040
ID Number(s): VB
Dimensions: 1 7x20 3/4x1-1/4 inches
Usage:
  Chevrolet: 1968 Nova with 327-ci V-8 or six-cylinder; 1968-1970 Chevelle with 327 or 350ci without heavy-duty cooling or air conditioning; 1968-1970 Chevelle six-cylinder with heavy-duty cooling; 1969-1971 Nova with 307-ci or 350-ci V-8; 1970-1971 Camaro with 307-ci or 350 ci except Z-28; 1970-1971 Monte Carlo with 350ci V-8 without air conditioning with heavy-duty cooling or air conditioning, all models have manual transmission.
  Buick: 1966-1967 Skylark with 340-ci V-8 without air conditioning; 1968-1969 Skylark six-cylinder without a/c all models have manual transmission.
  Oldsmobile: 1969 Cutlass (except 442) with 350-ci or 455-ci with automatic transmission without air conditioning, all models have manual transmission.
  Pontiac: 1969-1971 LeMans with six-cylinder without air conditioning; 1971 LeMans with 400-ci V-8 without air condition; 1971 Ventura with 307ci V-8, all models have manual transmission.
Notes: Interchange Number 29 will fit.

Interchange Number: 22
Part Number(s): 3017258
Dimensions: 17x28-3/8x1/4
Usage:
  Chevrolet: 1968 Chevelle SS 396 with manual transmission without air conditioning or heavy-duty cooling; 1968-1969 Chevelle with 307-ci 327-ci, or 350-ci V-8 with air conditioning or heavy-duty cooling; 1970-1971 Monte Carlo with 350-ci or 400-ci SMALL BLOCK V-8 with heavy-duty cooling or air conditioning; 1970-1971 Chevelle with 307-ci or 350-ci V-8 with air conditioning or heavy-duty cooling; all with manual transmission
  Buick: 1970-1971 Le Sabre with 350ci V-8 without air conditioning with manual transmission.
  Oldsmobile: 1971 442 with 455ci without air conditioning; 1971 Cutlass with 350ci V-8 with air conditioning or Heavy-Duty cooling with manual transmission.
Notes: Interchange Number 23 will fit

Interchange Number: 23
Part Number(s): 3014609
Dimensions: 17x28 3/8 x2
Usage:
  Chevrolet: 1968 Chevelle SS 396 with air conditioning or Heavy-Duty cooling; 1968 Chevelle SS 396 with automatic without air conditioning or heavy-duty cooling
  Oldsmobile: 1968 full-size Oldsmobile with 350-ci or 455-ci without air conditioning or heavy-duty cooling

Interchange Number: 24
Part Number(s): 3019205
ID Number(s): BR
Dimensions: 17x28-3/8x2 inches
Usage:
  Chevrolet: 1969-1970 SS 396 (402-ci) 375hp; 1969-1971 SS 396 (402-ci) with automatic transmission with heavy-duty cooling or air conditioning; 1970 Monte Carlo with 396/402ci V-8 with automatic transmission with air conditioning;1970-1971 Chevelle SS 454 with 450 or 425-hp LS-6; 1970-1971 Monte Carlo SS 454;1971 Chevelle SS 454
  Pontiac: 1968 LeMans with 400-ci 2bbl V-8 or 350 4bbl V-8; 1968-1969 Lemans with 350-ci V-8 with air conditioning; 1969 Bonneville with 428ci V-8; 1969 Pontiac Grand Prix with 400-ci V-8 or 428-ci V-8; 1969 Lemans 400-ci 2bbl V-8 with heavy-duty cooling or air conditioning; 1970 GTO with 400-ci with RAM AIR III but without air conditioning or heavy-duty cooling; 1971 Lemans 400-ci V-8 with air conditioning, except with Ram Air; 1970 GTO with 455-ci without air conditioning or heavy-duty cooling; 1970-1971 LeMans with 350-ci with automatic transmission with air conditioning or heavy-duty cooling; 1970-1971 Pontiac Grand Prix with 455-ci V-8 without air conditioning; 1970-1971 Bonneville with 350-ci or 400-ci V-8 with air conditioning or heavy-duty cooling; 1971 Lemans with 455ci 335hp without air conditioning
Notes: Part number is listed as 3020143 in Pontiac but will fit the Chevelle.

Interchange Number: 25
Part Number(s): 3016908
Usage:
  Chevrolet: 1969-1970 Chevelle SS 396, except for 375hp or with heavy-duty cooling or air conditioning; 1970 Monte Carlo 402-ci four-speed; 1971 Chevelle SS 402-ci with air conditioning
  Pontiac: 1970 Lemans with 350-ci V-8 without air conditioning; 1970 Bonneville with 350-ci or 400-ci with manual transmission without air conditioning

Interchange Number: 26
Part Number(s): 3017248
Usage:
  Chevrolet: 1970 Chevelle SS 454 with heavy-duty cooling or air conditioning; 1970 Chevelle SS with 402-ci with heavy-duty cooling or air conditioning
  Pontiac: 1968-1969 Lemans with 350 with air conditioning or heavy-duty; 1968 Lemans with 400-ci 2-bbl or 350-hp 4bbl;
1969 Pontiac Grand Prix with 400-ci or 428-ci V8; 1969 Bonneville with 428-ci V-8; 1969 Lemans with 400-ci 2bbl with heavy-duty cooling or air conditioning; 1970 GTO with 400-ci with RAM AIR II with air conditioning or heavy-duty cooling; 1970 Lemans with 400ci with air conditioning but without Ram Air; 1970 GTO with 455-ci with air conditioning or heavy-duty cooling, 1970-1971 Lemans with 350-ci V-8 with automatic transmission with air conditioning or heavy-duty cooling;
1970-1971 Grand Prix with 455- ci with air conditioning or heavy-duty cooling; 1970-1971 Bonneville with 350-ci or 400ci V-8 with air conditioning or Heavy-Duty cooling; 1971 Lemans with 455-ci 335-hp V-8 with air conditioning or Heavy-Duty cooling

Interchange Number: 27
Part Number(s): 3017248
Usage:
  Chevrolet: 1970 Chevelle SS 454 automatic with heavy-duty cooling or air conditioning; 1970 Chevelle SS396 (402-ci) with automatic transmission and air conditioning or Heavy-Duty cooling

Interchange Number: 28
Part Number(s): 3007613
ID Number(s):
Dimensions: 15 ½ x 23 x 1 -1/4 inches
Usage: 1966 Chevelle with 327-ci manual transmission
Notes: Interchange number 29 will fit.

Interchange Number: 29
Part Number(s): 3007615
Dimensions: 15 ½ x 23 x 2 inches
Usage: 1966 Chevelle with 327-ci with automatic transmission

Interchange Number: 30
Part Number(s): 3022041
ID Number(s): VC
Dimensions: 1 7x20 3/4x 2inches
Usage:
  Chevrolet: 1968 Nova with 327-ci V-8 or six-cylinder; 1968-1970 Chevelle with 327 or 350ci without heavy-duty cooling or air conditioning; 1968-1970 Chevelle six-cylinder with heavy-duty cooling; 1969-1971 Nova with 307-ci or 350-ci V-8; 1970-1971 Camaro with 307-ci or 350 ci except Z-28; 1970-1971 Monte Carlo with 350ci V-8 without air conditioning with heavy-duty cooling or air conditioning, all models have automatic transmission.
  Buick: 1966-1967 Skylark with 340-ci V-8 without air conditioning; 1968-1969 Skylark six-cylinder without a/c all models have automatic transmission.
  Oldsmobile: 1969 Cutlass (except 442) with 350-ci or 455-ci with automatic transmission without air conditioning, all models has an automatic transmission.
  Pontiac: 1969-1971 LeMans with six-cylinder without air conditioning; 1971 LeMans with 400-ci V-8 without air condition; 1971 Ventura with 307ci
V-8, all models have automatic transmission.

Interchange Number: 31
Part Number(s): 3017258
Dimensions: 17x28-3/8x2
Usage:
  Chevrolet: 1968 Chevelle SS 396 with automatic transmission without air conditioning or heavy-duty cooling; 1968-1969 Chevelle with 307-ci 327-ci, or 350-ci
V-8 with air conditioning or heavy-duty cooling; 1970-1971 Monte Carlo with 350-ci or 400-ci SMALL BLOCK V-8 with heavy-duty cooling or air conditioning; 1970-1971 Chevelle with 307-ci or 350-ci V-8 with air conditioning or heavy-duty cooling; all with automatic transmission
  Buick: 1970-1971 LeSabre with 350ci V-8 without air conditioning with automatic transmission.
  Oldsmobile: 1971 442 with 455ci without air conditioning; 1971 Cutlass with 350ci V-8 with air conditioning or Heavy-Duty cooling with automatic transmission.
Notes: Interchange Number 23 will fit

Interchange Number: 32
Part Number(s): 3016909
Usage:
   Chevrolet: 1969-1970 Chevelle SS 396, except for 375hp or with heavy-duty cooling or air conditioning; with automatic transmission; 1970 Monte Carlo 402-ci automatic; 1971 Chevelle SS 402-ci with air conditioning
   Pontiac: 1970 Lemans with 350-ci V-8 without air conditioning; 1970 Bonneville with 350-ci or 400-ci with automatic transmission without air conditioning

Interchange Number: 33
Part Number(s): 3025068
ID Codes:, VA,VB,VC, VD, VE, VG, VH,VI,VJ, VO,VS,
Usage:
1972 Chevelle full-size Chevrolet, Lemans with 6-cylinder; 1972 Chevelle with 307-ci without air conditioning or Heavy-Duty cooling; 1972 Nova with 350-ci with manual transmission except with air conditioning

Interchange Number: 34
Part Number(s): 3025230
ID Codes: CJ,CK,CL,CP,CQ,CR,CS,YG
Usage: 1972 Chevelle, full-size Chevrolet with 307-ci, 350-ci or 400 c- SMALL BLOCK V-8 with air conditioning or Heavy-Duty cooling; 1972 Sky lark or full-size Buick with 350-ci and air conditioning; 1972 Cutlass with 350-ci or 455-ci with air conditioning

Water pumps can be identified by their casting number

Water Pump

Model Identification   Interchange Number
Chevelle

1964
283-ci..1
327-ci..1
409-ci
Early..6
Late...7

1965
283-ci..2
327-ci..1
409-ci..7
396-ci..3

1966-1967
283-ci..2
327-ci..2
396-ci..3
427-ci..3

1968
307-ci..1
327-ci..2
350-ci..2
396-ci..3

1969
307-ci..5
350-ci..5
396-ci..4

1970-1972
307-ci..5
350-ci..5
396-ci..4
454-ci..4

Interchanges
Interchange Number: 1
Part Number(s): 3998207
Casting Number: 3859326
Usage: 1967-1968 Camaro Z-28 302-ci V-8; 1957-1965 full-size Chevrolet with 283-ci or 327-ci V-8, 1964-1965 Nova with 283-ci or 327-ci V-8; 1964-1965 Chevelle with 327-ci V-8 except 350-hp

Interchange Number: 2
Part Number(s): 3998206
Casting Number: 3738493
Usage: 1967-1968 Camaro with 327-ci, 350-ci V-8; 1964-1965 Chevelle with 283-c V-8; 1965 Chevelle with 327-ci 350-hp V-8 1966-1967 Chevelle, full-size Chevrolet Nova with 283-ci or 327-ci V-8

Interchange Number: 3
Part Number(s): 3990993
Casting Number: 3738493 or 3856284
Usage: 1967-1968 Camaro with 396-ci; 1965-1967 Chevelle SS 396; 1965-1967 full-size Chevrolet with 396-ci or 427-ci 1965-1967 Corvette with 396-ci or 427-ci.

Interchange Number: 4
Part Number(s): 6272159
Casting Number: 3969811
Usage: 1969-1972 Camaro, Chevelle, full-size Chevrolet, Nova, Corvette with 396-ci-, 402-ci 400-ci BIG BLOCK, 427-ci V-8; 1970-1975 Chevelle, Monte Carlo, full-size Chevrolet, Corvette with 454-ci V-8

Interchange Number: 5
Part Number(s): 474028
Casting Number: 3953692 or 3927170
Usage: 1969-1976 Camaro, Chevelle, full-size Chevrolet, Nova, Corvette with 307-ci, 327-ci, 350-ci or 400-ci SMALL BLOCK V-8; 1969 Z-28 with 302-ci V-8; 1976 Camaro, Chevelle, Nova, full-size Chevrolet with 305-ci V-8

Chapter 4 Exhaust Systems

Exhaust Manifolds

Exhaust manifolds are greatly interchangeable within their own family group. But certain restrictions do apply. Emissions systems-specifically the Air Injection Reactor, or AIR, System-greatly influence the interchange process. Transmission type may also affect certain applications. If any restrictions apply, they appear in the "Notes" section of each Interchange entry.

Manifolds from a car with AIR Emissions can be used on a car without AIR emissions if the holes are plugged, in fact factory-built cars have been found this way. However, those from a car without AIR cannot be used on a car with AIR emissions.

Model Identification   *Interchange Number*

Chevelle

1964
283-ci/ 327-ci V-8
LH..3
RH..4

1965
283-ci/ 327-ci V-8
LH..3
RH..4
396-ci
LH..21
RH..6

1966-1967
Without AIR Emissions
283-ci/ 327-ci V-8
LH..3
RH..4
396-ci
LH..7
RH..6

With AIR Emissions
283-ci/ 327-ci
LH..2
RH..1
396-ci
LH..8
RH..6

1968
307-ci/327-ci/350-ci
LH..1
RH..2
396-ci
Except High Performance or Special High Performance
LH..5
RH..6
High Performance or Special High-Performance
LH..8
RH..6

1969
307-ci/ 350-ci
Manual transmission
LH..9
RH..10
Automatic transmission
LH..11
RH..12
396-ci
Except High Performance or Special High Performance
LH..5
RH..6
High Performance or Special High-Performance
LH..8
RH..6

1970-1971
307-ci/ 350-ci V-8
LH..11
RH..13
396-ci/ 454-ci
Except Special High-Performance
LH..14
RH..17
375-hp 425-hp or 450-hp
LH..8
RH..17

1972
307-ci
LH..11
RH..13
Without NOX Emissions
350-ci
LH..11
RH..13
402-ci
LH..14
RH..15
With NOX Emissions
350-ci
LH..9
RH..16
402-ci/ 454-ci V-8
LH..8
RH..17

Interchanges

Interchange Number: 1
Part Number(s): RH, 3872730
Casting Number(s): 3750556
Notes: 1967 Camaro with 302-ci, 327-ci or 350-ci with AIR emissions; 1968 Camaro with 302-ci, 327-ci, 350-ci with manual transmission; 1966 Chevelle with 283-ci 4-bbl or 327-ci With AIR emissions; 1967 Chevelle with 283-ci or 327-ci V-8 with AIR emissions: 1968 Chevelle, Nova with 307-ci , 327-ci V-8 with manual transmission.
Notes: All manifolds use no choke tube.

Interchange Number: 2
Part Number(s): LH 3892683
Casting Number(s): 3749965
Notes: 1967 Camaro with 302-ci, 327-ci or 350-ci with AIR emissions; 1968 Camaro with 302-ci, 327-ci, 350-ci with manual transmission; 1966 Chevelle with 283-ci 4-bbl or 327-ci With AIR emissions; 1967 Chevelle with 283-ci or 327-ci V-8 with AIR emissions: 1968 Chevelle, Nova with 307-ci , 327-ci V-8 with manual transmission.
Notes: All manifolds use no choke tube.

Interchange Number: 3
Part Number(s): LH 389679
Casting Number: 3834947
Usage: 1967 Camaro, with 302-ci, 327-ci or 350-ci V-8 without AIR Emissions; 1968 Camaro with 327-ci or 350-ci with automatic transmission; 1964- 1965 Chevelle with 283-ci or 327-ci V-8; 1966-1967 Chevelle with 283-ci or 327-ci without AIR Emissions; 1968 Chevelle, Nova with 307-ci 327-ci or 350-ci V-8 with automatic transmission.

Interchange Number: 4
Part Number(s): RH 3893608
Casting Number: 3840912
Usage: 1967 Camaro, with 302-ci, 327-ci or 350-ci V-8 without AIR Emissions; 1968 Camaro with 327-ci or 350-ci with automatic transmission; 1964- 1965 Chevelle with 283-ci or 327-ci V-8; 1966-1967 Chevelle with 283-ci or 327-ci without AIR Emissions; 1968 Chevelle, Nova with 307-ci 327-ci or 350-ci V-8 with automatic transmission.

Interchange Number: 5
Part Number(s): LH 3969909
Casting Number: 3883999
Usage: 1967 Camaro, with 396-ci without AIR emissions; 1966-1967 Chevelle with 396-ci without AIR emissions; 1968-1969 Chevelle SS with 325-hp 396-ci V-8 and automatic transmission

Interchange Number: 6
Part Number(s): RH 3989312
Casting Number: 3916178
Usage: 1967-1970 Camaro with 396-ci V-8; 1972 Camaro, Nova, Chevelle, full-size Chevrolet with 402-ci with NOX emissions; 1965-1970 Chevelle with 396-ci V-8; 1968-1970 Nova with 396-ci V-8; 1968-1969 full-size Chevrolet with 396-ci 427-ci; 1970 Chevelle, Monte Carlo, full-size Chevrolet with 454-ci V-8; 1972 Chevelle, Monte Carlo, full-size Chevrolet with 454-ci V-8 with NOX emissions;

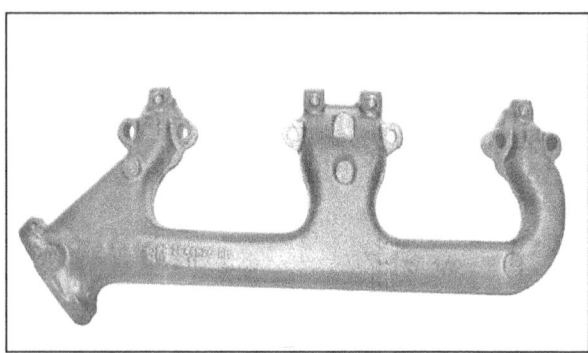

The 1967-1969 Z-28 Manifold can be found on a variety of other small block engines. Photo courtesy of YEAR ONE

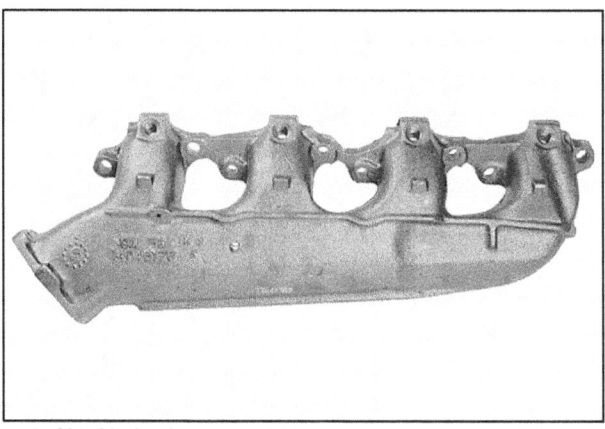
Typical big block exhaust manifolds. Photo courtesy of YEAR ONE

Interchange Number: 7
Part Number(s): LH 3969909
Casting Number: 3883999
Usage: 1967 Camaro, with 396-ci without AIR emissions; 1966-1969 Chevelle with 396-ci without AIR emissions.

Interchange Number: 8
Part Number(s): LH 3989345
Casting Number: 3909879
Usage: 1967 Camaro, Chevelle with 396-ci with AIR emissions; 1968-1970 Camaro with 396-ci V-8 ; 1968-1970 Chevelle SS 396 with 350-hp or 375-hp; 1970 Chevelle with 454-ci 450-hp V-8; 1971 Chevelle with 454-ci 425-hp V-8; 1970 Nova with 396-ci 375-hp

Interchange Number: 9
Part Number(s): LH 3989041
Casting Number(s): 3989041 or 3942529
Notes: 1969 Camaro with 302-ci, 307-ci, 327-ci or 350-ci with manual transmission; 1970-1972 Camaro Z-28; 1969 Nova with 307-ci or 350-ci V-8 with manual transmission; 1969 Chevelle with 307-ci or 350-ci V-8 with manual transmission; 1972 full-size Chevrolet, Camaro, Chevelle or Nova with 350-ci V-8 and with NOX emissions; 1973 Camaro, Chevelle, full-size Chevrolet or Nova with 307-ci, 350-ci or 400-ci SMALL BLOCK

Interchange Number: 10
Part Number(s): RH 3986330
Casting Number(s): 3946826
Notes: 1969 Camaro with 302-ci, 307-ci, 327-ci or 350-ci with manual transmission; 1969 Nova with 307-ci, 350-ci V-8 with manual transmission; 1969 Chevelle with 307-ci or 350-ci V-8; 1970-1972 Camaro Z-28

Interchange Number: 11
Part Number(s): LH 336706
Casting Number(s): 3989055
Notes: 1969 Camaro, Nova, Chevelle with 327-ci or 350-ci V-8 with automatic transmission; 1970-1971 Camaro, Nova and Chevelle with 307-ci, or 350-ci V-8 and automatic transmission; 1972 Camaro, Chevelle, and Nova with 307-ci V-8; 1972 Camaro, Chevelle, full-size Chevrolet, Nova with 350-ci V-8 without NOX emissions

Interchange Number: 12
Part Number(s): RH 3932376
Casting Number(s): 3942530 or 3932376
Notes: 1969 Camaro with 307, 327-ci or 350-ci with automatic transmission; 1969 Chevelle or Nova with 307-ci, 350-ci V-8 with automatic transmission

Interchange Number: 13
Part Number(s): RH 336708
Casting Number(s): 336708
Notes: 1970 Camaro, Chevelle or Nova with 307-ci or 350-ci with automatic transmission except Z-28; 1971 full-size Chevrolet with 350-ci or 400-ci SMALL BLOCK; 1972 Camaro, Chevelle, full-size Chevrolet, or Nova with 307-ci, 350-ci, or 400-ci SMALL BLOCK without NOX emissions except Z-28

Interchange Number: 14
Part Number(s): LH 3989343
Casting Number(s): 3989343
Notes: 1972 Camaro, Chevelle, full-size Chevrolet with 402-ci or 454-ci V-8 without NOX emissions; 1970 Chevelle with 396-ci or 454-ci V-8 except 450-hp; 1970 Nova with 396-ci except 375-hp

Interchange Number: 15
Part Number(s): RH 3989310
Casting Number(s): 3989310
Notes: 1972 Camaro, Chevelle, full-size Chevrolet with 402-ci or 454-ci V-8 without NOX emissions

Interchange Number: 16
Part Number(s): RH 3959562
Casting Number(s): 3959562
Notes: 1972 Camaro, Chevelle, full-size Chevrolet , Nova with 350-ci or 400-ci SMALL BLOCK with NOX emissions; 1973 Camaro, Chevelle, full-size Chevrolet or Nova with 307-ci, 350-ci or 400-ci SMALL BLOCK

Interchange Number: 17
Part Number(s): RH 353028
Casting Number(s): 3989310
Notes: 1972 Camaro, Chevelle, full-size Chevrolet with 402-ci or 454-ci V-8 with NOX emissions: 1973 Chevelle, full-size Chevrolet with 454-ci V-8; 1970 Chevelle with 396-ci or 454-ci 450-hp V-8; 1970 Nova with 396-ci except 375-hp

Exhaust manifolds are identified by a casting number

Chapter 5 Transmissions

Transmission

There are many ways to identify a transmission. One way is by its design or type, or by the manufacture and build date codes. Although this will not tell you what model of car the transmission came out of, it will tell you the assembly plant and the date the transmission was built. Another ID code was painted or stamped on the transmission for identification at the factory. However, note that the interchange here is based on the part number and the physical characteristics of the unit. Thus, many different code numbers can be used in the interchange.

Manual Transmission

To conserve space and due to a general lack of interest, three-speed manual transmissions- except when only that manual transmission was available for this model- have been left out of this book. Only four-speeds and automatics are listed.

The Saginaw design is a general-duty four-speed that saw wide usage. It has a cast-iron case and extension, and a seven-bolt cover with three shift rods.

The Muncie four-speed is a high-performance or heavy-duty transmission that also was widely used. There are two versions: wide-ratio and close-ratio. Wide ratio has twenty-four teeth on the input shaft; while the close-ratio has twenty-six teeth on shaft. Both versions have a seven-bolt cover with two shift rods. The case is aluminum. There is also a low-performance four-speed Muncie unit that was used in a number of cars. It has a cast-iron case but is not as desirable for performance applications as the aluminum case units.

A transmission's assembly plant and build date code location varied with the manufacturer. The 1962-1963 Warner four-speed ID was positioned on the cover side rear flange, where it began with the letter "W" for the Warner assembly plant. In 1963, when the Muncie transmission was first used, the build date code was stamped on the cover side of the case and began with the letter "P." Saginaw transmissions were stamped on the driver's side of the case, on a pad right below the side cover on the machined surface. Three speeds will begin with the letter "S" and 4-speed with the letter "R".

Both the Warner and Muncie codes were followed by the calendar build date of month and day. For example: "2 22" stood for February 22. The later letter code indicated the shift, on which the part was made, "D" for Day or "N" for Night.

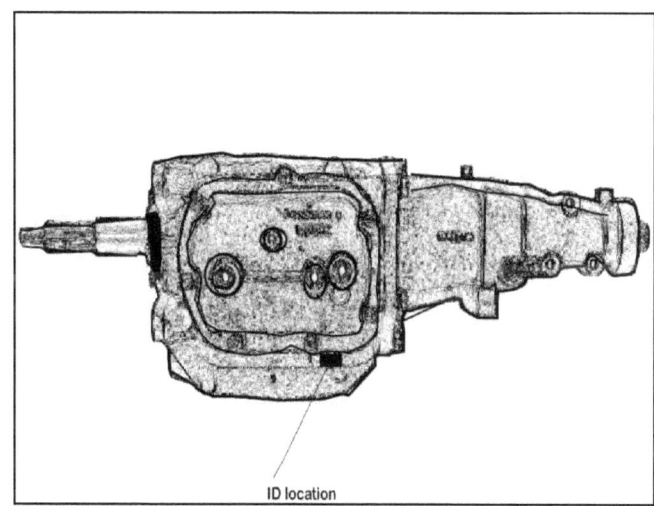

Saginaw transmission identification pad location

All 1964-1965 four-speeds were stamped on the top right-hand side of the flat area on the case assembly. From 1966 to 1968 the build date appeared on the right-hand side of the case, just ahead of the extension. On 1970 models, the ID can be found on a machined surface on the left-hand side of the case, just below the side cover for light-duty units. The ID on high-performance applications, the ID was stamped vertically on the right-hand side of the case, just ahead of the extension.

Muncie transmissions still used the "P" letter code and Warner used the "W," with the addition of the letter "R" to indicate the Saginaw plant. Build date code was the same as in earlier years-except for the Warner plant, which used a single letter to indicate the month ("A" for January to "M" for December), with the letter "I" not being used. Also, following the build day was the last digit of the year. Thus, the Code WC217 would translate as March 21, 1967. Also, the particular shift was represented by a single number (1-3).

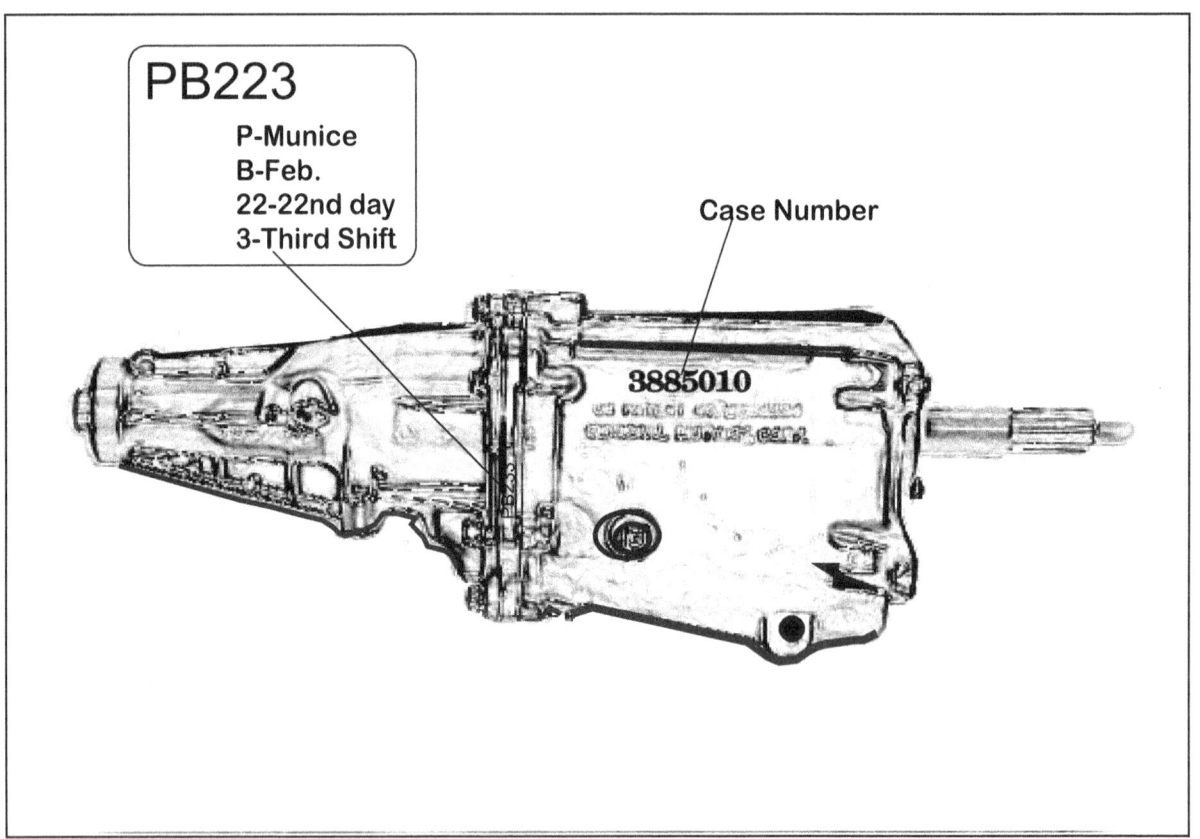

Muncie 4-speed transmission Identification location. Note some 1969, and 1970-1974 Muncie have and additional code at the end that identifies the transmission type (ratio) A=M20 B=M21, C=M22

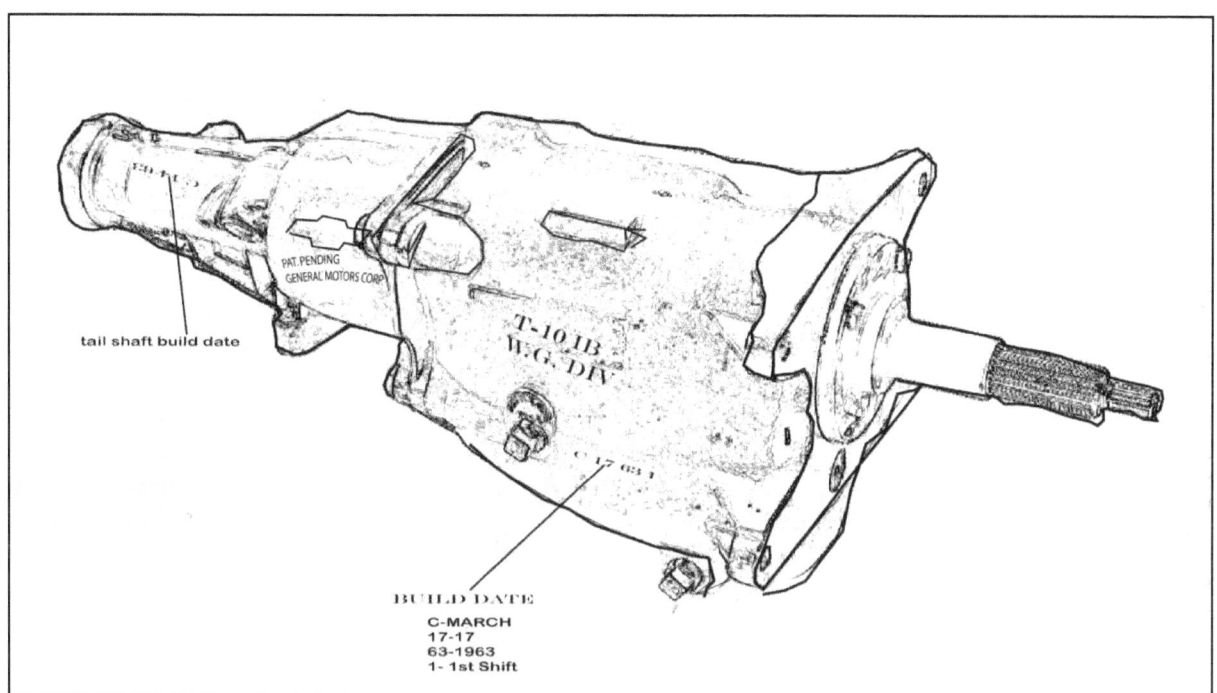

Early Warner transmissions build dates locations

Muncie Transmission Identification By Shaft

Year	Type	Input Shaft		Output Shaft		Notes
		Rings	Splines	Tooth#	Splines	
1963-1965	M20	None	10	24	27	
1966-1970	M20	Two	10	21	27	
1970-1974	M20	Two	26	21	32	
1963-1970	M21	One	10	26	27	
1970-1974	M21	One	26	26	32	
1967-1970	M22	None	10	26	27	

Manual Transmission Casting Numbers

Type	Years	Main Case	Extension Housing
Saginaw 4-Spd (IRON)	1970 - 1972	3925656	3873886
Muncie 4-Spd (aluminum)	1963-1964	3839606	3846429 Or 3843629
	1964-Early 1965	3851325	3846428
	1965	3864848	3846429
	1965	3864----* Last digits milled off	3846429
Muncie 4-Spd (aluminum)	1970	3925661	3857584
	1971 - 1975	3925661	3978764
Borg Warner	1974	1304 065 903	13.04.066.901

MANUAL TRANSMISSIONS

Model Identification   Interchange Number

Chevelle

1964
3-speed..1,2

1965
4-speed
2.52...3
2.20...4

1966
4-speed
283-ci..6
327-ci..5

1967-1968
4-speed
Saginaw..7
Muncie
2.20...4
2.52...3
Rock Crusher..8

1969
4-speed
Saginaw
307-ci
2.54...14
2.85 ratio..13
2.85
Except 2.73 rear axle...9
2.73 rear axle ratio..13
327-ci..10
350-ci..7
Muncie
2.20...12
2.52...11

1970
4-speed
Saginaw..15
Muncie
2.20...19
2.52...16
Rock Crusher..20

1971-1972
4-speed
Saginaw..17
Muncie
2.20...19
2.52...16
Rock Crusher..20

Muncie Build Date Codes	
Code	Month
A	January
B	February
C	March
D	April
E	May
H	June
K	July
M	August
P	September
R	October
S	November
T	December

Interchanges

Interchange Number: 1
Part Number(s):
Usage: 1964-1965 Chevelle with 3-speed

Interchange Number: 2
Part Number(s):
Usage: 1964 Chevelle with 3-speed overdrive

Interchange Number: 3
Part Number(s): 39645A2
ID Codes: P, FM, FE HP
Usage: 1964-1968 Nova; 1964-1968 full-size Chevrolet 1965-1968 Chevelle; 1965-1968 Oldsmobile Cutlass, except 442; 1967-1968 Camaro; 1967-1968 Buick Skylark; 1967-1968 Pontiac Firebird
Notes: Has 2.52:1 ratio. Muncie-built. See chart 1 for case numbers

Interchange Number: 4
Part Number(s): 3964506
ID Codes: N, HF, FX, FN
Usage: 1965-1968 Chevelle; 1965-1968 full-size Chevrolet; 1965-1968 Olds Cutlass 442; 1966-1968 Nova; 1967-1968 Camaro; 1967-1968 Buick Skylark; 1967-1968 Pontiac Firebird;
Notes: Has 2.20:1 ratio, cast-iron case, close-ratio transmission, excellent high-performance transmission. Muncie-built. See chart 2 for case numbers

Interchange Number: 5
Part Number(s) 3884603
Usage: 1966 Nova, Chevelle, full-size Chevrolet with 327-ciV-8 and 4-speed, except high-performance or special high-performance applications.
Notes: Saginaw unit cast-iron case, 2.54:1 ratio

Interchange Number: 6
Part Number(s):3916103
Usage: 1966 Nova, Chevelle, full-size Chevrolet with 283-ci V-8 and 4-speed, except with 3.55 or 3.70 rear axle ratios
Notes: Saginaw unit cast-iron case, 3.11:1 ratio.

Interchange Number: 7
Part Number(s): 3933853
ID Codes: R, FS, FH
Usage: 1967-1968 Nova, Camaro, or Chevelle with 327ci; 1969 Nova, Chevelle with 350ci; except with high-performance
Notes: Saginaw-built. Cast iron case

Interchange Number: 8
Part Number(s): 3964507
Usage: 1966-1968 Chevelle; 1967-1968 Camaro; 1968 Nova; 1968 Olds Cutlass; 1968 Pontiac Firebird; 1968 Corvette; all with heavy-duty Rock Crusher transmission
Notes: With aluminum case. Muncie-built. 26 spline no rings

Interchange Number: 9
Part Number(s): 3950376
ID Codes:
Usage: 1969 Nova, Camaro with 307-ci V-78 with 4-speed,
Notes: Saginaw-built. Cast iron case 2.85:1 ratio

Interchange Number: 10
Part Number(s): 3950379
ID Codes: R,FH
Usage: 1969 Nova, Camaro, with 327-ci or 350-ci V-8; 1969 Chevelle with 327-ci
Notes: Saginaw-built. Cast iron case 2.54:1 ratio

Interchange Number: 11
Part Number(s):3946797
ID Codes: P
Usage: 1969 Chevelle, Camaro, Nova
Notes: Muncie built 2.52:1 gear ratio in first gear. Interchange Number 15 will fit if cover is changed

Interchange Number: 12
Part Number(s): Chevrolet, 3946798
ID Codes: N, XE, XD
Usage: 1969 Chevelle, Camaro, Nova with 3.55, 3.73, and 4.10 rear axle ratios
Notes: Muncie built 2.20:1 gear ratio in first gear. Interchange Number 16 will fit if cover is changed.

Interchange Number: 13
Part Number(s): 3950376
Usage: 1969 Camaro, Nova Chevelle with 307-ci V-8 except with 2.73 rear axle ratio
Notes: Has 2.85:1 first gear ratio. Saginaw-built.

Interchange Number: 14
Part Number(s):3950379
ID Codes: R, FH
Usage: 1969 Camaro or Nova with 327 or 350ci with or 307-ci V-8 with 2.73 ratio
Notes: Saginaw-built. Has 2.54:1 first gear ratio. Interchange number 14 will fit if cover is changed

Interchange Number: 15
Part Number(s):3952658
Usage: 1970 Chevelle with 350-ci; 1970 Nova Camaro with 350-ci or 396-ci except 375-hp or Z-28
Notes: Saginaw-built cast iron cast

Interchange Number: 16
Part Number(s): 6271516
ID Codes: P, WB
Usage: 1970 Camaro, Chevelle, full-size Chevrolet, Nova; 1970 Oldsmobile Cutlass; 1970 Pontiac Firebird
Notes: Muncie wide-ratio 2.52:1 first gear ratio.

Interchange Number: 17
Part Number(s): 6273271
Usage: 1971-1979 Camaro, Chevelle, Nova with 4-speed
Notes: Saginaw-built cast iron cast

Interchange Number: 18
Part Number(s): 6271516
ID Codes: P, WB,WL
Usage: 1971-1972 Camaro, Chevelle, Nova, Firebird, Grand Prix, Lemans, Skylark, Corvette
Notes: Muncie built 2.52:1 first gear ratio

Interchange Number: 19
Part Number(s): 6271518
ID Codes: P, N, WC,WD, WY
Usage: 1970-1972 Camaro, Chevelle, Nova, Firebird, Grand Prix, Lemans, Skylark, Corvette
Notes: Muncie built 2.20:1 first gear ratio

Interchange Number: 20
Part Number(s): 6271517
Usage: 1970-1972 Camaro, Chevelle, Nova, Firebird, Grand Prix, Lemans, Skylark, Corvette
Notes: Muncie built 2.20:1 first gear ratio Heavy – duty Rock Crusher

Automatic Transmission

Chevelle's used three types of automatic transmissions: Powerglide, which has both have two forward speeds, and Turbo Hydra-Matic 350 and 400, both of which have three forward speeds. The transmissions can be identified by their visual characteristics.

Powerglide came in either a cast-iron or aluminum case with a flat, smooth, or rounded ridge top. A quick way to identify the transmission is to look for the word "POWERGLIDE" stamped into the case.

The Powerglide was the more popular unit and it used extensively after dismissal of the Turboglide until 1969 when Chevrolet began to phase it out in favor of the Turbo Hydra-Matic 350.

Powerglide is an excellent drag-racing transmission, even better than the Turbo Hydra-Matic. If you chose it for this purpose, opt for the aluminum case unit as it is much lighter.

Turbo Hydra-Matics (both 350 and 400) are easily identified by their design and their pan shape. The Turbo Hydra-Matic 350 uses a square-shaped oil pan that has a notched corner and is held on with thirteen bolts. The down-shift cable connector is located on the right-hand side of the unit.

The Turbo Hydra-Matic 400 has an oil pan that is also secured with thirteen bolts, but the pan is longer and has no uniform shape. The down-shift cable is located on the left-hand side of the unit and is controlled electronically.

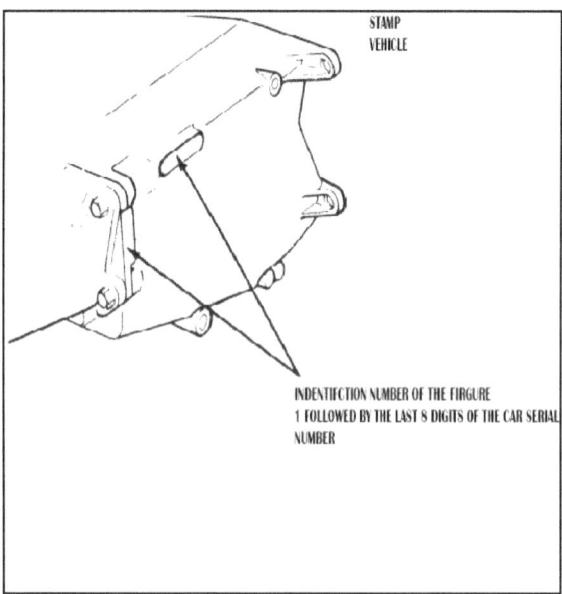

VIN was stamped on the manual transmissions these locations

The name 'POWERGLIDE' is stamped into the top of the case.

The Turbo Hydra-Matic 400 appeared in 1965 models. Be careful, though, because other GM makes (Pontiac, Buick, and Oldsmobile) also used Turbo Hydra-Matic 350 and 400 and have the same visual markings. In some cases an example from a Pontiac will fit, but a unit from a Buick uses a different bolt pattern that will not fit in a Chevrolet model. For the safest interchange, a Chevrolet unit is the best bet.

Unlike the Powerglide Turbo Hydra-Matics are also identified by their code letters or numbers. For the T.H. 350 these codes are found stamped on the servo cover on the right-hand side of the transmission. For the Turbo Hydra-Matic 400, the code can be found on a tag riveted to either the right-hand or the left-hand side of the case, depending on the model. The code can be helpful in locating a heavy-duty unit from a standard passenger car unit. You can use a heavy-duty unit in a non-high-performance car, but you really should not place a lighter duty unit behind the engine of a high-performance car. However, you can rebuild a standard-duty unit and make it a heavy-duty unit.

Automatic Transmissions
Chevelle
Model Identification   *Interchange Number*

1964
Powerglide
283-ci..2
327-ci..3

1965
Powerglide
283-ci..4
327-ci..5

1966
Powerglide
283-ci..4
327-ci..5
396-ci V-8..11
TH 400..10

1968
Powerglide
307-ci..7
327-ci..5
396-ci
Column Shift..8
Floor shift..9
TH400..10

1969
Powerglide
307-ci..14
350-ci..15
TH 350
350-ci 2-bbl..16
350-ci 4-bbl..17
Turbo Hydra Matic 400
350-ci
2bbl..18
4-bbl..19
396-ci
Except 375-hp..19
375-hp..20

1970
TH 350
350-ci 2-bbl..16
350-ci 4-bbl..17
Turbo Hydra Matic 400
350-ci
2bbl..18
4-bbl..19
396-ci/454-ci V-8
Except 375/ 450-hp-hp...................................21
375-hp/ 450-hp..20

1971
TH 350
350-ci 22
TH 400
402-ci..23
454-ci
Except 425-hp..24
425-hp..20
1972
TH 350
TH 400
350-ci 22
402-ci 23
454-ci..24

Interchanges

Interchange Number: 1
Part Number(s): 3791648
Type: Powerglide
Usage: 1962 Nova with 4-cylinder except wagon models.
Notes: Interchange number 2 will fit

Interchange Number: 2
Part Number(s): 3793704
Type: Powerglide
Usage: 1962 Nova with 6-cylinder
Note Do NOT use interchange number 1 in this application.

Interchange Number: 3
Part Number(s): 3793701
Type: Powerglide
Usage: 1963 Nova with 4-cylinder except wagon models.

Interchange Number: 4
Part Number(s): 3887080
Type: Powerglide
Usage: 1965-1967 full-size Chevrolet with 283-ci V-8; 1964-1967 Chevelle with 283-ci except with 3.55 or 3.70 axle ratios; 1965-1967 Nova with 283-ci V-8

Interchange Number: 5
Part Number(s): 3964596
Type: Powerglide
Usage: 1965-1968 full-size Chevrolet with 327-ci V-8; 1965-1968 Chevelle with 327-ci; 1966-1967 Nova with 327-ci V-8; 1968 Nova with 327-ci and floor shift; 1965-1967 Corvette with 327-ci

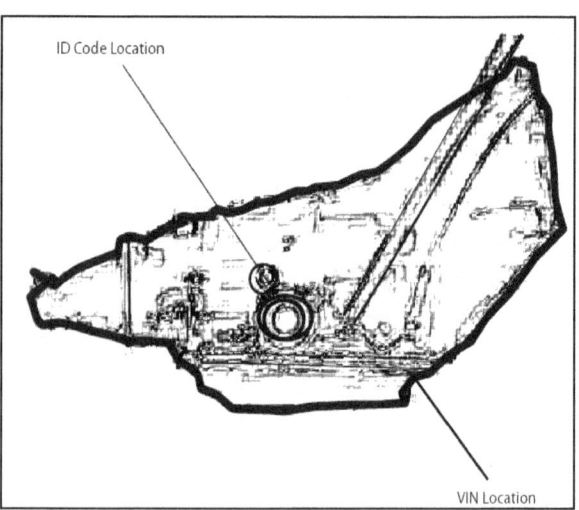

Turbo Hydra-Matic 350

Interchange Number: 6
Part Number(s): 3887076
Type: Powerglide
Usage: 1965-1967 full-size Chevrolet with 396ci; 1966-1967 Chevelle SS 396

Interchange Number: 7
Part Number(s): 3919310
Type: Powerglide
Usage: 1968 Nov with 307-ci floor shift; 1968 Chevelle or full-size Chevrolet with 307-ci column shift.

Interchange Number: 8
Part Number(s):3919342
Type: Powerglide
Usage: 1968 Chevelle SS 396 or Nova SS 396 with column shift

Interchange Number: 9
Part Number(s): 3919339
Type: Powerglide
Usage: 1968 Chevelle SS 396 with floor shift

Interchange Number: 10
Part Number(s): 8626648
Type T.H. 400
ID Codes: CA
Usage: 1965-1968 full-size Chevrolet with 396-ci, or 427-ci; 1967-1968 Chevelle SS 396; 1968 Camaro with 396-ci

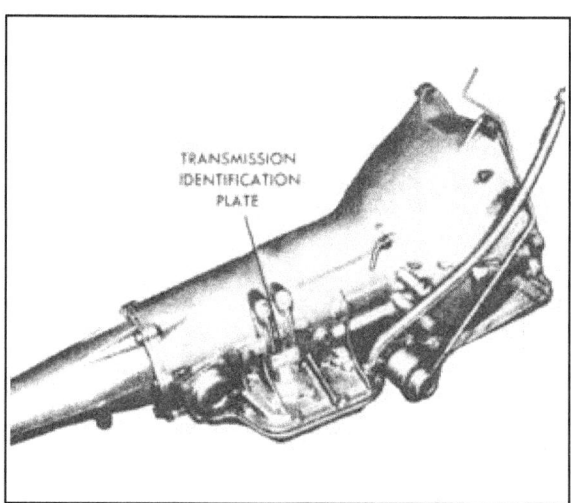

Turbo-Hydra-Matic's are identified by a code on a tag located here. (Chevrolet)

Interchange Number: 11
Part Number(s): 3887076
Type: Powerglide
Usage: 1965-1967 full-size Chevrolet with 396ci; 1966-1967 Chevelle SS 396

Interchange Number: 14
Part Number(s): 3950317
Type: Powerglide
Usage: 1969 Chevelle with 307-ci V-8

Interchange Number: 15
Part Number(s): 3950319
Type: Powerglide
Usage: 1969 Chevelle with 350-ci V-8

Interchange Number: 16
Part Number(s): 6261417
Type: TH350
ID: FU FQ
Usage: 1969-1970 Nova, Camaro, Chevelle, full-size Chevrolet with 350-ci 2-bbl V-8

Interchange Number: 17
Part Number(s): 6261721
Type: TH350
ID: FI
Usage: 1969-1970 Nova, Camaro, Chevelle, full-size Chevrolet with 350-ci 4-bbl V-8

Interchange Number: 18
Part Number(s): 8626412
Type: T.H. 400
ID Codes: CD
Usage: 1969-1970 full-size Chevrolet, Chevelle, Camaro, Nova with 350ci 2-bbl

Interchange Number: 19
Part Number(s): 862642
Type: T.H. 400
ID Codes: CA
Usage: 1969 full-size Chevrolet, Chevelle, Camaro, Nova with 350ci 4-bbl or 396-ci except 375-hp

Interchange Number: 20
Part Number(s): 8626793
Type: T.H. 400
ID Codes: CY
Usage: 1969 full-size Chevrolet with 427-ci; 1969-1970 Chevelle, Camaro, Nova with 396-ci 375-hp; 1970 Chevelle 454-ci 450-hp; 1971 Chevelle with 454-ci 425-hp

Interchange Number: 21
Part Number(s):8626795
Type: T.H. 400
ID Codes: CR
Usage: 1970 Chevelle, Camaro, Nova with 350ci 4-bbl or 396-ci except 375-hp; 1970 Chevelle with 454-ci except 450-hp.

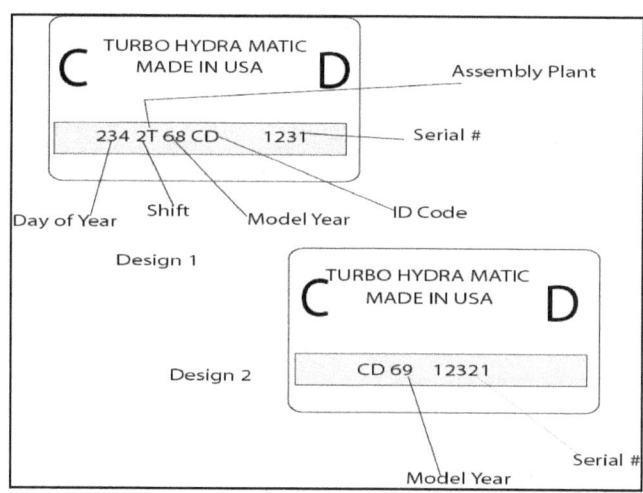

Typical breakdown of T.H. 400 tag.

Interchange Number: 22
Part Number(s):6272056
Type: T.H. 350
ID Codes: HW
Usage: 1971-1972 Chevelle, Camaro, Nova with 350ci

Interchange Number: 23
Part Number(s): 8627045
Type: T.H. 400
ID Codes: CD
Usage: 1971-1972 Chevelle, Camaro, with 400-ci BIG BLOCK V-8 OR 402-ci

Interchange Number: 24
Part Number(s): 8627048
Type: T.H. 400
ID Codes: CF
Usage: 1971-1972 Chevelle, with 454 ci except 425-hp

Interchange Number: 25
Part Number(s): 332564
Type: T.H. 350
ID Codes: FD, SA
Usage: 1972-1973 Chevelle, Camaro, Nova with 307-ci or 350ci 2-bbl

Interchange Number: 26
Part Number(s): 340662
Type: T.H. 350
ID Codes: FB, SB
Usage: 1972-1973 Chevelle, Camaro, Nova with 350-ci 4-bbl

Gearshift

Gearshift interchange is based on original part numbers. In most cases, it is for the entire lever assembly (lower mechanism and upper lever). Some models used different shift levers according to the type of seating arrangement used. Three speed levers are not listed.

1964-1966 Chevelle Shifter had more arc than the SS version

The 1964-1966 Super Sport Shifter

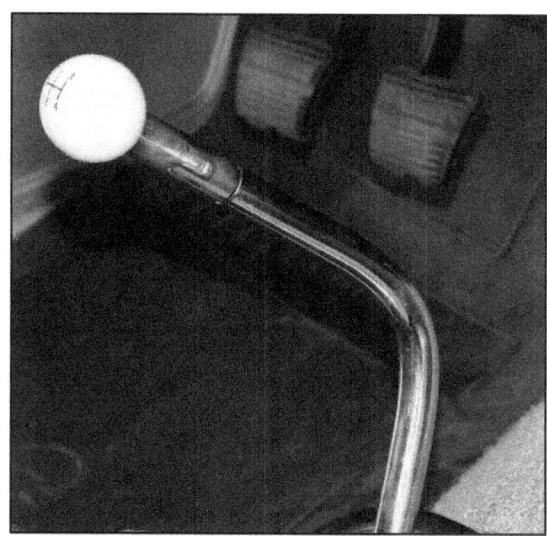

4-speed shifter for 1967

Chevelle

Model Identification *Interchange Number*

1964-1965
Manual
4-speed
Except Super Sport...1
Super Sport..2
Automatic
Column..25
Console..21

1966
Manual
4-speed
Except Super Sport...1
Super Sport..2
Automatic
Column
Without Tilt..12
Tilt..18
Floor..22

1967
Manual...3
Automatic
Column
Without Tilt..12
With Tilt..15
Floor
Powerglide..22
TH400..23

1968
Manual
Wide Ratio
Bench Seat..4
Bucket Seat..6
Close Ratio
Bench Seat..5
Bucket Seat..6
Automatic
Column
Without Tilt..13
With Tilt..16
Console..20

1969
Manual
4-speed
Bench Seat..5
Bucket seats..6
Automatic
Column
Without Tilt..14
With Tilt..17
Console..20
Sport shifter..24

1970-1972
Manual
4-speed
Bench Seat..7
Bucket seats
Without console..8
With Console..9
Automatic
Column
Without tilt..14
With tilt...18
Console..20

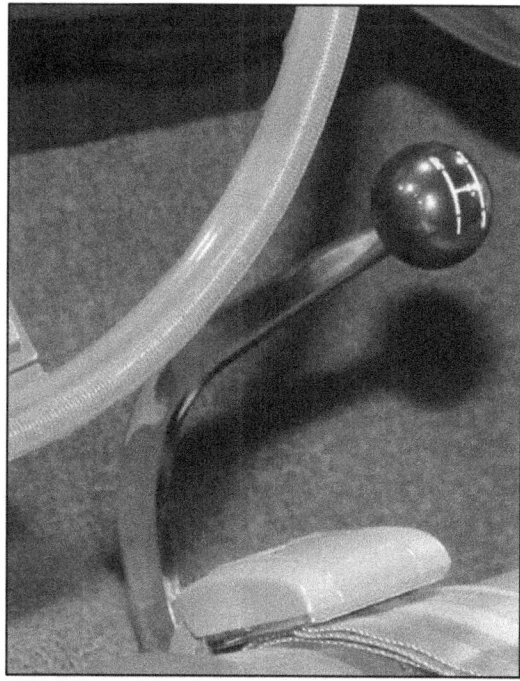

1968 shifter with bench seat

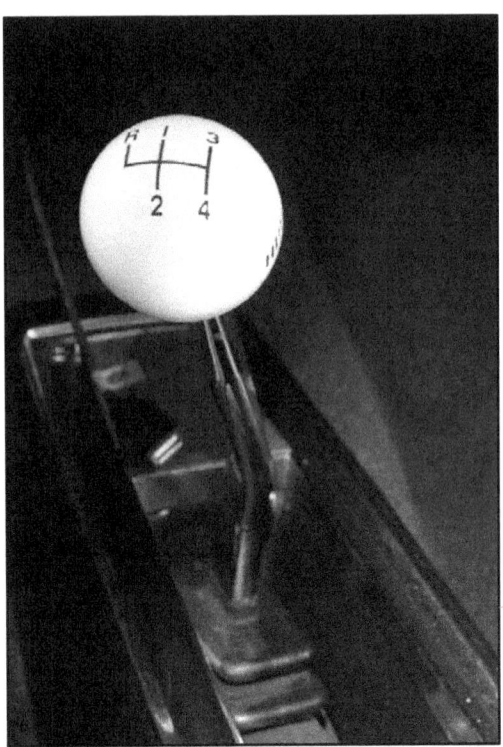

1968-1972 shifter with bucket seats

Interchange Number: 1
Part Number(s): 3853137
Usage: 1964-1966 Chevelle Super Sport
Note: Interchange Number 2 will fit and was replacement unit, but arc is different.

Interchange Number: 2
Part Number(s): 3853134
Usage: 1964-1966 Chevelle, except Super Sport
Notes: Has more arc than the SS unit in interchange

Interchange Number: 3
Part Number(s): 3903077
Usage: 1967 Chevelle

Interchange Number: 4
Part Number(s): 3922522
Usage: 1968 Chevelle with M20 four-speed with bench seats
Notes: Upper lever is the same unit used with 1968 three-speed; lower unit must be changed however.
Notes: Interchange number 6 will fit

Interchange Number: 5
Part Number(s): 3922523
Usage: 1968 Chevelle M21 or M22 four-speed with bench seats; 1969 Chevelle, all four-speeds, with bench seats
Notes: Interchange number 6 will fit

Interchange Number: 6
Part Number(s): 3922524
Usage: 1968-1969 Chevelle with bucket seats with wide or close ratio transmission
Notes: Used as a replacement shifter for the 1968-1969 Chevelle, regardless of seat type.

Interchange Number: 7
Part Number(s): 3973865
Usage: 1970-1972 Chevelle with bench seats

Interchange Number: 8
Part Number(s): 3973864
Usage: 1970-1972 Chevelle with bucket seats without console

1964 automatic shifter

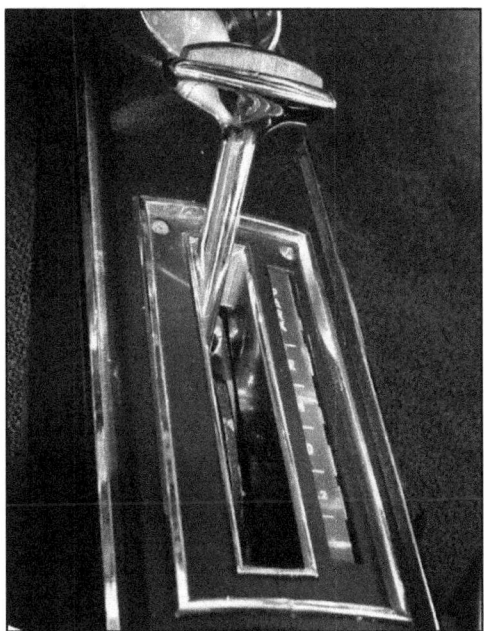
1966-1967 automatic console shifter. Shown is the 1967 version with the T.H. 400 transmission.

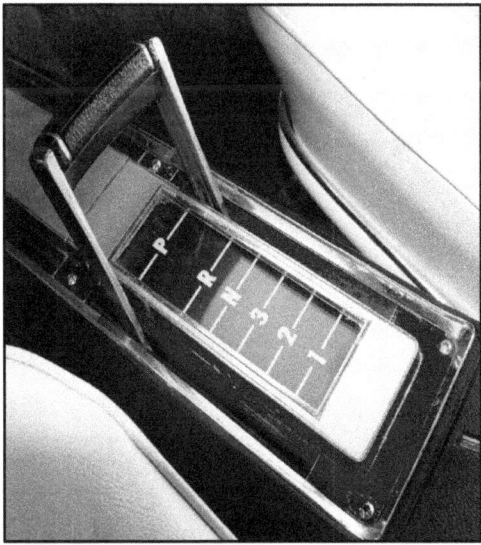
The 1968-1972 automatic console shifter

Interchange Number: 9
Part Number(s): 3973866
Usage: 1970-1972 Chevelle with console.

Interchange Number: 10
Part Number(s): 378265
Type: 4-speed floor
Usage: 1973-1975 Chevelle with close ratio transmission; 1974-1975 Nova with close ratio transmission without console.

Interchange Number: 11
Part Number(s): 378266
Type: 4-speed floor
Usage: 1973 Chevelle with wide ratio transmission; 1973 Nova with wide ratio transmission without console.

Interchange Number: 12
Part Number(s): 3904087
Type: Column automatic
Usage: 1966-1967 Chevelle; Late 1966-1967 full-size Chevrolet
Notes: This change occurred very late in the year. Interchange number 13 will fit.

Interchange Number: 13
Part Number(s): 3928319
Type: Column automatic
Usage: 1968 full-size Chevrolet; 1968 Chevelle

Interchange Number: 14
Part Number(s): 3939741
Type: Column automatic
Usage: 1969-1974 full-size Chevrolet, Chevelle, Camaro

Interchange Number: 15
Part Number(s): 3900565
Type: Column automatic
Usage: 1967 full-size Chevrolet, Chevelle with tilt steering

Interchange Number: 16
Part Number(s): 3928239
Type: Column automatic
Usage: 1968 full-size Chevrolet, Chevelle with tilt steering

Interchange Number: 17
Part Number(s): 7806159
Type: Column automatic
Usage: 1969 full-size Chevrolet, Chevelle with tilt steering

Interchange Number: 18
Part Number(s): 3884849
Type: Column automatic
Usage: 1966 Chevelle with tilt steering

Interchange Number: 19
Part Number(s): 3962727
Type: Column automatic
Usage: 1970-1974 Chevelle; 1969-1974 Camaro, nova; 1970-1974 full-size Chevrolet, Monte Carlo; 1971-1974 Ventura II all with tilt steering

Interchange Number: 20
Part Number(s): 3922577
Type: Console floor
Usage: 1968-1972 Chevelle or Monte Carlo with automatic in console; 1968-1969 full-size Chevrolet with bucket seats and console with automatic transmissions

Interchange Number: 21
Part Number(s): 3843285
Type: Console floor
Usage: 1964-1965 Chevelle with automatic in console

Interchange Number: 22
Part Number(s): 3880851
Type: Console floor
Usage: 1966-1967 Chevelle with Powerglide automatic in console

Interchange Number: 23
Part Number(s): 3909691
Type: Console floor
Usage: 1967 Chevelle with TH 400 automatic in console

Interchange Number: 24
Part Number(s): 3920267
Type: Console floor
Usage: 1969 Chevelle with Sport-shifter automatic in console.
Notes: Very rare ratchet type has no shift dial

Interchange Number: 25
Part Number(s): 383836
Type: Column automatic
Usage: 1964-1965 Chevelle; 1964 Cutlass with three speed on the column

Shift Patterns and Indicators

Shift patterns are used with manual transmissions, while shift indicators are used with automatics. Patterns are used only on cars with a console. On those without a console, the pattern appears on the knob.

Indicators are used for all shift lever locations. Again, interchange is based on the original part number. On-the-column types are usually unique to the car line; however, those that were used with consoles are more interchangeable. Note that sometime this is part of the lens on the cluster or below the speedometer.

Chevelle
Model Identification   Interchange Number
1964-1965
Automatic
Column..1
Console...15
1966
Automatic
Column..2
Console...13
4-speed..19
1967
Automatic
Column
Powerglide...2
Turbo-Hydra-Matic..3
Console
Powerglide...13
Turbo-Hydra-Matic..17
4-Speed..19
1968
Automatic
Column
Powerglide...4
Turbo-Hydra-Matic..5
Console
Powerglide...14
Turbo-Hydra-Matic..16
4-speed..18

1969
Automatic
Column
Powerglide..6
Turbo-Hydra-Matic...7
Console
Powerglide..14
Turbo-Hydra-Matic...16
4-speed...18

1970-1972
Automatic
Column
Without Gauges or Super Sport
Powerglide..9
Turbo-Hydra-Matic...10
With Gauges or Super Sport
Powerglide..11
Turbo-Hydra-Matic...12
Console
Powerglide..14
Turbo-Hydra-Matic...16
4-speed...18

Interchanges

Interchange Number: 1
Part Number(s): 3863337
Type: Column automatic
Usage: 1964-1965 Chevelle with automatic on the column
Notes: Lens retainer from 1964-1965 full-size Chevrolet will fit

Interchange Number: 2
Part Number(s): 6457757
Type: Column automatic
Usage: 1966-1967 Chevelle with Powerglide automatic on the column
Notes: Part of the lens of the main instrument cluster

Interchange Number: 3
Part Number(s): 6457758
Type: Column automatic
Usage: 1967 Chevelle with Turbo-Hydra Matic automatic on the column
Notes: Part of the lens of the main instrument cluster

Interchange Number: 4
Part Number(s): 6480927
Type: Column automatic
Usage: 1968 Chevelle with Powerglide automatic on the column.

Interchange Number: 5
Part Number(s): 6480928
Type: Column automatic
Usage: 1968 Chevelle with Turbo-Hydra-Matic automatic on the column.

Interchange Number: 6
Part Number(s): 6483424
Type: Column automatic
Usage: 1969 Chevelle with Powerglide automatic on the column

Interchange Number: 7
Part Number(s): 6483425
Type: Column automatic
Usage: 1969 Chevelle with Turbo-Hydra-Matic automatic on the column

Interchange Number: 9
Part Number(s): 6496773
Type: Column automatic
Usage: 1970-1972 Chevelle with gauges and Powerglide on the column.

Interchange Number: 10
Part Number(s): 6496774
Type: Column automatic
Usage: 1970-1972 Chevelle SS; 1970-1972 Monte Carlo;1970-1972 Chevelle with gauges with Turbo-=Hydra-Matic transmission

Interchange Number: 11
Part Number(s): 6492182
Type: Column automatic
Usage: 1970-1972 Chevelle, all except SS or with gauges with Powerglide automatic

Interchange Number: 12
Part Number(s): 6492183
Type: Column automatic
Usage: 1970-1972 Chevelle, all except SS or with gauges with Turbo Hydra Matic automatic

Interchange Number: 13
Part Number(s): 3880904
Usage: 1966-1967 Chevelle with Powerglide with console

Interchange Number: 14
Part Number(s): 3990804
Usage: 1968-1972 Chevelle with Powerglide with console

Interchange Number: 15
Usage: 1964-1965 Chevelle with automatic and console

Interchange Number: 16
Part Number(s): 3921428
Usage: 1968-1972 Chevelle Turbo Hydra-Matic with console

Interchange Number: 17
Part Number(s): 3880905
Usage: 1967 Chevelle with Turbo-Hydra Matic with console

Interchange Number: 18
Part Number(s): 3919914
Usage: 1968-1972 Chevelle with four-speed manual with console

Interchange Number: 19
Part Number(s): 3880912
Usage: 1966-1967 Chevelle with four-speed manual with console

Chapter 6 Frame, Suspension and Steering

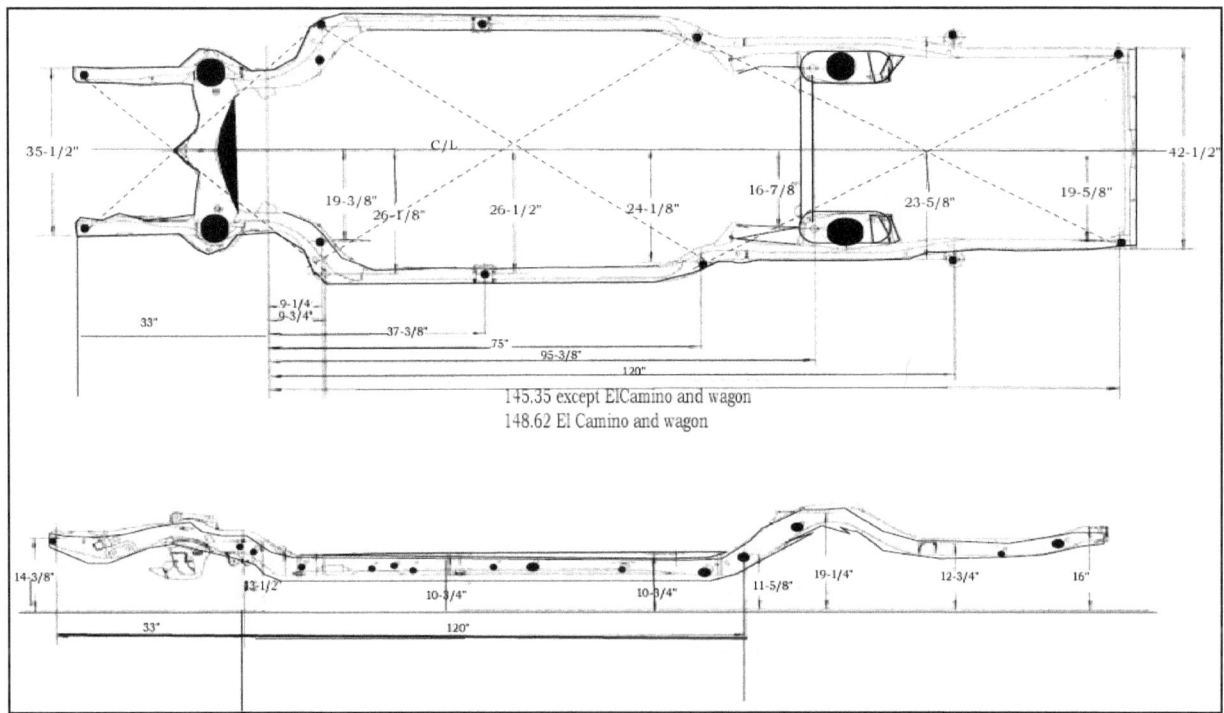

1964-1967 Frame specifications, measure on dotted lines to make sure it is square.

Frame

Several different manufacturers were used to assemble frames for various GM makes and models, including Chevelle. Thus, the same frame can sometimes be found on another Chevrolet or Pontiac or Oldsmobile's.

A frame's identification number is usually found stamped on the outer left-hand side-member, just ahead of the rear bumper bracket attaching slot.

The part number appears along with an abbreviated version of the manufacturer's name. For example, if Pontiac were the manufacturer, the ID would read: Pon. (for Pontiac), S- A.O. Smith, or P.P.S or Parish for-Parish Pressed Steel. This is followed by the part number, build date and shift.

The VIN or a partial VIN is also stamped on the frame it is located usually on top of the left-hand frame rail just under the driver's door, but some frame manufactures used other locations that can include: on top of the right-hand frame rail just in front of the rear bumper bracket or just behind the control arm.

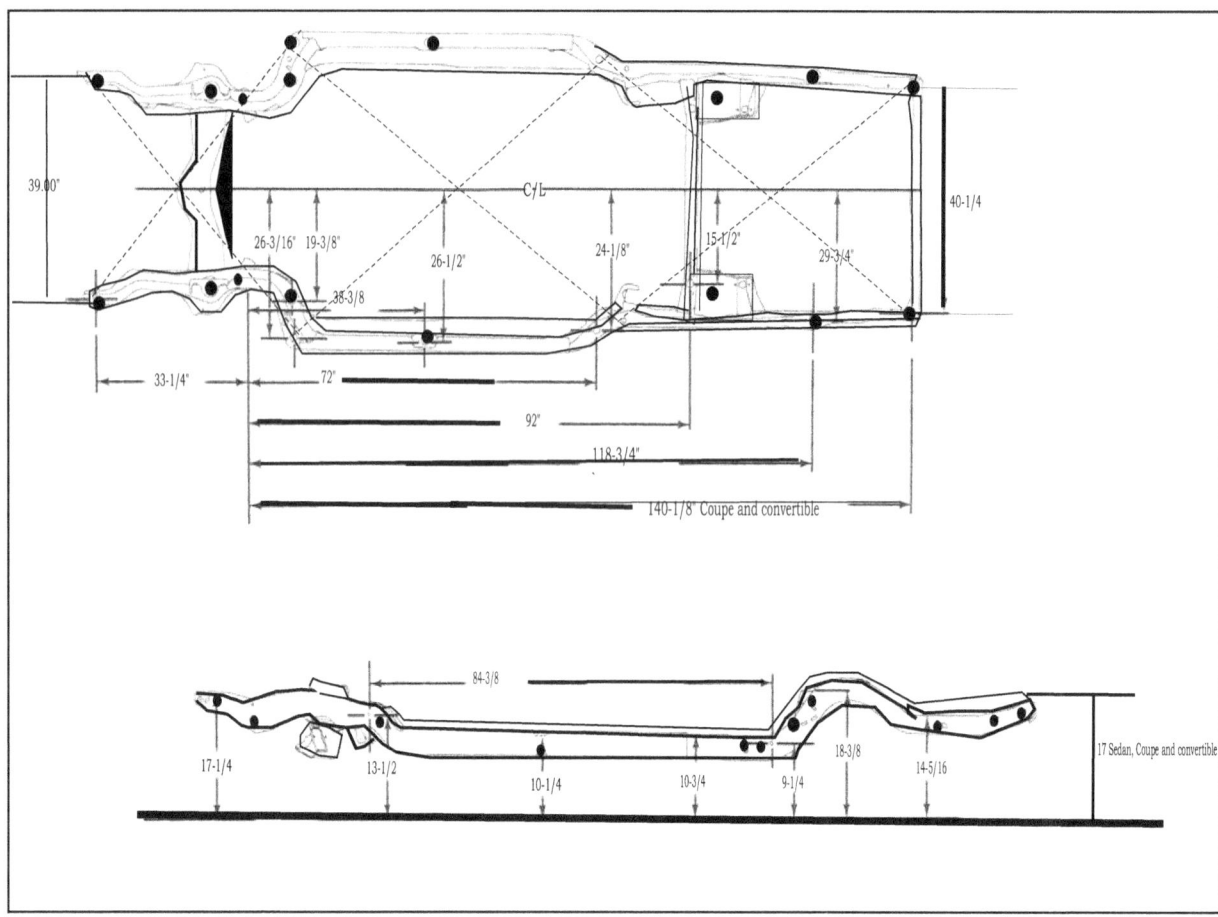

1968-1972 Frame specifications for coupe and 2-dr hardtop, Measure on dotted lines to make sure it is square.

Sometimes more than one-part number may be listed in the interchange charts. That is because the frame was changed midyear. However, either will fit unless otherwise noted.
Note sometimes body style can affect the interchange.

INSPECTING THE FRAME

Two things can destroy a frame. Rust is the most common. If the drain holes become plugged with dirt then the water cannot escape, and rust will eat the frame alive from the inside out. Common areas of rust are near the ends, especially the rear. Be sure to check thoroughly. Taking a hard object like a screwdriver blade and poking around on the frame rail to make sure it is solid. If the driver goes through the rail, or there are obvious signs of rust dismiss the frame and look for another one.

Second thing to watch for is damage. If there is excessive damage to the body, take care consideration in inspecting the frame. In addition, it is recommended that you check the alignment of the frame. This is best done with a specialty tool called a tramming bar, but can be done with a plumb bob and tape measure.

To do the tape measure you have to make sure that the floor is flat. Use the plum bob to make sure that measurement will be straight. Then use a tape measure and measure the distance from the extreme front end of one side of the frame rail to the floor. Note measurement then repeat this procedure for the other side. Repeat this measurement at the midpoint of the frame and at the extreme rear end of the frame from the top to the floor on one side and note the measurement. Then repeat for the other side. If there is a major difference in between the side

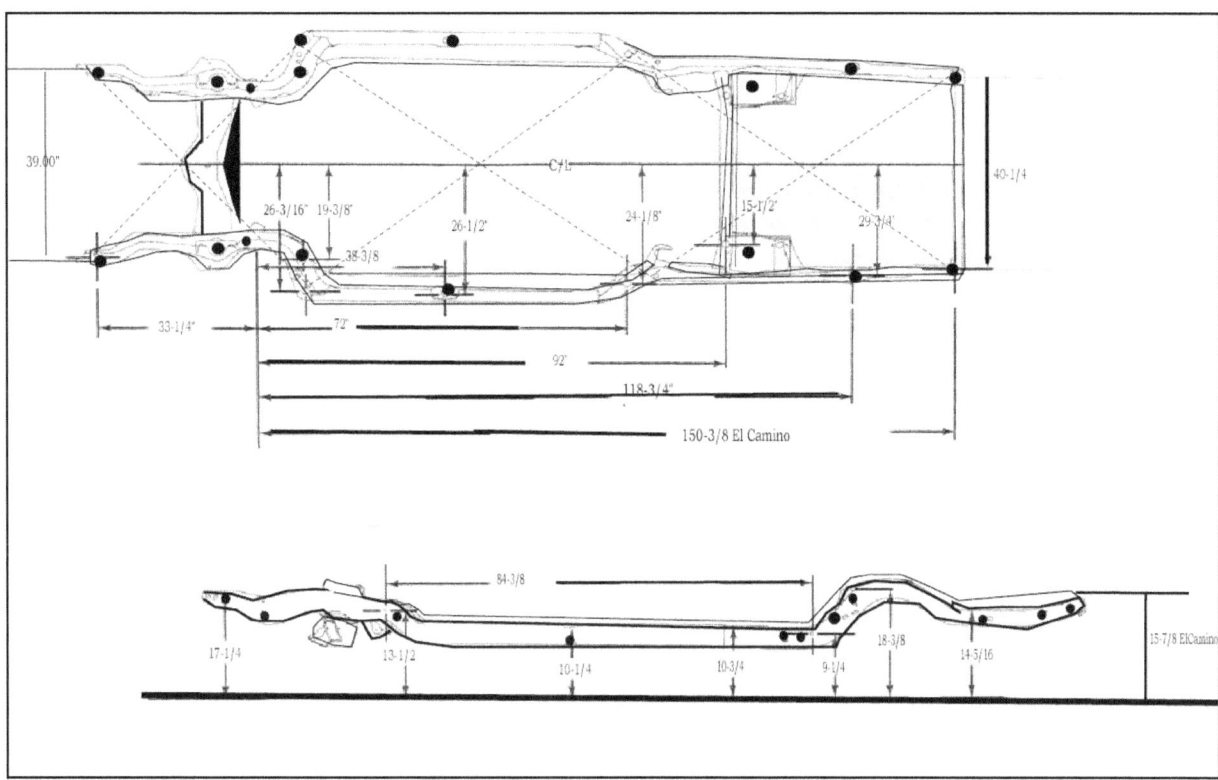
1968-1972 Frame specifications for El Camino. Measure on dotted lines to make sure it is square.

then the frame is twisted and considered unusable. Also check the measurement from the extreme right-hand front rail to midpoint of the frame on the left-hand side then from there to the extreme rear end of the frame on the right-hand. Repeat these measurements starting with the left front end to the mid right-hand side then end with the rear left-hand side. Compare these readings they should be the same. If not the difference is how much the frame is twisted. There are also specific measurements that can be made this will require a service manual for your particular model or follow our illustrations.

Model Identification   Interchange Number
Chevelle
1964-1965
Except convertible or El Camino..................................1
Convertible..2
El Camino..3
1966
Except convertible or El Camino..................................4
Convertible..6
El Camino..5
1967
Except convertible or El Camino..................................4
Convertible..6
El Camino..7
1968-1972
Except El Camino or sedan..8
El Camino..9

Typical frame part number with build date placed under it.

Interchanges

Interchange Number: 1
Part Number(s): 3837537 or 9773003
Usage: 1964-1965 Chevelle all body styles except convertible, or El Camino or station wagon

Interchange Number: 2
Part Number(s): 3837597
Usage: 1964-1965 Chevelle convertible

Interchange Number: 3
Part Number(s): 3854299
Usage: 1964-1965 El Camino
Notes: Station wagon frame will interchange but used part number 3837595

Interchange Number: 4
Part Number(s): 3837327
Usage: 1966-1967 Chevelle all body styles except convertible, or El Camino or station wagon

Interchange Number: 5
Part Number(s): 3876907
Usage: 1966 Chevelle El Camino or station wagon

Interchange Number: 6
Part Number(s): 3893333
Usage: 1966-1967 Chevelle convertible

Interchange Number: 7
Part Number(s): 3893329
Usage: 1967 Chevelle El Camino or station wagon

Interchange Number: 8
Part Number(s): 6263666
Usage: 1968-1972 Chevelle 2-door hardtop, sport coupe or convertible; 1968-1972 Skylark 2-dr hardtop, coupe or convertible except 400 or 455-ci V-8; 1968-1972 Cutlass coupe, 2-dr hardtop or convertible; 1968-1972 Lemans 2-dr hardtop, coupe or convertible except with 455-ci V-8
Note: Sedan frame is longer and will not interchange.

Interchange Number: 9
Part Number(s): 6263665
Usage: 1968-1972 El Camino or station wagon

Control Arms, Front

Chevelle

Model Identification   *Interchange Number*

1964-1969
Upper..1
Lower..2

1970-1971
Upper..1
Lower
With 307 or 350-ci...3
With 402-ci or 454-ci......................................2

1972
Upper..1
Lower
With 307 or 350-ci...4
With 402-ci or 454-ci......................................2

Interchanges

Interchange Number: 1
Part Number(s): 3974217 LH 3974218 RH
Position: Upper
Usage: 1964-1972 Chevelle; 1970-1972 Monte Carlo; 1971-1972 Sprint

Interchange Number: 2
Part Number(s): 3990509 LH 3990510 RH
Position: Lower
Usage: 1964-1969 Chevelle, all models and body styles; 1970-1972 Chevelle with 396-ci, 402-ci or 454-ci V-8; 1970-1972 Chevelle station wagon with all powerplants; 1970-1972 Monte Carlo with 396-ci, 402-ci or 454-ci; 1971-1972 GMC Sprint.

Interchange Number: 3
Part Number(s): 3990509 LH 3990510 RH
Position: Lower
Usage: 1970-1971 Chevelle except station wagon with 307-ci or 350-ci; 1970-1971 Monte Carlo with 350-ci or 400-ci SMALL BLOCK
Notes: oval bushings

Interchange Number: 4
Part Number(s): 6263617 LH 6263618 RH
Position: Lower
Usage: 1972 Chevelle except station wagon with 307-ci or 350-ci; 1972 Monte Carlo with 350-ci V-8

Front Springs, Coil

Note that all Nova, Camaro and Chevelle front springs will interchange as will other GM A-bodies. The interchange charts are simply a guide to alert you to what models and makes used the same coil springs.

However, there are different tensions available that were used with certain suspension options and/or other options. Thus, springs must be replaced in pairs from a car that has options similar to your own car. Never replace only one spring, even if you only need one spring. This could cause an imbalance in the car's suspension. Also, never swap one spring from one car and the second from another, even if they have the same options, because springs settle over the years and no two sets of springs settle the same.

Beginning in 1969, springs were selected by a computer and more springs were used per car. When selecting springs from 1969 to 1973 cars, try to match the same options including engine and body style or use the following charts to help you select your springs.

1964 Front Coil Springs			
Model	Code	Part Number	Notes
Without F40 Suspension			
Coupe	GP	3856585	
Convertible	AH	3843588	
Coupe with A/C	GQ	3856586	
Coupe with 327-ci	GX	3859074	
Convertible w/327	AJ	3843589	Wire diameter .619
Coupe with 327 and A/C	GW	3859075	Wire diameter .619
Convertible w 327 and A/C	AL	3849723	Wire diameter .619
El Camino	AH	3866286	
El Camino with A/C	GI	3895815	

1964 Front Coil Springs			
Model	Code	Part Number	Notes
With F40 Suspension			
Coupe	GS	3856588	
Coupe with A/C	AU	3851077	
Convertible	AU	3851077	
Convertible with A/C	GT	3856589	
Coupe with 327	AN	3850965	
Convertible with 327	AP	3850966	Wire diameter .619
Coupe 327 w/ A/C	AP	3850966	Wire diameter .619
Convertible with 327 A/C	AQ	3850967	Wire diameter .619
El Camino	AA	3856589	
El Camino w/ A/C	GJ	3895816	2449 lbs.
El Camino w/327	AQ	3850967	
El Camino 327 with A/C	GJ	3895816	

1965 Front Coil Springs

Model	Code	Part Number	Notes
Without F40 Suspension			
Coupe	GS	3856588	
Coupe with A/C or convertible without A/C	AM	3866287	
Convertible with A/C or coupe with 327-ci	AS	3866291	
Convertible with 327	AN	3850965	
Coupe with 327 and A/C	AS	3866291	
Convertible 327 A/C	AT	3866292	
El Camino	AH	3866286	
El Camino with A/C	GI	3895815	
With F40 Suspension			
Coupe/Convertible	GT	3856589	
Coupe Convertible w/327	AO	3850967	
Coupe with A/C	GZ	3859077	
Convertible with A/C	AY	3866296	
Coupe with 327 A/C	AY	3866296	
Convertible 327 A/C	AY	3866296	
Z-16 SS396	AY	3866296	
El Camino	AA	3856589	
El Camino w/ A/C	GJ	3895816	2449 lbs.
El Camino w/327	AQ	3850967	
El Camino 327 with A/C	GJ	3895816	

1966 Front Coil Springs

Model	Code	Part Number	Notes
Without F40 Suspension			
Coupe	GS	3856588	
Coupe with A/C or convertible without A/C	AM	3866287	
Convertible with A/C or coupe with 327-ci	AS	3866291	
Convertible with 327	AN	3850965	
Coupe with 327 and A/C	AS	3866291	
Convertible 327 A/C	AT	3866292	
El Camino	AH	3866286	
El Camino with A/C	GI	3895815	
Coupe/ Conv. with 396	GK	3895817	
Coupe/Conv. with A/C and 396	AB	3890620	
El Camino with 396	GS	3870477	
El Camino with A/C with 396-ci	GT	3870479	

1966 Front Coil Springs

Model	Code	Part Number	Notes
With F40 Suspension			
Coupe	GS	3856588	
Coupe with A/C or convertible without A/C	AM	3866287	
Convertible with A/C or coupe with 327-ci	AS	3866291	
Convertible with 327	AN	3850965	
Coupe with 327 and A/C	AS	3866291	
Convertible 327 A/C	AT	3866292	
El Camino	AH	3866286	
El Camino with A/C	GI	3895815	
Coupe with 396-ci	AB	3890620	2818 lbs*
Convertible with 396-ci	AB	3890620	2818 lbs*
Coupe	AJ	3857692	2818 lbs**
Convertible	GR	3851065	2818 lbs**
El Camino	AA	3856589	
El Camino w/ A/C	GJ	3895816	2449 lbs
El Camino w/327	AQ	3850967	
El Camino 327 with A/C	GJ	3895816	
*- 1 st design **-2nd design			

1967 SS 396 Front Coil Springs

Model	Code	Part Number	Notes
Without F40 Suspension			
Coupe	GD		
Convertible/Sedan	GG		
With A/C Coupe	GE		
With A/C Conv/sedan	GF		
El Camino	AH		
El Camino with A/C	GI		
Coupe with 396-ci	AA	3850967	2,729 lbs.
Convertible	AQ	3850967	2,729 lbs
El Camino	AZ	3850967	2,729 lbs
Coupe w/ A/C	GJ	3895836	2,729 lbs
Convertible	GJ	3850967	2,729 lbs
El Camino	GM	3881627	2,859 lbs
With F40 Suspension			
Coupe/Conv	AJ	3857688	
Coupe/Conv. With A/C	AA	3856589	
El Camino	AQ	3850967	2,729 lbs
El Camino with A/C	GJ	3850967	
Coupe with 396	AB	3890620	2818 lbs*
Convertible with 396	AB	3890620	2818 lbs*
El Camino with 396	GS	3870477	3,017 lbs
Coupe w/ A/C and 396-ci	AC	3890620	2818 lbs
Convertible w A/C and 396-ci	AA	3890620	2818 lbs
El Camino with 396-ci and A/C	GM	3870479	3,117 lbs

1968 Front Coil Springs			
Model	Code	Part Number	Notes
Without F-40 or F41			
Coupe	BJ	3866287	
Convertible	BE	3866287	
Coupe with A/C	CC	3866285	
Convertible with A/C	CC	3866285	
With 327-H.P.	CC	3866285	
With F41 Except 396	CE	3851077	
Coupe with 396	CQ	3952824	2,761 lbs
Convertible with 396	CQ	3952824	2,761 lbs
El Camino with 396	CQ	3952824	2,761 lbs
Coupe w/ A/C with 396	CR	3952824	2,761 lbs
Convertible with 396	CR	3952824	2,761 lbs
El Camino with 396	CR	3952824	2,761 lbs
H.D. Suspension was standard on SS 396 models			

RPO	Equipment	Chevelle Front	Chevelle Rear
L22	L-6 Eng. 250 Cu. In. - 155 H.P.	16	–
L34	V-8 Eng. 396 Cu. In. - 350 H.P.	194	46
L35	V-8 Eng. 396 Cu. In. - 325 H.P.	196	46
L48	V-8 Eng. 350 Cu. In. - 300 H.P.	27	44
L65	V-8 Eng. 350 Cu. In. - 250 H.P.	24	44
L78	V-8 Eng. 396 Cu. In. - 375 H.P.	179	44
L78	V-8 Eng. 396 Cu. In. 375 H.P. (w/L89 Al. Head)	–	–
M20	4-Speed Trans.	13	5
M35	Powerglide Trans. (L6)	-14	2
M35	Powerglide Trans. (V8)	-6	2
M38	3-Speed Auto. Trans.	–	–
M38	3-Speed Auto. Trans.	18	6
M40	3-Speed Auto. Trans.	23	9
MB1	2-Speed Trans.	–	–
MC1	HD 3-Speed Trans.	16	3
A31	Elect. Windows (exc. Pick-up)	11	13
A31	Elect. Windows (Pick-up)	6	4
A33	Elect. Tailgate Window	-2	7
A51	Astro Bucket Seats	11	10
A67	Folding Rear Seat	–	–
A81	Head Rest (Spec. Contour)	–	–
A93	Vacuum Door Locks (2 Dr.)	5	3
A93	Vacuum Door Locks (4 Dr.)	7	4
B37	Floor Mats (Front & Rear)	7	5
B37	Floor Mats (Front)	5	2
C06	Elect. Folding Top	–	–
C-8	Vinyl Top (exc. Pick-up)	2	5
C60	Air Conditioning	101	7
D55	Console (exc. M40)	7	4
D55	Console (w/M40)	12	4
D80	Aux. Panel & Valance	–	–
F40	HD Suspension	–	–
G31	Spl. Rear Spring	–	–
J50	Power Brakes	10	2
J52	Disc Brakes	–	–
N10	Dual Exhaust (exc. Sta. Wag., Pick-up, L78)	4	37
N10	Dual Exhaust (Sta. Wag., Pick-up, L78)	3	29
N40	Power Steering	30	0
N65	Space Saver Spare	–	–
T60	HD Battery	18	-3
T60	HD Battery (Base Eng.)	–	–
T60	HD Battery (RPO Eng.)	–	–
T60	HD Battery (L6 & Z28)	–	–
T60	HD Battery (307, 350, 396)	–	–
U57	Tape Player (w/U79)	12	4
U57	Tape Player (exc. U79)	9	3
U57	Tape Player	–	–
U63	Radio (Pushbutton)	6	2
U69	Radio (AM-FM)	6	3
U79	Stereo	7	2
V01	HD Radiator (L6)	8	-1
V01	HD Radiator (V-8)	7	-1
V31	Front Bumper Guard	–	–
V32	Rear Bumper Guard	–	–
V55	Luggage Carrier (Sta. Wag.)	2	14

1969 Option weight list table 1 (Chevrolet)

1969 Option Weights Table 2

Model	Susp.	Front		Rear	
		Weight	Code	Weight	Code
Coupe/ Conver.	Std	0-264 265-326 327-372 373-456 457-Over	GW GX GY GZ AA	0-130 131-Over	BL BM
	HD	0-304 305-422 423-over	AB AC AD	ALL	BT
El Camino	Std.	0-270 271-334 335-400 401-464 465-over	GW GX GY GZ AA	ALL	BR
	HD	0-310 311-428 429-Over	AB AC AD	ALL	BX

1969 Spring Part Numbers Table 3

FRONT			REAR		
Code	Part #	Rate	Code	Part #	Rate
AA	3983304	320	BL	3952828	130
AB	3960665	390	BM	3952828	130
AC	3952824	390	BT	3960652	160
AD	3952824	390	BR, BX	3952831	130
GW	3952818	320			
GX	3952818	320			
GY	3952820	320			
GZ	3952820	320			

1970 Spring Part Numbers

FRONT			REAR		
Code	Part #	Rate	Code	Part #	Rate
Coupe Convertible					
GA	3960665	390	OQ	3960652	160
GB	3960665	390		3987800	160
El Camino					
GC	3960686	435	--	3952834	160

Table 1 1971-1972 Base Weight

Model	Base Weight	
	Front	Rear
Coupe V-8	834.0	615.0
Convertible V-8	829	647.0
El Camino	836.5	622.0

Table 2: 1971-1972 Option Weight List

RPO	Option	Front	Rear
A-31	Power windows	5.5	6.0
A-46	Power Seats	7.5	4.5
A 51	Bucket Seats	10	8.0
C 60	A/C	48	3.0
D 55	Console	6.5	6.5
G-67	Level control	4.0	1.5
k-30	Cruise control	7.5	0
LS3	402-ci V-8	106.5	25.0
LS5	454-ci V-8	104.5	24.5
L48	350-ci 4bbl	11.5	1.5
MC1	H.D 3-spd	12.0	3.0
M20	4-SPD	6.0	2.5
M38	TH 350	14.0	3.0
M40	TH 400	30	9.5
N40	P/S	13.5	0.5
YF3	Heavy Chevy	7.0	0.5

Table 3: 1971-1972 Spring Part Numbers

Front			Rear		
Sprung Weight	Code	Part #	Sprung Weight	Code	Part #
SS 350 OR SS 402					
Coupe Convertible					
0-822	AR AF AH AI	39521808	0-665	BM BU BE	3952828
			666-OVER	BW BR BF BI	3952831
823-902	GI AJ AO	3952811			
903-1048	AK GQ AQ GD	3952813			
1049-OVER	AP AL	383304			
El Camino					
0-914	AZ GI GO	3952811	ALL	BR BW	3952831
915-990	AK GQ	3952813			
991-OVER	AP AL	3983304			

Table 3: 1971-1972 Spring Part Numbers

Front			Rear		
Sprung Weight	Code	Part #	Sprung Weight	Code	Part #
SS 454					
Coupe Convertible					
0-1040	GB GC	3960665	0-620	OQ	3960652
			622-OVER	OH OG	3987800
1041-OVER	GP	3987798			
El Camino					
0-972	GW GX	3952818	ALL	BR	3952831
973-1036	GY GZ	3952820			
1037-OVER	AA AP	3983304			

To interchange the 1964-1968 springs after finding your application on the proper chart for your model, then look over the other charts for a matching part number for example you have a 1967 SS396 coupe without air conditioning with the Heavy-Duty F40 suspension and your front spring part number is 3890620, by looking over the other charts we find that was also used in the 1966 SS 396.

For 1969-1972 spring were computer selected according to the weight of the vehicle. This was done by the weight of the options in 1969. You will have to use table 1 first then add up your options then with the total weight, go to table 2 using the total weight added up in table one find the spring code, and the go to table 3 and find the part number you can then cross reference the other charts to find where else the spring was use.

For the 1970-1972 models use the charts like you did in 1969, but first you will have to add the basic weight of the car then the options and find the proper spring.

For example, you have a 1971 SS 350 hardtop coupe. You go to table 1 and find the basic weight is 834 lbs, now go to table two and added the options, with the total weight go to table 2 finding the spring code then go to table 3, and the cross reference the other 1969-1972 charts to find an interchange.

A tip is that there are two basic interchanges for cars in this guide; the 1964-1967 and the 1968-1972 models. The springs from a 1966 SS96 will not fit your 1969 SS 396. For basic fit the interchange also goes into other models. For the 1964-1967 models those from the 1967-1969 Camaro will fit, as will the 1968-1972 Nova, along with other 1964-1967 GM mid-sized models like the Buick Skylark, Pontiac Lemans and the Oldsmobile Cutlass. Just be sure to pick a similar equipped car. For example, pick a Cutlass with a 400-ci or a Lemans with a 389 or 400-ci for swapping into your SS 396. Other possibilities are a 350-ci with air conditioning and Heavy-Duty suspension. Note when swapping for other GM models the ride height may not be the same as those when using Chevrolet springs, as the rating may not be the same.

Note that the 1968-1972 springs can also be found in Monte Carlo, and other GM models like Skylarks, Cutlasses, Lemans and Grand Prix just make sure it is similarly equipped model, look for cars with heavy-duty suspension or heavily optioned cars with a big block.

Rear Springs, Coil

Chevelle used rear coil springs and the interchange is the same as with the front coil springs. However, other GM or Chevrolet models will not fit the 1964-1967 Chevelle models only the springs from a 1964-1967 Chevelle will fit. However other mid-sized GM models will fit the 1968-1972 models.

When interchanging the spring use all the precautions that are listed with front springs. Use the below charts for 1964-1968 models for a 1969-1972 see charts listed with front springs.

1964-1965 Rear Coil Springs			
Model	Code	Part Number	Notes
Coupe	BB	3866298	1123 lbs
Coupe with 327	BW	3857643	
Convertible or 4-door sedan	BU	3856590	Without F40 Suspension
Convertible with 327 or 4-door sedan with 327	BY	3859078	
El Camino	BD	3851066	With F40 Suspension
El Camino	BU	3890626	Without F40 Suspension
Convertible	BV	3843674	With F40 Suspension
Coupe	BV	3851067	With F40 Suspension
With 327-ci	BK	3851067	With F40 Suspension

1965 Rear Coil Springs			
Model	Code	Part Number	Notes
Coupe	BB	3866298	
Coupe with 327	BV	3856591	
Convertible	BJ	3866259	Without F40 Suspension
Convertible with A/C	BL	3866276	
El Camino	BM	3851066	With F40 Suspension
El Camino	BG	3890626	Without F40 Suspension
Convertible w 327	BL	3866276	With or w/o A/C
Coupe	BV	3851067	With F40 Suspension
Z-16	BY	3870488	

1966-1967 Rear Coil Springs			
Model	Code	Part Number	Notes
Coupe	OA, BJ	3883641	W OR W/O A/C
Convertible	OD, BF	3895819	
Convertible with A/C	OG, BE	3895820	
Coupe/Conv. with F40	OE BZ[1]	3851067	W OR W/O A/C
El Camino	OG, BW	3895820	W OR W/O A/C
El Camino with F-40	OP, BB	3893398	W OR W/O A/C
Coupe with 396-ci	OI, BH[1]	3895821	W OR W/O A/C
Convertible with 396-ci	OM, BV	3895822	W OR W/O A/C
Coupe 396 with F40 Suspension	OT, BZ	3895825	W OR W/O A/C
Convertible 396 w F40 suspension	OV, BP	3895826	W OR W/O A/C
El Camino with 396	OP, BS	3893398	W OR W/O A/C
(1) Used with or without A/C Also found on 1966-1967 Chevelles with Heavy-Duty suspension with V-8 rated 1,469 lbs.			

1968 Rear Coil Springs			
Model	Code	Part Number	Notes
Coupe	BZ, BL	3952828	(1)
Convertible	BP, BM	3952828	(1)
Coupe	BT	3960652	With F40 suspension
El Camino	BR, BX	3952831	W or W/O A/C Or F40 suspension
(1) Used with or without A/C			

Only one rear sway bar was used on all applications from the 1965 Z-16, to the 1969-1972 models with F41 suspension package. The 1964-1967 did not have this option

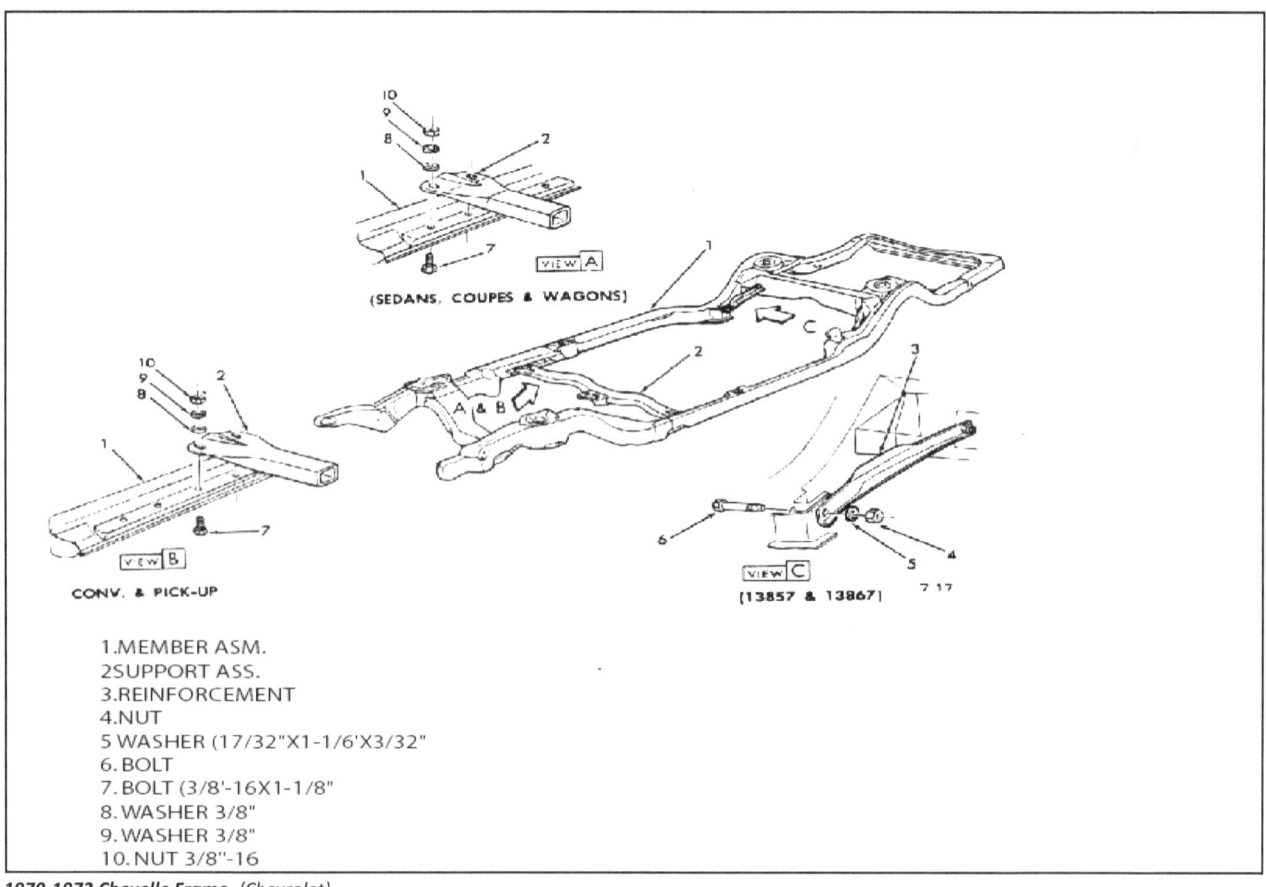

1. MEMBER ASM.
2. SUPPORT ASS.
3. REINFORCEMENT
4. NUT
5. WASHER (17/32"X1-1/6'X3/32"
6. BOLT
7. BOLT (3/8'-16X1-1/8"
8. WASHER 3/8"
9. WASHER 3/8"
10. NUT 3/8"-16

1970-1972 Chevelle Frame. (Chevrolet)

Steering Knuckle

Chevelle

Model Identification	Interchange Number
1964	
Drum Brakes	1
1965	
Drum Brakes	
Early	1
Late	2
1966	
Drum Brakes	2
1967-1972	
Drum Brakes	3
Disc Brakes	4

Interchanges

Interchange Number: 1
Part Number(s): 3855282 fits either side)
Brake Type: Drum
Usage: 1964- early 1965 Chevelle, all body styles.
Notes: Has ½ inch anchor hole. Number 2 will fit. But number 1 will not fit interchange number 2. Change occurred around May 1965.

Interchange Number: 2
Part Number(s): 38815124 (fits either side)
Brake Type: Drum
Usage: Late 1965-1966 Chevelle

Interchange Number: 3
Part Number(s): 3966159 (fits either side)
Brake Type: Drum
Usage: 1968-1974 Nova; 1967-1969 Camaro; 1971-1974 Ventura II; 1973-1974 Apollo; 1967-1972 Chevelle; 1971-1972 GMC Sprint; 1973-1974 Omega.

Interchange Number: 4
Part Number(s): 3966151 (fits either side)
Brake Type: Disc
Usage: 1968-1974 Nova; 1967-1969 Camaro; 1971-1974 Ventura II; 1967-1972 Chevelle; 1971-1972 GMC Sprint

Sway Bar, Front

Chevelle

Model Identification	Interchange Number
1964	
All	1
1965	
Except SS 396	1
SS 396	2
1966	
Except SS 396	1
1967	
Except SS 396	1
1968	
All	3
1969-1972	
Except SS 396	
Without F41	3
With F41	4
SS 396	4

Front sway bar

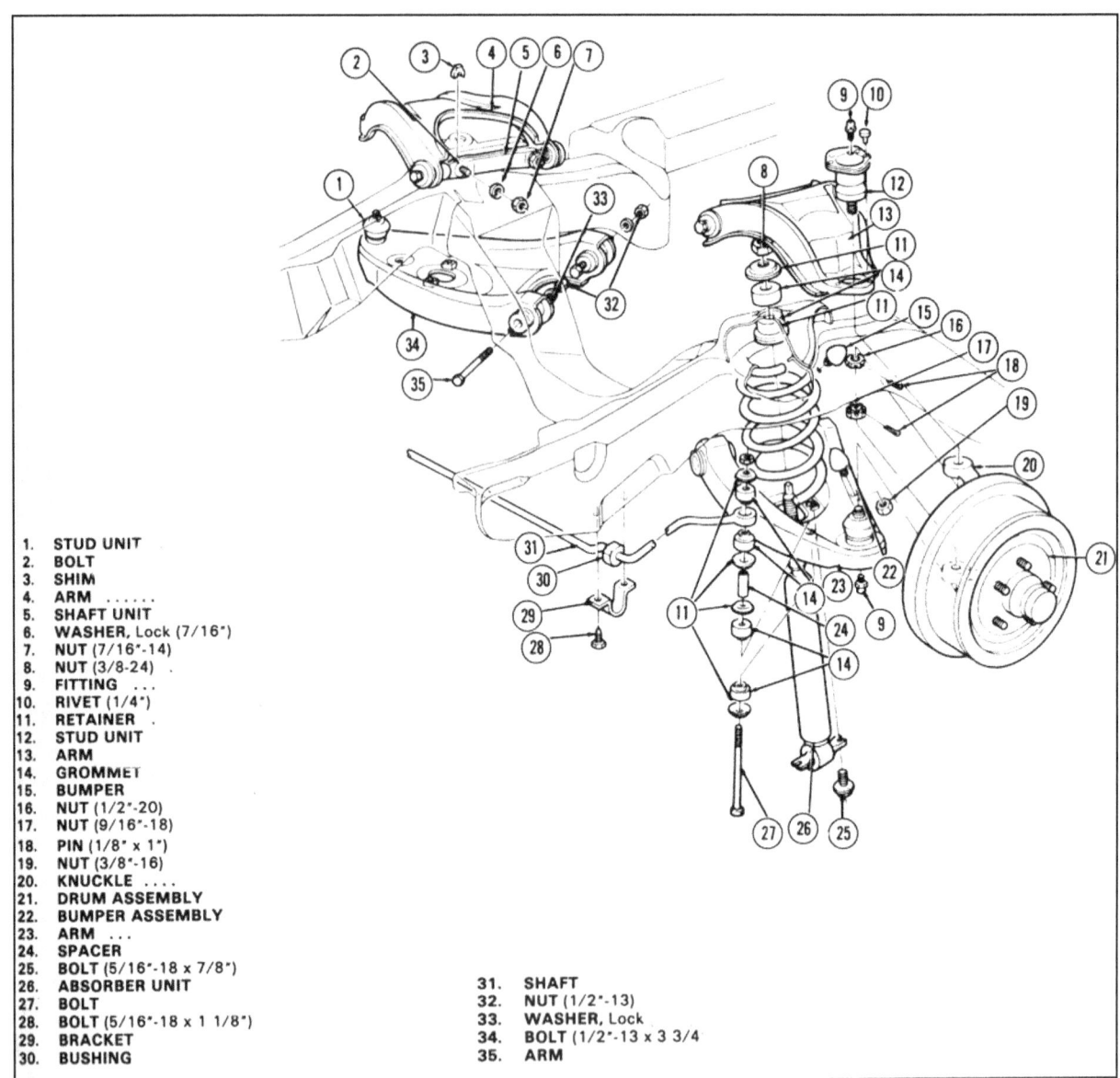

1964-1972 Front suspension. (Chevrolet)

1. STUD UNIT
2. BOLT
3. SHIM
4. ARM
5. SHAFT UNIT
6. WASHER, Lock (7/16")
7. NUT (7/16"-14)
8. NUT (3/8-24)
9. FITTING
10. RIVET (1/4")
11. RETAINER
12. STUD UNIT
13. ARM
14. GROMMET
15. BUMPER
16. NUT (1/2"-20)
17. NUT (9/16"-18)
18. PIN (1/8" x 1")
19. NUT (3/8"-16)
20. KNUCKLE
21. DRUM ASSEMBLY
22. BUMPER ASSEMBLY
23. ARM
24. SPACER
25. BOLT (5/16"-18 x 7/8")
26. ABSORBER UNIT
27. BOLT
28. BOLT (5/16"-18 x 1 1/8")
29. BRACKET
30. BUSHING
31. SHAFT
32. NUT (1/2"-13)
33. WASHER, Lock
34. BOLT (1/2"-13 x 3 3/4)
35. ARM

Interchange Number: 1
Part Number(s): 397703
Diameter: 0.8125"
Usage: 1964-1967 Chevelle, except SS 396; 1964-1967 Cutlass six cylinder

Interchange Number: 2
Part Number(s): 397705
Diameter: 0.9375"
Usage: 1965-1967 Chevelle SS 396; 1964-1966 Cutlass station wagon; 1964-1967 442

Interchange Number: 3
Part Number(s): 401194
Diameter: 1.00
Usage: 1968-1972 Chevelle without F41 suspension or SS 396 SS 454; 1968-1970 Cutlass with Rallye suspension; 1968-1972 Buick Skylark except GSX or with Stage Iv package; 1969-1972 442 convertibles; 1970-1971 Monte Carlo except SS models 1970-1972 Lemans, except Station wagon or GTO

Interchange Number: 4
Part Number(s): 402544
Diameter: 1-1/4"
Usage: 1969-1972 Chevelle with F41 suspension or SS 396 SS 454; 1970-1971 Monte Carlo SS 454; 1970-1972 GTO

Chevelle 1964-1972

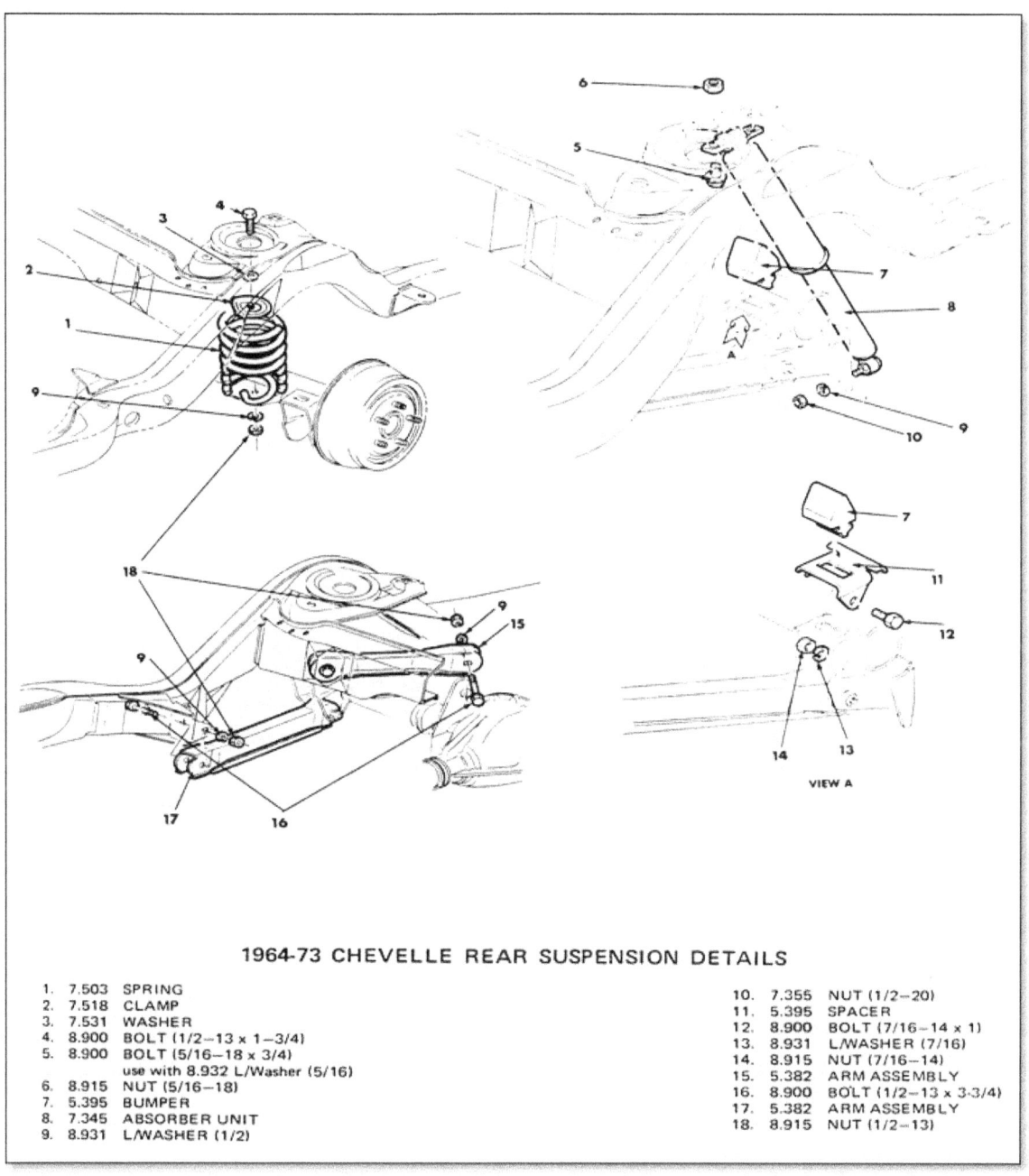

1864-1972 Chevelle Rear suspension (Chevrolet)

Steering Gearbox

Interchange for the steering gearbox is categorized by the type of steering used (manual or power assisted) It is based on the part number and fit. Ratio is given when it is needed. Made by Saginaw and used the type 800 with large gears and has a rectangular shaped cover held in place with 4-bolts.

There is no way to identify the steering gear boxes by casting as the casting was used for different ratio. A stamped ink code letters can be used, but the codes are worn off over time. Most Camaro used the type 800 power steering gear box, a build date can be stamped on top of the aluminum cover and it will be in a Julian form with the day of the year.

99

Remember this is the day of the year not necessarily the model year for example the date of 147-9 would be the 147th day of 1969 which would be May 27, 1969 and would be for a late built model, while the date of 330-9 would be November 26, 1969 and would be for a 1970 model.

Chevelle

Model Identification	Interchange Number

1964
Manual..1
Power Steering..5

1965
Manual
Except Z-16..1
Z-16..2
Power Steering..6

1966
Manual..1
Power Steering..6

1967-1968
Manual..1
Power Steering..8

1969
Manual..1
Power Steering..7

1970
Manual..3
Power Steering
Except El Camino..9
El Camino..10

1971-1972
Manual..12
Power Steering..11

Interchanges

Interchange Number: 1
Part Number(s): 5679270
Type: Manual
Usage: 1964-1969 Chevelle, except 1965 Z16; 19614-1969 Lemans, except quick-ratio; 1964-1969 Cutlass, except police car; 1964-1969 full-size Chevrolet, Oldsmobile. All without power steering.

Interchange Number: 2
Part Number(s): 7806396
Type: Manual
Usage: 1967-1969 Camaro Z-28; 1965 Chevelle SS 396 (Z16); 1967-1969 Firebird with quick-ratio steering; 1967-1969 Cutlass police car or with Heavy-duty steering option; 1967-1969 Lemans with Heavy-duty steering or police car package; 1967-1969 Chevelle with Police car package; 1965-1969 full-size Chevrolet police car manual steering

Interchange Number: 3
Part Number(s): 7812897
Type: Manual
Usage: 1970 Chevelle without power steering ;1970 Camaro with six cylinder; 1970 Camaro Z-28; 1970 Firebird six-cylinder or Formula 400 or Trans Am

Interchange Number: 4
Part Number(s): 7815770
Type: Manual
Usage: 1971-1972 Chevelle without power steering; 1972 Camaro without power steering except Z-28; 1972 Nova without power steering

Interchange Number: 5
Part Number(s): 5692398
Type: Power
Usage: 1964 Chevelle with power steering
Notes: Interchange Number 6 will fit was replacement unit.

Interchange Number: 6
Part Number(s): 5696113
Type: Power
Usage: 1965-1966 Chevelle with power steering
Notes: 17.5:1 ratio

Interchange Number: 7
Part Number(s): 7806671
Type: Power
Usage: 1969 Chevelle with power steering; 1969 Lemans with power steering except GTO; 1969 Skylark, except GS 400; 1969 Cutlass except 442
Notes: 17.5:1 ratio part number is different for BOP but they will fit. Code AH

Interchange Number: 8
Part Number(s): 7801584
Type: Power
Usage: 1967-1968 Chevelle with power steering; 1967-1968 Lemans with power steering except GTO; 1967-1968 Skylark, except GS 400; 1964-1968 Cutlass except 442
Notes: 17.5:1 ratio part number is different for BOP but they will fit. Code AH

Interchange Number: 9
Part Number(s): 7811176
Type: Power
Usage: 1970 Chevelle with power steering except El Camino or station wagon; 1970 Monte Carlo; 1970 Impala with variable ratio steering, except station wagon
Notes: 16-12.4:1 Code BA CF

Interchange Number: 10
Part Number(s): 7811177
Type: Power
Usage: 1970 El Camino or Chevelle station wagon with Power steering
Notes: 17.5:1 ratio code BH or CE

Interchange Number: 11
Part Number(s): 7815069
Type: Power
Usage: 1971-1972 Chevelle with power steering
Notes: 16-13:1 Code CL, CA

Interchange Number: 12
Part Number(s): 7809557
Type: Manual
Usage: 1971-1972 Chevelle without power steering

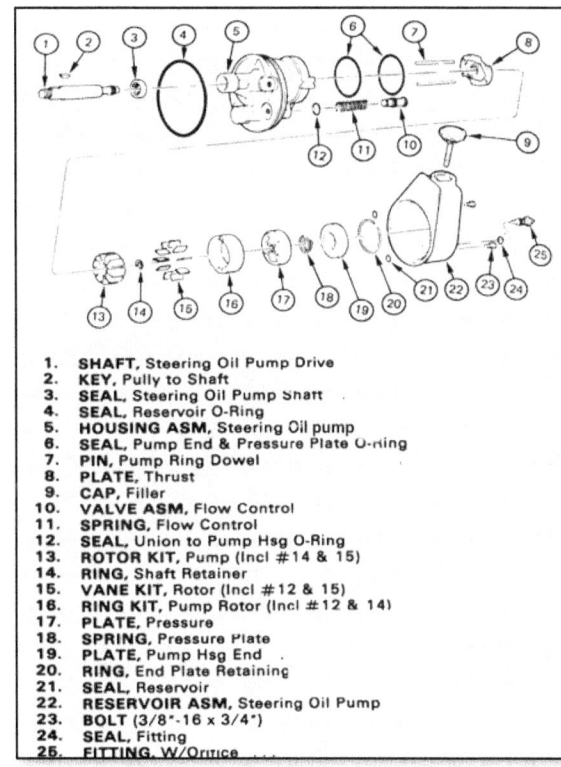

Typical power steering pump *(Chevrolet)*

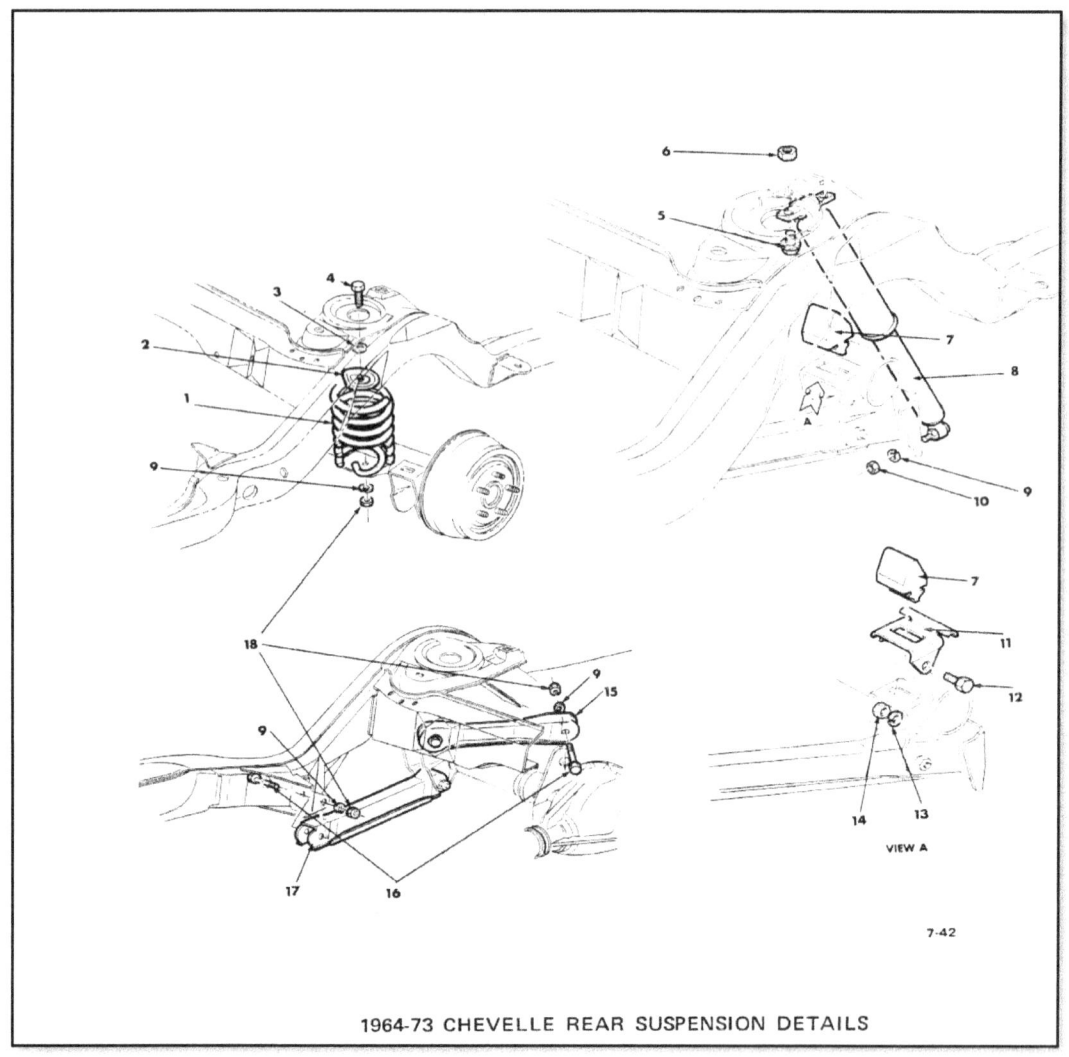

1964-73 CHEVELLE REAR SUSPENSION DETAILS

(Chevrolet)

Power Steering Pump

Chevelle
Model Identification *Interchange Number*
1964
All...1
1965-1967
Except 396-ci..1
396-ci..2
1968
Except 396-ci..1
396-ci..3
1969
Except 396-ci..5
396-ci
Except Variable-ratio..6
Variable-ratio...5

1970
Except El Camino..7
El Camino...8
1971-1972
All...7

Interchanges

Interchange Number: 1
Part Number(s): 5698076
Usage: 1964-1968 Chevelle, with 283, 307 or 327-ci V-8

Interchange Number: 2
Part Number(s): 5698077
Usage: 1965-1967 Chevelle SS 396

Interchange Number: 3
Part Number(s): 7803404
Usage: 1968 Chevelle SS 396

Interchange Number: 4
Part Number(s): 7806371
Usage: 1969 Chevelle with 307-ci or 350-ci V-8

Interchange Number: 5
Part Number(s): 7806370
Usage: 1969 Chevelle SS 396; 1969 Camaro with 396-ci.
Notes: Variable ratio

Interchange Number: 6
Part Number(s): 7806372
Usage: 1969 Chevelle SS 396; 1969 Nova with 396-ci.
Notes: Except variable ratio

Interchange Number: 7
Part Number(s): 7813397
Usage: 1970 Chevelle with V-8, except El Camino or station wagon; 1971-1972 Chevelle all models with V-8 SS 396; 1970-1974 Camaro with V-8; 1973-1974 Chevelle with 307-ci or 350-ci V-8; 1970-1972 Monte Carlo with V-8; 1973-1974 Monte Carlo with 350-ci V-8; 1971-1972 full-size Chevrolet with 350-ci or 400-ci SMALL BLOCK 1971-1972 GMC Sprint with V-8; 1971-1972 Ventura II with 307-ci V-8

1964-1966 wood rim steering wheel

1964-1965 Malibu and Super Sport steering wheel

Steering Wheel

Steering wheel interchange is based on the overall design and style number. Both design and color can vary from year to year and model to mode, as well as usage. Thus, color is not part of the interchange, and the interchange is based on the part number for the black steering wheel to give you the most interchanges possible.

You can hunt for the proper shade for your car or you can opt for another color and paint the steering wheel to match. If you are looking to paint steering wheels look for a light-colored wheel as it is easier to cover with paint. Also inspect the steering wheel for cracks and make sure the plastic is not dry rotted. Steering wheels can be repaired with epoxy, but it is best to start with a good base.

Basically, three different types of steering wheels were used. The standard wheel, which was used in low level models like Biscayne and Bel-Air and the Deluxe wheel which was option in the low trim models and standard on high trim models like the Impala and the Super Sport. The third type is the sport wheel which is a wood rim steering wheel.

Chevelle

Model Identification   Interchange Number

1964-1965
Standard
Chevelle..1
Deluxe..2
Malibu..2
Sport..3

1966
Standard
Chevelle..4
Deluxe..5
Malibu..5
Sport..3

1967
Standard...16
Deluxe..6
Sport..7

1968
Standard...17
Deluxe..8
Sport..7

1969
Standard...10
Deluxe..10
Sport..11

1970
Standard...10
Deluxe..12

1971-1972
Standard...13
Deluxe..14
Sport..15

Interchanges

Interchange Number: 1
Part Number(s): 9740378
Type: Standard wheel
Usage: 1964-1965 Chevelle 300

1966 Steering wheel on Malibu and Super Sport not the rings on the rim.

Interchange Number: 2
Part Number(s): 9740388
Type: Standard wheel
Usage: 1964-1965 Chevelle Malibu and Super Sport

Interchange Number: 3
Part Number(s): 9741033
Type: Sport wheel
Usage: 1964-1966 full-size Chevrolet, Chevelle; 1966-1967, Nova with RPO N34 wood rim steering wheel.

Interchange Number: 4
Part Number(s): 3878031
Type: Standard wheel
Usage: 1966 Biscayne, Chevelle except Malibu or Super Sport.
Notes: Deluxe wheel interchange number 8

1967 Steering wheel

1967-1968 Sport Steering wheel has a walnut rim

1968 Standard steering wheel

Interchange Number: 5
Part Number(s): 3878002
Type: Standard wheel/Deluxe Wheel
Usage: 1966 Impala, Nova, Chevelle Malibu or Super Sport

Interchange Number: 6
Part Number(s): 9745760
Type: Standard wheel/Deluxe
Usage: 1967 Impala, Nova, Chevelle Malibu or Super Sport; 1968 Biscayne, Bel Air, Chevelle except Malibu or SS 396, 1967 Camaro; 1967-1968 Nova
Notes:

Interchange Number: 7
Part Number(s): 9746195
Type: Sport wheel
Usage: 1967-1968 Camaro, Chevelle, full-size Chevrolet, Nova with N34 wood rim steering wheel.
Notes: Walnut rim

1968 Deluxe steering wheel, Standard on higher trim models

Interchange Number: 8
Part Number(s): 9747689
Usage: 1968 Impala Chevelle Malibu or Super Sport; Nova, Camaro with deluxe steering wheel.

Interchange Number: 9
Part Number(s): 3997584
Usage: 1969-1970 Camaro, Chevelle, full-size Chevrolet Nova, except 1970 with Deluxe steering wheel.

Interchange Number: 10
Part Number(s): 3960722
Type: Sport wheel
Usage: 1969 Camaro, Chevelle, full-size Chevrolet, Nova with N34 wood rim steering wheel.
Notes: Rosewood rim

Interchange Number: 11
Part Number(s): 3960722
Type: Sport wheel
Usage: 1969 Camaro, Chevelle, full-size Chevrolet, Nova with N34 wood rim steering wheel.
Notes: Rosewood rim

Interchange Number: 12
Part Number(s): 9752131
Type: Deluxe
Usage: 1970 Camaro, Chevelle, full-size Chevrolet, Monte Carlo and Nova with Vinyl grip steering wheel.

Interchange Number: 13
Part Number(s): 3989115
Type: Standard wheel
Usage: 1971-1972 Camaro, Chevelle, full-size Chevrolet, Nova; 1970 Camaro

1969-1970 Steering wheel

1969 Rosewood wood rim steering wheel.

The 1971-1972 Sport wheel was used on all Chevrolets models. But most commonly found on Camano's.

1970 Deluxe steering wheel.

The standard steering wheel used in many Chevrolet models

Interchange Number: 14
Part Number(s): 9752131
Type: Deluxe wheel
Usage: 1971-1972 Camaro, Chevelle, full-size Chevrolet, Monte Carlo, Nova

Interchange Number: 15
Part Number(s): 3978125
Type: Sport wheel
Usage: 1971-1972 Camaro, Chevelle, full-size Chevrolet, Monte Carlo, Nova
Notes: X spokes

Interchange Number: 16
Part Number(s):
Type: Standard
Usage: 1967 Chevelle except Malibu or Super Sport; 1967 Biscayne; 1967 Chevy II except Nova
Notes: two spoke

Interchange Number: 17
Part Number(s):
Type: Standard
Usage: 1968 Chevelle except Malibu or Super Sport; 1968 Biscayne
Notes: two spoke

Steering Column

Chevelle

Model Identification   Interchange Number

1964-1965
Shift on Column
Manual..1
Automatic...1
Shift on Floor
Without tilt...2
With Tilt..4

1966
Shift on Column
Manual..5
Automatic
Without tilt...7
With tilt...8
Floor
Without tilt...6
With tilt...9

1967
Shift on Column
Manual..11
Automatic
Without tilt...10
With tilt..8
Floor
Without tilt
Except SS 396..12
SS 396..13
With tilt..9

1968
Shift on Column
Except SS 396
Without tilt...22
With tilt...21
Without tilt
SS 396
Powerglide...16
T.H. 400
Without tilt...14
With tilt...15
Floor
Except SS 396
Without tilt...19
With tilt...20
SS 396
Without tilt...17
With tilt...18

1969
Shift on Column
Manual..33
Automatic
Except SS 396
Without tilt...31
With tilt...29
SS 396..26
Floor
Without Tilt
Except SS 396..23
SS 396
Powerglide...27
T.H. 400..28
Manual. 29
With Tilt
Except SS 396..24
SS 396..25

1970-1972
Shift on Column
Manual..33
Automatic
Without tilt...32
With tilt...31
With tilt...29
Floor
Except SS 396/SS 454
Without tilt...34
With tilt...23

SS 396/SS 454
Without tilt..32
With tilt
4speed..34
Automatic...35

Interchanges

Interchange Number: 1
Part Number(s): 3854381
Transmission Type: Manual three-speed
Shifter Location: Column
Usage: 1964 Chevelle, all models

Interchange Number: 2
Part Number(s): 3854244
Transmission Type: All
Shifter Location: Floor
Usage: 1964 Chevelle, all models

Interchange Number: 3
Part Number(s): 3864545
Transmission Type: All
Shifter Location: Floor
Usage: 1965 Chevelle, all models
Without tilt-steering

Interchange Number: 4
Part Number(s): 5693760
Transmission Type: All
Shifter Location: Floor
Usage: 1964-1965 Chevelle with tilt wheel

Interchange Number: 5
Part Number(s): 5691416
Transmission Type: Manual three-speed
Shifter Location: Column
Usage: 1966 Chevelle, except SS 396

Interchange Number: 6
Part Number(s): 5692597
Transmission Type: All
Shifter Location: floor
Usage: 1966 Chevelle

Interchange Number: 7
Part Number(s): 5692598
Transmission Type: Automatic
Shifter Location: Column
Usage: 1966 Chevelle

Interchange Number: 8
Part Number(s): 5697070
Transmission Type: Automatic
Shifter Location: Column
Usage: 1966-1967 Chevelle with tilt wheel

Interchange Number. 9
Part Number(s): 5697065
Transmission Type: All
Shifter Location: Floor
Usage: 1966-1967 Chevelle with tilt wheel

Interchange Number: 10
Part Number(s): 7802716
Transmission Type: Automatic
Shifter Location: Column
Usage: 1967 Chevelle

Interchange Number: 11
Part Number(s): 7802717
Transmission Type: Manual three-speed
Shifter Location: Column
Usage: 1967 Chevelle

Interchange Number: 12
Part Number(s): 7802718
Transmission Type: All
Shifter Location: Floor
Usage: 1967 Chevelle, except SS 396

Interchange Number: 13
Part Number(s): 7802722
Transmission Type: All
Shifter Location: Floor
Usage: 1967 SS 396 only

Interchange Number: 14
Part Number(s): 7802416
Transmission Type: Turbo Hydra-Matic 400
Shifter Location: Column
Usage: 1968 Chevelle SS 396

Interchange Number: 15
Part Number(s): 7802909
Transmission Type: Turbo Hydra-Matic 400
Shifter Location: Column
Usage: 1968 SS 396 with tilt wheel

Interchange Number: 16
Part Number(s): 7803695
Transmission Type: Powerglide
Shifter Location: Column
Usage: 1968 SS 396 without tilt wheel

Interchange Number: 17
Part Number(s): 7803696
Transmission Type: All
Shifter Location: Floor
Usage: 1968 SS 396 without tilt

Interchange Number: 18
Part Number(s): 7803752
Transmission Type: All
Shifter Location: Floor
Usage: 1968 SS 396 with tilt wheel

Interchange Number: 19
Part Number(s): 7802059
Transmission Type: All
Shifter Location: Floor
Usage: 1968 Chevelle, without tilt all but SS 396

Interchange Number: 20
Part Number(s): 7801973
Transmission Type: All
Shifter Location: Floor
Usage: 1968 Chevelle with tilt wheel, all but SS 396

Interchange Number: 21
Part Number(s): 7801972
Transmission Type: Powerglide
Shifter Location: Column
Usage: 1968 Chevelle with tilt wheel, except SS 396

Interchange Number: 22
Part Number(s): 7802068
Transmission Type: Powerglide
Shifter Location: Column
Usage: 1968 Chevelle, without tilt all but SS 396

Interchange Number: 23
Part Number(s): 7812236
Transmission Type: Automatic
Shifter Location: Floor
Usage: 1969-1972 Chevelle, except SS 396
Notes: without tilt

Interchange Number: 24
Part Number(s): 7808147
Transmission Type: All
Shifter Location: Floor
Usage: 1969 Chevelle with tilt wheel, except SS 396

Interchange Number: 25
Part Number(s): 7808150
Transmission Type: Automatic
Shifter Location: Floor
Usage: 1969 SS 396 with tilt wheel

Interchange Number: 26
Part Number(s): 7804954
Transmission Type: Automatic
Shifter Location: Column
Usage: 1969 Chevelle SS 396 without tilt

Interchange Number: 27
Part Number(s): 7804956
Transmission Type: Powerglide
Shifter Location: Floor
Usage: 1969 Chevelle SS 396 without tilt

Interchange Number: 28
Part Number(s): 7808149
Transmission Type: Turbo Hydra-Matic 400
Location floor
Usage 1969 SS 396 without tilt wheel

Interchange Number: 29
Part Number(s): 7813111
Transmission Type: Automatic
Shifter Location: Column
Usage: 1969-1972 Chevelle with tilt wheel, except Super Sport 396

Interchange Number: 30
Part Number(s): 7813112
Transmission Type: Automatic
Shifter Location: Floor
Usage: 1970-1972 Chevelle; 1970 Monte Carlo; both with tilt wheel, except Super Sport 396

Interchange Number: 31
Part Number(s): 7810631
Transmission Type: Automatic
Shifter Location: Column
Usage: 1969-1972 Chevelle without tilt wheel, except SS 396 in 1969

Interchange Number: 32
Part Number(s): 7812237
Transmission Type: Manual
Shifter Location: Floor
Usage: 1969 SS 396 without tilt wheel; 1970-1972 Chevelle with 4-speed or auto in the floor without tilt steering

Interchange Number: 33
Part Number(s): 7812234
Transmission Type: Manual three-speed
Shifter Location: Column
Usage: 1969-1972 Chevelle without tilt wheel, except SS 396 or SS 454

Interchange Number: 34
Part Number(s): 7813113
Transmission Type: Manual
Shifter Location: Floor
Usage: 1970-1972 Chevelle with 350-ci and 4-speed with tilt steering

Interchange Number: 34
Part Number(s): 7813116
Transmission Type: Manual
Shifter Location: Floor
Usage: 1970-1972 Chevelle with 396 ci or 454-ci 4-speed with tilt steering

Interchange Number: 35
Part Number(s): 7813115
Transmission Type: automatic
Shifter Location: Floor
Usage: 1970-1972 Chevelle automatic with tilt steering

Chapter 7 Drive Shafts and Rear Axles

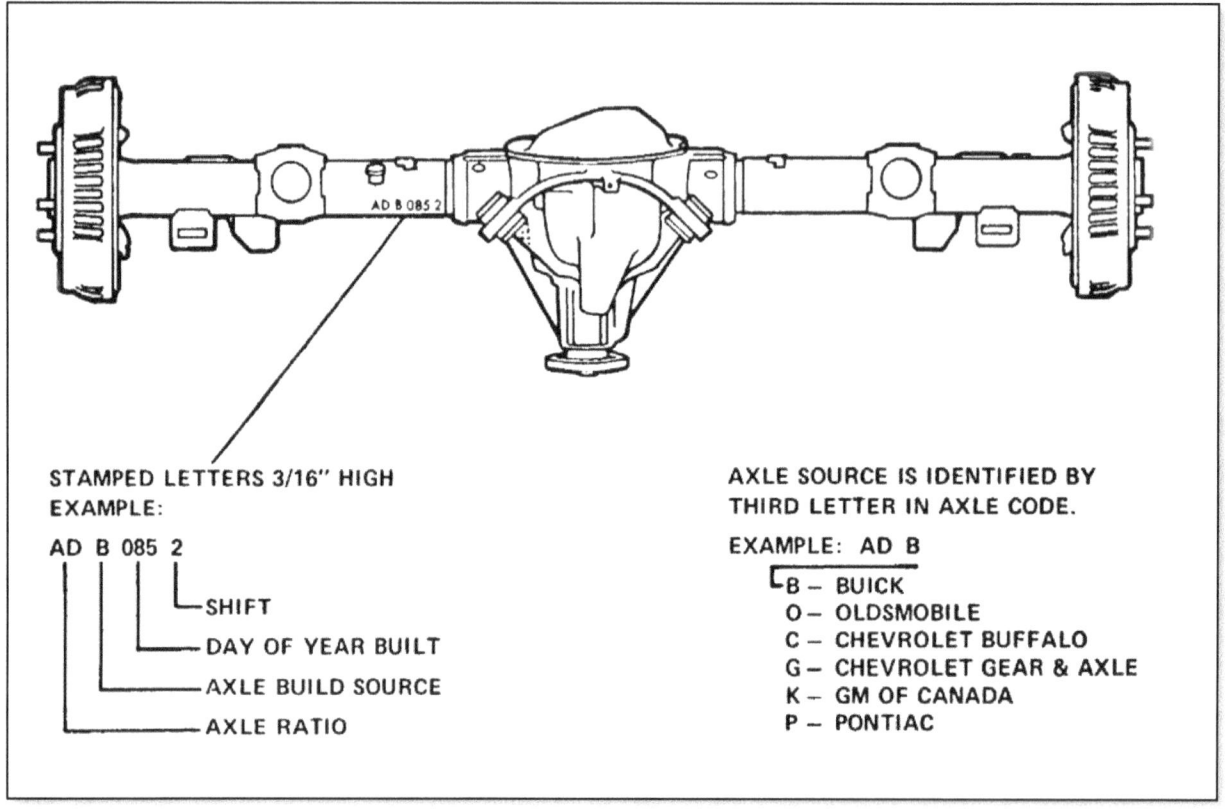

GM axle manufacturer and axle ratio can be identified by a code stamped into the axle tube. (Chevrolet)

Drive Shafts

The driveshafts fit into two basic interchanges for 1964-1967, and 1968-1972. However, body style, transmission and engine sizes can affect the interchange.

Chevelle

Model Identification   *Interchange Number*
1964-1966
Manual..1
Automatic...1
1967
Manual..1
Automatic
Powerglide...10
T.H. 400..11
1968
Except El Camino
Manual..2
Powerglide...6
T.H. 350...3
T.H. 400...8
El Camino
Manual..1
Powerglide...10
T.H. 350...7
T.H. 400...8
1969
Except El Camino
Except SS 396
Manual..3
Automatic..3

SS 396
Except El Camino
Manual..12
Automatic..9
El Camino
Except SS 396..7
SS 396
Manual..5
Automatic..4

1970
Except El Camino
Except SS 396
Except T.H.400..3
T.H. 400..9
El Camino
Except SS 396 or SS 454....................................7
SS 396 SS 454
Manual..5
Automatic
396-ci...4
454-ci...13

1971-1972
Except El Camino
Except SS 396
Manual..3
Automatic
307-ci...3
350-ci
Powerglide..3
TH. 350...12
T.H. 400..9
SS 396
Manual..15
Automatic..9
El Camino
Except SS 396 or SS 454
Manual
3-speed..7
4-speed..14
Automatic..7
SS 396 SS 454
Manual..5
Automatic
396-ci...4
454-ci
4-speed..16
Automatic..13

Interchanges

Interchange Number: 1
Part Number(s): 3898244
Usage: 1964-1966 Chevelle; 1967 Chevelle with manual transmission; 1968 Chevelle four-door sedan with manual transmission; 1968 El Camino with manual transmission

Interchange Number: 2
Part Number(s): 3924126
Usage: 1968 Chevelle coupe or two-door hardtop

Interchange Number: 3
Part Number(s): 3955598
Usage: 1969-1972 Chevelle two-door, except El Camino, all engines except 396 or 454ci; 1968 Chevelle 2-dr with T.H, 350; 1971-1972 Chevelle 2 dr with 307-ci or 350-ci V-8 except T.H. 350 1970 Monte Carlo with Powerglide; 197 Monte Carlo with manual or T.H. 400

Interchange Number: 4
Part Number(s): 3970519
Usage: 1969-1970 El Camino or Chevelle four-door or station wagon with 396ci and Turbo Hydra-Matic 400

Interchange Number: 5
Part Number(s): 3970518
Usage: 1969-1972 El Camino or Chevelle four-door or station wagon with 396ci four-speed

Interchange Number: 6
Part Number(s): 3966951
Usage: 1968 Chevelle two-door with Powerglide transmission.

Interchange Number: 7
Part Number(s): 3955597
Usage: 1969-1972 El Camino with except 396 or 454ci; 1968-1972 Chevelle four-door with 307-ci or 350-ci V-8; 1968 El Camino Chevelle 4 door sedan with 307-ci or 350-ci with T.H. 350 automatic

Interchange Number: 8

Part Number(s): 7801646

Usage: 1968 Chevelle two-door or convertible with Turbo-Hydra-Matic 400; 1971-1972 Chevelle SS 454 with Turbo Hydra-Matic 400 except El Camino

Interchange Number: 9

Part Number(s): 3949163

Usage: 1969-1972 Chevelle two-door, all except El Camino with 396 or 402ci with Turbo Hydra-Matic 400

Interchange Number: 10

Part Number(s): 3895845

Usage: 1967 Chevelle with Powerglide; 1968 Chevelle and El Camino with Powerglide

Interchange Number: 11

Part Number(s): 780541

Usage: 1967 Chevelle SS 396 with T.H. 400 automatic

Interchange Number: 12

Part Number(s): 3949161

Usage: 1969 Chevelle two-door, with 396-ci with manual transmission; 1970-1972 Chevelle with 3-speed manual trnamisison1970-1972 Chevelle 2-dr. 350-ci V-8 and T.H. 350 automatic; 1971-1972 Monte Carlo with 350-ci and automatic transmission

Interchange Number: 13

Part Number(s): 7802607

Usage: 1970-1972 El Camino with 454-ci and T.H. 400 automatic

Interchange Number: 14

Part Number(s): 3997574

Usage: 1971-1972 El Camino with 4-speed except 402-ci or 454-ci; 1971-972 Chevelle sedan with 350-ci 4-bbl and 4-speed

Interchange Number: 15

Part Number(s): 3997575

Usage: 1971-1972 Chevelle with 396-ci 402-ci with 4-speed except El Camino.

Interchange Number: 16

Part Number(s): 789870

Usage: 1971-1972 El Camino with 454-ci and manual transmission

Rear Axle Identification

Axle assembly can be identified quickly and easily by the code that is stamped on the axle housing. This code is located on one of the axle tubes (usually on the driver's side) in numerals that are approximately three inches from the carrier.

The codes represent the manufacturer plant date, build date, and axle gear ratio. You should be aware that ring gears are easily changed, and that the ratio may not be the same as that of the factory unit. Thus, the code can be used for locating the proper axle housing.

Axle housings are also categorized by their basic design. They will often be referred to as a ten-bolt and a twelve-bolt assembly. This refers to the number of bolts that secure the carrier cover. A ten-bolt axle is a fairly good assembly, but for extreme high-performance applications the twelve-bolt is better. Ten-and twelve-bolt axles were used with all 1965-1972 models.

Interchange is based on the fit of the axle and its basic design. Codes are given in the charts to help you identify the axle, but the interchange is for the basic axle housing assembly without gears.

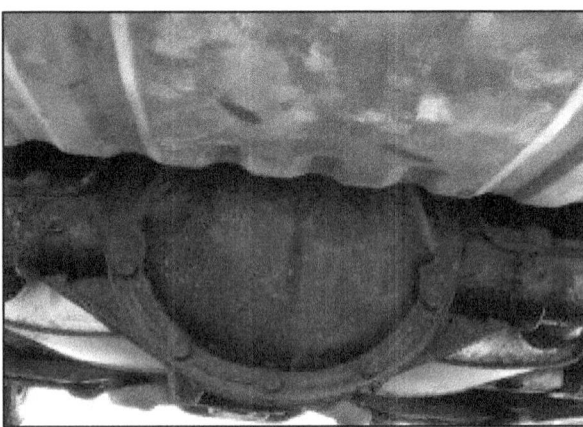

10 bolt axle has a smooth round cover held on with 10-bolts. They are used only on Chevrolet A-bodies

1964 Rear Axle Codes

3.08	LA,YA,ZA ZC*
LOCKING 3.08	LG,YG,ZG ZE*
3.36	LB,YB,ZB ZD*
LOCKING 3.36	LH,YH,ZH ZF*
3.70	ZJ, ZL*
LOCKING 3.70	ZK, ZM*

*-WITH METALLIC BRAKES

1965 Rear Axle Codes

327 w/Powerglide (2.73 ratio)	GB
Positraction (2.73 ratio)	GC
Metallic Brakes (2.73 ratio)	GD
Positraction w/Metallic Brakes (2.73 ratio)	GE
(3.08 ratio)	CA
(3.36 ratio)	CB
(3.73 ratio)	CC
Positraction (3.07 ratio)	CD
Positraction (3.08 ratio)	CE
Positraction (3.31 ratio)	CF
Positraction (3.36 ratio)	CG
Positraction (3.70 ratio)	CR
Positraction (3.73 ratio)	CI
w/Metallic Brakes (3.07 ratio)	CJ
Positraction w/Metallic Brakes (3.07 ratio)	CK
w/Metallic Brakes (3.08 ratio)	CL
Positraction w/Metallic Brakes (3.08 ratio)	CM
w/Metallic Brakes (3.31 ratio)	CN
Positraction w/Metallic Brakes (3.31 ratio)	CO
w/Metallic Brakes (3.36 ratio)	CP
Positraction w/Metallic Brakes (3.36 ratio)	CQ
w/Metallic Brakes (3.70 ratio)	CH
Positraction w/Metallic Brakes (3.70 ratio)	CS
w/Metallic Brakes (3.73 ratio)	CT
Positraction w/Metallic Brakes (3.73 ratio)	CU
Overdrive (3.70 ratio)	CV
(3.31 ratio) "327" w/Air Cond.	CW
(3.07 ratio) "327"	CX

1966 Rear Axle Codes

(3.08 ratio)	CA
(3.36 ratio)	CB
(3.73 ratio)	CC
Positraction (3.07 ratio)	CD
Positraction (3.08 ratio)	CE
Positraction (3.31 ratio)	CF
Positraction (3.36 ratio)	CG
w/Metallic Brakes (3.70 ratio)	CH
Positraction (3.73 ratio)	CI
w/Metallic Brakes (3.07 ratio)	CJ
Positraction w/Metallic Brakes (3.07 ratio)	CK
w/Metallic Brakes (3.08 ratio)	CL
Positraction w/Metallic Brakes (3.08 ratio)	CM
w/Metallic Brakes (3.31 ratio)	CN
Positraction w/Metallic Brakes (3.31 ratio)	CO
w/Metallic Brakes (3.36 ratio)	CP
Positraction w/Metallic Brakes (3.36 ratio)	CQ
Positraction (3.70 ratio)	CR
Positraction w/Metallic Brakes (3.70 ratio)	CS
w/Metallic Brakes (3.73 ratio)	CT
Positraction w/Metallic Brakes (3.73 ratio)	CU
Overdrive (3.70 ratio)	CV
(3.31 ratio) "396" w/Air Cond.	CW
(3.07 ratio) "396" w/Air Cond. and PG	CX
w/Metallic Brakes (3.55 ratio)	KF
Positraction w/Metallic Brakes (3.55 ratio)	KG
Positraction (3.55 ratio)	KH
"396" w/PG (2.73 ratio)	KI

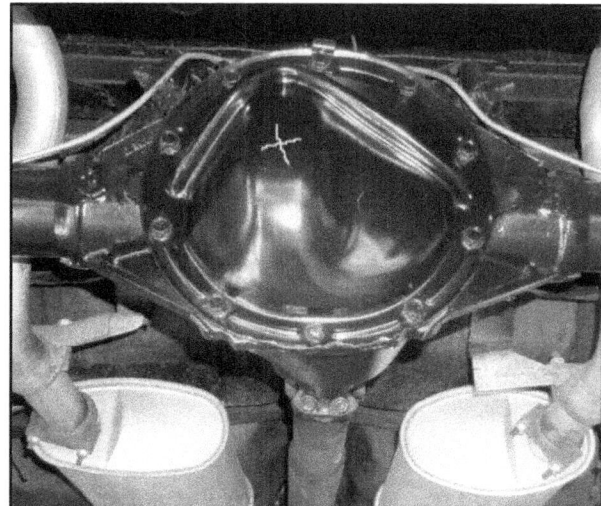

!2-BOLT Axles are usually found under the SS 396 and SS 454. They have a humped cover that is held on with 12 bolts. And also under several different GM A-Bodies

1967 Rear Axle Codes

Description	Code
(3.08 ratio)	CA
(3.36 ratio)	CB
(3.73 ratio)	CC
Positraction (3.07 ratio)	CD
Positraction (3.08 ratio)	CE
Positraction (3.31 ratio)	CF
Positraction (3.36 ratio)	CG
Positraction (2.73 ratio)	CH
Positraction (3.73 ratio)	CI
w/Metallic Brakes (3.07 ratio)	CJ
Positraction w/Metallic Brakes (3.07 ratio)	CK
w/Metallic Brakes (3.31 ratio)	CN
Positraction w/Metallic Brakes (3.31 ratio)	CO
Positraction (3.70 ratio)	CR
w/Metallic Brakes (3.73 ratio)	CT
Positraction w/Metallic Brakes (3.73 ratio)	CU
(3.70 ratio)	CV
(3.31 ratio)	CW
(3.07 ratio)	CX
(2.73 ratio)	CZ
Positraction (3.55 ratio)	KF
Positraction w/Metallic Brakes (3.55 ratio)	KG
w/Metallic Brakes (3.55 ratio)	KH
(3.55 ratio)	KJ
Positraction (4.10 ratio)	KK
w/Metallic Brakes (4.10 ratio)	KL
Positraction (4.56 ratio)	KM
w/Metallic Brakes (4.56 ratio)	KN
Positraction (4.88 ratio)	KO
w/Metallic Brakes (4.88 ratio)	KP

1968 Rear Axle Codes

Description	Code
(3.08 ratio)	CA
(3.36 ratio)	CB
(3.73 ratio)	CC
Positraction (3.07 ratio)	CD
Positraction (3.08 ratio)	CE
Positraction (3.31 ratio)	CF
Positraction (3.36 ratio)	CG
Positraction (2.73 ratio)	CH
Positraction (3.73 ratio)	CI
(2.73 ratio), (2.73 ratio)	CP
Positraction (3.70 ratio)	CR
Positraction w/Metallic Brakes (3.73 ratio)	CU
(3.70 ratio)	CV
(3.31 ratio)	CW
(3.07 ratio)	CX
(3.07 ratio)	CY
(2.73 ratio)	CZ
(2.73 ratio) (small ring gear)	FH
Positraction (2.73 ratio) (small ring gear)	FI
(3.08 ratio)	FJ
Positraction (3.08 ratio)	FK
(3.36 ratio)	FL
Positraction (3.36 ratio)	FM
(3.55 ratio) (small ring gear)	FN
Positraction (3.55 ratio) (small ring gear)	FO
(3.70 ratio)	FP
Positraction (3.70 ratio)	FQ
(3.55 ratio) (small ring gear)	KA
Positraction (3.55 ratio) (small ring gear)	KB
Positraction (2.73 ratio) (small ring gear)	KC
(2.73 ratio) (large ring gear)	KD
Positraction (3.55 ratio) (large ring gear)	KF
(3.55 ratio) (large ring gear)	KJ
Positraction (4.10 ratio)	KK
Positraction (4.56 ratio)	KM
Positraction (4.88 ratio)	KO
w/Metallic Brakes (2.73 ratio)	KW
Positraction (3.07 ratio)	KX
Positraction (3.31 ratio)	KY
(3.31 ratio)	KZ
(3.55 ratio) (large ring gear)	K2
Positraction (3.55 ratio) (large ring gear)	K3
(3.73 ratio)	K4
Positraction (3.73 ratio)	K5
Positraction (4.10 ratio)	K6
Positraction (4.56 ratio)	K7
Positraction (4.88 ratio)	K8

1969 Rear Axle Codes

(3.08 ratio)	CA
(3.36 ratio)	CB
(3.73 ratio)	CC
Positraction (3.07 ratio)	CD
Positraction (3.08 ratio)	CE
Positraction (3.31 ratio)	CF
Positraction (3.36 ratio)	CG
Positraction (2.73 ratio)	CH
Positraction (3.73 ratio)	CI
(2.56 ratio)	CJ
Positraction (2.56 ratio)	CK
(2.56 ratio)	CL
Positraction (2.56 ratio)	CM
(2.56 ratio)	CN
Positraction (2.56 ratio)	CO
(2.73 ratio)	CP
(2.56 ratio)	CQ
Positraction (2.56 ratio)	CS
(2.73 ratio)	CT
(3.31 ratio)	CW
(3.07 ratio)	CX
(3.55 ratio) (small ring gear)	KA
Positraction (2.55 ratio) (small ring gear)	KB
Positraction (2.73 ratio) (small ring gear)	KC
(2.73 ratio) (large ring gear)	KD
Positraction (2.73 ratio) (small ring gear)	KE
Positraction (3.55 ratio) (large ring gear)	KF
(3.08 ratio) (small ring gear)	KG
Positraction (3.08 ratio) (small ring gear)	KH
(3.36 ratio)	KI
(3.55 ratio) (large ring gear)	KJ
Positraction (4.10 ratio)	KK
Positraction (3.36 ratio) (small ring gear)	KL
Positraction (4.56 ratio)	KM
(3.55 ratio) (small ring gear)	KN
Positraction (4.88 ratio)	KO
Positraction (3.55 ratio) (small ring gear)	KP
Positraction (3.07 ratio)	KX
(2.73 ratio)	FH
Positraction (2.73 ratio)	FI
(3.08 ratio)	FJ
Positraction (3.08 ratio)	FK
(3.36 ratio)	FL
Positraction (3.36 ratio)	FM
(3.55 ratio)	FN
Positraction (3.55 ratio)	FO

1970 Rear Axle Codes

Positraction (2.73 Ratio)	CGD
Positraction (2.73 Ratio)	CCH
Positraction (3.07 Ratio)	CCD
(2.73 Ratio)	CCP
(3.08 Ratio)	CCA
(2.56 Ratio)	CGA
(2.73 Ratio)	CGC
(3.36 Ratio)	CGG
Positraction (2.56 Ratio)	CGB
Positraction (3.36 Ratio)	CGI
(2.56 Ratio)	CCN
(2.73 Ratio)	CKD
(3.07 Ratio)	CCX
(3.31 Ratio)	CCW
(3.55 Ratio)	CKJ
Positraction (2.56 Ratio)	CCO
Positraction (3.31 Ratio)	CCF
Positraction (3.55 Ratio)	CKF
(4.10 Ratio)	CKK
Positraction (2.73 Ratio)	CKC
Positraction (3.08 Ratio)	CCE
(2.56 Ratio)	CRJ
Positraction (2.56 Ratio)	CRK
(3.31 Ratio)	CRU
Positraction (3.31 Ratio)	CRV
(4.10 Ratio)	CRW

1971 Rear Axle Codes

Positraction (2.73)	GD
(3.08)	GF
Positraction (2.73)	CH
(2.56)	GA
(2.73)	GC
(3.36)	GG
Positraction (2.56)	GB
Positraction (3.36)	GI
(2.73)	KD
(3.31)	CW
Positraction (3.31)	CF
(3.31)	RU
Positraction (3.31)	RV
(4.10)	RW
(2.73)	GH
(3.08)	GN

1972 Rear Axle Codes	
Positraction (2.73) (G-97, GS1)	GD
(3.08) (G92)	GF
Positraction (2.73)	GH
(2.73)	GC
(3.36)	GG
Positraction (3.36)	GI
(2.73)	GI
(3.31)	CW
Positraction	CF
(3.31)	RU
Positraction (3.31)	RV
(4.10)	RW
(2.73)	GH
(3.08)	GN

REAR AXLE INTERCHANGE

Chevelle

Model Identification   *Interchange Number*

1964
All...1

1965
10- bolt..2
12-bolt..3

1966
10- bolt..2
12-bolt..3

1967
10- bolt..4
12-bolt..5

1968-1972
10- bolt..7
12-bolt..6

Interchanges

Interchange Number: 1
Part Number(s): 3846574
Usage: 1964 Chevelle, all models and body styles

Interchange Number: 2
Part Number(s): 3917878
Usage: 1965-1966 Chevelle with ten-bolt axle, all models and body styles.

Interchange Number: 3
Part Number(s); 3917877
Usage: 1965-1966 Chevelle with twelve-bolt axle all models and body styles.

Interchange Number: 4
Part Number(s): 3917876
Usage: 1967 Chevelle with ten-bolt axle, all models and body styles.

Interchange Number: 5
Part Number(s): 3917875
Usage: 1967 Chevelle with twelve-bolt axle, all models and body styles.

Interchange Number: 6
Part Number(s): 3981669
Usage: 1968-1972 Chevelle; 1970-1972 Monte Carlo; 1970-1972 Pontiac LeMans; 1968,1970 Buick Skylark;1970-1972 Pontiac Grand Prix; 1971-1972 CMC Sprint; all with twelve-bolt axle. All models and body styles.

Interchange Number: 7
Part Number(s): 3981668
Usage: 1968-1972 Chevelle; 1970-1972 Monte Carlo; both with ten-bolt axle with round cover
Notes: Some Monte Carlos came with the Pontiac-built ten-bolt axle with a notched cover. This unit will not fit a Chevelle.

Differential Case

Chevelle

Model Identification   *Interchange Number*

1964
Without Locking Axle...9
Locking Axle..2

1965
10-bolt
Without Locking Axle
3.08,3.36,3.55,or 3.70..9
2.56, 2.73..8
Locking Axle
3.08,3.36 or 3.70 ratios
Early...2
Late..3
2.73 ratio..7
12-bolt
Locking Axle
3.07, 3.31,3.55,3.73..4
4.10, 4.56 4.88...5

1966
10-bolt
Without Locking Axle
3.08,3.36,355, or 3.70...9
2.56, 2.73..8

118

Locking Axle
3.08,3.36 or 3.70 ratios..................................3
2.73 ratio..7
12-bolt
Locking Axle
3.07, 3.31,3.55,3.73.....................................4
4.10, 4.56 4.88...5

1967
10-bolt
Without Locking Axle
3.08,3.36,3.55,or 3.70................................9
2.56, 2.73...8
Locking Axle
3.08,3.36 or 3.70 ratios..............................3
2.73 ratio..7
12-bolt
Locking Axle
3.07, 3.31,3.55,3.73....................................4
4.10, 4.56 4.88...5

1968-1972
10-bolt
Without Locking Axle
3.08,3.36,355, or 3.70................................9
2.56, 2.73...8
Locking Axle
3.08,3.36 or 3.70 ratios..............................3
2.73 ratio..7
12-bolt
Locking Axle
3.07, 3.31,3.55,3.73....................................4
4.10, 4.56 4.88...5

Interchanges

Interchange Number: 1
Part Number(s): 3863432
Type: Postitraction
Usage; 1964-early 1965 Chevy II, Chevelle, full-size Chevrolet; all with 3.08, 3.36, 3.55 or 3.70 rear axle ratios, ten-bolt axle

Interchange Number: 2
Part Number(s): 3863433
Type: Postitraction
Usage; 1964-early 1965 Chevy II, Chevelle, full-size Chevrolet; all with 3.08, 3.36, 3.55 or 3.70 rear axle ratios, ten-bolt axle

Interchange Number: 3
Part Number(s): 3993502
Type: Postitraction
Usage: Late 1965-1971 Nova; 1965-1970 full-size Chevrolet; 1967-1970 Camaro; 1965-1972 Chevelle; 1971 Pontiac Ventura II; all with ten-bolt axle, and 3.08 or 3.36 rear axle ratios
Notes: Round cover

Interchange Number: 4
Part Number(s): 3993516
Type: Postitraction
Usage: 1966-1967 Nova; 1966-1970 full-size Chevrolet; 1966-1972 Chevelle; 1967-1970 Camaro; 1968-1970 Nova; all with 3.07, 3.31, 3.55, or 3.73 rear axle ratios. With twelve-bolt axle.

Interchange Number: 5
Part Number(s): 3993517
Type: Postitraction
Usage: 1965-1967 Nova; 1966-1970 full-size Chevrolet; 1966-1972 Chevelle; 1967-1970 Camaro; 1968-1970 Nova; all with 4.10 4.56 or 4.88 rear axle ratios. With twelve-bolt axle.

Interchange Number: 6
Part Number(s): 3993504
Type: Postitraction
Usage: 1967-1969 Camaro; 1967-1972 Chevelle; 1971 Nova; 1968-1969 full-size Chevrolet; all with 2.56 or 2.73 rear axle ratios, ten-bolt axle,

Interchange Number: 7
Part Number(s); 3936444
Type: Postitraction
Usage: 1966-1970 Chevelle; 1967-1970 Nova; 1967-1970 Camaro; 1968-1970 Nova; 1968-1970 full-size Chevrolet with 2.29, 2.56, or 2.73 rear axle, twelve-bolt axle

Interchange Number: 8
Part Number(s): 3869789
Type: Standard
Usage: 1965-1967 Nova; 1965-1970 full-size Chevrolet; 1965-1972 Chevelle; 1967-1969 Camaro; 1968-1970 Nova; all with 2.73, 2.29, and 2.56 rear axle ratios,, and twelve-bolt axle

Interchange Number: 9
Part Number(s): 3958109
Type: Standard
Usage: 1964-1971 Nova; 1964-1971 full-size Chevrolet; 1964-1972 Chevelle; 1967-1971 Camaro; 1968-1971 Nova; all with 3.08,3.36,3.55, or 3.70 rear axle ratios and ten-bolt axle

Interchange Number: 10
Part Number(s): 3852989
Type: Standard
Usage: 1965-1970 Nova; 1965-1970 full-size Chevrolet; 1965-1972 Chevelle; 1967-1969 Camaro; all with 3.07, 3.31, 3.55, and 3.73 rear axle ratios and twelve-bolt axle

Interchange Number: 11
Part Number(s): 3790627
Type: Postitraction
Usage: 1962-1963 Nova

Interchange Number: 12
Part Number(s): 3936444
Type: Postitraction
Usage: 1966-1969 Chevelle; 1967-1970 Nova; 1967-1969 Camaro; 1968-1970 full-size Chevrolet with 2.29, 2.56, 2.73 12-bolt axles

Rear Axle Shafts

Chevelle

Model Identification	Interchange Number
1964	
All	1
1965-1967	
10-bolt	2
12-bolt	3
1968-1972	
10-bolt	4
12-bolt	5

Interchanges

Interchange Number: 1
Part Number(s): 3832417 (fits either side) (28 splines)
Overall Length: 29 inches (fits either side)
Usage: 1964 Chevelle, all models and body styles

Interchange Number: 2
Part Number(s): 3969348 (fits either side) (28 splines)
Overall Length: 29 33/64 inches (fits either side)
Usage: 1965-1967 Chevelle; 1967-1969 Camaro; 1968-1971 Nova; 1971-1973 Ventura II; 1973 Omega; all with ten-bolt axle

Interchange Number: 3
Part Number(s): 3969349 (fits either side) (30 splines)
Overall Length: 30 1 /2 inches (fits either side)
Usage: 1965-1967 Chevelle; 1967-1969 Camaro except with four-wheel disc brakes
; 1968-1971 Nova; 1971-1973 Ventura II; 1973 Omega; all with twelve-bolt axle

Interchange Number: 4
Part Number(s): 3969284 (fits either side) (28 splines)
Overall Length: 30 5/32 inches (fits either side)
Usage: 1968-1972 Chevelle; 1970-1972 Monte Carlo;1970- 1973 Camaro; 1970-1973 Pontiac Firebird; 1971- 1972 CMC Sprint; all with ten-bolt axle
Notes: Must have round cover. Notched cover axles are different.

Interchange Number: 5
Part Number(s): 3969285 (fits either side) (30 splines)
Overall Length: 30 5/32 inches (fits either side)
Usage: 1968-1972 Chevelle; 1970-1972 Monte Carlo; 1970-1973 Camaro; 1970-1973 Pontiac Firebird; 1971- 1972 CMC Sprint; all with twelve-bolt axle

Chapter 8 Brakes

Master Cylinder

Interchange for the master cylinder is based on part number. Type of braking system is an important factor in interchange. Two types were used, drum and disc, and they are not interchangeable.

Thus, a drum brake master cylinder cannot be used on a car with disc brakes, and vice versa. Beginning in 1967, all master cylinders were restyled to a dual-circuit system. This system is easily recognized by its two separate reservoirs. Single-reservoir master cylinders should never be used on a 1967 or newer model.

Master cylinder manufacture must also be considered. Chevrolet used the Moraine brand from Delco, and the Bendix brand. For best braking operation, the proper manufacture should be used.

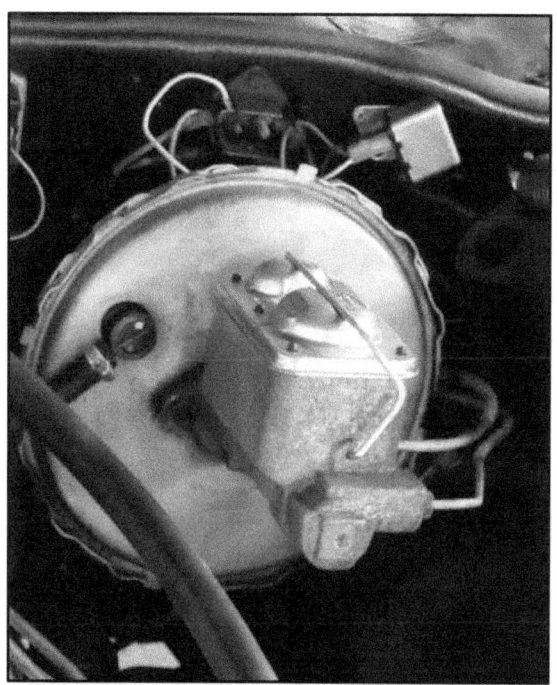
Typical dual circuit master cylinder with Delco-Moraine master cylinder and booster chamber

Single circuit master cylinder used from 1964-1966

Bendix master cylinder and Booster chamber

121

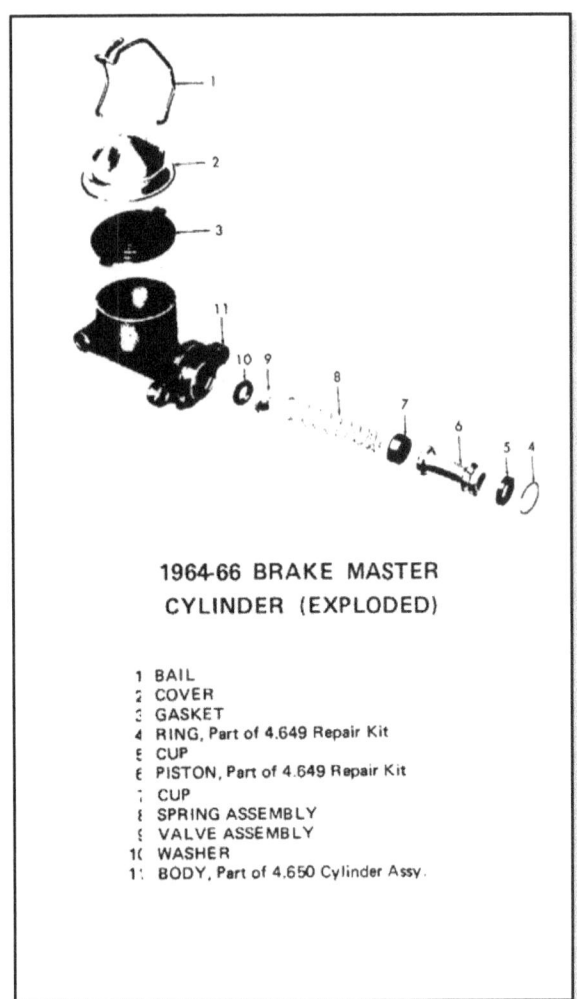

1962-1966 master cylinder (Chevrolet)

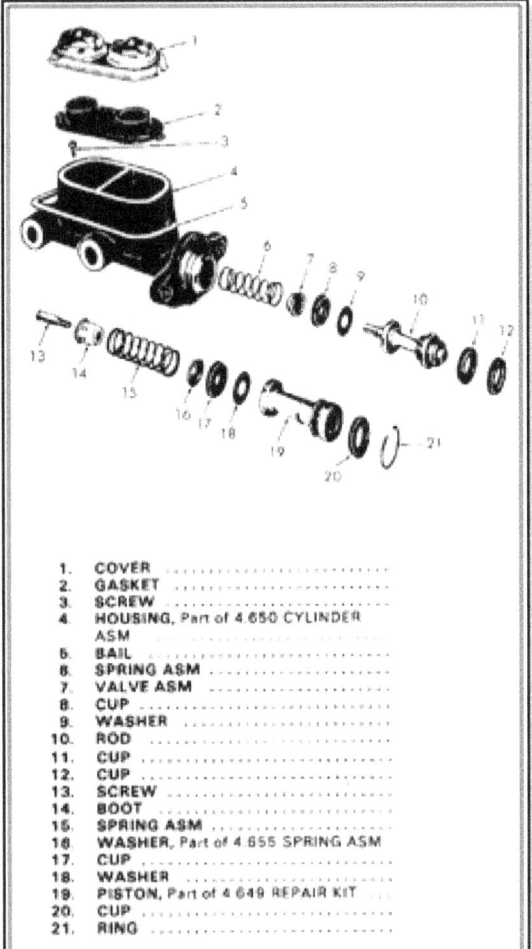

Typical `1967-1972 master cylinder (Chevrolet)

Chevelle

Model Identification   *Interchange Number*

1964-1966
Without Metallic Linings
Bendix..1
Moraine...2
With Metallic Linings..3

1967
Drum Brakes
Without Metallic Linings..4
With Metallic Linings...5
Disc Brakes..6

1968
Drum Brakes
Moraine...4
Disc Brakes
Bendix...12
Moraine...7

1969
Drum Brakes...4
Disc Brakes
Bendix...12
Moraine...8

1970
Drum Brakes...4
Disc Brakes
Bendix...12
Moraine...9

1971-1972
Drum Brakes...11
Disc Brakes
Moraine...10

Interchanges

Interchange Number: 1
Part Number(s): 3853776
Manufacturer: Bendix (618105)
Type: Drum
Usage: 1964-1966 full-size Chevrolet; 1964-1966 Chevelle; 1964-1966 Nova; 1964-1966 C-10 to C-30 pickup
Notes: All have Bendix power brake systems.

Interchange Number: 2
Part Number(s): 5465489
Manufacture: Moraine
Type: Drum
Usage: 1962-1966 full-size Chevrolet; 1962-1966 Nova; 1963-1966 C10 pick up or G10 van; 1964-1966 Chevelle
Notes: All are without metallic linings

Interchange Number: 3
Part Number(s): 5464275
Manufacturer: Moraine
Type: Drum
Usage: 1962-1963 full-size Chevrolet; 1964-1966 Chevelle; 1962-1966 Nova with Metallic linings

Interchange Number: 4
Part Number(s): 5458523
Manufacturer: Moraine Stamped BS
Type: Drum
Usage: 1967-1970 Chevelle, Camaro, Nova 1967-1969 Corvair; 1967 Firebird
Notes: Dual-circuit type. All are without metallic linings.

Interchange Number: 5
Part Number(s): 5463284
Manufacturer: Moraine Stamped AU
Type: Drum
Usage: 1967 Chevelle, Camaro with metallic brakes

Interchange Number: 6
Part Number(s): 5463492
Manufacturer: Moraine
Type: Disc
Usage; 1967-early 1968 full-size Chevrolet; 1967 Chevelle; 1968 Nova

Interchange Number: 7
Part Number(s): 5468811
Manufacture: Moraine
Type: Disc
Usage: 1968 Chevelle

Interchange Number: 8
Part Number(s): 5461184
Manufacture: Moraine
Type: Disc
Usage: 1969 Chevelle; 1969-1974 Corvette

Interchange Number: 9
Part Number(s): 5470665
Manufacture: Moraine
Type: Disc
Usage: 1970 Chevelle, Monte Carlo

Interchange Number: 10
Part Number(s): 5471802
Manufacture: Moraine Stamped BE
Type: Disc
Usage: 1971-1974 Chevelle, Monte Carlo, full-size Chevrolet, Lemans, Cutlass, Skylark, Grand Prix. All with Moraine booster

Interchange Number: 11
Part Number(s): 5472651
Manufacturer: Moraine
Type: Drum
Usage: 1971-1972 Chevelle; 1971-1974 Nova; 1973-1974 Omega, Apollo; 1971-1974 Ventura II; 1971-1972 GMC Sprint

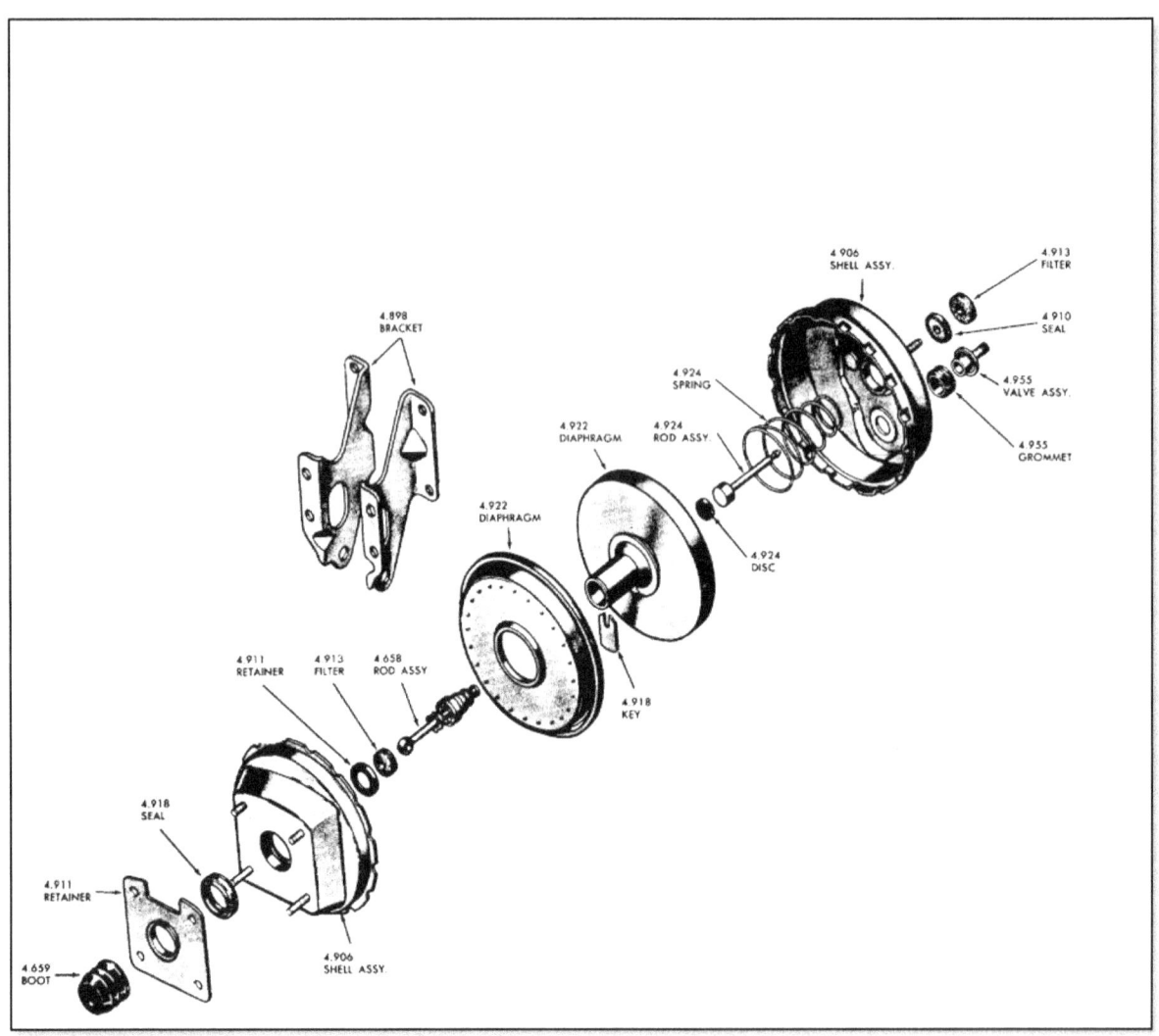

1962-1971 Bendix brake booster (Chevrolet)

Interchange Number: 12
Part Number(s): 3922509
Manufacturer: Bendix
Type: Disc
Usage: 1967-1970 Chevelle, Camaro, Nova
 1967-1969 Corvair; 1967 Firebird
Notes: Dual-circuit type. All are without metallic linings.

Booster Chamber

Vacuum chambers, often called booster chambers, were keyed to the type of brake system used on a car. Disc brakes and drum brakes used a different chamber and are not interchangeable. However, unlike the master cylinder, the same vacuum chamber was used on both metallic drum and nonmetallic brakes.

There are two boost chamber manufacturers, Moraine and Bendix. The two brands cannot be interchanged and must be used with the identical brand of master cylinder. Chambers are clearly marked either Moraine Delco or Bendix. Some chambers may also be coded with a letter or number that is used for identification.

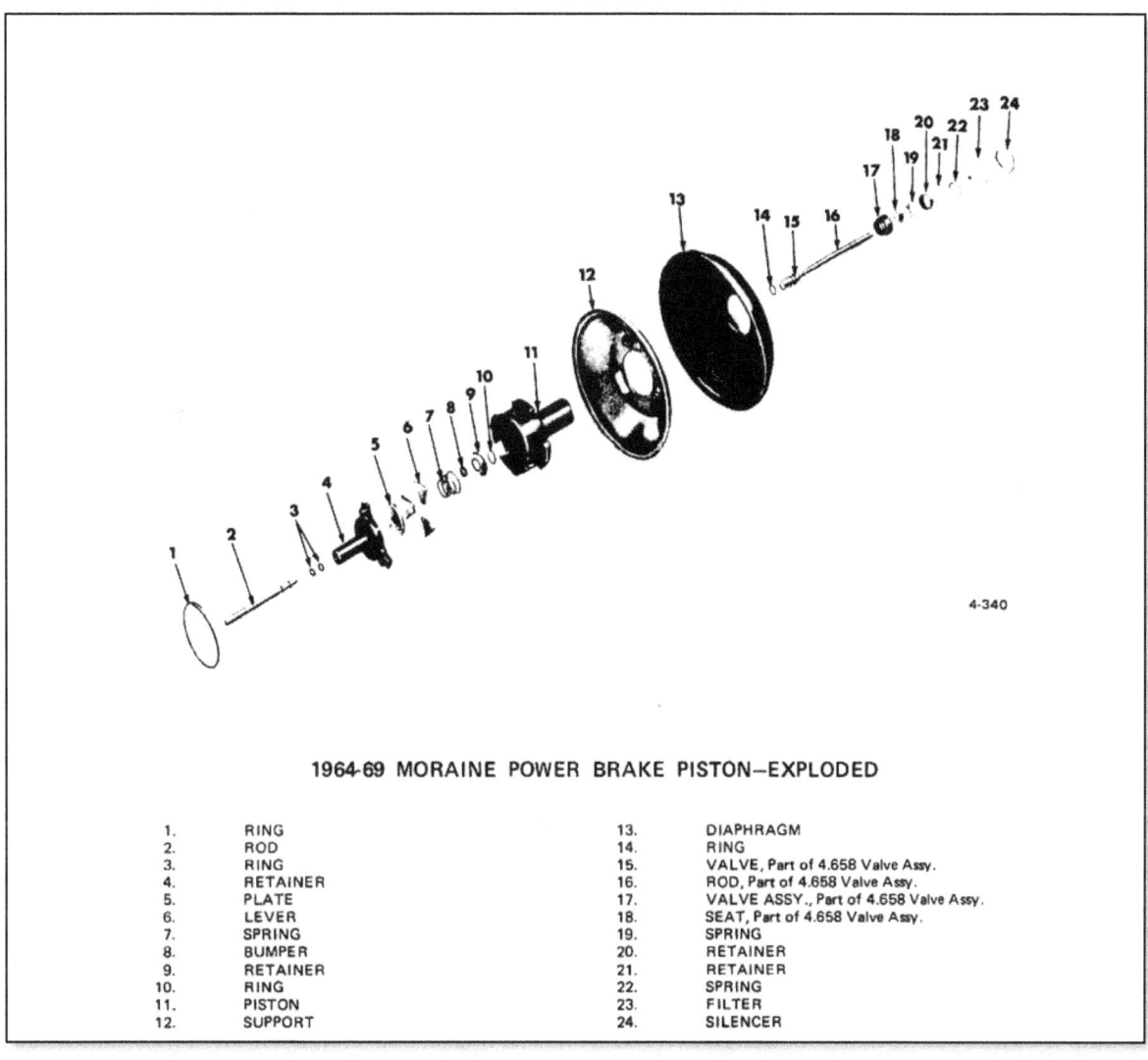

1964-69 MORAINE POWER BRAKE PISTON—EXPLODED

1.	RING	13.	DIAPHRAGM
2.	ROD	14.	RING
3.	RING	15.	VALVE, Part of 4.658 Valve Assy.
4.	RETAINER	16.	ROD, Part of 4.658 Valve Assy.
5.	PLATE	17.	VALVE ASSY., Part of 4.658 Valve Assy.
6.	LEVER	18.	SEAT, Part of 4.658 Valve Assy.
7.	SPRING	19.	SPRING
8.	BUMPER	20.	RETAINER
9.	RETAINER	21.	RETAINER
10.	RING	22.	SPRING
11.	PISTON	23.	FILTER
12.	SUPPORT	24.	SILENCER

(Chevrolet)

BRAKE BOOSTER INTERCHANGE
Chevelle
Model Identification   *Interchange Number*

1964
Drum
Bendix..1
Moraine..2

1965-1966
Drum
Bendix..1
Moraine..3

1967
Drum
Bendix..8
Moraine..9
Disc...7

1968
Drum..10
Disc
Bendix..12
Moraine..4

1969
Drum..8
Disc
Bendix..12

1970
Drum..8
Disc
Bendix..12
Moraine..6

1971-1972
Drum..11
Disc..6

Interchanges

Interchange Number: 1
Part Number(s): 3848934
Manufacturer; Bendix (stamped C-4)
Type: Drum
Usage: 1964-1966 Chevelle with all models and body styles.

Interchange Number: 2
Part Number(s): 5464361
Manufacturer: Moraine (stamped 5464900)
Type: Drum
Usage; 1964 Chevelle, all models and body styles.
Notes: Interchange number 3 will fit

Interchange Number: 3
Part Number(s): 5465341
Manufacturer: Moraine (stamped 5464901)
Type: Drum
Usage: 1965-1966 Chevelle, all models and body styles

Interchange Number: 4
Part Number(s): 5468819
Manufacturer: Moraine (tagged CL)
Type: Disc
Usage: 1968 Chevelle all models and body styles
Notes:

Interchange Number: 5
Part Number(s): 3848934
Manufacturer; Bendix (stamped C-4)
Usage: 1964-1966 Chevelle, all models and models styles

Interchange Number: 6
Part Number(s): 5469400
Manufacturer; Moraine
Type: Disc
Usage: 1969-1970 Chevelle, all models and models styles

Interchange Number: 7
Part Number(s): 5460428
Manufacturer; Moraine
Type: Disc
Usage: 1967 Chevelle, all models and models styles

Interchange Number: 8
Part Number(s): 3979596
Manufacturer: Bendix
Type: Drum
Usage: 1967-1971 Chevelle; 1971 GMC Sprint
Notes: This is replacement part number. Original varies but all the same unit.

Interchange Number: 9
Part Number(s); 5462030
Manufacturer: Moraine
Usage: 1967 Chevelle all models and body styles

Interchange Number: 10
Part Number(s): 5468804
Manufacturer: Moraine
Usage: 1968 Chevelle with finned brake drums
Notes: Interchange Number 11 will fit

Interchange Number: 11
Part Number(s): 5472408
Manufacturer: Moraine
Type: Drum
Usage: 1971-1972 Chevelle; 1971-1972 Sprint

Interchange Number: 12
Part Number(s): 3922585
Manufacturer: Bendix
Type: Disc
Usage: 1968-1971 Chevelle; 1971 Sprint

Brake Drum

Brake drums are largely interchangeable. However, front and rear drum brakes are different and will not interchange. Models with metallic brakes used special drums and therefore cannot use nonmetallic brake drums.

Chevelle

Model Identification   *Interchange Number*

1964
Without Metallic Brakes
Front..1
Rear..5
With Metallic Brakes
Front..2
Rear..6

1965
Except Z-16
Without Metallic Brakes
Front..1
Rear..5
With Metallic Brakes
Front..2
Rear..6
Z-16 SS 396
Front..4
Rear..5
With Metallic Brakes
Front..4
Rear..6

1966-1967
Except SS 396
Without Metallic Brakes
Front..1
Rear..5
With Metallic Brakes
Front..2
Rear..6
SS 396
Front..4
Rear..5
With Metallic Brakes
Front..2
Rear..6

1968
Front
Without Fins...1
With Fins..3
Rear..5

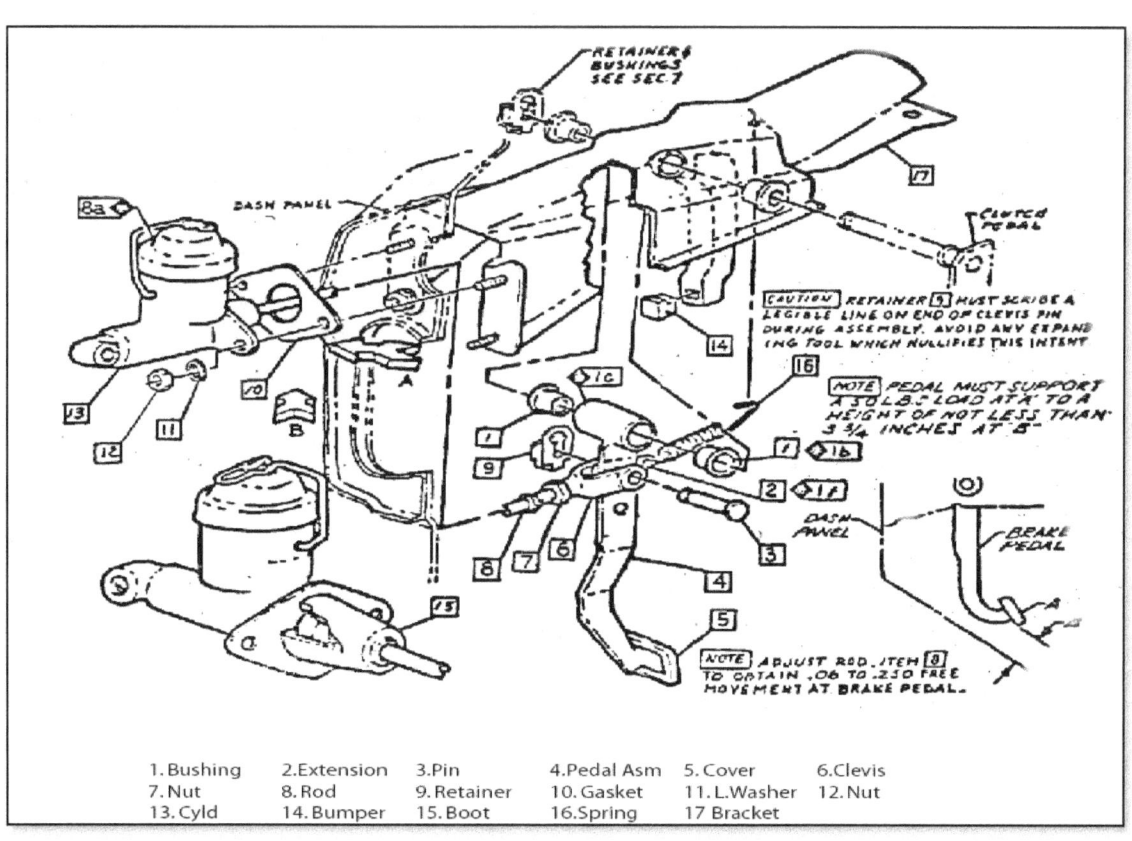

1. Bushing 2. Extension 3. Pin 4. Pedal Asm 5. Cover 6. Clevis
7. Nut 8. Rod 9. Retainer 10. Gasket 11. L.Washer 12. Nut
13. Cyld 14. Bumper 15. Boot 16. Spring 17. Bracket

1964-1967 Brake pedal (Chevrolet)

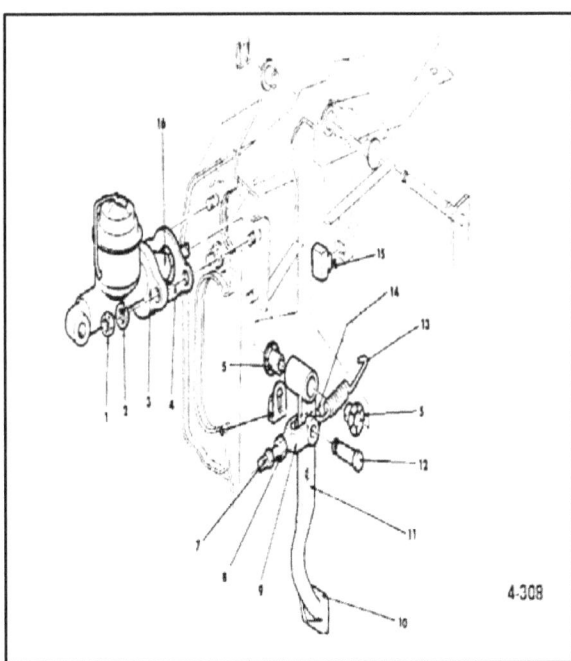

1968-1972 Brake Pedal (Chevrolet)

1969
Front..3
Rear...7

1970-1972
Front..3
Rear...5

Interchanges

Interchange Number: 1
Part Number(s): 3845258
Position: Front
Usage: 1964-1967 Chevelle, except 1965-1966 SS 396 ;1 964-1967 Nova; 1967 Camaro; 1968 Camaro, Chevelle, Nova without finned drums
Notes: Without metallic linings

Interchange Number: 2
Part Number(s): 3845282
Position: Front
Usage: 1964-1968 Chevelle, except 1965 Z-16 SS 396 ;1964-1968 Nova; 1967-1968 Camaro; all with metallic brakes

Interchange Number: 3
Part Number(s): 3996670
Position: Front
Usage: 1968 Chevelle, Camaro, Nova with Finned drums; 1969-1972 Chevelle, except 1969-1972 SS; 1969-1970 Camaro; 1968 Firebird; 1969-1974 Nova; 1971-1974 Ventura II; 1973-1974 Apollo; 1973-1974 Omega

Interchange Number: 4
Part Number(s): 3872398
Position: Front
Usage: 1965-1966 Chevelle SS

Interchange Number: 5
Part Number(s): 3987445
Position: Rear
Usage: 1964-1967 Chevelle;1964-1967 Nova; 1967 Camaro; 1968 1969- 74 Nova with front disc brakes; 1970-1972 Chevelle with 10-bolt axle cover; all without metallic brakes

Rotors are interchange from 1967-1972. They can also be found on 1967-1969 Camaro; 1967-1972 Chevelle; 1967-1974 Nova; 1967-1969 Pontiac Firebird; 1967-1968 Lemans;1967-1969 Cutlass; 1967-1971Skylark; 1970-1972 Monte Carlo; 1971-1972 GMC Sprint; 1971-1974 Pontiac Ventura II; 1973-1974 Apollo

Interchange Number: 6
Part Number(s): 3998266
Usage: 1964-1967 Chevelle, 1967 Camaro; 1964-1966 Nova; all with metallic brakes
Notes: A few 1968 models were built with metallic brakes using these drums.

Interchange Number: 7
Part Number(s): 3996135
Usage: 1969 Chevelle; 1969-1970 Nova with front drums; 1969-1974 Camaro; 1971-1974 Nova; 197-1974 Firebird;1971- 1974 Ventura II; 1973 Apollo; 1973-1974 Omega

Calipers

For calipers, interchange is based on right- and left-hand sides and on the number of pistons. Early models used a four-piston design, while the later ones used a single-piston design. Single-piston calipers must be used with the single-piston-rotors; four-piston calipers must be used with corresponding rotors.

Chevelle
Model   Interchange Number
1964-1966
All..not used
1967-1968
All..1
1969-1972
All..2

Interchange Number: 1
Part Number(s): Inner. RH, 5468364, LH,5468365
Outer: 5456076 (fits either side)
Type: 4-piston
Usage:1967-1968 Chevelle; 1967-1968 Cutlass; 1967-1968 Lemans, Skylark
Notes: Some cast with 838

Interchange Number: 2
Part Number(s): RH, 5472162; LH, 5472161
Type: Single piston design
Usage: 1969-1972 Chevelle; 1970-1972 Monte Carlo; 1969-1972 LeMans, Grand Prix, Cutlass; Skylark; 1971- 72 CMC Sprint
Notes Casting numbers 5469636 and 5469637

Brake Pedal
Chevelle
Model   Interchange Number
1964-1966
Manual Transmission....................................1
Automatic Transmission...............................4
1967-1972
Manual Transmission....................................2
Automatic Transmission...............................3

Interchanges

Interchange Number: 1
Part Number(s): 3843931
Usage: 1964-1966 Chevelle with manual transmission

Interchange Number: 2
Part Number(s): 3937889
Usage: 1967-1972 Chevelle; 1967-1970 Cutlass; 1970-1972 Monte Carlo; all with manual transmission

Interchange Number: 3
Part Number(s): 3937893
Usage: 1967-1972 Chevelle, Cutlass, LeMans, Skylark all with automatic transmission

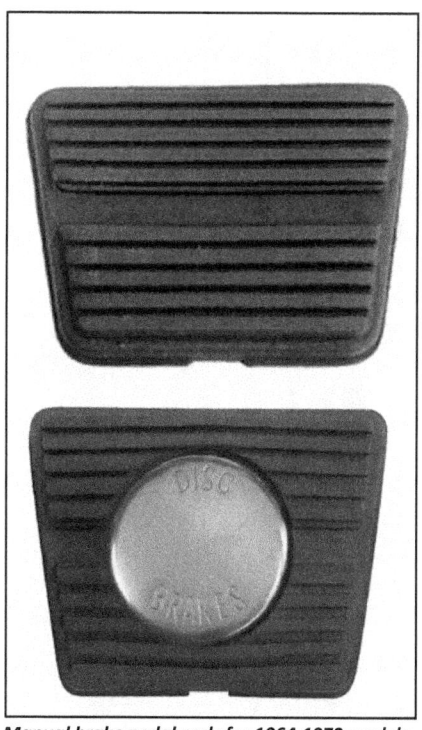

Manual brake pedal pads for 1964-1972 models

Interchange Number: 4
Part Number(s): 3843935
Usage: 1964-1966 Chevelle, LeMans, Cutlass, Skylark all with automatic transmission

Brake Pedal Pad

Even though the brake pedal was changed many times, the brake pedal pad, or cover, was not. As a result, there is ample interchange available. This section is not so much for salvage yard hunting, but for NOS or reproduction parts. Another point of interest is that those pads used with manual transmissions are the exact same covers used on the clutch. Models with disc brakes used a special pad that featured trim identifying it for use with disc brakes.

Chevelle

Model	Interchange Number
1964-1966	
Manual Transmission	1
Automatic Transmission	2
1967-1972	
Drum Brakes	
Manual Transmission	1
Automatic Transmission	2
Disc Brakes	
Manual Transmission	3
Automatic Transmission	4

Brake pedal pads for 1964-1972 models with automatic transmission.

Interchanges

Interchange Number: 1
Part Number(s): 3858198
Transmission type: Manual
Usage: 1964-1972 Chevelle; 1962-1967 Nova 1964-1972 Cutlass, Skylark; 1971 Buick LeSabre; 1975-1976 Astre; 1975-1976 Monza/Vega; all with drum brakes

Interchange Number: 2
Part Number(s): 3858199
Transmission type: Automatic
Usage: 1962-1967 Chevy II; 1964-1972 Chevelle, Cutlass, Skylark; 1971 Buick LeSabre; 1975-1976 Astre; 1975-1976 Monza, Vega; all with drum brakes

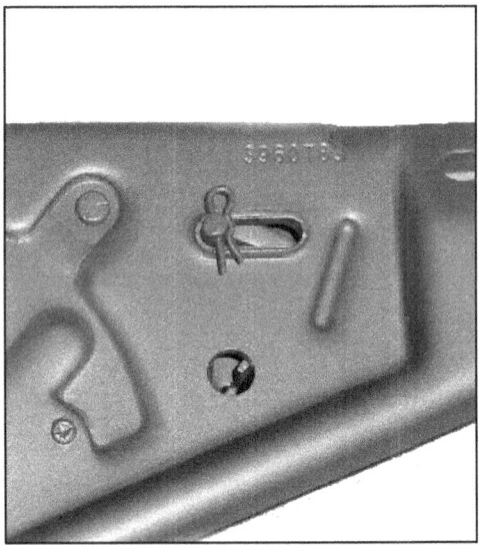

Some parking brake units maybe stamped with the part number. This is for the 1970-1972 models.

Interchange Number: 3
Part Number(s); 3934000
Transmission type: Manual
Usage: 1967 Chevy II; 1967-1972 Chevelle Cutlass, Skylark; 1971 Buick LeSabre; 1975-1976 Astre; 1975-1976 Monza or Vega; all with disc brakes
Notes: Pad has bright circle with the words "disc brakes" on it.

Interchange Number: 4
Part Number(s): 3934002
Type: Automatic
Usage: 1967 Nova; 1967-1972 Chevelle, Cutlass, Skylark; 1971 Buick LeSabre; 1975-1976 Astre; 1975-1976 Monza or Vega; all with disc brakes
Notes: Pad has bright circle with the words "disc brakes" on it.

Parking Brake
Chevelle

Model	Interchange Number
1964	
All	1
1965	
Early	1
Late	2
1966	
All	2
1967	
All	3
1968-1969	
All	4
1970-1972	
All	5

Interchanges

Interchange Number: 1
Part Number(s): 3845501
Usage: 1964-early 1965 Chevelle, Skylark, Cutlass, Lemans all models and body styles
Notes: Interchange number 2 or 3 will fit

Interchange Number: 2
Part Number(s): 3871191
Usage: Late 1965-1966 Chevelle, Skylark, Cutlass, Lemans all models and body styles
Notes: Interchange number 3 will fit

Interchange Number: 3
Part Number(s): 3908775
Usage: 1967 Chevelle, Skylark, Cutlass, Lemans all models and body styles
Notes:

Interchange Number: 2
Part Number(s): 3949154
Usage: 1968-1969 Chevelle, all models and body styles

Interchange Number: 3
Part Number(s): 3960783
Usage: 1970-1972 Chevelle, all models and body styles

Chapter 9 Electrical Systems

Delco-Ramey starters are identified by a part number stamped on the case.

Starter

Chevrolet's starter motor is a GM-built unit that can be found on many different CM models, so there is ample interchange. Starters can be identified by a number stamped on the side of the housing. While a starter may "physically fit," it may not have enough power to properly turn over a high-performance engine. The rule when interchanging is that the output should be the same as or greater than the original unit. A starter that is able to start a car in the summertime may not prove as capable in the middle of a cold Midwest winter.

Chevelle

Model	Interchange Number
1964	
Alli	8
1965-1967	
283-ci	8
327-ci	5
396-ci	4
1968	
307-ci	8
327-ci	
Except Turbo-Hydra-Matic	6
Turbo-Hydra-Matic	4
396-ci	4
1969-1972	
307-ci	8
350-ci	
Except Turbo Hydra-Matic	6
Turbo-Hydra-Matic	7
396-ci	4

Interchanges

Interchange Number: 1
Part Number(s): 1108429
ID Number(s): 1108427, 1108429, 1108430, 1108480, 1108502
Usage: 1970-early 1975 Camaro with automatic transmission; 1970-early 1975 Chevelle with 350-ci, 396-ci, 402-ci or 454-ci V-8 and automatic transmission; 1970 Nova with 396-ci and automatic transmission; 1971-1974 Nova with 350-ci and automatic transmission; 1970-1974 Corvette with automatic transmission;1970-1974 C10-C30 or 1500-3500 GMC with 396-ci or 350-ci V-8 with automatic transmission

Interchange Number: 2
Part Number(s): 1109068
ID Number(s): 1109068
Usage: Late 1975-1980 Camaro with V-8; 1980 Camaro with 305-ci V-8; 1980-1981 Camaro with 350-ci V-8 and automatic transmission; Late 1975-1979 full-size Chevrolet with V-8; 1980 full-size Chevrolet with 305-ci California or high altitude; late 1975-1977 Chevelle with 305-ci, 350-ci or 400-ci SMALL BLOCK V-8 with automatic transmission; Late 1975-1979 Nova with V-8 and automatic transmission; Late 1975-1980 Monte Carlo with V-8 and automatic transmission, 1977, 1979 Monza, Starfire, ; 1875-1980 Cutlass, Regal with 305-ci and automatic transmission; Late 1975-1976 Ventura II with V-8 and automatic transmission; 1977-1979 Phoenix with 305-ci and automatic transmission; Late 1975-1980 C10-C30 1500-3500 GMC with V-8 and automatic transmission

Interchange Number: 3
Part Number(s): 1109524
ID Number(s): 1109524
Usage: 1980 Camaro with 305-ci except California; 1981 Camaro with 305-ci V-8 ; 1980-1981 Camaro with 267-ci V-8; 1980-1981 full-size Chevrolet with 305-ci except California or high altitude; 1978-1980 Malibu with 305-ci except California; 1979-1980 Monte Carlo with 305-ci except California; 1979-1980 Grand Prix with 305-ci except California; 1979-1980 Cutlass with 305-ci except California; 1980 Fire bird with 305-ci V-8

Interchange Number: 4
Part Number(s): 1107365
ID Number(s): 1107365, 1108400, 1107342,1107660, 1107687, 1107694, 1107890, 1107892, 1108338, 1108382, 1108418, 1109067, 1107365, 1108520, 1108775, 1108788, 1108799, 1109059, 1109066, 1109074, 198225,
Usage: 1965-1969 full-size Chevrolet with 396-ci; 1966-1969 full-size Chevrolet with 427-ci V-8; 1968-1969 full-size Chevrolet with 307-ci or 350-ci with TH 350/400; 1969 full-size ch3evroelt with 350-ci 4-bbl; 1967-1969 Camaro with 396-ci or 350-ci ; 1970-1972 Camaro with 396-ci or 402-ci with manual transmission; 1970-1974 Camaro with 350-ci and manual transmission; 1965-1969 Chevelle SS 396; 1970-1972 Chevelle with 396-ci or 402-ci and manual transmission; 1970-1973 Chevelle, Monte Carlo with 454-ci V-8 an manual transmission; 1968-1969 Nova with 396-ci V-8; 1970 Nova with 396-ci and manual transmission; 1969-1970 Nova with 350-ci 4-bbl with manual transmission; 1968-1969 Corvette with 327-ci or 3427-ci except 425-hp; 1970-1972 Corvette with manual transmission except M22 rock crusher; 1968-1969 C10-C30 GMC 1500-3500 with 327-ci and T.H. transmission; 1970-1971 C10-C30 GMC 1500-3500 manual transmission ; 1974-1981 Camaro with 350-ci V-8 and manual transmission; 1975-1977 Chevelle with 350-ci V-8 with manual transmission; 1974-1975 Monte Carlo with manual transmission; 1974-1979 Nova with V-8 and manual transmission1975-1981 Corvette with 350-ci V-8 and manual transmission; 1975-1979 Ventura II/Phoenix with 350-ci with maul transmission; 1978 Firebird with 305-ci V-8 with manual transmission; 1977, 1979 Sunbird with V-8 and manual transmission

Distributors can be identified by a number stamped into the housing. This fits the 1969 350- with automatic transmission

Interchange Number: 5
Part Number(s): 1107320
ID Number(s): 1107320
Usage: 1965-1967 full-size Chevrolet with 327-ci; 1966-1967 Nova with 327-ci; 1967 Camaro with 327-ci; 1965-1967 Corvette with 327-ci; 1965-1967 Chevelle with 327-ci V-8
Notes: Interchange number 10 will fit

Interchange Number: 6
Part Number(s): 1108361
ID Number(s): 1108361
Usage: 1968-1969 full-size Chevrolet, Chevelle, Camaro, Nova with 327-ci or 350-ci V-8 except high performance; 1968 Corvette with 327-ci V-8 and manual trnamission1969-1970 C10-C30 or 1500-3500 GMC with standard duty 350-ci; early 1969 Camaro with 350-ci 300-hp V-8 with T.H. 400

Interchange Number: 7
Part Number(s): 1180420
ID Number(s): 1108420
Usage: 1969 Nova, Chevelle, or full-size Chevrolet; all 350-ci 300 hp V-8 with Turbo Hydra-Matic 350/400 transmission
Notes: Second design only in 1969 Camaro

Interchange Number: 8
Part Number(s): 1108366
ID Number(s):1108365,1108366,1108367
Usage: 1966-1967 full-size Chevrolet with 283-ci; 1968-1969 Chevrolet with 307-ci V-8; 1969 full-size Chevrolet with 327-ci except with T.H. transmission; 1972-1973 full-size Chevrolet with six cylinder; 1967-1969 Camaro with 6 cylinder or 302-ci V-8; 1968-1969 Camaro with 327-ci; 1969-1972 Camaro with 307-ci V-8; 1970-1974 Camaro with six cylinder; 1964 Chevelle; 1965-1973 Chevelle with six cylinder; 1965-1967 Chevelle with 283-ci V-8 1968-1973 Chevelle with 307-ci V-8; 1962-1967 Nova with 4-cylinder, six cylinder 283-ci ; 1968-1973 Nova with 307ci; 1971-1974 Nova with six cylinder; 1970-1974 firebird with six cylinder; 1964-1967 Skylark with six cylinder; 1964-1965 Cutlass with six cylinder with automatic transmission; 1964-1967 Le Sabre or skylark with 300-ci 340-ci ; 1971-1974 Ventura II with six cylinder or 307-ci V-8; 1973-1974 Omega, Apollo with six cylinder or 307-ci V-8

Distributor Housing

The unit described here is a bare distributor housing without cap, breaker plate, points, condenser, or vacuum control. Engine size and output, and in some cases emission controls, will influence distributor interchange.

Distributors are grouped together under their replacement part number. Identification numbers, stamped on a band on the distributor housing itself, can be used to identify the assembly, but should not be relied on since more than one ID number can be used in the same interchange.

Chevelle
Model   Interchange Number
1964
283-ci
2-bbl..1
4-bbl..34
1965
283-ci..1
327-ci
Except 350 hp Special High performance..................19
350 hp Special high performance
    Without transistorized ignition 15
    With transistorized ignition..................................16

1966
283-ci..2
327-ci
275-hp
    Without AIR emissions...20
    With AIR Emissions..29
325-hp
    Without transistorized ignition 15
    With transistorized ignition..................................16
396-ci
325-hp
    Without transistorized ignition............................22
    With transistorized ignition..................................25
360-hp
    Without transistorized ignition 26
    With transistorized ignition....................................4
375-hp
    Without transistorized ignition 26
    With transistorized ignition..................................20
1967
283-ci
    Without AIR Emissions...2
    With AIR emissions..3
327-ci
Except Special High Performance
    Without AIR Emissions...19
    With AIR emissions..34
Special High Performance...15
396-ci
325-hp..22
350/375 hp
Without transistorized ignition 22
With transistorized ignition...25
1968
307-ci...9
327-ci
275 hp
Manual...6
Automatic..7
325-hp..17
350-ci
Manual...11
Automatic..12
396-ci
325-hp..22
350-hp
Manual...18
Automatic..22
375-hp..26

1969
307-ci..9
350-ci
2-bbl
  Manual...13
  Automatic...14
4-bbl
255-hp
  Manual...29
  Automatic...30
300-hp
  Manual...11
  Automatic...12
396-ci V-8
Except 375-hp
  Manual transmission.................................18
  Automatic transmission.............................26
375-hp..26

1970
307-ci
  Manual...9
  Automatic...10
350-ci
2-bbl
  Manual...13
  Automatic...14
4-bbl
255-hp
  Manual...29
  Automatic...30
396-ci V-8
Except 375-hp
  Manual transmission.................................18
  Automatic transmission.............................35
375-hp..35
454-ci
  390-hp..5
  LS6 450 hp..8

1971
307-ci
  Manual...10
  Automatic...36
350-ci
2-bbl
  Manual...37
  Automatic...10
4-bbl
  Manual...38
  Automatic...39
402-ci..41

454-ci
  Except 425-hp..42
425-hp
  Manual transmission.................................43
  Automatic...44

1972
307-ci
  Manual...10
  Automatic...40
350-ci
2-bbl..10
4-bbl
  Manual...38
  Automatic...39
402-ci..45
454-ci..42

Interchanges

Interchange Number: 1
Part Number(s): 1111015
ID Number(s): 1110946, 1110947, 1111015
Usage: 1959-1965 full-size Chevrolet with 283-ci V-8 ; 1964-1965 Chevelle, Nova with 283-ci V-8; 1959-1961 Corvette with 283-ci V-8 except 2x4-bbl

Interchange Number: 2
Part Number(s): 1111500
ID Number(s): 1111150
Usage: 1966-1967 full-size Chevrolet, Chevelle, Nova with 283i without AIR; 1968 full-size Chevrolet with 327-ci 250hp Except Special high performance.

Interchange Number: 3
Part Number(s): 1111256
ID Number(s): 1111256
Usage: 1967 full-size Chevrolet, Chevelle, Nova with 283 ci with AIR emissions

Interchange Number: 4
Part Number(s): 1111139
ID Number(s): 1111139
Usage: 1966 Chevelle 396-ci 360-hp with transistorized ignition

Interchange Number: 5
Part Number(s): 1111963
ID Number(s): 1111963
Usage: 1970 Chevelle, full-size Chevrolet, Monte Carlo with 454-ci 4-bbl 390-hp

Interchange Number: 6
Part Number(s): 1111298
ID Number(s): 1111298
Usage: 1968 Camaro, Chevelle, full-size Chevrolet, Nova, C10-C30, 1500-3500 with 327-ci 4-bbl V-8 and manual transmission

Interchange Number: 7
Part Number(s): 1111297
ID Number(s): 1111297
Usage: 1968 Camaro, Chevelle, full-size Chevrolet, Nova, C10-C30, 1500-3500 with 327-ci 4-bbl V-8 and automatic transmission

Interchange Number: 8
Part Number(s): 1111437
ID Number(s): 1111437
Usage: 1970 Chevelle, Monte Carlo with 454-ci 450-hp V-8.

Interchange Number: 9
Part Number(s): 1111995
ID Number(s): 1111995, 1111439, 1111257
Usage: 1968-1969 Chevelle, Camaro, full-size Chevrolet, Nova with 307-ci ; 1970 Chevelle, Camaro, Nova with 307-ci and manual transmission

Interchange Number: 10
Part Number(s): 1112005
ID Number(s): 1112005, 1111483
Usage: 1969-1970 Camaro, Chevelle, Nova with 307-ci V-8 and automatic transmission; 1969 full-size Chevrolet with 327-ci 2-bbl with automatic transmission; 1971-1972 Camaro; 1971-1972 Monte Carlo with 350-ci 2-bbl V-8; 1971-1972 Ventura II with 307-ci V-8; 1971-1972, Chevelle with 307-ci or 350-ci 2-bbl V-8 1971 full-size Chevrolet with 350-ci 2-bbl and automatic transmission; ;

Interchange Number: 11
Part Number(s): 1111996
ID Number(s): 1111996, 1111488, 1111264
Usage: 1968-1970 Camaro, Chevelle, Nova with 350 ci 4bbl 300-hp with manual, except 1970 Z-28; 1969-1970 Full-size Chevrolet with 350-ci 300 high performance V-8 with manual transmission

Interchange Number: 12
Part Number(s): 1111997
ID Number(s): 1111997, 1111489, 1111265
Usage: 1968-1970 Camaro, Chevelle, Nova with 350 ci 4bbl 300-hp with automatic, except 1970 Z-28; 1969-1970 Full-size Chevrolet with 350-ci 300 high performance V-8 with automatic transmission

Interchange Number: 13
Part Number(s): 1112001
ID Number(s): 1112001, 1111486
Usage: 1969-1970 Camaro, Chevelle, full-size Chevrolet, Nova with 350ci 2bbl manual transmission; 1970 Monte Carlo with 350-ci 2-bbl with manual transmission

Interchange Number: 14
Part Number(s): 1112002
ID Number(s): 1111487,1112002
Usage: 1969-1970 Camaro, Chevelle, full-size Chevrolet, Nova with 350ci 2bbl manual transmission; 1970 Monte Carlo with 350-ci 2-bbl with manual transmission

Interchange Number: 15
Part Number(s): 1111195
ID Number(s): 1111195
Usage: 1966-1967 Nova, Chevelle with 327-ci special high-performance without transistorized ignition; 1965 Chevelle with 327-ci special high-performance without transistorized ignition

Interchange Number: 16
Part Number(s): 1111155
ID Number(s): 1111155
Usage: 1966 Nova, Chevelle with 327-ci Special high performance -with transistorized ignition
1965 Chevelle with 327-ci special high-performance with transistorized ignition

Interchange Number: 17
Part Number(s): 1111478
ID Number(s): 1111478
Usage: 1968 Camaro, Chevelle, Nova with 325-hp 327-ci Special high performance.

Interchange Number: 18
Part Number(s): 1111999
ID Number(s): 1111999, 1111498, 1111445
Usage: 1968-1970 Camaro, Chevelle, Nova with 396-ci 350-hp.

Interchange Number: 19
Part Number(s): 1111249
ID Number(s): 1111107, 1111249, 1111152, 1111193, 1111075
Usage: 1965-1967 full-size Chevrolet with 327ci without AIR; 1965-1967 Chevelle with 327-ci except special high performance; 1966-1967 Nova with 327-ci V-8 except special high performance

Interchange Number: 20
Part Number(s): 1111100
ID Number(s): 1111100
Usage: 1965 full-size Chevrolet with 396-ci 425-hp V-8; 1966 Chevelle SS396 375 hp; 1966 full-size Chevrolet with 427-ci 425-hp.
Notes: All without transistorized ignition

Interchange Number: 21
Part Number(s): 1111098
ID Number(s): 1111073
Usage: 1965 full-size Chevrolet with 396-ci except with special high performance 425-hp V-8 without transistorized ignition
Notes: Interchange number 22 will fit

Interchange Number: 22
Part Number(s): 1111497
ID Number(s): 1111109, 11111073, 1111169, 1111497
Usage: 1966-1969 full-size Chevrolet with 396-ci except with special high performance; 1966-1969 Chevelle with 396-ci V-8 except 375-hp; 1967-1969 Camaro with 396-ci V-8 except 375-hp; 1968-1969 Nova with 396-ci except 375-hp
Notes: All without transistorized ignition

Interchange Number: 23
Part Number(s): 1111074
ID Number(s): 1111074
Usage: 1965-1966 full-size Chevrolet with 396-ci Special high performance; 1966 full-size Chevrolet with 427-ci 425-hp V-8; 1966 Chevelle SS396 375-hp all with transistorized ignition

Interchange Number: 24
Part Number(s): 1111098
ID Number(s): 1111098
Usage: 1965 full-size Chevrolet with 396-ci with transistorized ignition except Special high performance.

Interchange Number: 25
Part Number(s): 1111137
ID Number(s): 1111137
Usage: 1966 full-size Chevrolet, Chevelle with 396-ci 325-hp with transistorized ignition

Interchange Number: 26
Part Number(s): 1111499
ID Number(s): 1111278, 11111170, 1111138, 1111112, 1111499
Usage: 1967-1969 full-size Chevrolet with 427-ci 425-hp V-8; 1967-1969 Chevelle SS 396 with 396-ci 350-hp or 375 hp; 1967-1969 Camaro with 396-ci 350-hp or 375-hp; 1969 Nova with 396-ci 350-hp 375-hp automatic transmission.; 1966 full-size Chevrolet with 427-ci 390 hp V-8; 1966 Chevelle 396 with 350-hp
Notes: All without transistorized ignition

Interchange Number: 27
Part Number(s): 1111140
ID Number(s): 1111140
Usage: 1966 full-size Chevrolet with 427-ci 390-hp V-8 and transistorized ignition

Interchange Number: 28
Part Number(s): 1111116
ID Number(s): 1111116
Usage: 1966 Chevelle, full-size Chevrolet, Nova with 327-ci V-8 with AIR emissions

Interchange Number: 29
Part Number(s): 1111956
ID Number(s): 1111956
Usage: 1969 Camaro, Chevelle, full-size Chevrolet Nova with 350-ci 4-bbl 255-hp and manual transmission

Interchange Number: 30
Part Number(s): 1111955
ID Number(s): 1111955
Usage: 1969 Camaro, Chevelle, full-size Chevrolet Nova with 350-ci 4-bbl 255-hp and automatic transmission

Interchange Number: 31
Part Number(s): 1111949
ID Number(s): 1111949
Usage: 1969 full-size Chevrolet with 396-ci and manual transmission

Interchange Number: 32
Part Number(s): 1111950
ID Number(s): 1111950
Usage: 1969 full-size Chevrolet with 396-ci and automatic transmission

Interchange Number: 33
Part Number(s): 1111497
ID Number(s): 1111497
Usage: 1969 full-size Chevrolet with 427-ci 335-hp V-8; 1969 Camaro, Chevelle, Nova with 396-ci 325-hp

Interchange Number: 34
Part Number(s): 1111051
ID Number(s): 11111051
Usage: 1967 Nova, Camaro, Chevelle with 327-ci 4-bbl , with AIR emission except special high performance.

Interchange Number: 35
Part Number(s): 1112000
ID Number(s): 1112000
Usage: 1970 Camaro, Chevelle, Nova with 396-ci 350-hp with automatic transmission; 1970 Chevelle, Camaro, Nova with 396-ci 375-hp V-8

Interchange Number: 36
Part Number(s): 1112039
ID Number(s): 1112039
Usage: 19701Camaro, Chevelle, Nova, Ventura, Sprint with 307-ci V-8 with automatic transmission

Interchange Number: 37
Part Number(s): 1112042
ID Number(s): 1112042
Usage: 1971 Camaro, Chevelle, Nova, Monte Carlo, Sprint with 350-ci 2-bbl V-8 with manual transmission

Interchange Number: 38
Part Number(s): 1112044
ID Number(s): 1112044
Usage: 1971-1972 Camaro, Chevelle, full-size Chevrolet, Nova, Monte Carlo, Sprint with 350-ci 4-bbl V-8 with manual transmission

Interchange Number: 39
Part Number(s): 1112045
ID Number(s): 1112045
Usage: 1971-1972 Camaro, Chevelle, full-size Chevrolet, Nova, Monte Carlo, Sprint with 350-ci 4-bbl V-8 with automatic transmission

Interchange Number: 40
Part Number(s): 1112147
ID Number(s): 1112147
Usage: 1972 Camaro, Chevelle, full-size Chevrolet, Nova, Ventura II, Sprint with 307-ci 2-bbl V-8 with automatic transmission

Interchange Number: 41
Part Number(s): 1112057
ID Number(s): 1112057
Usage: 1971 Camaro, Chevelle, full-size Chevrolet, Monte Carlo, Sprint with 402-ci V-8

Interchange Number: 42
Part Number(s): 1112052
ID Number(s): 1112052
Usage: 1971-1972 Chevelle, full-size Chevrolet, Monte Carlo, Sprint with 454-ci V-8, except LS6 425-hp

Interchange Number: 43
Part Number(s): 1112075
ID Number(s): 1112075
Usage: 1971 Chevelle, Monte Carlo, Sprint with 454-ci 425-hp V-8 and manual transmission

Interchange Number: 44
Part Number(s): 1112054
ID Number(s): 1112054
Usage: 1971 Chevelle, Monte Carlo, Sprint with 454-ci 425-hp V-8 and automatic transmission

Interchange Number: 45
Part Number(s): 1112162
ID Number(s): 1112162
Usage: 1971 Camaro, Chevelle, full-size Chevrolet, Monte Carlo, Sprint with 402-ci V-8

Ignition Coil

Several different coils were used originally and were based on according to engine size and output. However, they were grouped together under three different original coils as certified replacements. Part number 1115202 was used with 1.8 OHM wire from 1955-1969 and part number 1115238 was used from 1967-1969 with 1.3 OHM wire. While those with transistorized ignition used a special coil listed as part number 1115207.

Listed below is the original coil that was installed on the car at the factory. Information was taken from assembly manuals.

Chevelle

Model   *Interchange Number*

1964
Without Transistorized Ignition
283-ci..1
327-ci
Except Special High Performance...............................1
Special High Performance...3
Transistorized Ignition..2

1965
Without Transistorized Ignition
283-ci..4
327-ci
Except Special High Performance...............................4
Special High Performance...5
396-ci
Early...4
Late...7
Transistorized Ignition..6

1966
Without Transistorized Ignition
283-ci..4
327-ci..4
396-ci..7
427-ci..7
Transistorized Ignition..8

1967
All V-8's
Very early...4
Early...9
Late...7
Very Late..9

1968
307,327, 350-ci...10
396-ci...9
427-ci...9

1969-1972
All Powerplants..10

Interchanges

Interchange Number: 1
Part Number(s): 1115115
ID Number(s): 115
Usage: 1955-1964 full-size Chevrolet; 1964 Nova; 1964 Chevelle, all with 283-ci or 327-ci V-8

Interchange Number: 2
Part Number(s): 1115176
ID Number(s): 176
Usage: 1964 full-size Chevrolet, Chevelle, Nova with V-8 and transistorized ignition.

Interchange Number: 3
Part Number(s): 1115087
ID Number(s): 087
Usage: 1964 full-size Chevrolet, Chevelle, Nova with 327-ci special high performance

Interchange Number: 4
Part Number(s): 1115204
ID Number(s): 204
Usage: 1965-1966 full-size Chevrolet, Chevelle, Nova with v-8 except 327-ci with special high performance; Early 1965-1966 full-size Chevrolet, Chevelle, Corvette with 396-ci or 427-ci; Very early 1967 Camaro, Chevelle, full-size Chevrolet with all V-8's
Notes: Used up until Feb 23, 1966 with 396-ci or 427-ci Then used up to Aug 7, 1966 in 1967 models.

Interchange Number: 5
Part Number(s): 1115202
ID Number(s): 202
Usage: 1965 full-size Chevrolet, Chevelle, Nova with 327-ci with special high performance
Notes: Replacement coil

Interchange Number: 6
Part Number(s): 1115207
ID Number(s): 207
Usage: 1965 full-size Chevrolet, Chevelle, Nova with V-8 and transistorized ignition.

Interchange Number: 7
Part Number(s): 1115242
ID Number(s): 242
Usage: Late 1966 full-size Chevrolet, Chevelle with 396-ci or 427-ci without transistorized ignition; Early 1967 Camaro, Chevelle, full-size Chevrolet, Nova with 283-ci, 302-ci, or 327-ci V-8; Late 1967 Camaro, Chevelle, full-size Chevrolet with V-8
Notes: Used after February 23, 1966 with 396-ci
Up to Oct 20, 1966 with small blocks in 1967
Used after Oct 20, 1966 and up to October 10, 1966

Interchange Number: 8
Part Number(s): 1115210
ID Number(s): 210
Usage: 1966 full-size Chevrolet, Chevelle, Nova with V-8 and transistorized ignition.

Interchange Number: 9
Part Number(s): 1115267
ID Number(s): 267
Usage: Early 1967 Camaro, Chevelle, full-size Chevrolet, Nova with V-8; Very late Camaro, Chevelle, full-size Chevrolet, Nova with V-8
Notes: Used after Aug 5, 1966 up to September 3, 1966, then after Oct 5, 1966

Interchange Number: 10
Part Number(s): 1115293
ID Number(s): 293
Usage:1968 Camaro, Chevelle, full-size Chevrolet, Nova with 302-ci, 307-ci, 350-ci; 1969-1972 Camaro, Chevelle, full-size Chevrolet, Nova with V-8; 1970-1972 Monte Carlo with V-8

Interchange Number: 11
Part Number(s): 1115267
ID Number(s): 267
Usage:1968 Camaro, Chevelle, full-size Chevrolet, Nova with 396-ci or 427-ci

Alternator

Interchanging factors for alternators Include the Output range and the original factory-Installed options on the car, like air conditioning, also Heavy-Duty alternators were also an option.

Dealer-installed options such as air conditioning may have required a different alternator that would have come from the factory. As is the norm, interchange is based on the original part number. When and if a change was made during the model year, the date of the change is given if known in most cases, the part number is the also the identification number.

Chevelle
Model   *Interchange Number*
1964
37 amp..16
42 amp..17
55 amp..18
1965
37amp..1
42 amp...2
55 amp..19
60 amp..20
1966
37 amp..1
42 amp..2
61 amp..3
62 amp..6
1967
37 amp..1
42 amp..2
61 amp..3
62 amp..4
1968
37 amp
    Single Pulley..5
    Two Groove Pulley..7
42 amp..8
61 amp
    Single Pulley..9
    Dual Pulley...10
62 amp..4
1969
37 amp
Single Pulley
    Except 396 375 hp..12
    396 375-hp..11
61 amp..14
1970
37 amp
Single Pulley
    Except 396 375 hp or 454-ci 450 hp..........................12
    396/375-hp...11
61 amp..14
1971
37 amp
Except 454-ci 425 -hp..16
425-hp...11
61 amp..14
1972
37 amp
307-ci/ 350 V-8...17
402-ci or 454-ci..18
61 amp..19

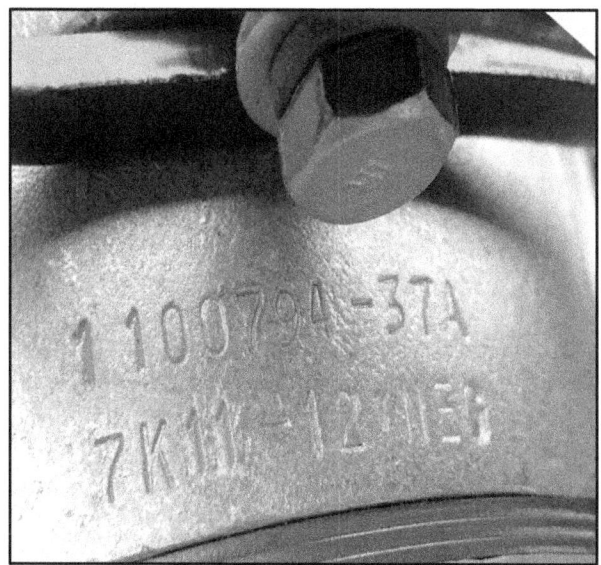

Alternators can be identified by the part number and the output that is stamped on the case. This is a pretty standard 37 amp- unit for 1968 models

Interchanges

Interchange Number: 1
Part Number(s): 1100693
Output: 37-amp
ID Number(s): 1100693
Usage: 1965-1967 Chevelle, full-size Chevrolet, Nova; 1967 Camaro
Notes: Standard alternator

Interchange Number: 2
Part Number(s): 1100696
Output: 42-amp
ID Number(s): 1100696
Usage: 1965-1967 full-size Chevrolet, Chevelle, Nova with air conditioning; 1967 Camaro with air conditioning

Interchange Number: 3
Part Number(s): 1100750
Output: 61 –amp
ID Number(s): 1100750
Usage: 1967 full-size Chevrolet, Chevelle; 1967 Camaro, Nova

Interchange Number: 4
Part Number(s): 1117767
Output: 62-amp
ID Number(s): 1117767
Usage: 1967 Camaro, Chevelle, full-size Chevrolet; 1968 Camaro, Chevelle full-size Chevrolet, Nova

Interchange Number: 5
Part Number(s): 1100794
Output: 37-amp
ID Number(s): 1100794
Usage: 1968 Camaro, except 302-ci, Chevelle full-size Chevrolet, Nova; all with single-groove pulley.
Notes: Will fit interchange number 7. Will fit if pulleys are swapped.

Interchange Number: 6
Part Number(s): 1117765
Output: 62-amp
ID Number(s): 1117765
Usage: 1966 Chevelle, full-size Chevrolet or Nova

Interchange Number: 7
Part Number(s): 1100813
Output: 37-amp
ID Number(s): 1100813
Usage: 1968 full-size Chevrolet, Chevelle, Camaro, Nova; all with dual-groove pulley.
Notes: Will fit interchange number 5. Will fit if pulleys are swapped.

Interchange Number: 8
Part Number(s): 1100696
Output: 42-amp
ID Number(s): 1100696, 1100795
Usage: 1968 Camaro, Chevelle, full-size Chevrolet, Nova with air conditioning

Interchange Number: 9
Part Number(s): 1100796
Output: 61 -amp
ID Number(s):1100796
Usage: 1968 Camaro, Chevelle full-size Chevrolet, Nova with RPO K76 61 amp alternator without air conditioning.
Notes: Has single groove pulley. Will fit interchange number 10 if pulleys are switched.

Interchange Number: 10
Part Number(s): 1100817
Output: 61 -amp
ID Number(s): 1100817
Usage: 1968 Camaro, Chevelle, full-size Chevrolet, Nova with RPO K76 alternator and air conditioning
Notes: Has dual groove pulley. Will fit interchange number 9 if pulleys are switched.

Interchange Number: 11
Part Number(s): 1100837
Output: 37-amp
ID Number(s): 1100837
Usage: 1969 Camaro Z-28; 1969-1970 Chevelle SS 396 with 375-hp; 1969 full-size Chevrolet with 427-ci 425-hp; 1969 Nova with 396ci 375hp 1970-1971 Chevelle SS 454 with 450 hp or 425hp (LS-6 option); 1970 Camaro with 350-ci V-8; 1971 Camaro Z-28; 1970-1971 Full-size Chevrolet with 454-ci V-8; 1970 Monte Carlo with 400-ci SMALL BLOCK
Note: Has single grove pulley

Interchange Number: 12
Part Number(s): 1100834
Output: 37-amp
ID Number(s): 1100834
Usage: 1969-1970 Camaro except 302-ci, Chevelle except SS 396 or SS 454; 1969-1970 full-size Chevrolet except 427-ci or 454-ci V-8 1969-1970 Nova except SS 396 with 375 hp; 1970 Camaro, except with 350-ci V-8
Notes: All have single groove pulley Interchange number 13 will fit if pulleys are switched

Interchange Number: 13
Part Number(s): 1100836
Output: 37-amp
ID Number(s): 1100836
Usage: 1969-1970 Camaro, Chevelle full-size Chevrolet, Nova
Notes: All have dual groove pulley
Interchange number 12 will fit if pulleys are switched

Interchange Number: 14
Part Number(s): 1100843
Output: 61-amp
ID Number(s): 1100843
Usage: 1969-1970 Camaro, Chevelle, full-size Chevrolet, Nova with RPO K76 alternator

Interchange Number: 15
Part Number(s): 1100842
Output: 42-amp
ID Number(s): 1100842
Usage: 1969-1970 Camaro, Chevelle, full-size Chevrolet, Nova with air conditioning

Interchange Number: 16
Part Number(s): 1100668
Output: 37-amp
ID Number(s): 1100668
Usage: 1964 Chevelle, full-size Chevrolet, Nova; 1964 Lemans with V-8 without air conditioning

Interchange Number: 17
Part Number(s): 1100669
Output: 42-amp
ID Number(s): 1100669
Usage: 1964 Chevelle, full-size Chevrolet, Nova with air conditioning

Interchange Number: 18
Part Number(s): 1100665
Output: 55-amp
ID Number(s): 1100665
Usage: 1964 Chevelle, full-size Chevrolet, Nova; 1964 Pontiac Tempest

Interchange Number: 19
Part Number(s): 1100694
Output: 55-amp
ID Number(s): 1100694
Usage: 1965 Chevelle, full-size Chevrolet, Nova

Interchange Number: 20
Part Number(s): 1100697
Output: 60-amp
ID Number(s): 1100697
Usage: 1965-1967 Chevelle, full-size Chevrolet; 1965-1967 full-size Pontiac; 1966 Chevelle SS 396; 1966 Impala SS 427

Battery Tray
Chevelle
Model   Interchange Number
1964-1965
All..1
1966
All..2
1967
All..3
1968-1972
All..4

Interchanges

Interchange Number: 1
Part Number(s): 3848270
Usage: 1964-1965 full-size Chevrolet, Chevelle

Interchange Number: 2
Part Number(s): 3893882
Usage: 1966 full-size Chevrolet; 1966 Chevelle; 1967-1969 Camaro; 1967-1969 Pontiac Firebird

Interchange Number: 3
Part Number(s): 3895138
Usage: 1967 full-size Chevrolet or Chevelle

Interchange Number: 4
Part Number(s): 3915471
Usage: 1968 full-size Chevrolet, 1968-1972 Chevelle

Interchange Number: 6
Part Number(s): 3916658
Part Number(s): 3938000
Usage: 1969 full-size Chevrolet

Windshield Wiper Motor

Several different types of windshield wiper motors were used by Chevrolet. Interchange variables include the number of blade speeds and the type. Concealed and non-concealed wipers are not interchangeable. Concealed wipers became available on 1968 models. They were standard on the higher trim models like the Malibu and optional on the lower trim models. Concealed wipers differed from the non-concealed type in that the resting position of the blades was underneath the rear edge of the hood. The motor itself was responsible for the positioning of the wipers, not the hood.

Chevelle

Model	Interchange Number
1964	
Single Speed	2
Two Speed	1
1965	
Single Speed	4
Two Speed	3
1966-1967	
Two Speed	3
1968	
Non-concealed	5
Concealed	7

1969-1972
Without Headlamp washers
Non-concealed 5
Concealed 7
With headlamp washers 6

1964 two-speed wiper motor

1966-1967 wiper motor

Interchange

Interchange Number: 1
Motor Type: Two-speed
Part Number(s): 4914164
ID Number(s): 4914164, 5044594,
Usage: 1964 Chevelle (round type)

Interchange Number: 2
Motor Type: Single-speed
Part Number(s): 4911945
ID Number(s): 4911945, 5045325
Usage: 1964-1965 Chevelle; 1963-1965 Nova; 1963-1965 Corvair; 1964-1965 Cutlass, Skylark or Lemans

Interchange Number: 3
Motor Type: Two-speed
Part Number(s): 4911476
ID Number(s): 4911476, 5045430, 5045508, 5045462, 9899321
Usage: 1963-1967 Nova; 1965-1967 Chevelle; 1967 Camaro

Interchange Number: 4
Motor Type: Single-speed
Part Number(s): 4911945
ID Number(s): 4911945, 5045325
Usage: 1963-1965 Nova, Corvair; 1964-1965 Chevelle, Cutlass, Skylark, Lemans

Interchange Number; 5
Motor Type: Two-speed non-concealed wipers
Part Number(s): 4918442
ID Number: 5045555, 5045619, 5045573 4914507, 5045430
Usage; 1968-1972 Chevelle; 1968-1974 Nova 1968-1972 LeMans, Cutlass, Skylark without shaft lever control; 1968-1974 Camaro;; 1970-1972 Monte Carlo; 1970-1974 Firebird; 1971-1974 Vega; 1971-1974 Ventura II; 1973-1974 Omega, Apollo

Interchange Number: 6
Motor Type: Two-speed with headlamp washer
Part Number(s): 4919624
ID Number(s); 4919642, 5045605
Usage: 1969 Camaro, Chevelle, or Nova
Notes: Unit has additional nipple for headlamp washer outlet.

Interchange Number; 7
Motor Type: Two-speed concealed wipers
Part Number(s): 4939586
ID Numbers: 5044681, 504756, 4918077, 4939300, 5944756
Usage: 1968-1972 Chevelle, LeMans, Cutlass, Skylark without shaft lever control; 1970-1972 Camaro; 1970-19772 Monte Carlo; 1970-1972 Pontiac Firebird; 1970-1972 CMC Sprint

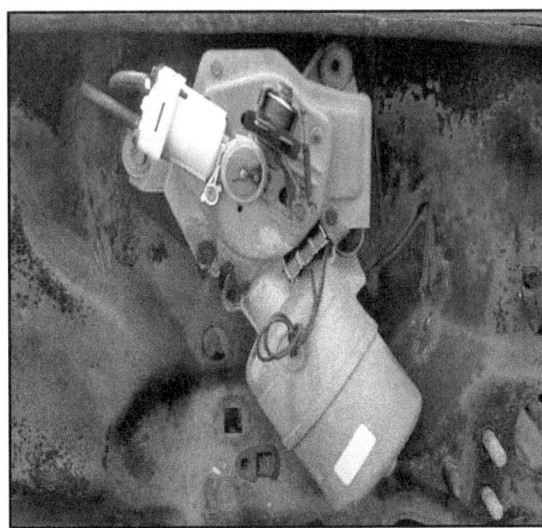
Concealed wiper motor

The 1968-1972 wipers can be identified by a casting number that is cast into the back of the motor. A part number may be stamped into the hub or the back frame of the motor, or a label stuck to it. Do not use the number stamped on the black cover. It is for the cover, not the wiper itself.

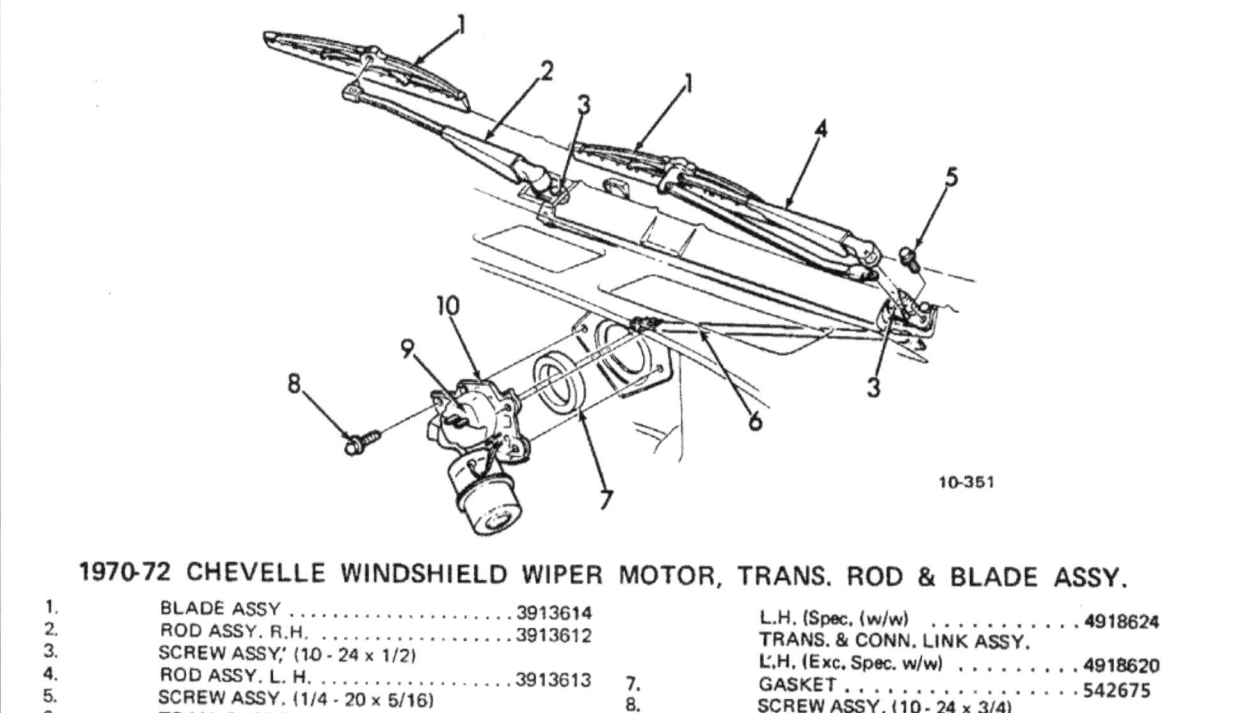

1970-72 CHEVELLE WINDSHIELD WIPER MOTOR, TRANS. ROD & BLADE ASSY.

1. BLADE ASSY 3913614
2. ROD ASSY. R.H. 3913612
3. SCREW ASSY. (10 - 24 x 1/2)
4. ROD ASSY. L.H. 3913613
5. SCREW ASSY. (1/4 - 20 x 5/16)
6. TRAN. & MOTOR DRIVE LINK ASSY. R.H. 4918758
   TRANS. & CONN. LINK ASSY.
   L.H. (EXC. CONN. LINK ASSY.)
   L.H. (Spec. (w/w) 4918624
   TRANS. & CONN. LINK ASSY.
   L.H. (Exc. Spec. w/w) 4918620
7. GASKET 542675
8. SCREW ASSY. (10 - 24 x 3/4)
9. MOTOR ASSY. 4939586
10. PUMP ASSY.. 4918180

(Chevrolet)

1964-1969 washer jar

Windshield Washer Jar

Interchange parts include the white plastic jar and lid. Some 1964-1967 models did come with a black plastic washer jug as optional equipment. The 1964-1972 jars were used on more models except the Chevelle, so this increases the interchange range.

Chevelle
Model	Interchange Number
1967-1969	
All	1
1970-1972	
All	2

1970-1972 washer jar

Interchanges

Interchange Number: 1
Part Number(s): 3840083
Usage: 1967-1969 Camaro; Late 1963-1970 Nova; Late 1963-1969 full-size Chevrolet; 1964-1969 Chevelle; 1964-1967 Cutlass, LeMans, Skylark
Notes: Used after November 30, 1962. All used bracket part number 548935. Location varies and makes the bracket appear different, but it is the same bracket. Exceptions: 1965-1967 Nova with two-speed wipers, which used bracket pan number 3863488; 1965-1966 full-size Chevrolet with two-speed wipers, which used bracket part number 3833218

Interchange Number: 2
Part Number(s): 3961557
Usage: 1970 full-size Chevrolet; 1970-1972 Chevelle, 1970 Camaro; 1970-1974 Pontiac Firebird; 1971-1974 Nova; 1971-1974 Ventura II
Notes: Bracket was not required; jar supported itself.

Windshield Wiper Linkage

These are the bars that transfer the power from the motor to the wiper arms. Some bars were coded, while others were not. They are largely interchangeable because they are of GM design.

Chevelle
Model	Interchange Number
1964-1965	
Single Speed Wipers	4
Two Speed Wipers	3
1966-1967	
Two Speed Wipers	3
1968-1972	
All	1

Interchanges

Interchange Number: 1
Part Number(s): LH, 4918758; RH, 4918620
Usage: 1968-1972 Chevelle, Cutlass, Skylark LeMans, Grand Prix; 1970-1972 Monte Carlo
Notes: All without concealed wipers Note RH same as in interchange number 2

Interchange Number: 2
Part Number(s): LH, 4918624; RH, 4918620
Usage: 1968-1972 Chevelle, Cutlass, Skylark LeMans, Grand Prix; 1970-1972 Monte Carlo
Notes: All with concealed wipers Note RH same as in interchange number 1

Interchange Number: 3
Part Number(s): RH, 4913654; LH, 4913665
Usage: 1964-1967 Chevelle, LeMans, Cutlass, Skylark
Notes: Two-speed wipers.

Interchange Number: 4
Part Number(s): 4913871
Usage: 1964-1965 Chevelle, LeMans; Cutlass, Skylark
Notes: Single-speed wipers.

Windshield Wiper Switch

The wiper switch interchange is the bare switch without its decorative knob. Interchange is based on part number. Type and number of wiper blade speeds will affect interchangeability as will those with a windshield washer.

Chevelle
Model	Interchange Number
1964	
Single Speed	1
Two Speed	
Without washer	
Early	2

Late..3
With Washer...4
1965
Single Speed
With Washer...5
Two Speed
Without washer..3
With Washer...6
1966
Two Speed..7
1967
Two Speed..8
1968
Without Concealed Wipers.............................8
With Concealed Wipers..................................9
1969-1971
Without Concealed Wipers...........................10
With Concealed Wipers................................11
1972
Without Concealed Wipers...........................12
With Concealed Wipers................................14

Interchanges

Interchange Number: 1
Part Number(s): 1993634
Usage: 1964 Chevelle, Cutlass, Lemans Skylark; all with single-speed wipers.

Interchange Number: 2
Part Number(s): 1993633
Usage: Early 1964 Chevelle, Cutlass, Skylark, LeMans; all with two-speed wipers
Notes: First design. Interchange 3 will fit.

Interchange Number: 3
Part Number(s): 1993665
Usage: Late 1964-1965 Chevelle, Cutlass, Skylark, LeMans; all with two-speed wipers without washers

Interchange Number: 4
Part Number(s): 1993677
Usage: 1965 Chevelle, full-size Chevrolet, or Nova, with single-speed wipers without washers

Interchange Number: 5
Part Number(s): 1993680
Usage: 1965 Chevelle, Chevy II, or full-size Chevrolet, all with single-speed wipers and washers

Interchange Number: 6
Part Number(s): 1993678
Usage: 1965-1966 full-size Chevrolet; 1965 Chevelle with two-speed wiper and washer

Interchange Number: 7
Part Number(s): 1993679
Usage: 1965-1966 Nova; 1966 Chevelle with two speed wipers with washers

Interchange Number: 8
Part Number(s): 1993395
Usage: 1967-1968 Camaro; 1967-1968 Chevelle, without concealed wipers; 1968 Nova

Interchange Number: 9
Part Number(s): 1993442
Usage: 1968 Chevelle; 1968-70 full-size Chevrolet both with concealed wipers

Interchange Number: 10
Part Number(s): 1993464
Usage: 1969 Camaro; 1969-1971 Nova; 1969-1971 Chevelle (except Malibu or SS or with concealed wipers);1971 Pontiac Ventura II

Interchange Number: 11
Part Number(s): 1993465
Usage: 1969-1971 Chevelle Malibu, SS, or those with concealed wipers; 1970-1971 Monte Carlo

Interchange Number: 12
Part Number(s): 1994180
Usage: 1972-1974 Nova; 1972 Chevelle (except Malibu or SS or with concealed wipers); 1972-1974 Pontiac Ventura II; 1973-1974 Omega, Apollo

Interchange Number: 14
Part Number(s): 1994131
Usage: 1972 Malibu ,SS or with concealed wipers

Heater motors are stamped with an identification number and sometime a build date, this motor did not have a build date.

Heater Motor Assembly

The biggest determining factor in interchanging the heater motor assembly is whether or not it was installed with factory air conditioning. The dealer-installed air conditioning used the same unit as those models that came from the factory without air conditioning. Motors with factory air conditioning are not interchangeable with cars without factory air or with dealer-installed air.

If the air conditioning unit looks like it has been added on, then it is a dealer-installed unit. Those integrated into the dash—often called Four Seasons—are factory-installed units.

Motors are identified by a number stamped onto the case. This number usually matches the part number, and is followed by the build date represented by the month and last two digits of the year. For example, "11 68" would represent November 1968.

Chevelle

Model	Interchange Number
1964-1972	
Without Air Conditioning	1
With Air Conditioning	2

Interchanges

Interchange Number: 1
Part Number(s): 4960505
ID Number(s): 5044555, 5044695, 5044531
Type: Without Air Conditioning
Usage: 1964-1977 Chevelle;1964-1982 full-size Chevrolet; 1964-1977 LeMans, Cutlass, Skylark, 1967-1981 Camaro, Firebird; 1968-1979 Nova; 1969-1983 Grand Prix; 1969-1983 full-size Oldsmobile; 1969- 1978 full-size Buick, except 1969-1970 Riviera; 1970- 1983 Monte Carlo; 1970-1982 full-size Pontiac;1971- 1976 Pontiac Ventura II; 1971-1974 CMC Sprint; 1973-19745 Buick Apollo; 1973-1979 Olds Omega; 1977-1979 Phoenix, Skylark; 1975-1980 Monza; 1973-1981 Regal; 1971-1977 Vega;197-1978 Blazer, Jimmy; 1966-1978 C10-C30 or 1500- 3500 GMC truck; 1971-1974 Eldorado ; 1967-1970 C10-C30 or GMC van

Interchange Number: 2
Part Number(s): 4960538
ID Number(s): 5044559, 4960538, 89977733
Type: With Air Conditioning
Usage: 1963-1976 full-size Chevrolet; Usage: 1964-early 1977 Chevelle;1964-1976 full-size Chevrolet; 1964- early 1977 LeMans, Cutlass, Skylark, 1967-early 1977 Camaro, Firebird; 1968-early 1977 Nova; 1969-early 1977 Grand Prix; 1969-1976 full-size Oldsmobile; 1969- 1976 full-size Buick, except 1969-1970 Riviera; 1970- early 1977 Monte Carlo; 1970-1976 full-size Pontiac; 1971- 1976 Pontiac Ventura II; 1971-1974 CMC Sprint; 1973-1975 Buick Apollo; 1973-early Omega; early 1977 Phoenix, Skylark; 1975- early 1977 Monza; 1973-1976 Regal; 1971-early 1977 Vega;197-1977 Blazer, Jimmy; 1966-1977 C10-C30 or 1500- 3500 GMC truck; 1971-1974 Eldorado ; 1967-1970 C10-C30 or GMC van

Heater Core Assembly

Interchange of the heater core is determined by whether or not factory (integrated) air conditioning was installed. Hang on or dealer installed air used the same core as those units without factory air conditioning, so the early 1962-1967 models only used one type of core. Engine size may also affect interchange.

Chevelle

Model	Interchange Number
1964-1967	
Without Air Conditioning	1
With Air Conditioning	2
1968	
Without Air Conditioning	3
With Air Conditioning	4
1969-1972	
Without Air Conditioning	3
With Air Conditioning	5

Interchanges

Interchange Number: 1
Part Number(s): 3022069
Usage: 1963-1968 full-size Chevrolet; 1964-1967 Chevelle, LeMans, Cutlass, Skylark; all without air conditioning

Interchange Number: 2
Part Number(s): 3004817
Usage: 1964-1967 Chevelle, Cutlass, Lemans, Skylark all with air conditioning

Interchange Number: 3
Part Number(s): 3014083
Usage: 1968-1972 Chevelle; 1970-1972 Monte Carlo; 1968-1972 Cutlass, Lemans, Skylark; 1971-1972 GMC Sprint; all without air conditioning

Interchange Number: 4
Part Number(s): 3021826
Usage: 1965-1968 full-size Chevrolet; 1968 Chevelle; 1965-1968 full-size Pontiac; all with air conditioning.

Interchange Number: 5
Part Number(s): 3014782
Usage: 1969-1970 full-size Chevrolet; 1969-72 Chevelle, Cutlass, Lemans, Skylark; 1970-1972 Monte Carlo; 1971-1972 GMC Sprint all with with air conditioning

Air Conditioning Compressor

The interchange for an air conditioning compressor is based on the original part number for the entire compressor. Interchange is quite large if you go by fit alone. In fact, compressors from other GM makes and models will interchange. For example, a compressor from a 1966-1974 Cutlass will fit the 1966 and up Chevelle. Although it may fit properly, the number may be incorrect for that particular model year. If you want to go the route of using the correct part number, try to focus your interchange on the same model year and engine type. For example, if you are looking for a compressor for your 1969 SS 396, you might try a unit from a 1969 full-size car (remember, other GM makes will fit). Part numbers were generally the same for all models for that particular compressor.

Factory-installed air conditioning and dealer-installed or "hang on" units used two different compressors, thus they are not interchangeable. The Four Seasons integrated units are much more common than the hang-on type. If your car is equipped with a dealer-installed unit, your search is going to be somewhat limited.

Chevelle

Model	Interchange Number
1964-1971	
Dealer Installed Air Conditioning	1
Factory Air Conditioning	2
1972	
Factory Air Conditioning	3

Interchanges

Interchange Number: 1
Part/ID Number(s): 5910432
Usage: 1962-1965 full-size Chevrolet, Pontiac with hang-on air conditioning; 1962-1967 Nova with air conditioning; 1962-1967 Buick Skylark with hang-on air conditioning; 1964-1967 Cutlass with hang-on air conditioning; 1964-1970 Chevelle, LeMans with hang-on a/c; 1967-1970 Camaro with hang-on air conditioning; 1968-1970 Nova with hang-on air conditioning
Notes: Will not fit cars with factory-integrated (Four Seasons) systems.
Used with dealer-installed a/c. Factory-installed in 1962-1967 Nova.

Interchange Number: 2
Part Number(s): 5910486
Id Numbers: 5910486, 6598423, 5910435, 5910495, 5910431
Usage: 1962-1971 full-size Chevrolet, full-size Pontiac, full-size Buick, Full-size Oldsmobile; 1962-1971 Olds Cutlass; 1964-1971 Chevelle, Lemans; 1967-1971 Camaro, Firebird; 1968-1971 Nova; 1969-1971 Grand Prix; 1971 GMC Sprint; all with factory-installed air condition
Notes: Compressors in interchange number 3 will fit, but have a heat switch while the earlier compressor has no heat switch. Bypass heat switch when installing

Interchange Number: 3
Part Number(s): 6598423
ID Numbers: 1131008, 1131009, 1131012, 1131016, 1131017, 1131026, 1131027, 1131049, 1131050, , 1131051, 1131058, 1131060, 1131086, 1131087, 1131111, 1131243, 5910781, 5910782, 5910783, 5910784, 5910785, 5910787, 5910789, 5910790, 5910793, 5910796
Usage: 1972-1975 Camaro, Chevelle, full-size Chevrolet, Monte Carlo, Nova, C10-C-30 or 1500-23500 GMC truck; -1972-1976 full-size Buick, Oldsmobile, Pontiac, 1972-1975 Firebird, Ventura II; 1972-1976 Lemans, Cutlass, Skylark, Century, 1972-1976 Grand Prix; 1972-1976 GMC Sprint; 1972-1976 Toranado; 1972-1976 Cadillac; 1973-1976 Regal All with factory installed air conditioning.
Notes: Axis type

Air Conditioning Condenser

Chevelle
Model	Interchange Number
1964-1966	
All	1
1967	
All	5
1968	
All	2
1969	
All	3
1970-1972	
All	4

Interchanges

Interchange Number: 1
Part Number(s): 3859770
Usage: 1964-1966 Chevelle, all models and body styles

Interchange Number: 2
Part Number(s): 3919596
Usage: 1968 Chevelle with factory-installed air conditioning

Interchange Number: 3
Part Number(s): 3937140
Usage: 1969 Chevelle with factory-installed a/c

Interchange Number: 4
Part Number(s): 3967948
Usage: 1970-1972 Chevelle; 1970-1972 Monte Carlo; 1970-1972 CMC Sprint; all with factory-installed air conditioning

Interchange Number: 5
Part Number(s): 3899793
Usage: 1967 Camaro; 1967 Chevelle; 1967 full-size Chevrolet; 1968 Nova; 1967-1968 Pontiac Firebird; all with factory air conditioning
Notes: Also used on 1968 Chevelle, Camaro, and full size Chevrolet with dealer-installed air conditioning.

Horns

The car horn has fewer interchange possibilities than you would expect—if you interchange the horn along with its mounting bracket, that is. Each model and model year had various mounting locations, so the only interchange is usually the same model and same model year. An exception is the 1968- 1972 Nova, which used the same exact horn assembly for all five years.

Interchange likelihood becomes much greater, however, if you remove the horn from the bracket and crosses over models. Full-size Chevrolets from 1955 to 1964 and Chevy II models from 1962 to 1964 used the same two horns. The high-note horn was listed as part number 9000239 and stamped the same. The low-note horn was listed as part number 9000011 and stamped 9000014.

Beginning in 1965, the high-note horn was listed as part number 1892164 (A note), and the low-note horn was part number 1892162 (D Note. The high note continued into the 1981 model year. These horns were used on all GM makes and will interchange.

Signal Lever

The biggest concern with the signal lever is the column type. The levers used with the tilt steering column differed from those units used without the option. Also, the levers with speed control used a special stalk that doubled as the speed control switch. Another factor to watch for includes model usage, for some types.

Chevelle

Model	Interchange Number
1964-1965	
Without tilt steering	1
With tilt steering	2
1966	
Without tilt steering	3
With tilt steering	2
1967-1968	
Without Speed Control	4
With Speed Control	5
1969-1972	
Without Speed Control	1
With Speed Control	5

Interchanges

Interchange Number: 1
Part Number(s): 470320
Usage: 1971-1975 Camaro, Chevelle, full-size Chevrolet, Monte Carlo, Nova all without cruise control

Interchange Number: 2
Part Number(s): 3783459
Usage: 1959-1966 full-size Chevrolet; 1962-1966 Nova; 1964-1966 Chevelle; all with tilt column

Interchange Number: 3
Part Number(s): 3840903
Usage: 1964-1967 Chevelle; 1966 Nova both without tilt column

Interchange Number: 4
Part Number: 3909580
Usage: 1967-1968 Nova; 1967 Pontiac Firebird; 1967-1968 full-size Chevrolet; 1967-1968 Camaro; 1968 Chevelle all without cruise control

Interchange Number: 5
Part Number(s): 6465256
Usage: 1967-1975 full-size Chevrolet, Chevelle, Nova, Camaro, LeMans, Skylark; 1968-1975 full-size Pontiac; 1970-1975 Monte Carlo; all with cruise control
Notes: Look for this option in full-size cars or personal luxury models like the Monte Carlo. It was more commonly used on those models.

Interchange Number: 5
Part Number(s): 3961517
Usage: 1969-1970 full-size Chevrolet, Camaro Chevelle, or Nova; 1970 Monte Carlo; all with cruise control

Convertible Top Motor

Only one motor was used from 1964-1972 listed as part number 5044586 it was used on all GM A-bodies from 1964-1972 and 1967-1969 Firebird and Camaros. However, beware that early 1964 Skylarks used part number 5044573. The motors are stamped with the part number

Interchange Number: 1
Part Number(s): 7710923
Usage: 1964-1972 Chevelle, Lemans, Cutlass, Skylark; 1967-1969 Camaro; 1967-1969 Pontiac Firebird

Convertible Top Switch

This is the power switch that was placed on the instrument panel that operated the top. It is the bare switch without the bezel. Tip: Look at Chevelle or full-size station wagons with a power rear window; the switch is the same.

Chevelle

Model	Interchange Number
1964-1966	
All	1
1967-1968	
All	2
1969	
All	3
1970-1972	
All	4

Interchanges

Interchange Number: 1
Part Number(s): 3840095
Usage: 1964-1966 Chevelle, Pontiac Tempest, Olds Cutlass ,or Buick Skylark convertible or station wagon with power rear window; 1965-1966 full-size convertible; 1965-66 full-size wagon with power rear window; 1968 Camaro or Pontiac Firebird; 1968 Malibu or SS 396 convertible; 1968 Chevelle Concours wagon

Interchange Number: 2
Part Number(s): 3906118
Usage: 1967 Chevelle or Camaro; 1967-1968 full-size Chevrolet convertible or station wagon with power rear window

Interchange Number: 3
Part Number(s): 3959230
Usage: 1969 Camaro or Chevelle convertible; 1969 Pontiac Lemans, Skylark, Cutlass convertible; 1969 Chevelle, Cutlass, Skylark, Lemans station wagon with power rear window;
1969-1970 full-size Chevrolet convertible or station wagon with power rear window

Interchange Number: 4
Part Number(s): 3973644
Usage: 1970-72 Chevelle convertible; 1970-1972 Chevelle station wagon with power rear window

Power Window Motor

Chevelle

Model	Interchange Number
1964-1968	
All	1
1969-1972	
Door	
Except El Camino	2
El Camino	1
Quarters	1

Interchanges

Interchange Number: 1
Part Number(s): 40902201 RH 4092202 LH
ID Stamped 5045191, 5045192, 5045238, 5045239, 5945585, 5945586, 5045191, 5045192
Usage: 1964-1968 Chevelle, Cutlass, Lemans, Skylark-except 1966-1968 4 door hardtop; 1961-1968 full-size Chevrolet, Buick, Oldsmobile, except 98, Pontiac except tailgate; 1961-1965 Cadillac; 1967-1968 Firebird; 1969-1972 Chevelle, Cutlass, Lemans, Skylark rear quarter windows; 1970-1972 El Camino or two door sedan
Notes Fits doors or quarters

Interchange Number: 2
Part Number(s): 5045639 RH 5045640 LH
ID Numbers: 3676095 3676096,
Usage: 1969-1972 Chevelle, Cutlass, Lemans, Skylark 2-door except El Camino; 1966-1968 Chevelle, Cutlass, Lemans, Skylark 4-door hardtop1967-1968 Cadillac quarter windows only; 1965-1968 Wildcat or LeSabre except 4-door hardtop

Some power window motors are stamped with an ID number and build date code, this translates to October 1965 and is for a 1966 model

1964-1965 Speedometer

Perfectly good speedometers can be found in salvage yards like this one in a 1967 that will also fit your 1966.

1968 Speedometer

1969 Speedometer

Speedometer
Chevelle
Model   *Interchange Number*

1964-1965
All..1
1966
All..2
1967
Without Speed Warning.......................................2
With Speed Warning...3
1968
Without Speed Warning.......................................4
With Speed Warning...5
1969
Without Speed Warning.......................................6
With Speed Warning...7
1970-1972
Without Gauges or Super Sport Models
Column automatic...8
With Gauges or Super Sport Models
Column automatic...10
Floor Shift...9

Used Parts Buyers Guide

1970-1972 Standard speedometer without gauge or SS package

Interchanges

Interchange Number: 1
Part Number(s): 6408655
Usage: 1964-1965 Chevelle all models and body styles

Interchange Number: 2
Part Number(s): 6456882
Usage: 1966 Chevelle; 1967 Chevelle without speed warning, all models and body styles

Interchange Number: 3
Part Number(s): 6459395
Usage: 1967 Chevelle with speed warning, all models and body styles

Interchange Number: 4
Part Number(s): 6492545
Usage: 1968 Chevelle; without speed warning, all models and body styles

Interchange Number: 5
Part Number(s): 6480637
Usage: 1968 Chevelle; with speed warning, all models and body styles

Interchange Number: 6
Part Number(s): 6492542
Usage: 1969 Chevelle; without speed warning, all models and body styles

1970-1972 SS speedometer with column automatic

1970-1972 SS speedometer with floor shift.

Interchange Number: 7
Part Number(s): 6492544
Usage: 1969 Chevelle; with speed warning, all models and body styles

Interchange Number: 8
Part Number(s): 6497814
Usage: 1970-1972 Chevelle; except without gauges or SS models

Interchange Number: 9
Part Number(s): 6496702
Usage: 1970-1972 Chevelle; with gauge or SS models with manual or floor shift

Interchange Number: 10
Part Number(s): 6496643
Usage: 1970-1972 Chevelle; with gauge or SS models with column shift automatic

Tachometer
Chevelle
Model   Interchange Number
1964
Except Transistorized ignition.........................1
Transistorized Ignition....................................2
1965
Except 327-ci 350 hp or 396-ci
Except Transistorized ignition.........................1
Transistorized Ignition....................................2
350-hp...3
396-ci...2
1966
Except 396-ci/ 350 or 375-hp..........................4
396-ci 350/375-hp..5
1967
Except 396-ci or 327-ci special high performance......6
327-ci Special High Performance................18
396-ci
325-hp...6
350-hp or 375 hp...7
1968
Except 396-ci or 327-ci Special High Performance.....8
327-ci Special High Performance................10
396-ci
Except 375-hp...9
375-hp...10
1969
Except 396-ci...11
396-ci
Except 375-hp...12
375-hp...13

1970
Except 396-ci or 454-ci
Early..20
Late...14
396-ci/454-ci
Except 375-hp/450-hp
Early..19
Late...15
375-hp/450-hp...16

Interchanges

Interchange Number: 1
Part Number(s):6412221
Usage: 1964-1965 Chevelle except with transistorized ignition or special high performance in 1965

Interchange Number: 2
Part Number(s):6412218
Usage: 1964-1965 Chevelle with transistorized ignition; 1965 SS 396

Interchange Number: 3
Part Number(s):6412504
Usage: 1965 Chevelle with 327-ci Special High performance.

Interchange Number: 4
Part Number(s) 6412759
Usage: 1966 Chevelle except with 396-ci 350-hp or 375-hp

Interchange Number: 5
Part Number(s) 6412816
Usage: 1966 Chevelle with 396-ci 350-hp or 375-hp

Interchange Number: 6
Part Number(s) 6468319
Usage: 1967 Chevelle except with 396-ci 350-hp or 375-hp or 327-ci special high performance.

Interchange Number: 7
Part Number(s) 6468499
Usage: 1967 Chevelle with 350- hp or 375 hp 396-ci

Interchange Number: 8
Part Number(s) 6468821
Usage: 1968 Chevelle except 396-ci or 327-ci special high performance
Notes: Stamped with part number Red lines at 5,000 rpm

Interchange Number: 9
Part Number(s) 6468822
Usage: 1968 Chevelle with 396-ci except 375 hp; 1968 Chevelle with 327-ci special high performance
Notes: Stamped with part number red lines at 5,500 rpm

Interchange Number: 10
Part Number(s) 6468823
Usage: 1968 Chevelle with 396-ci 375-hp
Notes: Stamped with part number redlines at 6,000 rpm

Interchange Number: 11
Part Number(s) 6469397 or 3469312
Usage: 1969 Chevelle except 396-ci or 350-ci
Notes: Red lines at 5,000 rpm

1967 tachometer, because it covered up the left-hand turn indicator on the dash it contained a signal indicator at the bottom

Interchange Number: 12
Part Number(s) 6491313
Usage: 1969 Chevelle with 396-ci except 375-hp; 1969 Chevelle with 350-ci V-8
Red lines at 5,500 rpm

Interchange Number: 13
Part Number(s) 6491314
Usage: 1969 Chevelle 396-ci 375-hp
Notes: Red lines at 6,000 rpm

Interchange Number: 14
Part Number(s) 5667405
Usage: Late 1970-1972 Chevelle except 396-ci or 454
Notes: Used after July 1970 stamped with part number redlines at 5,000 rpm

Interchange Number: 15
Part Number(s) 5667406
Usage: Late 1970 Chevelle Monte Carlo with 396-ci or 454, except 375-hp or 450-hp; 1971-1972 Chevelle, Monte Carlo with 402-ci or 454 ci except 425-hp
Notes: Used after July 1970 stamped with part number red lines at 5,500 rpm

1966 tachometer was housed in a bright metal case

Interchange Number: 16
Part Number(s) 5667407
Usage: 1970 Chevelle or Monte Carlo with 396-ci 375-hp or 454, 450-hp; 1971 Chevelle, Monte Carlo with 454-ci 425-hp
Notes: Stamped with part number red lines at 6,500 rpm

Interchange Number: 18
Part Number(s) 6468500
Usage: 1967 Chevelle with 327-ci special high performance.

Interchange Number: 19
Part Number(s) 6469985
Usage: Early 1970 Chevelle Monte Carlo with 396-ci or 454, except 375-hp or 450-hp
Notes: Used before July 1970 Interchange number 15 will fit. Stamped with part number. Red lines at 5,500 rpm.

Interchange Number: 20
Part Number(s) 6469940
Usage: Late 1970 Chevelle except 396-ci or 454
Notes: Used before July 1970 Interchange number 14 will fit. Stamped 6469940 Red lines at 5,000 rpm

1969 Tachometer was housed in the instrument cluster to the far right and displaced the standard fuel gauge.

1970 tachometer used with 375 hp 396 or 450-hp 454 note the red line marking

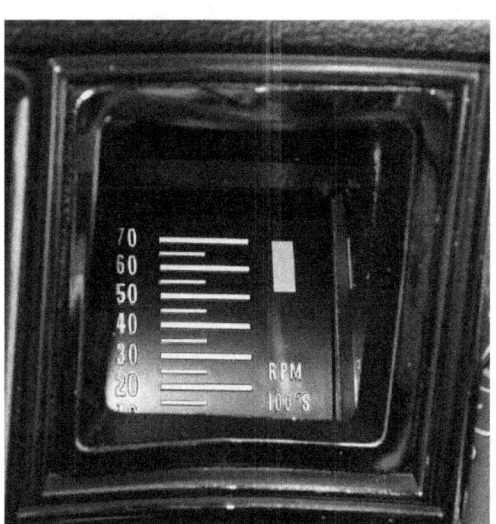
1968 tachometer is an unusual design. Red line differs between various engines. This is for 396-ci engine except thee 375-hp V-8

Late 1970-1972 Tachometer for 350-ci and 402-ci

Ammeter

Listed here is the gauge assembly only, usually had when the car was ordered with the optional gauge package. The idiot or tell-tale lights are not listed here. If the model is not listed then only tell-tale lights were used.

Chevelle

Model	Interchange Number
1964	
All	1
1965	
All	2
1966-1967	
All	3
1968	
All	4
1969	
All	5
1970-1972	
All	6

Interchanges

Interchange Number: 1
Part Number(s) 1502873
Usage: 1964 Chevelle, with gauge package

Interchange Number: 2
Part Number(s) 1503013
Usage: 1965 Chevelle, with gauge package

Interchange Number: 3
Part Number(s) 1503251
Usage: 1966-1967 Chevelle, with gauge package

Interchange Number: 4
Part Number(s) 6473105
Usage: 1968 Chevelle, with gauge package

Interchange Number: 5
Part Number(s) 6473402
Usage: 1969 Chevelle, with gauge package

Interchange Number: 6
Part Number(s) 6473843
Usage: 1970-197 Chevelle, with gauge package; 1970-1972 Monte Carlo with gauge package.

1964 optional gauges standard unit has warning lights for Gen. Oil and temp. 1965 is similar

1966-1967 with optional ammeter meter and temp gauge

1968 optional gauges and clock

1970-1972 Ammeter with optional gauge package

Fuel Gauge
The fuel gauge was moved many times when optional gauge clusters were used, and thus is not interchangeable with those with the standard gauge cluster in many cases.

Chevelle
Model   Interchange Number
1964
Except SS..1
SS...2
1965
Without Gauges..3
With Gauges..4
1966-1967
Without Gauges..5
With Gauges..6
1968
All...7
1969
Without Gauges..8
With Gauges..9
1970-1972
Without Gauges..10
With Gauges..11

Interchanges

Interchange Number: 1
Part Number(s) 5644870
Usage: 1964 Chevelle without gauges.

Interchange Number: 2
Part Number(s) 5644871
Usage: 1964 Chevelle with gauges.

Interchange Number: 3
Part Number(s)
Usage: 1965 Chevelle without gauges.

Interchange Number: 4
Part Number(s)
Usage: 1965 Chevelle with gauges.

Interchange Number: 5
Part Number(s) 6430420
Usage: 1966-1967 Chevelle without gauges.

Interchange Number: 6
Part Number(s) 6430421
Usage: 1966-1967 Chevelle with gauges.

Interchange Number: 7
Part Number(s) 6431251
Usage: 1969 Chevelle without gauges.

Interchange Number: 8
Part Number(s) 6431252
Usage: 1969 Chevelle with gauges.

Interchange Number: 8
Part Number(s) 6431251
Usage: 1969 Chevelle without gauges.

Interchange Number: 9
Part Number(s) 6431586
Usage: 1970-1972 Chevelle SS without gauges package; 1970-1972 Monte Carlo

Interchange Number: 10
Part Number(s) 6431584
Usage: 1970-1972 Chevelle except with SS package or gauge package.

Interchange Number: 11
Part Number(s) 6431581
Usage: 1970-1972 Chevelle with gauge package

1966-1967 fuel gauge without gauge package

1964 Standard fuel gauge. 1965 is similar

1969 fuel gauge without gauge package.

1970-1972 fuel gauge and clock except SS models or with gauge package.

Standard SS fuel gauges can also be found on 1970-1972 Monte Carlos

Oil Pressure

The idiot light or tell-tale warning lights are not listed here, only the gauge assembly is. If an oil pressure gauge was not offered, it is not listed.

Chevelle
Model	Interchange Number

1964
With Gauges..1
1965
With Gauges..2
1966-1967
With Gauges..3
1968
With Gauges..3
1969
With Gauges..4

With the optional gauge package, the fuel gauge was much smaller and located just below the temp gauge.

Interchange Number: 1
Part Number(s) 5644875
Usage: 1964 Chevelle with gauges.

Interchange Number: 3
Part Number(s) 565466
Usage: 1965 Chevelle with gauges.

Interchange Number: 5
Part Number(s) 6460142
Usage: 1966-1967 Chevelle with gauges.

Interchange Number: 6
Part Number(s) 6461238
Usage: 1968 Chevelle with gauges

Interchange Number: 7
Part Number(s) 6462069
Usage: 1969 Chevelle with gauges

Temperature Gauge

The temperature gauge was moved many times when optional gauge clusters were used, and thus is not interchangeable with those with the standard gauge cluster in many cases. If no temp gauge was offered then it is not listed.

Chevelle

Model	Interchange Number
1964	
All	1
1965	
All	2
1966-1967	
All	3
1968	
All	4
1969	
All	5
1970-1972	
All	6

Interchanges

Interchange Number: 1
Part Number(s) 6400423
Usage: 1964 Chevelle with gauges

Interchange Number: 2
Part Number(s) 6401598
Usage: 1965 Chevelle with gauges

Interchange Number: 3
Part Number(s) 6402466
Usage: 1966-1967 Chevelle with gauges

Interchange Number: 4
Part Number(s) 6488813
Usage: 1968 Chevelle with gauges

Interchange Number: 5
Part Number(s) 6489398
Usage: 1969 Chevelle with gauges

Interchange Number: 6
Part Number(s) 6490087
Usage: 1970-1972 Chevelle with gauges; 1970-1972 Monte Carlo with gauges

1966-1967 Temp and oil pressure gauges

1965 clock, the 1964 is similar

Clock

The Clock was offered as separation option or as part of gauge package in the 1970-1972 models

Chevelle

Model	Interchange Number
1964-1965	
In Dash	1
On dash	2
On console	5
1966-1967	
In Dash	3
On console	4
On floor	5
1968	
Without gauges	6
With Gauges	7
1969	
All	8
1970	
Except SS	
Without gauges	9
With Gauges	10
SS	10

Interchanges

Interchange Number: 1
Part Number(s) 3863459
Usage: 1964-1965 Chevelle without a tachometer. In dash.
Notes: Stamped 2542430

Interchange Number: 2
Part Number(s) 3840439
Usage: 1964-1965 Chevelle; 1963-1965 full-size Chevrolet, Nova clock was mounted in housing on dash
Note: this item is rare.

Interchange Number: 3
Part Number(s) 3874552
Usage: 1966-1967 Chevelle with clock in dash

Interchange Number: 4
Part Number(s) 3880972
Usage: 1966-1967 Chevelle clock in console

Interchange Number: 5
Part Number(s) 3901632
Usage: 1966-1967 Chevelle clocked mounted on floor without console
Notes: Item is very rare.

Interchange Number: 6
Part Number(s) 3919015
Usage: 1968 Chevelle without optional gauges or with tachometer. Is housed in the center pod.

Interchange Number: 7
Part Number(s) 6481543
Usage: 1968 Chevelle with optional gauge cluster without tachometer. Housed in far right of instrument cluster.

Interchange Number: 8
Part Number(s) 3948956
Usage: 1969 Chevelle

Interchange Number: 9
Part Number(s) 3990802
Usage: 1970-1972 Chevelle, except SS or with optional gauges.

Interchange Number: 10
Part Number(s) 3990803
Usage: 1970-1972 Chevelle with optional gauges; 1970-1972 Chevelle SS; 1970-1972 Monte Carlo

1966-1967 in dash clock in the dash

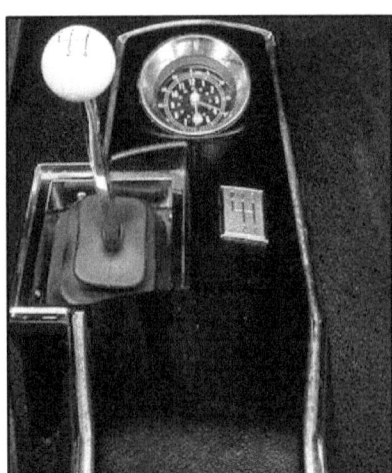

1966-1967 clock in console

1969 Clock in the center of the dash

The 1970-1972 SS clock can be found in 1970-1972 Monte Carlo, the SS bezel is behind the Woodgrain trim As the case of this unit we found in a salvage yard

Headlamp, Switch

Chevelle

Model	Interchange Number
1964-1969	
All	1
1970-1971	
All	2
1972	
All	1

Interchanges

Interchange Number: 1
Part Number(s): 1995179
Usage: 1964-1967 full size Chevrolet; 1964-1974 Nova; 1964-1969 Chevelle; 1967-1968 Camaro except RS models; 1964-1967 Cutlass, Lemans, Skylark; 1967 Firebird; 1967 full-size Oldsmobile, except Toranado; 1968-1974 full size Pontiac; 1971-1974 Ventura II; 1973-1974 Apollo, Omega; 1972 Chevelle

1964 Front parking lamps fit either side. Amber colored lens

Interchange Number: 2
Part Number(s): 19951183
Usage: 1969 Camaro with console gauges, except Rally Sport; 1969-1972 full-size Chevrolet, except with hidden headlamps; 1970-1971 Chevelle; 1970-1972 Camaro

Lamps, Front Parking

Chevelle

Model	Interchange Number
1964	
All	1
1965	
All	2
1966	
All	3
1967	
All	4
1968	
Except with Lamp Monitoring	5
With Monitoring	6
1969	
Except SS 396 Or El Camino	7
SS 396	8
El Camino	9
1970	
Except El Camino	11
El Camino	10
SS	12
1971	
Except El Camino	13
El Camino	14
1972	
Except El Camino or Malibu	15
El Camino	
Except Custom	17
Custom	
Early	17
Late	18
Malibu	
Early	15
Late	16

Interchanges

Interchange Number: 1
Part Number(s) 910850 (fits either side)
Usage: 1964 Chevelle, all models and body styles

Interchange Number: 2
Part Number(s) 910659 LH 910660 RH
Usage: 1965 Chevelle, all models and body styles

Interchange Number: 3
Part Number(s) 911243 LH 911244 RH
Usage: 1966 Chevelle, all models and body styles

Interchange Number: 4
Part Number(s) 911271 LH 911272 RH
Usage: 1967 Chevelle, all models and body styles

Interchange Number: 5
Part Number(s) 916173 (either side)
Usage: 1968 Chevelle, all models and body styles, except with lamp monitoring

Interchange Number: 6
Part Number(s) 916355 LH 916356 RH
Usage: 1968 Chevelle, all models and body styles, with lamp monitoring

1965 front parking lamp, lens is amber in color

1966 front parking lamp, amber colored lens.

1967 front parking lamp, lens amber in color

1968 front parking lamp, amber in color.

The 1969 El Camino used different front parking lamps then the other Chevelle models even with the SS package.

1969 Chevelles without the SS package used this clear front parking lamp

1969 SS 396 models used this clear front parking lamp. It was not used on El Camino with the SS package

The 1970 El Camino used a round shaped front parking lamp

Interchange Number: 7
Part Number(s) 916791 LH 916792 RH
Usage: 1969 Chevelle, except SS 396 or El Camino

Interchange Number: 8
Part Number(s) 916795 LH 916796 RH
Usage: 1969 El Camino

Interchange Number: 9
Part Number(s) 916901 LH 916902 RH
Usage: 1969 SS 396, except El Camino's

Interchange Number: 10
Part Number(s) 917194 (fits either side)
Usage: 1970 El Camino

Interchange Number: 11
Part Number(s) 5962103- Housing 5962107 Lenses
Usage: 1970 Chevelle, except SS models or El Camino

Interchange Number: 12
Part Number(s) 5962103- Housing 5961555 Lenses
Usage: 1970 Chevelle SS models
Note: housing the same in interchange 11

Interchange Number: 13
Part Number(s) 5963817 LH 5963818 RH Lenses
Usage: 1971 Chevelle, except El Camino or wagon

Interchange Number: 14
Part Number(s) 5963821 LH 5963822 RH Lenses
Usage: 1971 El Camino or Chevelle station wagon

Interchange Number: 15
Part Number(s) 5965269 LH 5965270 RH Lenses
Usage: 1972 Chevelle except El Camino or Chevelle station wagon; Early 1972 Malibu

Interchange Number: 16
Part Number(s) 5965683 LH 5965684 RH Lenses
Usage: Late 1972 Malibu

1971 Front marker lamps for El Camino were wider than those for other Chevelles.

1970 Chevelle's all used the front parking lamp except El Camino's

1971 Chevelle front parking lamp except El Camino or wagons. There is a difference in the width of the lens.

1972 Chevelle amber colored lens were used on early 1972 models up to build date 11D72.

Beginning with build date 12A72 lens were switched to clear lens. Dates are just approx.

Once again El Camino's and wagons used wider front lamps than regular Chevelle models did. Early models used Amber lens and the later used clear.

Interchange Number: 17
Part Number(s) 5965275 LH 5965276 RH Lenses
Usage: 1972 El Camino or Chevelle station wagon; early 1972 Custom El Camino or Concours Station wagon

Interchange Number: 18
Part Number(s) 5965687 LH 5965688 RH Lenses
Usage: Late 1972 Custom El Camino or Concours Station wagon

Lamps, Side Marker

Beginning with the 1968 models side marker lamps or reflectors were used on the front fenders and rear quarter panels. Some used engine call out bezels on the front, the bezel is not part of the interchange. Only the lamp assembly or reflector is interchange here. For bezels see the emblem section of this guide.

Chevelle

Model	Interchange Number
1968	
Front	1
Rear	
Except El Camino	part of taillight
El Camino	2

1969
Front..3
Rear
Except El Camino..4
El Camino..2
1970
Front..5
Rear
Except El Camino..6
El Camino..part of taillight
1971-1972
Front.....................................part of front parking lamp
Rear
Except El Camino..6
El Camino..part of taillight

1968 front side marker lamp was used on all 1968 Chevrolet car models.

1969 front side lamp was also used on Camaros

Interchanges
Interchange Number: 1
Part Number(s): 916581
Part: Front lamp assembly
Usage: 1968 Camaro, Chevelle, full-size Chevrolet, Nova

Interchange Number: 2
Part Number(s): 916632
Part: Rear lamp assembly
Usage: Early 1968 El Camino, 1968-1969 Chevelle station wagon; 1968-1969 Nova

Interchange Number: 3
Part Number(s): 916813 (fits either side)
Part: Front lamp assembly
Usage: 1969 Camaro, Chevelle

Interchange Number: 4
Part Number(s): 916847 (fits either side)
Part: Rear lamp assembly
Usage: 1969 Camaro, Chevelle, except wagon and El Camino

Interchange Number: 5
Part Number(s): 917093 LH 917094 RH
Part: Front lamp assembly
Usage: 1970 Chevelle, all models and body styles

Interchange Number: 6
Part Number(s): 917101 LH 917102 RH
Part: Rear reflector assembly
Usage: 1970-1972 Chevelle, all models and body styles, except wagon or El Camino

1970 front side lamp

Chevelle 1964-1972

Lamps, Taillights

Chevelle
Model   *Interchange Number*
1964
Except El Camino..1
El Camino..2
1965
Except El Camino Or Malibu..3
Malibu...4
El Camino..5
1966
Except El Camino 7
El Camino..6
1967
Except El Camino 10
El Camino
Except Deluxe...8
Deluxe..9
1968
Except El Camino 13
El Camino
Except Deluxe...12
Deluxe..11
1969
Except El Camino 17
El Camino
Deluxe..15
Custom...16

1970-1972 Rear side marker

1964 taillight

1966 taillight used a two-part lens.

1970
Except El Camino or Malibu..1
El Camino
Deluxe..15
Custom..16
1970
Except El Camino or Malibu..20
Malibu..19
El Camino
Except Custom...21
Custom..18
1971
Except El Camino or Malibu..22
Malibu..23
El Camino
Except Custom...21
Custom..18
1972
Except El Camino or Malibu..24
Malibu..25
El Camino
Except Custom...21
Custom..18

Interchanges

Interchange Number: 1
Part Number(s) 910267 LH 910268 RH
Usage: 1964 Chevelle, all models and body styles except wagon and El Camino

Interchange Number: 2
Part Number(s) 910441 LH 910442 RH
Usage: 1964 El Camino or Chevelle station wagon

Interchange Number: 3
Part Number(s) 910723 LH 910724 RH
Usage: 1965 Chevelle, all models and body styles except Malibu, wagon and El Camino

Interchange Number: 4
Part Number(s) 910725 LH 910726 RH
Usage: 1965 Malibu styles except wagon and El Camino

Interchange Number: 5
Part Number(s) 910863 LH 910864 RH
Usage: 1965 Chevelle station wagon or El Camino

1967 taillight except El Camino

The 1968 Chevelle Deluxe taillight contains the backup lamp.

1968 Malibu and SS 396 taillight assembly

1969 Chevelle Deluxe taillight

Interchange Number: 6
Part Number(s) Housing: 5958367 LH 5958368 RH
Lenses: 5957819 LH 5957820 RH
Usage: 1966 El Camino or Chevelle Station wagon

Interchange Number: 7
Part Number(s) Lenses: Inner: 5957814 Outer: 597819
Usage: 1966 Chevelle except El Camino or Chevelle Station wagon

Interchange Number: 8
Part Number(s) Housing: 5959063 LH 5959064 RH
Lenses: 5959069 LH 5959070 RH
Usage: 1967 El Camino or Chevelle Station wagon, except Deluxe models
Notes: Housing same as in interchange number 9

Interchange Number: 9
Part Number(s) Housing: 5959063 LH 5959064 RH
Lenses: 5957823 LH 5957824 RH
Usage: 1967 El Camino or Chevelle Station wagon, Deluxe models
Notes: Housing same as in interchange number 8

Interchange Number: 10
Part Number(s) Lenses: 5958449)fits either side)
Usage: 1967 Chevelle except El Camino or Chevelle Station wagon

Interchange Number: 11
Part Number(s) Housings: 5960313 LH 5960314 RH Lenses: 5961793 LH 5961794 LH
Usage: 1968 Deluxe El Camino or Nomad station wagons
Notes: Lens are the same as in interchange number 12,15 and 16

Interchange Number: 12
Part Number(s) Housings: 5959945LH 5959946 RH Lenses: 5961793 LH 5961794 LH
Usage: 1968 El Camino except Deluxe; 1968 Malibu or Concours wagon
Notes: Lenses are the same as in interchange number 11, 15 and 16

Interchange Number: 13
Part Number(s) Lenses: 5959993 LH 5959994 LH
Usage: 1968 Chevelle Deluxe, except wagon or El Camino

Interchange Number: 14
Part Number(s) Lenses: 5959995 LH 5959996 LH
Usage: 1968 Malibu or SS 396, except El Camino or wagon models

Interchange Number: 15
Part Number(s) Housings: 5961648 LH 5961649 RH Lenses: 5961793 LH 5961794 LH
Usage: 1969 Deluxe El Camino or Nomad station wagons
Notes: Lens are the same as in interchange number 12,11 and 16

Interchange Number: 16
Part Number(s) Housings: 5961651 LH 5961652 RH Lenses: 5961793 LH 5961794 LH
Usage: 1969 El Camino Custom
Notes: Lens are the same as in interchange number 12,11 and 15

1970 Malibu and SS taillight

Interchange Number: 17
Part Number(s) Lenses: 5961097 LH 5961098 LH
Usage: 1969 Chevelle, except wagon or El Camino

Interchange Number: 18
Part Number(s): Housing: 5964203 LH 5964204 RH Lenses: 5964159 LH 5964120 LH
Usage: 1970-1972 El Camino Custom, Concours Station wagon
Notes: Lens the same as in interchange number 21

1970-1972 El Camino taillight

Early 1971 Malibu taillights. Note the circle pattern on the back up light.

Interchange Number: 19
Part Number(s): Housing: 5962793 LH 5962794 RH
 Lenses: L 5964287 LH 5964288 LH
Usage: 1970 Malibu, except wagon or El Camino
Notes: Housing same as in interchange number 20

Interchange Number: 20
Part Number(s): Housing: 5962793 LH 5962794 RH
 Lenses: 5964361 LH 5964362 LH
Usage: 1970 Chevelle, except Malibu, wagon or El Camino
Notes: Housing same as in interchange number 19

Interchange Number: 21
Part Number(s): Housing: 5964197 LH 5964198 RH
 Lenses: 5964159 LH 5964120 LH
Usage: 1970-1972 El Camino except Custom, except Concours Station wagon
Notes: Lens the same as in interchange number 18

Interchange Number: 22
Part Number(s): Housing: 5963421 LH 5963422 RH
 Lenses: 5963427 LH 5963428 LH
Usage: 1971 Chevelle, except Malibu, wagon or El Camino
Notes: Housing same as in interchange number 23

Interchange Number: 23
Part Number(s): Housing: 5963421 LH 5963422 RH
 Lenses: 5963425 LH 5963426 LH
Usage: 1971 Malibu, except wagon or El Camino
Notes: Housing same as in interchange number 22, 24, and 25

Interchange Number: 24
Part Number(s): Housing: 5963421 LH 5963422 RH
 Lenses: 5964503 LH 5964504 LH
Usage: 1972 Chevelle, except Malibu, wagon or El Camino
Notes: Housing same as in interchange number 23, 22, and 25

Interchange Number: 25
Part Number(s): Housing: 5963421 LH 5963422 RH
 Lenses: 5964497 LH 5964498 LH
Usage: 1972 Malibu, except wagon or El Camino
Notes: Housing same as in interchange number 22, 23. And 24

Late 1971-1972 Malibu taillights note the slight change in the back up lens

Lamps, Back Up

Many times, the backup lamp is part of the taillight assembly only separate lamp assemblies are listed here. If not listed the lamp is part of the taillight assembly, see that section for the interchanges.

Chevelle

Model	Interchange Number
1964	
Except El Camino	1
El Camino	3
1965	
Except El Camino	4
El Camino	2
1966	
Except El Camino	5
El Camino	7
1967	
Except El Camino	6
El Camino	2
1968	
Malibu	8
El Camino	8
1969-1970	
El Camino	9
1971	
Deluxe	10
Malibu	11
El Camino	9
1972	
Deluxe	12
Malibu	13
El Camino	14

1965 El Camino back up lamps were used again on the 1967 El Camino

Interchanges

Interchange Number: 1
Part Number(s): Housing: 910531 LH 910532 RH
Lenses 5955883 LH 5955884 RH
Usage: 1964 Chevelle, except wagon or El Camino

Interchange Number: 2
Part Number(s): Housing: 910798
Usage: 1965, 1967 El Camino or Chevelle station wagon

Interchange Number: 3
Part Number(s): Lens: 5955059 LH 5955060 RH
Usage: 1964 El Camino or Chevelle station wagon

Interchange Number: 4
Part Number(s): 910729 fits either side
Lens: 5956582
Usage: 1965 Chevelle, except El Camino or Chevelle station wagon
Notes: Lens same interchange number 6

Interchange Number: 5
Part Number(s): Lens: 5957813
Usage: 1966 Chevelle except El Camino or Chevelle station wagon

Interchange Number: 6
Part Number(s): Housing: 911417
Lens: 5956582
Usage: 1967 Chevelle except El Camino or Chevelle station wagon
Notes: Lens same interchange number 4

Interchange Number: 7
Part Number(s): Lens: 5957825 LH 5957826 RH
Usage: 1966 El Camino or Chevelle station wagon

Interchange Number: 8
Part Number(s): Lens: 5960079
Usage: 1968 Malibu, SS 396, El Camino or Chevelle station wagon

1969-1971 El Camino back up lamps were in the tailgate.

Interchange Number: 9
Part Number(s): Lens: 5961725
Usage: 1969-1971, El Camino or Chevelle station wagon

Interchange Number: 10
Part Number(s): Lens: 5964071 LH 5964072 RH
Usage: 1971 Chevelle Deluxe

Interchange Number: 11
Part Number(s): Lens: 5963431 LH 5963432 RH
Usage: 1971 Malibu

Interchange Number: 12
Part Number(s): Lens: 5964511 LH 5964512 RH
Usage: 1972 Chevelle Deluxe

Interchange Number: 13
Part Number(s): Lens: 5964505 LH 5964506 RH
Usage: 1972 Malibu

Interchange Number: 14
Part Number(s): Lens: 5961725 fits either side
Usage: 1972 El Camino

1964-1967 El Camino dome lamp

1968-1972 El Camino dome lamp

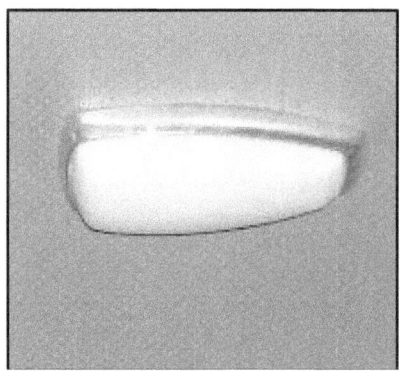
1964-1967 dome lamp

1968-1970 Dome lamp

1971-1972 dome lamp

Lamps, Dome
Chevelle

Model	Interchange Number
1964-1967	
Except El Camino	1
El Camino	3
1968-1970	
Except El Camino	5
El Camino	4
1971-1972	
Except El Camino	2
El Camino	4

Interchanges

Interchange Number: 1
Part Number(s): Housing: 4866918
Lens: 6279669
Usage: 1962-1971 Nova; 1964-1967 Chevelle; 1967-1969 Camaro, except convertibles or El Camino

Interchange Number: 2
Part Number(s): Housing: 20030351
Lens: 8732777
Usage: 1970-1976 Camaro; 1971-1976 Chevelle, except convertible or El Camino; 1971-1976 Nova; 1971-1976 full-size Chevrolet, except convertible; 1971-1976 Vega; 1971-1976 Monte Carlo

Interchange Number: 3
Part Number(s): Housing: 4866920
Lens: 6279671
Usage: 1964-1967 El Camino

Interchange Number: 4
Part Number(s): Housing: 8732781
Lens: 7731130
Usage: 1968-1975 El Camino; 1971-1975 GMC Sprint

Interchange Number: 5
Part Number(s): 7731128
Usage: 1968-1970 Chevelle, except El Camino or convertible

Chapter 10 Wheels, and Trim Rings

Wheels are sometimes marked with a ID code, this code is usually near the valve steam opening, but can be on the back of the spider of the wheel, however not all wheels were stamped.

Wheels

Two determining factors in wheel interchange are diameter and width. A third important consideration is offset, the distance the wheel is set back from the brake drum or rotor. Offset can be measured by noting the distance from the centerline of the rim to the inner side of the wheel. Incorrect offset can interfere with brake operation or cause tire clearance problems. (When offsets are known, they are given in the charts.) There is generally a "one-plus" rule in swapping wheels. This means you can usually, but not always, go up one-wheel size without a problem. For example, if your car is equipped with 14x5 inch wheels, you can usually install 14x6 inch wheels. Try to avoid large offset changes, though. If you have a wheel with, say, a 1/4-inch offset, you should not go to a wheel with a 3.00 inch offset.

Another suggestion for wheel swapping: If the wheels in question were an option on your model, they will usually fit your car.

Chevelle

Model	Interchange Number
1964-1965	
Stamped Steel Wheels	
14x5	1
14x6	2
1966	
Stamped Steel Wheels	
14x5	1
14x6	
Except SS 396	2
SS 396	3
1967	
Stamped Steel Wheels	
14x5	1
14x6	
Drum brakes	
Except SS 396	2
SS 396	3
Disc Brakes	6
Rally Wheel	
14x5	7
14x6	8
1968	
Stamped Steel Wheels	
Drum Brakes	
14x5	1
14x6	
Except SS 396	2

1967 Rally Wheel

SS 396..3
Disc Brakes..9
Rally Wheels
14x6
Except El Camino..10
El Camino..11

1969
Stamped Steel Wheels
Drum Brakes
14x5..1
14x6
Except SS 396..2
SS 396..3
Disc Brakes..9
Rally Wheels
14x6
Except El Camino..10
El Camino..11
SS Mag Wheel...12

1970
Stamped Steel Wheels
14x5..5
14x6..4
Rally Wheels
14x6
Except El Camino..10
El Camino..11
14x7
SS Mag Wheel...12

1971-1972
Stamped Steel Wheels
14x5..5
14x6..15
Rally Wheels
14x6..13
14x7..14
15x7
 5spoke Mag Wheel.....................................16

Interchanges

Interchange Number: 1
Part Number(s): 3872276
Size: 14x5 inches
ID: J
Usage: 1964-1969 Nova, except SS 396; 1964-1968 Chevelle;1964-1968 Buick Skylark, except GS 350 or GS 400; 1964-1968 Pontiac LeMans, except GTO; 1964-1968 Cutlass, except 442.
Notes: All with drum brakes

Interchange Number: 2
Part Number(s): 3928297
Size: 14x6 inches (11/32 inch offset)
ID:
Usage: 1965 Chevelle Z-16; 1966-1969 Chevelle, except SS 396

1968 Rally wheel with drum brakes

1968 Rally wheel with disc brakes.

1969-1970 SS style wheel

Interchange Number: 3
Part Number(s): 3871919
Size: 14x6 inches (1 inch offset)
ID: JK
Usage: 1966-1969 Chevelle SS 396; 1968-1969 Chevelle with F70x14 tires; 1964-1966 Pontiac GTO; 1964-1966 Oldsmobile 88; 1965-1970 Chevrolet C-10 or 1500 GMC C-10 van; 1966 Buick Gran Sport; 1966-1968 Skylark with heavy-duty suspension; 1966-1968 Cutlass with heavy-duty suspension; 1967 Pontiac LeMans; all with drum brakes

Interchange Number: 4
Part Number(s): 9791450
Size: 14x6 inches
ID: YB, CZ
Usage: 1970-1972 Chevelle; 1968 Cutlass with disc brakes; 1968 Skylark with disc brakes; 1968 LeMans with disc brakes; 1968-1972 LeMans; 1969-1972 Skylark; 1970-1972 Cutlass; 1970-1972 Grand Prix
Notes: This is the standard painted wheel.

Interchange Number: 5
Part Number(s): 3960336
Size: 14x5 inches
ID: YD, YF, DD
Usage: 1970-1972 Chevelle; 1969-1972 Nova; 1971-1972 Lemans, Ventura II

Interchange Number: 6
Part Number(s): 3901326
Size: 14x6 inches
ID:
Usage: 1967 Camaro, Chevelle, Skylark with disc brakes.
Notes: Stamped steel wheel

1971-1972 Rally wheels

1971-1972 Five spoke wheel

Interchange Number: 7
Part Number(5): 3901325
Size: 14x5 inches (0.88 inch offset)
ID: DA
Type: Rally
Usage: 1967 Camaro, Chevelle, Nova all with disc brakes

Interchange Number: 8
Part Number(s): 3918078
Size: 14x6 inches (0.88 inch offset)
ID: DG
Type: Rally
Usage: 1967 Camaro, Chevelle, Nova all with disc brakes

Interchange Number: 9
Part Number(s): 3928294
Size: 14x5 inches
ID: XE
Usage: 1968 Chevelle, except SS 396; 1968 Nova, except SS; both with disc brakes

Interchange Number: 10
Part Number(s): 3918077
Size: 14x6 inches
ID: XB
Type: Rally
Usage: 1968 Chevelle except El Camino; 1968 Camaro with drum brakes

Interchange Number: 11
Part Number(s): 3938984
Size: 14x6 inches
ID: YW
Type: Rally
Usage: 1968-1969 El Camino; 1968-1969 Camaro with disc brakes; 1968-1970 Nova

Interchange Number: 12
Part Number(s): 3975671
Size: 14x7 inches
ID: YA, YO
Type: SS wheel
Usage: 1969-1970 Chevelle, Camaro, Nova

Interchange Number: 13
Part Number(s): 334329
Size: 14x6 inches
ID: DE
Type: Rally wheel
Usage: 1971-1972 Chevelle; 1973-1974 Camaro; 1971-1974 Nova

Interchange Number: 14
Part Number(s): 334330
Size: 14x7 inches
ID:
Type: Rally wheel
Usage: 1971-1972 Chevelle; 1970-1974 Camaro; 1971-1974 Nova

Interchange Number: 15
Part Number(s): 9791450
Size: 14x6 inches
ID: HB, HF
Usage: 1971-1972 Chevelle. Cutlass, Skylark, Lemans without rally wheels

Interchange Number: 16
Part Number(s): 3998532
Size: 15x7 inches
ID:
Type: Five spoke
Usage: 1971-1972 Chevelle; 1970-1974 Camaro; 1971-1972 GMC Sprint

RPO N95 1966-1969 simulated mag wheel, 1970-1972 is similar

Wheels Covers

Wheel covers should not be confused with hubcaps. Hubcaps cover only the inner portion of the wheel and the lug nuts, while wheel covers cover the entire face of the steel wheel.

Wheel covers are identified by their design and size (diameter). Sometimes a wheel cover can be modified, by painting or changing the center domes to allow more interchanges. A description is given in the interchange charts under the note section if this is the case Note the diameter given is for the wheel not the diameter of the cover itself.

Chevelle
Model   **Interchange Number**
1964
PO1 Cover
Except Super Sport..1
Super Sport...2
RPO PO2 Wire Wheel..3
1965
RPO N96 Mag Wheel..6
PO1 Cover
Except Super Sport..4
Super Sport...5
RPO PO2 Wire Wheel..3
1966
RPO N96 Mag Wheel..6
PO1 Cover..10
RPO PO1 Wire Wheel..3

1967
RPO N96 Mag Wheel..11
PO1 Cover
Except Concurs or SS 396.................................7
Concours..8
SS 396...9
RPO PO2 Wire Wheel..12
1968
RPO N95 Wire Wheel...12
RPO N96 Mag style...11
RPO PO1 Cover..13
RPO PA2 Mag II cover...14
1969
RPO N95 Wire Wheel...15
RPO N96 Mag style...12
RPO PO1 Cover..16
RPO PA2 Mag II cover...14
1970
RPO N95 Wire Wheel...15
RPO N96 Mag style...12
RPO PO1 Cover..17
1971-1972
10 slots..18
Wire Cover...19
Ribbed Wire Cover..20
15-inch..21

1964 Standard SS wheel cover

1965 SS wheel covers.

The PO2 wire wheel cover for 1964-1966

1967 PO1 Wheel covers used different inserts, but the same basic wheel cover. Shown is the standard Chevelle unit.

Interchanges

Interchange Number: 1
Part Number(s): 3840900
Size: 14 inches
Description: Multiple spokes with starburst center
RPO PO1
Usage: 1964 Chevelle except Super Sport models

Interchange Number: 2
Part Number(s): 3840976
Diameter: 14 inches
RPO PO1
Description: Tri-spoke design emitting from a center cap that has a red SS log housed in a ribbed center cap, and nine slots along the outer edge
Usage: 1964 Impala with RPO Z03 Super Sport package; 1964 Malibu Super Sport

Interchange Number: 3
Part Number(s): 3839767
Diameter: 14 inches
RPO P02
Description: Wire spoke wheel cover, with tri-spinner center cap.
Usage: 1964-1966 full-size Chevrolet, Chevelle, Nova or Corvair

Interchange Number: 4
Part Number(s): 3860209
Size: 14 inches
Description: 24 indentions surrounding a center dome with 24 holes on the outer edge
RPO PO1
Usage: 1965 Chevelle except Super Sport models

Interchange Number: 5
Part Number(s): 3860240
Size: 14 inches
Description: Tri-spoke pattern with seven indentions between spokes, SS logo in the center
RPO PO1
Usage: 1965 Chevelle Super Sport models

Interchange Number: 6
Part Number(s): 3872860
Diameter: 14 inches
RPO N96
Description: Simulated mag wheel, dark gray with bow tie symbol in the center
Usage: 1965-1966 full-size Chevrolet, Chevelle, Nova

Interchange Number: 7
Part Number(s): 3890690
Size: 14 inches
Description: Red, White and blue stripes circling the bow-tie symbol in the center, with five slots with ribs
RPO PO1
Usage: 1967 Chevelle, except SS or Concours models
Notes: Interchanges 8 and 9 will fit if center inserts are changed.

Interchange Number: 8
Part Number(s): 3895851
Size: 14 inches
Description: Red, White and blue medallion symbol in the center, with five slots with ribs
RPO PO1
Usage: 1967 Chevelle Concours models
Notes: Interchanges 7 and 9 will fit if center inserts are changed.

Interchange Number: 9
Part Number(s): 3893340
Size: 14 inches
Description: Black and white SS logo in the center, with five slots with ribs
RPO PO1
Usage: 1967 Chevelle SS 396
Notes: Interchanges 7 and 8 will fit if center inserts are changed.

Interchange Number: 10
Part Number(s): 3875040
Size: 14 inches
Description: Starburst design with bow-tie symbol in the center with 12 slots on the pouter edge.
RPO PO1
Usage: 1966 Chevelle, all models

Interchange Number: 11
Part Number(s): 3903085
Diameter: 14 inches
RPO N96
Description: Simulated mag wheel, light gray with bow tie symbol in the center and brightly plated simulated lug nuts
Usage: 1967-1969 Camaro, full-size Chevrolet, Chevelle, Nova

You can swap out the wheel cover insert and have more interchanges. *By carefully unbending the tabs and swap out the center inserts of some wheel covers.*

1968 SS 396 wheel cover

Some wheel covers the center is bolted into place, when it is rusty like this use a penetrating solution before trying to remove.

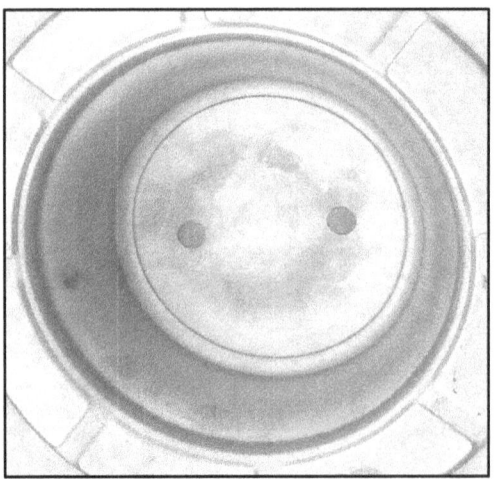

Some inserts are glued into place, they can be removed sometimes by applying heat with a heat gun, but the inserts are sometimes damaged, so use care.

1969-1970 PO2 wheel covers, are more commonly found on 1969-1974 Corvettes

Interchange Number: 12
Part Number(s): 3908760
Size: 14 inches
RPO N95
Description: Simulated wire wheel with round center dome with bow-tie symbol imprinted with the words "Chevrolet Motor Division"
Usage: 1967-1968 Camaro; 1967-1968, 1970-1971 Nova; 1967-1968 Chevelle

Interchange Number: 13
Part Number(s): 3918054
Size: 14 inches
Description: Five elongated slots along the outer edge. Logo center.
RPO PO1
Usage: 1968 Chevelle, all models
Notes: Regular Chevelle used insert part number 3890693 and features a bow-tie symbol, Concours uses part number 3898242 with the medallion and SS 396 uses part number 3920604 and reads SS396. To switch between the makes, swap out the center inserts.

Interchange Number: 14
Part Number(s): 3918079
Diameter: 14 inches
RPO PA2
Description: Simulated mag wheel, with six-spoke design with two slots in between the spokes,
Usage: 1968-1969 Camaro, full-size Chevrolet, Chevelle, Nova

Interchange Number: 15
Part Number(s): 3957060
Diameter: 14 inches
RPO N95
Description: Simulated wire wheel cover with large center dome imprinted with the words "Chevrolet Motor Division"
Usage: 1969 full-size Chevrolet; 1969-1970 Chevelle; 1969 Nova; 1969-1970 Camaro

Interchange Number: 16
Part Number(s): 3937878
Diameter: 14 inches
RPO PO1
Description: Eight Slots around the center dome, with 30 slots around the outer edge of the cover
Usage: 1969 Chevelle

Interchange Number: 17
Part Number(s): 3883390
Diameter: 14 inches
RPO PO1
Description: Six double slot divided by bars protruding from the center dome with the bow-tie symbol and the words "Chevrolet Motor Division"
Usage: 1970 Chevelle

Interchange Number: 18
Part Number(s): 3990554
Diameter: 14 inches
Description: 10 slot cover
Usage: 1971-1973 Camaro, Nova, Chevelle,

Interchange Number: 19
Part Number(s): 9942205
Diameter: 14 inches
Description: Simulated wire cover, with knobbed center hub. Imprinted with the words "Chevrolet Motor Division"
Usage: 1971-1975 Camaro, Nova, Chevelle,

Interchange Number: 20
Part Number(s): 3972260
Diameter: 14 inches
Description: Multiple wire spoke cover with cross flags in the center
Usage: 1971-1972 Camaro, Nova, Chevelle,

Interchange Number: 21
Part Number(s): 3972645
Diameter: 15 inches
Description: Multiple spokes surrounding a large center dome
Usage: 1972 Chevelle with 15-inch wheels; 1970-1972 Monte Carlo

1971-1972 Wire wheel cover

Caps, Styled Wheels

Chevelle

Model	Interchange Number
1967	
With Rally wheel	1
1968-1969	
With Rally wheel	2
With SS wheel	3
1970	
With Rally wheel	7
With SS wheel	
Early	3
Late	4
1971-1972	
With Rally wheel	7
With 5 spoke wheel	5

Interchanges

Interchange Number 1
Part Number(s): Cap, 3901710
Type: Rally
Description: Chrome-plated ornament; cap reads "disc brakes."
Usage: 1967 Chevelle; 1967 full-size Chevrolet
Notes:

Interchange Number: 2
Part Number(s): 3925800
Type: Rally
Description: Die-cast brightly plated. Ribbed sides. Imprinted with "Chevrolet Motor Division."
Usage: 1968-1969 Camaro; 1968-1970 Chevelle, 1968-1970 Nova, 1968-1970 full-size Chevrolet;1968-1970 Corvette; 1972-1973 Monte Carlo with 15 inch wheels; 1974-1975 Chevelle with 15 inch Rally wheels

Interchange Number: 3
Part Number(s): 3956770
Diameter: 14 inches
Type: Super Sport
Usage; 1969- early 1970 Camaro with SS package; 1969-early 1970 Nova with SS package; 1969- Early 1970 Chevelle Super Sport
Notes: First design. Change in 1970. Attaches with retainer.

Interchange Number: 4
Part Number(s): 3983323
Description: Cap holds SS long insert.
Type: Super Sport
Usage: Late 1970 Chevelle SS 396 or Nova SS; Camaro SS 350 or SS 396
Notes: Second design. Attaches with three screws.

Interchange Number: 5
Part Number(s): 3989478
Description: Small cap.
Type: With five spoke wheels
Usage: 1971-1972 Chevelle; 1971-1972 Nova; 1971-1979 Camaro

Trim Rings

Chevelle
Model   *Interchange Number*
1967-1970
Rally Wheels
14-inch
14x6..2
14x7..3
15-inch
15x6..4
15x7..1
SS wheel (1969-1970 only).............................6
1971-1972
Rally Wheels
14-inch
14x6..2
14x7..3
15-inch Wheel
15x6..4
15x7..1
Five Spoke Wheels..5

Interchanges

Interchange Number: 1
Part Number(s): 3901703
Type: Rally (15x7 inch)
Diameter Width: 2 3/8x16 5/8-inch overall diameter
Usage: 1967-1970 full-size Chevrolet; 1970-1975 Monte Carlo; 1973-1975 Chevelle; 1968-1975 Camaro all with 15 x7 inch Rally wheels

Interchange Number: 2
Part Number(s): 475019
Type: Rally (14x6 inch)
Diameter/Width: 15 5/8-inch overall diameter; 1.86-inch offset
Usage: 1967-1979 Camaro; 1967-1975, Chevelle, Nova; 1968-1970 full-size Chevrolet; 1967-1969 Corvette with 14-inchs; with rally wheels or PO6 wheel trim and hub cap option
Notes: Attaches with four clips

Interchange Number: 3
Part Number(s): 475020
Type: 14 x7 Rally wheels
Diameter/Width: 15 5/8-inch overall diameter; 2.24-inch offset
Usage; 1968-1975 Chevelle; 1968-1981 Camaro; 1968-1979 Nova with 14x7 inch Rally wheels

Interchange Number: 4
Part Number(s): 3901702
Type: Rally 15x6
Width: 16 5/8-inch overall diameter; 2-3/8-inch offset
Usage; 1967 Full-size Chevrolet station wagon with disc brakes; 1968-1969 Camaro; 1971-1974 Monte Carlo; 1975 Chevelle

Interchange Number: 5
Part Number(s): 3984523
Type: Steel spoke (15x7 inch)
Usage: 1971-1978 Camaro; 1971-1972 Chevelle; 1971-1972 Nova; all with SS package or Z-28 Camaro or with RPO Z86 Gymkhana; 1979-1981 Z-28

Chapter 11 Sheet Metal

1964-1965 Chevelles all used a plain flat hood, including the Super Sport models.

Hood

Hood interchange means the bare hood only without trim, emblems, or hinges. It is based on the original replacement part number and on original model usage. For example, some performance models such as the Chevelle SS 396 came with a special hood. Even though the interchange will say SS 396 only, the hood can be adapted to fit a regular Chevelle but may not be historically correct.

Chevelle
Model   *Interchange Number*
1964-1965
All 1
1966
Except SS 396 3
SS 396 4
1967
Except SS 396 5
SS 396 6
1968
Except SS 396 7
SS 396 8
1969
Except SS 396 9
SS 396 10

1970-1972
Except SS 11
SS
Without Cowl Induction 12
With Cowl Induction 13

Interchanges

Interchange Number: 1
Part Number(s): 3854140
Special Usage Description: Standard flat hood
Usage: 1964 Chevelle, all models and body styles.

Interchange Number: 2
Part Number(s): 3856895
Special Usage Description: Standard flat hood
Usage: 1965 Chevelle, all models and body styles.

Interchange Number: 3
Part Number(s): 3896557
Special Usage Description: Standard flat hood
Usage: 1966 Chevelle, all models and body style except SS 396

Interchange Number: 4
Part Number(s): 3896559
Special Usage Description: Super Sport hood with special indentations to hold louvers.
Usage: 1966 Chevelle SS 396

The 1966 SS 396 hood used two special vents part numbers 3891431 LH and 3891432 RH. They are stamped with the part numbers

Some trim is stamped with a part number as is the case of this 1967 simulated hood vent

Interchange Number: 5
Part Number(s): 3885987
Special Usage Description: Standard flat hood
Usage: 1967 Chevelle, all models and body styles except SS 396

Interchange Number: 6
Part Number(s): 3897504
Special Usage Description: Super Sport hood with special indention on each side to hold simulated air vent.
Usage; 1967 Chevelle SS 396

Interchange Number: 7
Part Number(s): 3940657
Special Usage Description: Standard flat hood
Usage: 1968 Chevelle, all models and body styles except SS 396

Interchange Number: 8
Part Number(s): 3940660
Special Usage Description: Super Sport hood; twin dome design with cutouts at rear edge of hood to support louvers
Usage: 1968 Chevelle SS 396
Notes: Use caution: Two different hoods were used. Both will fit, but each used unique hinges and hood springs. You will need those parts to interchange as they will not interchange between the hood types.

Interchange Number: 9
Part Number(s): 3940631
Special Usage Description: Standard flat hood
Usage: 1969 Chevelle, all models and body style except SS 396

Interchange Number: 10
Part Number(s): 3940632
Special Usage Description: Super Sport hood; twin dome design with cutouts at rear edge
Usage: 1969 Chevelle SS 396
Notes: Although similar, 1968 and 1969 hood will not interchange.

Interchange Number: 11
Part Number(s): 3977767
Special Usage Description: Standard flat hood
Usage: 1970-1972 Chevelle, all models and body style except those with the SS package.

1967 SS 396 hood with simulated hood vents part number 3897500

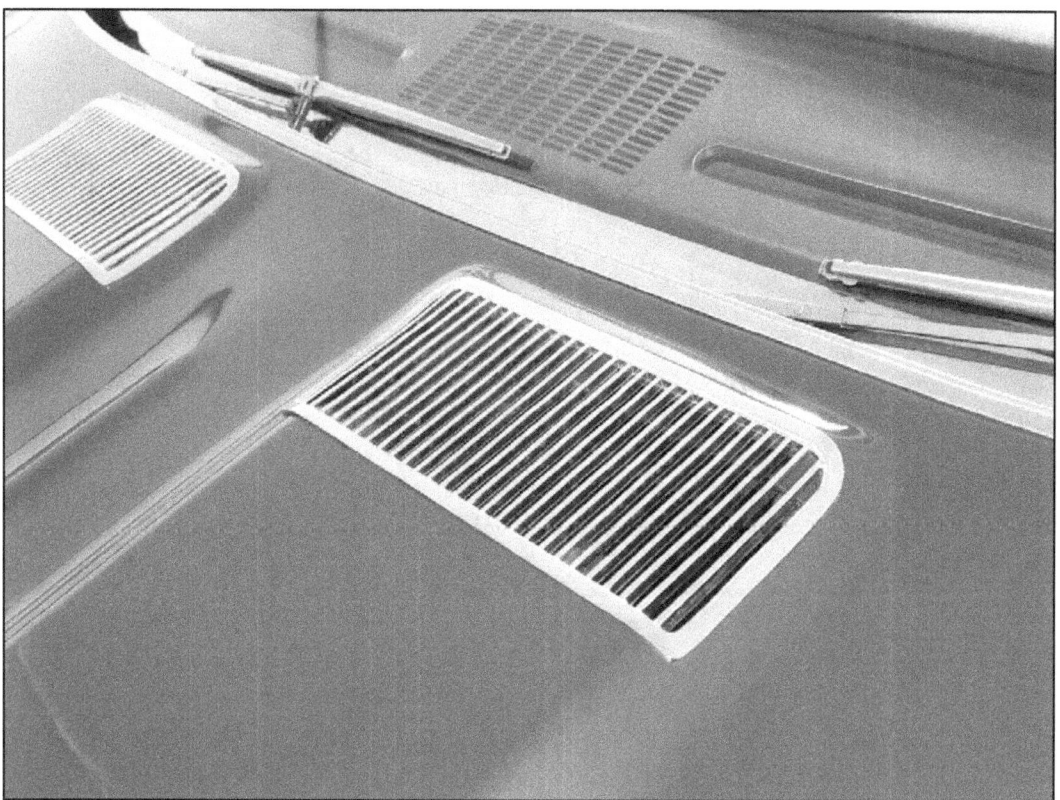

1968-1969 SS 396 models used a twin dome design hood. Shown is the 1968 version with 3915489 LH and 3915490 RH both years. They are stamped with part numbers

The standard Super Sport Hood for 1970-1972 models.

1970-1972 ZL2 hood was available on all big blocks.

Interchange Number: 12
Part Number(s): 3987022
Special Usage Description: Super Sport hood with center dome but without induction cutout
Usage: 1970-1972 Chevelle with SS package
Notes: Not for those with cowl induction.

Interchange Number: 14
Part Number(s): 3987028
Special Usage Description: Super Sport hood with ZL-2 cowl induction. Features cutout on center dome.
Usage: 1970-1972 Chevelle SS, except 1971-72 SS 350

Hinges, Hood

Chevelle

Model	Interchange Number
1964	
All	5
1965-1967	
All	1
1968	
Early	2
Late	3
1969	
All	4
1970-1972	
All	5

Interchanges

Interchange Number: 1
Part Number(s): RH, 3910668; LH, 3910667
Usage: 1965-1967 Chevelle; 1965-1967 full-size Chevrolet; 1966-1967 Nova; 1967-1969 Camaro, Firebird

Interchange Number: 2
Part Number(s): RH, 3910680; LH, 3910679
Usage: Early-built 1968 Chevelle
Notes: (before 11-30-67) has longer rear bolt slot. Interchange 3 will fit if rear bolt slot is elongate to fit

Interchange Number: 3
Part Number(s): RH, 39266830; LH, 39126829
Usage: Late-built (beginning 12-1-67) 1968 Chevelle; 1968 full-size Chevrolet; 1968-1974 Nova; 1971-1974 Ventura II; 1973-1974 Omega or Apollo

interchange Number: 4
Part Number(s): RH, 3949202; LH, 3949201
Usage: 1969 Chevelle; 1969 full-size Chevrolet

Interchange Number: 5
Part Number: 3825827 LH 3825828 RH
Usage: 1963-1964 full-size Chevrolet; 1963-1965 Chevy; 1964 Chevelle

Interchange Number: 6
Part Number(s): 3976675 LH 3976676 RH
Usage: 1970-1972 Chevelle; 1970-1972 Monte Carlo; 1970 full-size Chevrolet

Springs, Hood Hinge

Chevelle

Model	Interchange Number
1964-1965	
All	1
1966-1967	
Except SS 396	2
SS 396	1
1968	
Early	3
Late	2
1969-1970	
All	2
1971-1972	
Except SS or El Camino	2
El Camino	1
SS	1
Heavy Chevy	1

Interchanges

Interchange Number: 1
Part Number(s): 3848272
Usage: 1963-1966 full-size Chevrolet; 1963-1964 Nova; 1964-1965 Chevelle; 1964-1967 Chevelle SS 396; 1964-1967 Cutlass,; 1964-1967 Lemans;1967-68 Pontiac Firebird; 1967-1969 Camaro SS 350 or SS 396; 1969-1970 full-size Pontiac; 1969 Pontiac Firebird (except 400ci); 1970 full-size Chevrolet; 1970 Pontiac Firebird; 1971 Chevelle SS; 1971-1972 Monte Carlo; 1971-1972 El Camino; 1971-1972 Pontiac LeMans; 1972 Chevelle SS or Heavy Chevy
Notes: Do not use in 1963 Chevrolet with Z-11 option; severe hood damage will occur.

Interchange Number: 2
Part Number(s): 3864680
Free length: 8 1 3/32 inches
Usage: 1965 Chevy II; 1966-1967 Chevelle, except SS 396; Late 1968 Chevelle second design; 1968 full-size Chevrolet; 1969-1972 Chevelle, except 1971-1972 SS, El Camino, or Heavy Chevy
Notes: Beginning Dec 1, 1968 for Chevelle models.

Interchange Number: 3
Part Number(s): 3926800
Free length: 8-3/4 inches
Usage: Early 1968 Chevelle; 1968-1970 Pontiac LeMans; 1968-1975 Nova; 1971-1972 LeMans (with chrome bumper); 1971-1975 Pontiac Ventura II; 1973 LeMans
Notes: Up to Nov 30, 1968 for Chevelle models.

Front Fenders

Due to design changes such as side-marker lamps, then is very little interchanging in the front fenders. Also, in some cases a fender from a coupe or sedan Chevelle will not fit an El Camino or vice versa.

Interchange is for the bare unit only without nameplates, wheel well trim, or side moldings. However, these factors do come into play as side trim and nameplates require holes to be matched or drilled. To mount the fender, existing holes may have to be filled and new ones drilled, depending on your intended usage. Remember, it is always easier to drill new holes than it is to cover up existing ones. Look for a fender that matches your particular application or without any other trim, if possible. This can be a problem when swapping from a loaded model like Concours which was loaded with trim, to your SS 396. With new reproduction fenders this is not a problem.

Chevelle

Model	Interchange Number
1964	
All	1
1965	
All	2
1966	
All	3
1967	
All	4
1968	
All	5
1969	
All	6
1970	
Except El Camino	8
El Camino	7
1971-1972	
Except El Camino	9
El Camino	10

Interchanges

Interchange Number: 1
Part Number(s): RH, 3858944; LH, 38589943
Usage: 1964 Chevelle, all models and body styles.

Interchange Number: 2
Part Number(s): RH, 38737899; LH, 38737898
Usage: 1965 Chevelle, all models and body styles.

The underside of the 1970-1972 Cowl induction hood.

The 1970-1972 El Camino used a special fender and those from other body style (except wagons) will not fit.

Interchange Number: 3
Part Number(s): RH, 3886308; LH, 3886307
Usage: 1966 Chevelle, all models and body styles.

Interchange Number: 4
Part Number(s): RH, 3904677; LH, 3904676
Usage: 1967 Chevelle, all models and body styles

Interchange Number: 5
Part Number(s): RH, 3924118; LH, 3924117
Usage: 1968 Chevelle, all models and body styles

Interchange Number: 6
Part Number(s): RH, 3953854; LH, 3953853
Usage: 1969 Chevelle, all models and body styles

Interchange Number: 7
Part Number(s): RH, 3970612; LH, 3970611
Usage: 1970 Chevelle station wagon or El Camino
Notes: Sedan, coupe, or convertible fenders will not fit.

Interchange Number: 8
Part Number(s): RH, 3970610; LH,3970609
Usage: 1970 Chevelle sedan, coupe, or convertible
Notes: Fenders from El Camino or station wagon will not fit

Interchange Number: 9
Part Number(s): RH, 325038; LH,335037
Usage: 1971-1972 Chevelle sedan, coupe, or convertible
Notes: Fenders from El Camino or station wagon will not fit

Interchange Number: 10
Part Number(s): RH, 325040; LH, 35039
Usage: 19701-1972 Chevelle station wagon or El Camino
Notes: Sedan, coupe, or convertible fenders will not fit.

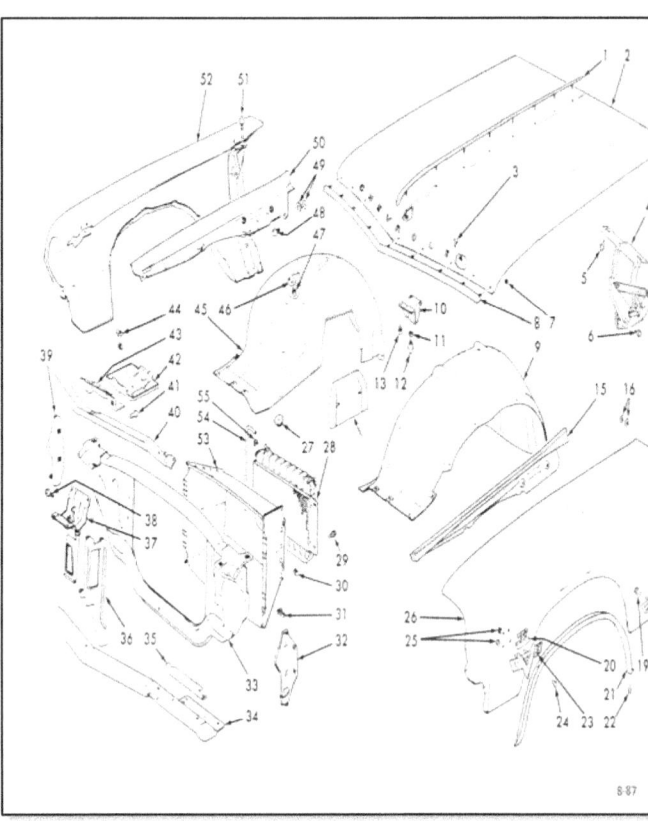

1965 front sheet metal. 1964 is similar. (Chevrolet)

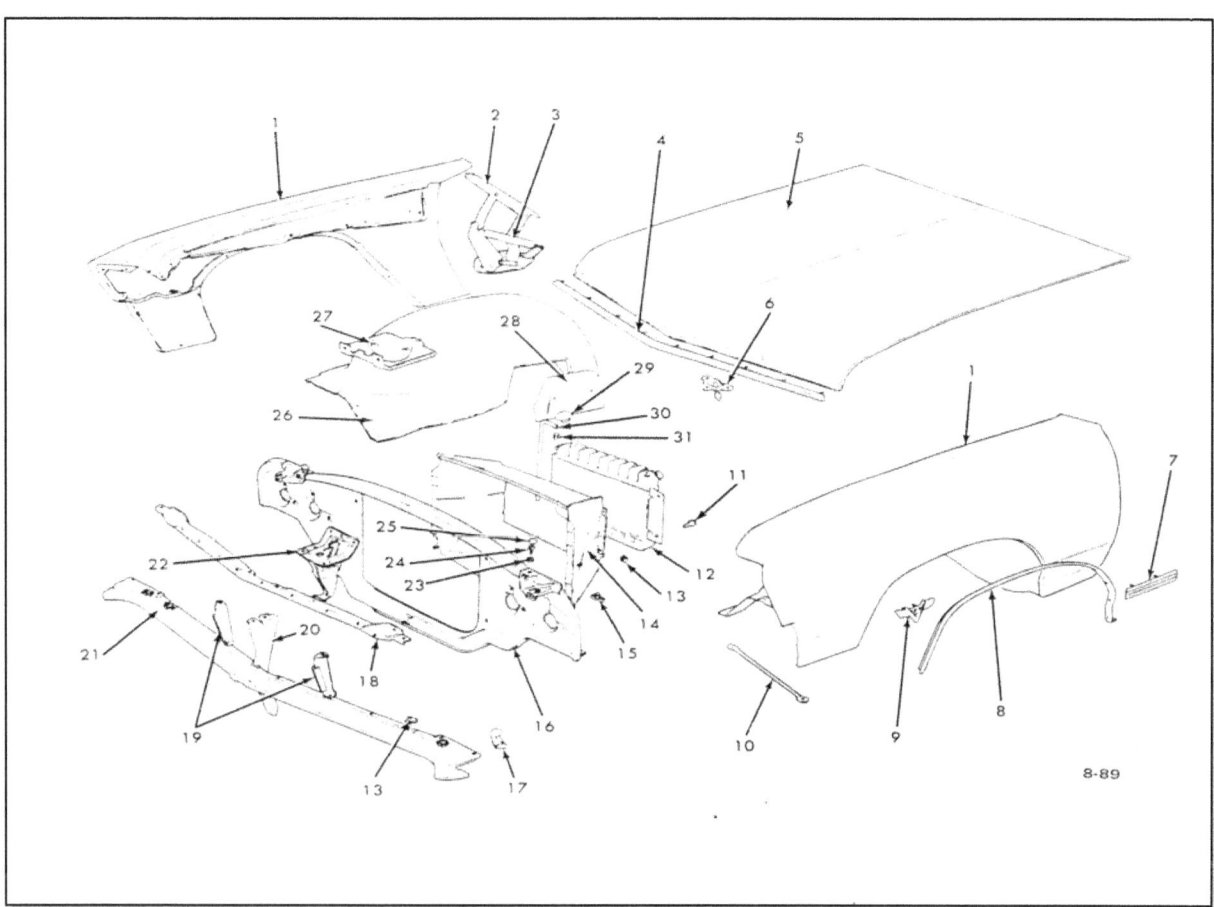

1967 Front sheet metal, 1966 is similar (Chevrolet)

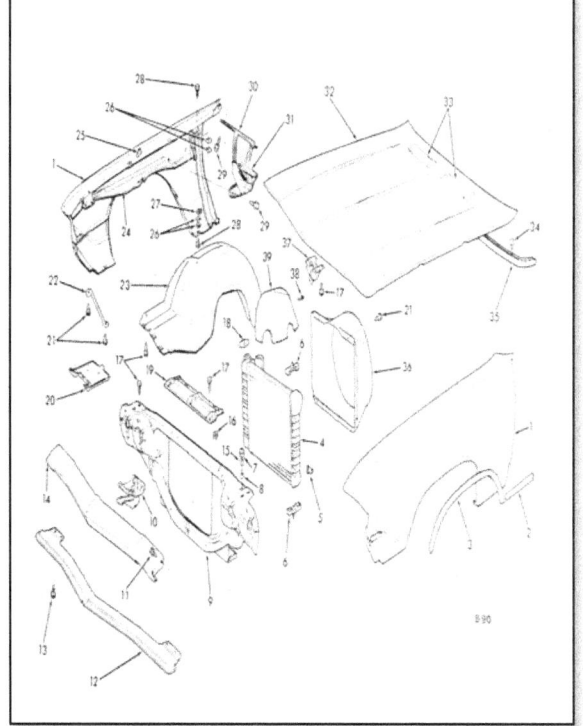

1968 Chevelle front sheet metal, 1969 is similar. (Chevrolet)

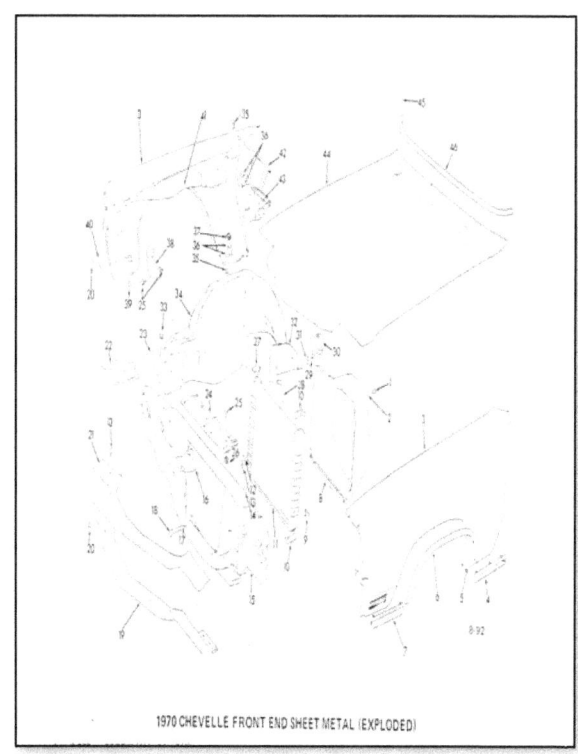

1970 Front sheet metal, 1971-1972 is is similar. (Chevrolet)

Skirts, Front Fenders

Also called an inner fender, or fender liner.

Chevelle

Model	Interchange Number
1964	
All	1
1965	
All	2
1966	
All	3
1967	
All	4
1968-1972	
All	5

Interchanges

Interchange Number: 1
Part Number(s): RH, 3864322; LH, 3853635
Usage: 1964 Chevelle, all models and body styles.

Interchange Number: 2
Part Number(s): RH, 3864324; LH, 3856893
Usage: 1965 Chevelle, all models and body styles.

Interchange Number: 3
Part Number(s): RH, 3872138; LH, 3872137
Usage: 1966 Chevelle, all models and body styles.

Interchange Number: 4
Part Number(s): RH, 3885986; LH, 3885985
Usage: 1967 Chevelle, all models and body styles.

Interchange Number: 5
Part Number(s): RH, 3992604 LH, 6264843
Usage: 1968-1972 Chevelle, all models and body styles.

Support Wall, Radiator

Chevelle

Model	Interchange Number
1964	
All	1
1965	
All	2
1966	
All	3
1967	
All	4
1968	
Except 396-ci	5
396-ci	6
1969	
All	5
1970	
350-ci	
Without Air Conditioning	7
With Air Conditioning	8
396-ci or 454-ci	
Without Air Conditioning	7
With Air Conditioning	9
1971-1972	
350-ci	
Without Air Conditioning	10
With Air Conditioning	11
396-ci or 454-ci	11

Interchange

Interchange Number: 1
Part Number(s):3853569
Usage: 1964 Chevelle, all models and body styles

Interchange Number: 2
Part Number(s):3856901
Usage: 1965 Chevelle, all models and body styles

Interchange Number: 3
Part Number(s):3897533
Usage: 1966 Chevelle, all models and body styles

Interchange Number: 4
Part Number(s):3907632
Usage: 1967 Chevelle, all models and body styles

Interchange Number: 5
Part Number(s):3956068
Usage: 1968 Chevelle six cylinder; 1968 Chevelle with T.H. 350 without air conditioning; 1968 Chevelle with V-8 except with Powerglide or 396-ci V-8; 1969 Chevelle all models and boy styles

Interchange Number: 6
Part Number(s):3956069
Usage: 1968 Chevelle with T.H. 350 with air conditioning; 1968 Chevelle with 396-ci V-8.

Interchange Number: 7
Part Number(s):3958368
Usage: 1970 Chevelle with six cylinder without air conditioning or H.D. cooling; 1970 Chevelle with 307-ci or 350-ci V-8 without air conditioning or H.D,. cooling

Interchange Number: 8
Part Number(s):3957351
Usage: 1970 Chevelle with 307-ci or 350-ci V-8 with air conditioning or H.D. cooling; 1970 Chevelle with 396-ci or 454-ci except with air conditioning or 4.10 rear gears

Interchange Number: 9
Part Number(s):3975388
Usage: 1970 Chevelle with 396-ci or 454-ci with 4.10 gears;1970 Chevelle with 396-ci or 454-ci with 4.10 gears; 1970 Chevelle with 396-ci or 454-ci with air conditioning or H.D. cooling

Interchange Number: 10
Part Number(s):6264807
Usage: 1971-1972 Chevelle with six cylinder, 307-ci or 350-ci without air conditioning or H.D. cooling

Interchange Number: 11
Part Number(s):6264811
Usage: 1971-1972 Chevelle with six cylinder, 307-ci or 350-ci with air conditioning or H.D. cooling; 1971-1972 Chevelle with 402-ci or 454-ci with or without air conditioning; 1971-1972 Chevelle with 4.10 gears

Front Doors

On most models, doors were changed only when a significant design change occurred, so the interchange is larger than it may at first appear. Factors to consider are that they are unique to each side of the car and to different body styles.

Interchange is the complete door, minus the interior door panel and any exterior trim moldings. In this chapter, two-door sedan means a pillar coupe.

Some doors may have to be stripped of their glass and other hardware to interchange. This is especially true when swapping a hardtop door to a convertible.

Chevelle

Model	Interchange Number
1964-1965	
2 door Sedan	1
2 door hardtop or convertible	2
El Camino	3
1966-1967	
2 door Sedan	4
2 door hardtop or convertible	5
El Camino	6
1968	
2 door Sedan	8
2 door hardtop or convertible	7
El Camino	9
1969	
2 door Sedan	8
2 door hardtop or convertible	10
El Camino	9
1970-1971	
2 door hardtop or convertible	11
El Camino	9
1972	
2 door hardtop or convertible	12
El Camino	9

Interchanges

Interchange Number: 1
Part Number(s): RH, 4492500; LH, 4492501
Usage: 1964-1965 Chevelle two-door sedan, except El Camino

Interchange Number: 2
Part Number(s): RH, 4492506; LH, 4492507
Usage: 1964-1965 Chevelle two-door hardtop or convertible
Notes: When swapping from hardtop to convertible, glass and all hardware must be removed and replaced with convertible components.

Interchange Number: 3
Part Number(s): RH, 4492504; LH, 4492505
Usage: 1964-1965 El Camino
Notes: Unique door. Station wagon door will not interchange

Interchange Number: 4
Part Number(s): RH, 7661576; LH, 7661577
Usage: 1966-67 Chevelle two-door sedan, except El Camino.

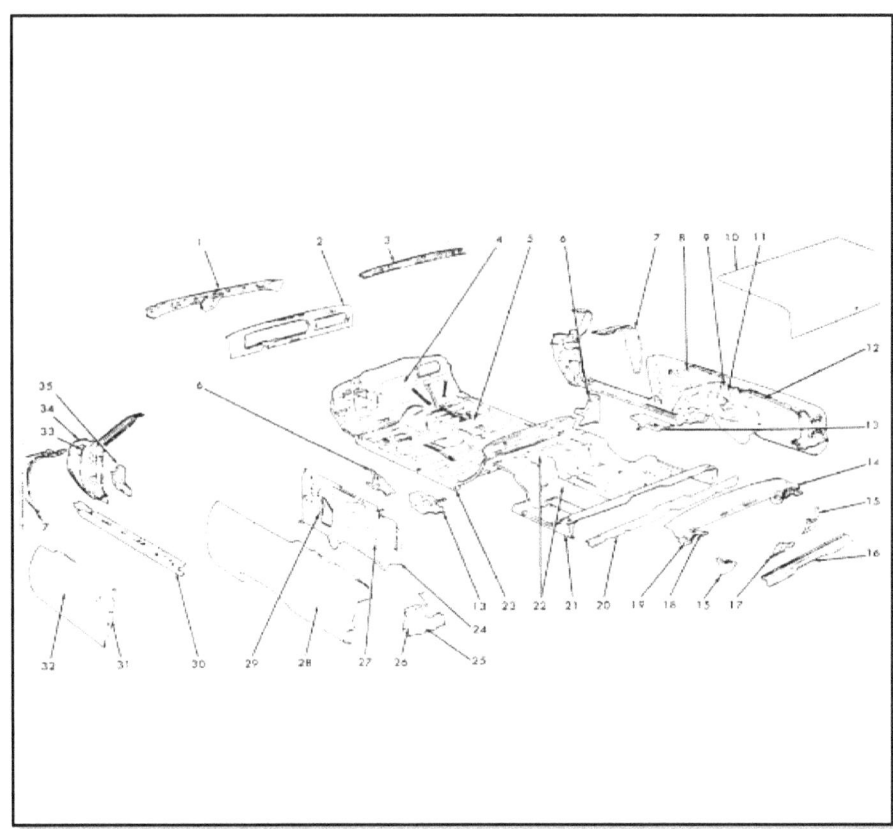

1964-1965 Convertible sheet metal (Chevrolet)

1964-1965 2-door coupe sheet metal hardtop is similar. (Chevrolet)

Interchange Number: 5
Part Number(s): RH, 7661578; LH, 7661579
Usage: 1966-1967 El Camino
Notes: Unique door assembly. Station wagon will not fit.

Interchange Number: 6
Part Number(s): RH, 7661580; LH, 76615181
Usage: 1966-1967 Chevelle two-door hardtop or convertible

Interchange Number: 7
Part Number(s): RH, 7742314; LH, 7742315
Usage: 1968 Chevelle two-door hardtop or convertible

interchange Number: 8
Part Number(s): RH, 8716906; LH, 8716907
Usage: 1968-1969 Chevelle two-door sedan, except El Camino

Interchange Number: 9
Part Number(s): RH, 9888121; LH, 9888122
Usage: 1968-1972 El Camino; 1971-1972 CMC Sprint
Notes: Unique door; station wagon will not fit.

Interchange Number: 10
Part Number(s): RH, 8716910; LH, 8716911
Usage: 1969 Chevelle two-door hardtop or convertible

Interchange Number: 11
Part Number(s): RH, 9861034; LH, 9888153
Usage: 1970-1971 Chevelle coupe or convertible
Notes: Driver's side door in interchange number 12 will interchange, but passenger's side will not fit

Interchange Number: 12
Part Number(s): RH, 9888152; LH, 9888153
Usage: 1972 Chevelle coupe or convertible
Notes: Driver's side door in interchange number 11 will interchange, but passenger's side will not fit

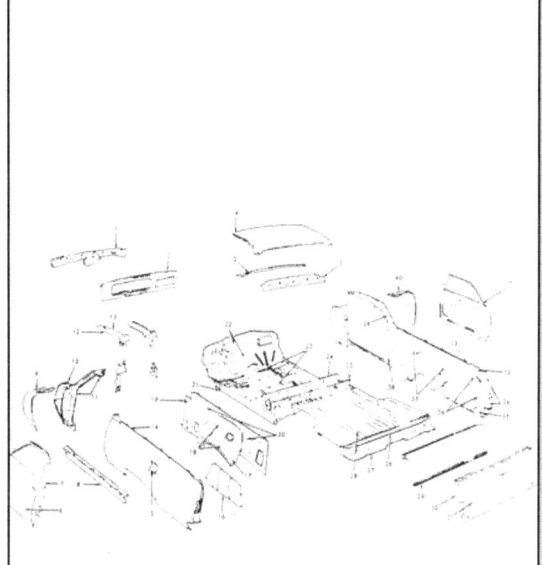

1964-1966 El Camino sheet metal (Chevrolet)

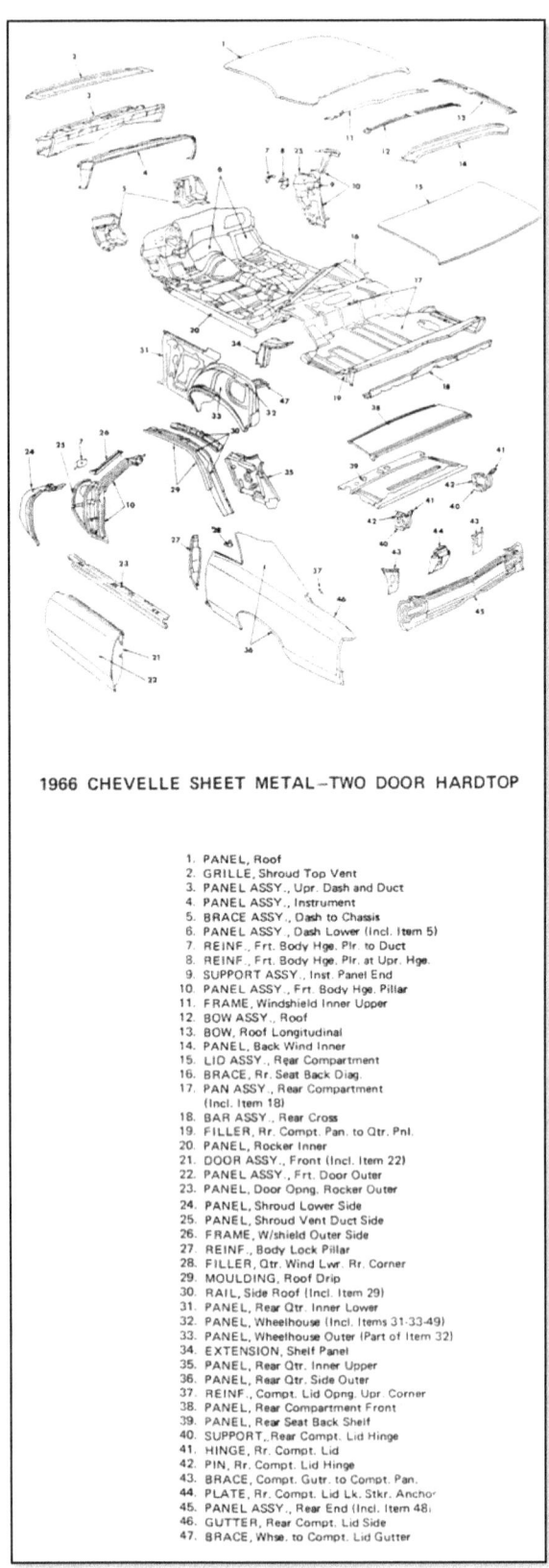

1966 CHEVELLE SHEET METAL—TWO DOOR HARDTOP

1. PANEL, Roof
2. GRILLE, Shroud Top Vent
3. PANEL ASSY., Upr. Dash and Duct
4. PANEL ASSY., Instrument
5. BRACE ASSY., Dash to Chassis
6. PANEL ASSY., Dash Lower (Incl. Item 5)
7. REINF., Frt. Body Hge. Plr. to Duct
8. REINF., Frt. Body Hge. Plr. at Upr. Hge.
9. SUPPORT ASSY., Inst. Panel End
10. PANEL ASSY., Frt. Body Hge. Pillar
11. FRAME, Windshield Inner Upper
12. BOW ASSY., Roof
13. BOW, Roof Longitudinal
14. PANEL, Back Wind Inner
15. LID ASSY., Rear Compartment
16. BRACE, Rr. Seat Back Diag.
17. PAN ASSY., Rear Compartment (Incl. Item 18)
18. BAR ASSY., Rear Cross
19. FILLER, Rr. Compt. Pan. to Qtr. Pnl.
20. PANEL, Rocker Inner
21. DOOR ASSY., Front (Incl. Item 22)
22. PANEL ASSY., Frt. Door Outer
23. PANEL, Door Opng. Rocker Outer
24. PANEL, Shroud Lower Side
25. PANEL, Shroud Vent Duct Side
26. FRAME, W/shield Outer Side
27. REINF., Body Lock Pillar
28. FILLER, Qtr. Wind Lwr. Rr. Corner
29. MOULDING, Roof Drip
30. RAIL, Side Roof (Incl. Item 29)
31. PANEL, Rear Qtr. Inner Lower
32. PANEL, Wheelhouse (Incl. Items 31-33-49)
33. PANEL, Wheelhouse Outer (Part of Item 32)
34. EXTENSION, Shelf Panel
35. PANEL, Rear Qtr. Inner Upper
36. PANEL, Rear Qtr. Side Outer
37. REINF., Compt. Lid Opng. Upr. Corner
38. PANEL, Rear Compartment Front
39. PANEL, Rear Seat Back Shelf
40. SUPPORT, Rear Compt. Lid Hinge
41. HINGE, Rr. Compt. Lid
42. PIN, Rr. Compt. Lid Hinge
43. BRACE, Compt. Gutr. to Compt. Pan.
44. PLATE, Rr. Compt. Lid Lk. Stkr. Anchor
45. PANEL ASSY., Rear End (Incl. Item 48)
46. GUTTER, Rear Compt. Lid Side
47. BRACE, Whse. to Compt. Lid Gutter

1966 2 door sheet metal, 1967 is similar. (Chevrolet)

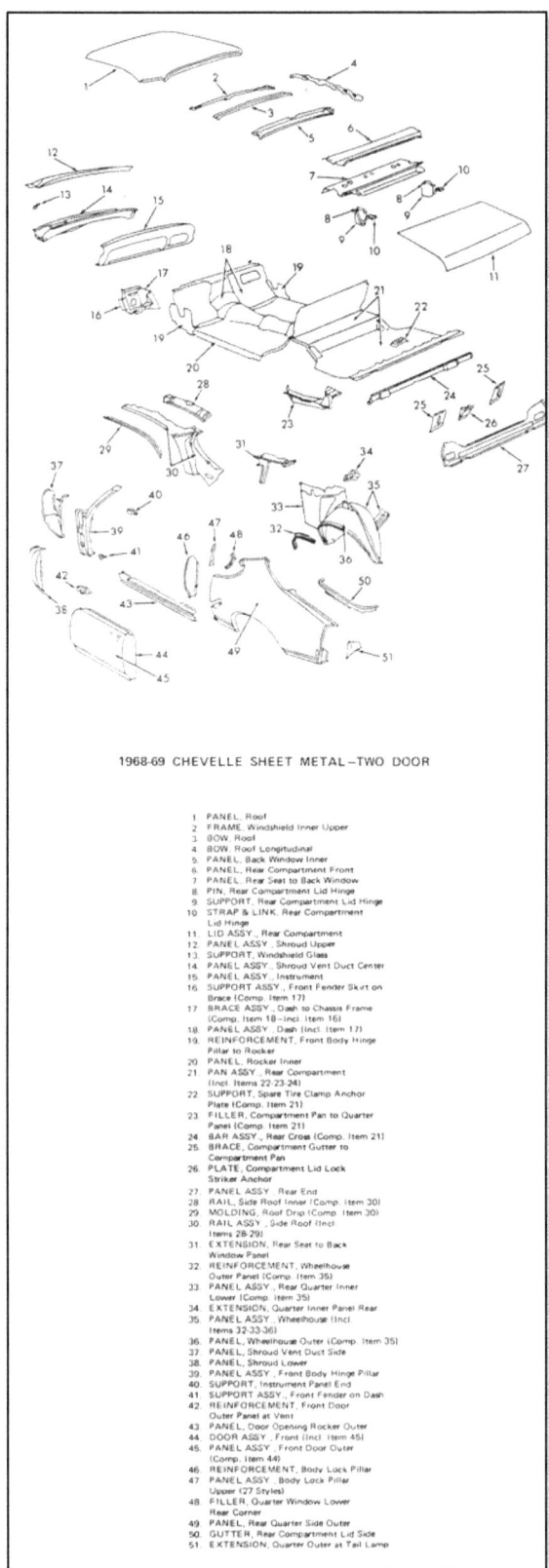

1968-69 CHEVELLE SHEET METAL—TWO DOOR

1. PANEL, Roof
2. FRAME, Windshield Inner Upper
3. BOW, Roof
4. BOW, Roof Longitudinal
5. PANEL, Back Window Inner
6. PANEL, Rear Compartment Front
7. PANEL, Rear Seat to Back Window
8. PIN, Rear Compartment Lid Hinge
9. SUPPORT, Rear Compartment Lid Hinge
10. STRAP & LINK, Rear Compartment Lid Hinge
11. LID ASSY., Rear Compartment
12. PANEL ASSY., Shroud Upper
13. SUPPORT, Windshield Glass
14. PANEL ASSY., Shroud Vent Duct Center
15. PANEL ASSY., Instrument
16. SUPPORT ASSY., Front Fender Skirt on Brace (Comp. Item 17)
17. BRACE ASSY., Dash to Chassis Frame (Comp. Item 18—Incl. Item 16)
18. PANEL ASSY., Dash (Incl. Item 17)
19. REINFORCEMENT, Front Body Hinge Pillar to Rocker
20. PANEL, Rocker Inner
21. PAN ASSY., Rear Compartment (Incl. Items 22-23-24)
22. SUPPORT, Spare Tire Clamp Anchor Plate (Comp. Item 21)
23. FILLER, Compartment Pan to Quarter Panel (Comp. Item 21)
24. BAR ASSY., Rear Cross (Comp. Item 21)
25. BRACE, Compartment Gutter to Compartment Pan
26. PLATE, Compartment Lid Lock Striker Anchor
27. PANEL ASSY., Rear End
28. RAIL, Side Roof Inner (Comp. Item 30)
29. MOLDING, Roof Drip (Comp. Item 30)
30. RAIL ASSY., Side Roof (Incl. Items 28-29)
31. EXTENSION, Rear Seat to Back Window Panel
32. REINFORCEMENT, Wheelhouse Outer Panel (Comp. Item 35)
33. PANEL ASSY., Rear Quarter Inner Lower (Comp. Item 35)
34. EXTENSION, Quarter Inner Panel Rear
35. PANEL ASSY., Wheelhouse (Incl. Items 32-33-36)
36. PANEL, Wheelhouse Outer (Comp. Item 35)
37. PANEL, Shroud Vent Duct Side
38. PANEL, Shroud Lower
39. PANEL ASSY., Front Body Hinge Pillar
40. SUPPORT, Instrument Panel End
41. SUPPORT ASSY., Front Fender on Dash
42. REINFORCEMENT, Front Door Outer Panel at Vent
43. PANEL, Door Opening Rocker Outer
44. DOOR ASSY., Front (Incl. Item 45)
45. PANEL ASSY., Front Door Outer
46. REINFORCEMENT, Body Lock Pillar
47. PANEL ASSY., Body Lock Pillar Upper (27 Styles)
48. FILLER, Quarter Window Lower Rear Corner
49. PANEL, Rear Quarter Side Outer
50. GUTTER, Rear Compartment Lid Side
51. EXTENSION, Quarter Outer at Tail Lamp

1968-1969 2 door sheet metal. (Chevrolet)

1970-72 EL CAMINO REAR END SHEET METAL

1. PANEL, OUTER
2. PANEL, rear inner front upper
3. PANEL, Rear Compartment
4. BAR ASSY., Rear Cross
5. BAR ASSY., Rear Cross Front
6. SCREW
7. PANEL
8. SCREW (8-18 x 3/8)
9. PLATE, Lock Striker upr.
10. PLATE, Lock Striker rear
11. SPACER, Lock Striker
12. STRIKER
13. SCREW
14. COVER
15. BOLT
16. WASHER (3/8 X1X 3/32)
17. CABLE
18. PANEL ASSY., Outer
19. SCREW (8-18 x 3/8)
20. SCREW
21. PLATE
22. SCREW
23. HANDLE
24. ESCUTCHEON
25. LOCK ASSY.
26. ROD, R.H.
    ROD, L.H.
27. LOCK ASSY.
28. SCREW
29. GATE ASSY.
30. PLUG, Black Plastic (5/16)
31. WASHER
32. SPRING
33. BOLT
34. BOLT
35. PIN
36. STRAP, Hinge Gate Side
37. STRAP, Hinge Body Side
38. PANEL, Rear Inner
39. PANEL, Rear Inner Front Upper
40. EXTENSION, Pan to oute Panel Filler Front
41. FILLER, Pan to Qtr. Panel
42. PANEL, Outer
43. PANEL, Wheelhouse Ou
44. PANEL, Wheelhouse
45. PANEL, Rear Qtr. Inner Front

(Chevrolet)

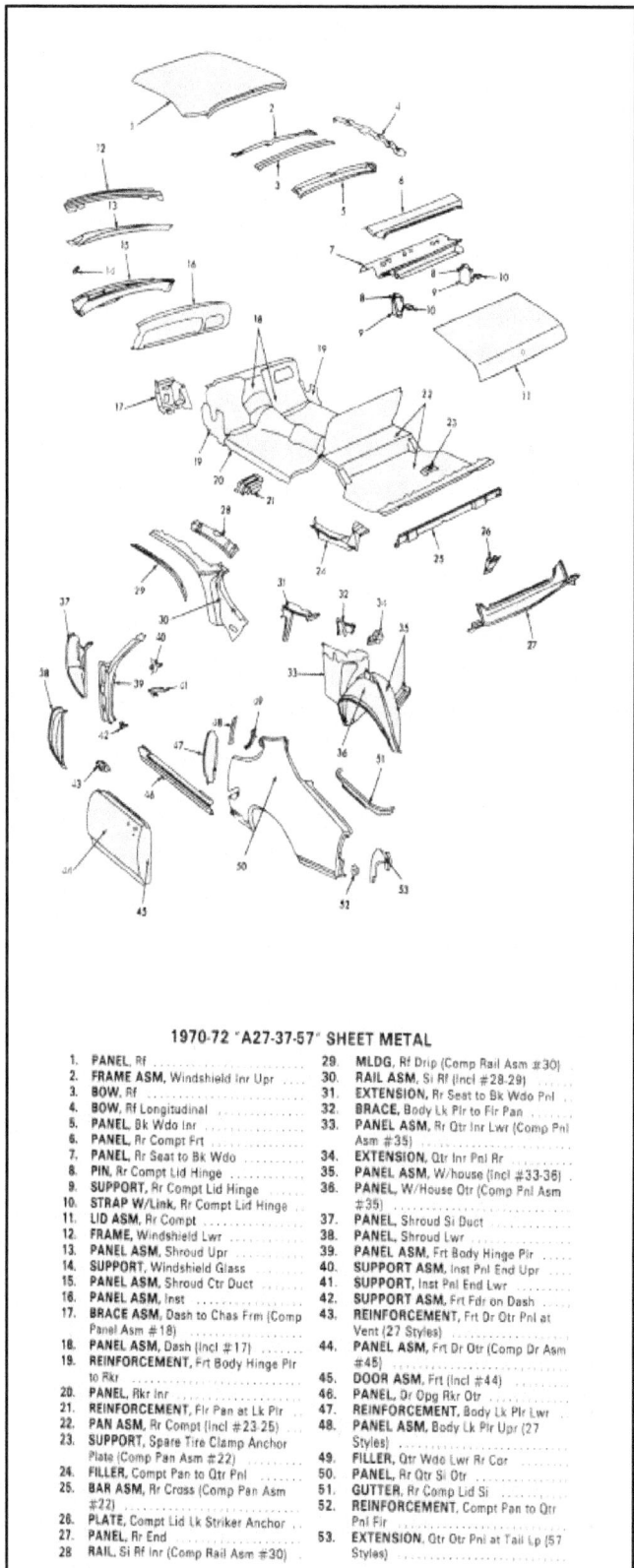

1970-72 "A27-37-57" SHEET METAL

1. PANEL, Rf
2. FRAME ASM, Windshield Inr Upr
3. BOW, Rf
4. BOW, Rf Longitudinal
5. PANEL, Bk Wdo Inr
6. PANEL, Rr Compt Frt
7. PANEL, Rr Seat to Bk Wdo
8. PIN, Rr Compt Lid Hinge
9. SUPPORT, Rr Compt Lid Hinge
10. STRAP W/Link, Rr Compt Lid Hinge
11. LID ASM, Rr Compt
12. FRAME, Windshield Lwr
13. PANEL ASM, Shroud Upr
14. SUPPORT, Windshield Glass
15. PANEL ASM, Shroud Ctr Duct
16. PANEL ASM, Inst
17. BRACE ASM, Dash to Chas Frm (Comp Panel Asm #18)
18. PANEL ASM, Dash (Incl #17)
19. REINFORCEMENT, Frt Body Hinge Plr to Rkr
20. PANEL, Rkr Inr
21. REINFORCEMENT, Flr Pan at Lk Plr
22. PAN ASM, Rr Compt (Incl #23-25)
23. SUPPORT, Spare Tire Clamp Anchor Plate (Comp Pan Asm #22)
24. FILLER, Compt Pan to Qtr Pnl
25. BAR ASM, Rr Cross (Comp Pan Asm #22)
26. PLATE, Compt Lid Lk Striker Anchor
27. PANEL, Rr End
28. RAIL, Si Rf Inr (Comp Rail Asm #30)
29. MLDG, Rf Drip (Comp Rail Asm #30)
30. RAIL ASM, Si Rf (Incl #28-29)
31. EXTENSION, Rr Seat to Bk Wdo Pnl
32. BRACE, Body Lk Plr to Flr Pan
33. PANEL ASM, Rr Qtr Inr Lwr (Comp Pnl Asm #35)
34. EXTENSION, Qtr Inr Pnl Rr
35. PANEL ASM, W/house (Incl #33-36)
36. PANEL, W/House Otr (Comp Pnl Asm #35)
37. PANEL, Shroud Si Duct
38. PANEL, Shroud Lwr
39. PANEL ASM, Frt Body Hinge Plr
40. SUPPORT ASM, Inst Pnl End Upr
41. SUPPORT, Inst Pnl End Lwr
42. SUPPORT ASM, Frt Fdr on Dash
43. REINFORCEMENT, Frt Dr Qtr Pnl at Vent (27 Styles)
44. PANEL, Frt Dr Qtr (Comp Dr Asm #45)
45. DOOR ASM, Frt (Incl #44)
46. PANEL, Dr Opg Rkr Otr
47. REINFORCEMENT, Body Lk Plr Lwr
48. PANEL ASM, Body Lk Plr Upr (27 Styles)
49. FILLER, Qtr Wdo Lwr Rr Cor
50. PANEL, Rr Qtr Si Otr
51. GUTTER, Rr Compt Lid Si
52. REINFORCEMENT, Compt Pan to Qtr Pnl Flr
53. EXTENSION, Qtr Otr Pnl at Tail Lp (57 Styles)

(Chevrolet)

Hinges, Front Door

Hinges are greatly interchangeable, and model or body style does not affect the interchange as much as you might think.

Hinges are differentiated by the position in which they are used: upper and lower. When replacing a hinge, upper and lower units should be replaced at the same Also, you should be aware that on some models there is a distinct difference between the right and left sides of the car. Thus, door hinges from the passenger's side may not driver's side door.

Chevelle
Model	Interchange Number
1964-1965	
Upper	2
Lower	5
1966-1967	
Upper	1
Lower	4
1968-1972	
Upper	3
Lower	6

Interchanges

Interchange Number: 1
Part Number(s): 7642529 (fits either side)
Position: Upper
Usage: 1966-67 Chevelle; 1966-67 Buick Skylark, LeMans; 1967 Camaro; 1967 Pontiac Firebird; 1966 Cutlass

Interchange Number: 2
Part Number(s): 4409743 (fits either side)
Position: Upper
Usage: 1964-1965 Chevelle Skylark, Cutlass LeMans

Interchange Number: 3
Part Number(s): 7722170 (fits either side)
Position: Upper
Usage: 1968-1972 Chevelle LeMans Cutlass, Skylark, Grand Prix; 1970-1972 Monte Carlo; 1971-1972 GMC Sprint

Interchange Number: 4
Part Number(s): RH, 7663424; LH, 7663425
Position: Lower
Usage: 1966-1967 Chevelle, Skylark, LeMans; 1966 Cutlass; 1967 Camaro; 1967 Pontiac Firebird

Interchange Number: 5
Part Number(s): RH, 4506971; LH, 4506972
Position: Lower
Usage: 1964-1965 Chevelle, Skylark, Cutlass, LeMans

Interchange Number: 6
Part Number(s): RH, 7722087; LH, 7722088
Position: Lower
Usage: 1968-1972 Chevelle, LeMans, Cutlass, Skylark, Grand Prix; 1970-1972 Monte Carlo; 1971-1972 GMC Sprint

Door Handle, Outside

Exterior door handles are widely interchangeable and can be found on other GM models besides Chevrolet. While this section deals with front door handles only, in some cases, and on some models, the same handle can be found on the rear door. Normally, handles are also reversible, meaning one side will fit the other. There are exceptions that are unique to each side. If there are special circumstances, they are listed in the charts under "Restrictions."

Chevelle
Model	Interchange Number
1964-1967	
All	1
1968-1969	
All	2
1970-1972	
Except El Camino	3
El Camino	2

Interchanges

Interchange Number: 1
Part Number(s): RH, 5716870; LH, 5716871
Usage: 1960 full-size Chevrolet (except sport SI) 1963-1964 full-size Buick; 1964-1967 Chevelle; 1966-1967 Pontiac LeMans; 1966-1967 Buick Skylark (**rear doors only**); 1967-1969 Pontiac Firebird; 1967-69 Camaro; 1968-1975 Nova; 1969-1970 Electra (**rear doors only**); 1970-19 72 Buick Skylark (**front and rear doors**); 1971- 75 Pontiac Ventura II; 1973-1975 Omega (front and rear doors)
Restrictions: See usage.

Interchange Number: 2
Part Number(s): RH, 9712350; LH, 9712351
Usage: 1968-1969 Chevelle; 1968-1969 Pontiac LeMans; 1969-1970 full-size Chevrolet four-doors only); 1970-1972 Chevelle station wagon or El Camino

Interchange Number: 3
Part Number(s): RH, 9717592; LH, 971 7593
Usage: 1970-1972 Chevelle 2-door, except El Camino; 1969-1970 full-size Chevrolet; 1969-70 full size Pontiac; 1969-1970 full-size Buick (front only; 1970-1972 Chevelle sedan (**Front Door only**)
Restrictions: Coupe or convertible on full-0size models

Rocker Panel

Chevelle
Model   Interchange Number
1964-1967
Inner..1
Outside..2
1968-1972
Inner..3
Outside
Except El Camino..4
El Camino..5

Interchanges

Interchange Number: 1
Part Number(s): 4537121 RH 4537122 LH
Position: Inner
Usage: 1964-1967 Chevelle, all models

Interchange Number: 2
Part Number(s): 7595782 RH 7595783 LH
Position: Outer
Usage: 1964-1967 Chevelle, all models

Interchange Number: 3
Part Number(s): 7704346 RH 7704347 LH
Position: Inner
Usage: 1972-1972 Chevelle, two door models,

Interchange Number: 4
Part Number(s): 7773846 RH 7773847 LH
Position: Outer
Usage: 1972-1972 Chevelle, two door models, except El Camino

Interchange Number: 5
Part Number(s): 7773840 RH 7773841 LH
Position: Outer
Usage: 1972-1972 El Camino

Roof

Chevelle
Model   Interchange Number
1964-1965
2-dr. Sedan..1
2-dr. hardtop..2
El Camino..3
1966-1967
2-dr. Sedan..4
2-dr. hardtop..5
El Camino..3
1968-1969
2-dr. Sedan..6
2-dr. hardtop..6
El Camino..7
1970-1972
2-dr. hardtop..6
El Camino..7

Interchanges

Interchange Number: 1
Part Number(s): 4533800
Usage: 1964-1965 Chevelle two-door sedans

Interchange Number: 2
Part Number(s): 4533802
Usage: 1964-1965 Chevelle; 1964-1965 Lemans Skylark, Cutlass; all two-door hardtops

Interchange Number: 3
Part Number(s): 7596481
Usage: 1964-1967 El Camino

Interchange Number: 4
Part Number(s): 4498668
Usage: 1966-1967 Chevelle two-door sedans

Interchange Number: 5
Part Number(s): 4534268
Usage: 1966-1967 Chevelle Lemans, Skylark, Cutlass all are two-door hardtops

Interchange Number: 6
Part Number(s): 7790418
Usage: 1968-1972 Chevelle two-door sedan, or two-door hardtop; 1968-1972 Cutlass except Supreme; 1968-1972 Pontiac LeMans or Skylark 2-door hardtops

Interchange Number: 7
Part Number(s): 7790424
Usage: 1968-1972 El Camino

Roof, Folding

Chevelle
Model	Interchange Number
1964-1965	
Manual top	1
Power top	7
1966-1967	
Manual top	2
Power top	3
1968-1969	
Manual top	4
Power top	5
1970	
Power top	5
1971-1972	
Power top	6

Interchanges

Interchange Number: 1
Part Number(s):
Usage: 1964-1965 Chevelle, Lemans, Cutlass, Skylark with manual top

Interchange Number: 2
Part Number(s): RH 4545507 LH 454508
Usage: 1966-1967 Chevelle, Lemans, Cutlass, Skylark convertible with power top

Interchange Number: 3
Part Number(s): RH 4545505 LH 4545506
Usage: 1966-1967 Chevelle, Lemans, Cutlass, Skylark convertible with manual top

Interchange Number: 4
Part Number(s): RH 9801876 LH 7745211
Usage: 1968-1969 Chevelle, Lemans, Cutlass, Skylark convertible with manual top

Interchange Number: 5
Part Number(s): RH 9801880 LH 9801881
Usage: 1968-1970 Chevelle, Lemans, Cutlass, Skylark convertible with power top

Interchange Number: 6
Part Number(s): RH 9842240 LH 9842241
Usage: 1971-1972 Chevelle, Lemans, Cutlass, Skylark convertible with manual top

Interchange Number: 7
Part Number(s):
Usage: 1964-1965 Chevelle, Lemans, Cutlass, Skylark with power top

Quarter Panel

Chevelle
Model	Interchange Number
1964	
2-dr Sedan	2
2-dr hardtop	1
Convertible	4
El Camino	3
1965	
2-dr Sedan	5
2-dr hardtop	6
Convertible	7
El Camino	3
1966	
2-dr Sedan	8
2-dr hardtop	9
Convertible	10
El Camino	11
1967	
2-dr Sedan	8
2-dr hardtop	9
Convertible	10
El Camino	12
1968	
2-dr Sedan	13
2-dr hardtop	14
Convertible	15
El Camino	
Early	16
Late	17
1969	
2-dr Sedan	18
2-dr hardtop	19
Convertible	20
El Camino	17

Early 1968 El Camino's had a hole for the rear side marker lamp. The change occurred in September 6, 1967 however it is possible these were used after this date as the supplies were used up. A later panel can be cut and made to fit using the early panel as a template.

1970-1972
2-dr hardtop	21
Convertible	22
El Camino	17

Interchanges

Interchange Number: 1
Part Number(s): RH, 4409810; LH, 4409811
Usage: 1964 Chevelle two-door hardtop

Interchange Number: 2
Part Number(s): RH, 4468406; LH, 4468407
Usage: 1964 Chevelle two-door sedan

Interchange Number: 3
Part Number(s): RH, 4490695; LH, 4490696
Usage: 1964-1965 El Camino

Interchange Number: 4
Part Number(s): RH, 4468404; LH, 4468405
Usage: 1964 Chevelle convertible

Interchange Number: 5
Part Number(s): RH, 4533825; LH, 4533826
Usage: 1965 Chevelle two-door sedan

Interchange Number: 6
Part Number(s): RH, 4484741; LH, 4484742 ,.
Usage: 1965 Chevelle two-door hardtop

Interchange Number: 7
Part Number(s): RH, 4484743; LH, 4484744
Usage: 1965 Chevelle convertible

Interchange Number: 8
Part Number(s): RH, 7580122; LH, 7580123
Usage: 1966-1967 Chevelle two-door sedan
Notes: Do not include tail lamp extension in interchange.

Interchange Number: 9
Part Number(s): RH, 7580162; LH, 7580163
Usage: 1966-1967 Chevelle two-door hardtop
Notes: Do not include tail lamp extension in interchange.

Interchange Number: 10
Part Number(s): RH, 7580164; LH, 7580165
Usage: 1966-1967 Chevelle convertible
Notes: Do not include tail lamp extension in interchange.

Interchange Number: 11
Part Number(s): RH, 4542622; LH, 4542623
Usage: 1966 El Camino

Interchange Number: 12
Part Number(s): RH, 7598638; LH, 7598639
Usage: 1967 El Camino

The late 1968-1972 El Camino's had no rear side markers.

Interchange Number: 13
Part Number(s): RH, 7761614; LH, 7761615
Usage: 1968 Chevelle two-door sedan

Interchange Number: 14
Part Number(s): RH, 7761616; LH, 776161 7
Usage: 1968 Chevelle two-door hardtop

Interchange Number: 15
Part Number(s): RH, 7793617; LH, 7793618
Usage: 1968 Chevelle convertible

Interchange Number: 16
Part Number(s): RH, 7671477; LH, 7671478
Usage: Early 1968 El Camino, first design

Interchange Number: 17
Part Number(s): RH, 8738084; LH, 8738085
Usage: Late 1968-1972 El Camino, second design

Interchange Number: 18
Part Number(s): RH, 7757064; LH, 7757065
Usage: 1969 Chevelle two-door sedan

Interchange Number: 19
Part Number(s): RH, 8768754; LH, 8768755
Usage: 1969 Chevelle two-door hardtop

Interchange Number: 20
Part Number(s): 8770136 RH, 8770137 LH,
Usage: 1969 Chevelle convertible

Interchange Number: 21
Part Number(s): RH, 9815404; LH, 9815405
Usage: 1970-1972 Chevelle two-door hardtop

Interchange Number: 22
Part Number(s): RH, 8735905; LH, 8735906
Usage: 1970-1972 Chevelle convertible

Interchange Number: 23
Part Number(s): RH, 9815404; LH, 9815405
Usage: 1970-1972 Chevelle two-door hardtop

Trunk, Lid

Chevelle

Model	Interchange Number
1964	
All	1
1964-1965	
Except Malibu SS	1
Malibu SS	2
1966-1967	
All	3
1968-1972	
All	4

Interchanges

Interchange Number: 1
Part Number(s): 4493013
Usage: 1964 Chevelle all models and body styles except El Camino or wagon; 1965 Chevelle 300, Deluxe all body styles except wagon or El Camino
Notes: Interchange 2 will fit but uses more trim.

Interchange Number: 2
Part Number(s): 4490148
Usage: 1965 Malibu Sport all body styles

Interchange Number: 3
Part Number(s): 4493013
Usage: 1966-1967 Chevelle all models and body styles except El Camino or wagon
Notes: Interchange without trim or nameplates

Interchange Number: 4
Part Number(s): 8761214
Usage: 1968-1972 Chevelle, Skylark, Monte Carlo all models and body styles except El Camino or wagon

Tailgate

El Camino

Model	Interchange Number
1964-1967	
All	1
1968	
All	2
1969-1972	
All	3

Interchanges

Interchange Number: 1
Part Number(s): 7660966
Usage: 1964-1967 El Camino

Interchange Number: 2
Part Number(s): 787327
Usage: 1968 El Camino
Notes: Interchange number 3 will fit but backup lamps will have to be rewired from the rear bumper to the tailgate.

Interchange Number: 3
Part Number(s): 9862703
Usage: 1969-1972 El Camino
Notes: Has two back up lights in the tailgate.

Hinges, Trunk Lid

Chevelle

Model	Interchange Number
1964-1965	
All	1
1966-1967	
All	2
1968	
All	3
1969-1972	
Except convertible	3
Convertible	4

Interchanges

Interchange Number: 1
Part Number(s): 5717153
Usage: 1964-1965 Chevelle, Lemans, Cutlass, Skylark all body styles except El Camino or wagon
Notes: Fits either side

Interchange Number: 2
Part Number(s): RH: 9706258 LH 9706259
Usage: 1966-1967 Chevelle, Lemans, Cutlass, Skylark all body styles except El Camino or wagon
Notes: Fits either side

Interchange Number: 3
Part Number(s): 9722033
Usage: 1968 Chevelle, Lemans, Cutlass, Skylark all body styles except El Camino or wagon; 1969-1972 Chevelle, except convertible, wagon or El Camino; 1969-1972 Cutlass, Lemans, Skylark except convertible or wagon
Notes: Fits either side

Interchange Number: 4
Part Number(s): 9720628
Usage: 1969-1972 Chevelle, Lemans, Cutlass, Skylark except convertible, wagon or El Camino
Notes: Fits either side

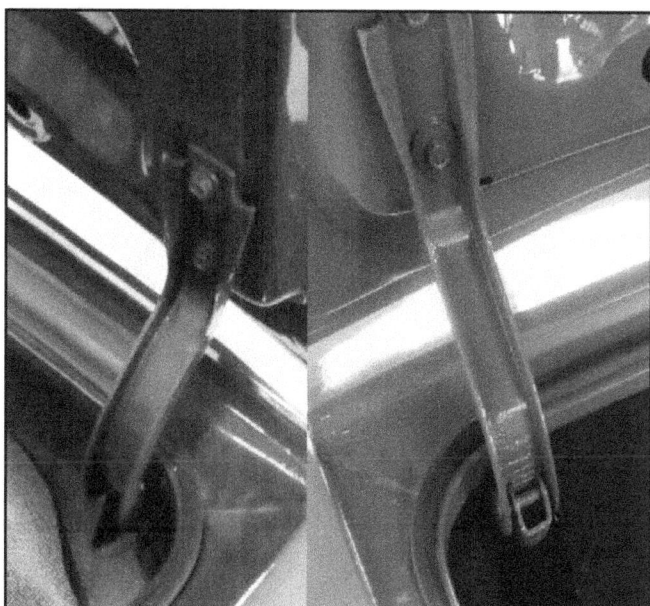
1968-1972 Hinges hardtop on the left and convertible on the right

1964-1967 Tailgate hinge

1968-1972 tailgate hinge. On wagon look for single action tailgate only

Hinges, Tailgate

Chevelle

Model	Interchange Number
1964-1967	
Gate Side	1
Body side	2
1968-1972	
Gate Side	3
Body side	4

Interchanges

Interchange Number: 1
Part Number(s): RH 5717018 LH 5717019
Usage: 1964-1967 Chevelle, Lemans, Cutlass, Skylark wagon; 1964-1967 El Camino
Notes: Gate side

Interchange Number: 2
Part Number(s): RH 5717022 LH 5717023
Usage: 1964-1967 Chevelle, Lemans, Cutlass, Skylark wagon; 1964-1967 El Camino
Notes: Body side

Interchange Number: 3
Part Number(s): RH 9712976 LH 9712977
Usage: 1968-1970 Chevelle, Lemans, Cutlass, Skylark wagon; 1968-1972 El Camino
Notes: Body side

Interchange Number: 4
Part Number(s): RH 979876 LH 9719877
Usage: 1968-1970 Chevelle, Lemans, Cutlass, Skylark wagon; 1968-1972 El Camino
Notes: Body side

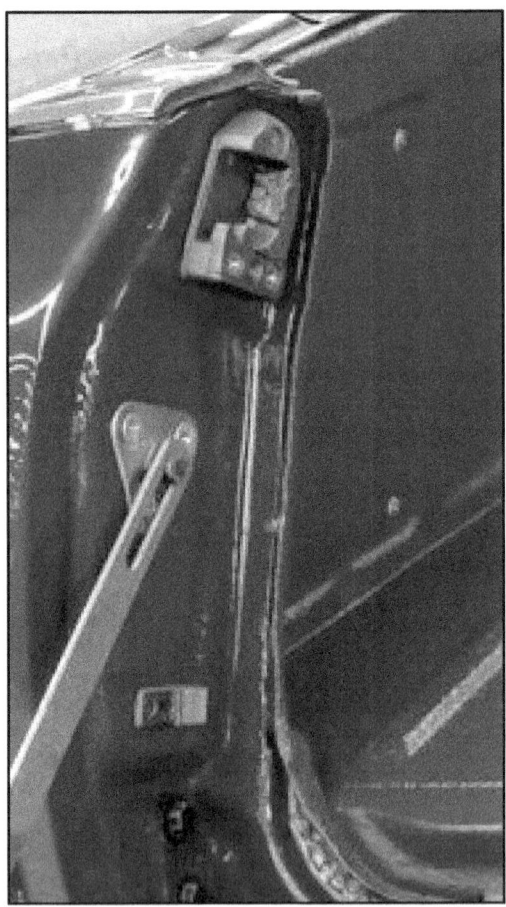
1964-1967 tailgate straps, and the tail gate strikers that were used on all 1964-1972 El Camino's; 1965-1968 full-size Chevrolet wagon; 1964-1969 Chevelle wagons 1962-1967 Nova wagons

Chapter 12 Grilles and Bumpers

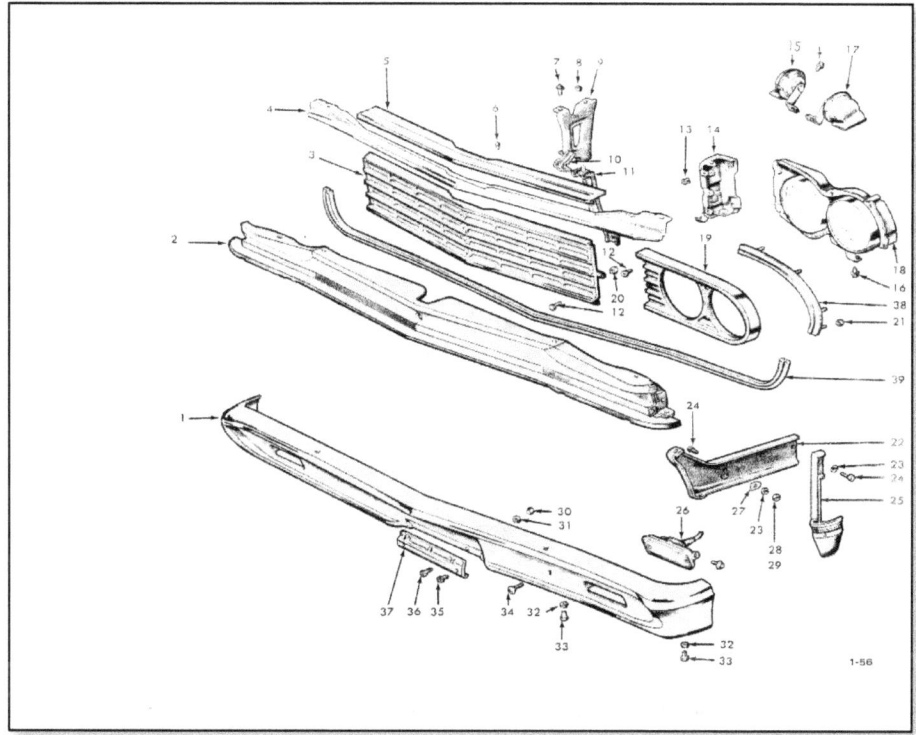

1964 Chevelle grille (Chevrolet)

Grille

Grille design usually changes from year to year and between some models and sub-models. However, you can modify (paint) some grilles to adapt to another model. For example, the 1968 Chevelle SS 396 used a black-accented grille while other models from the same year used a brightly plated one. Grille interchange includes headlamp bezels, as they were usually a continuation of the grille.

Chevelle
Model   *Interchange Number*
1964
All..1
1965
All..2
1966
All..3
1967
Except SS or Concours.................................4
SS..5
Concours...14
1968
Except SS or Concours.................................6
SS or Concours...12
1969
Except SS, Concours, or Malibu...................7
Malibu SS or Concours..................................8
1970
All..9
1971
All..10
1972
All..11

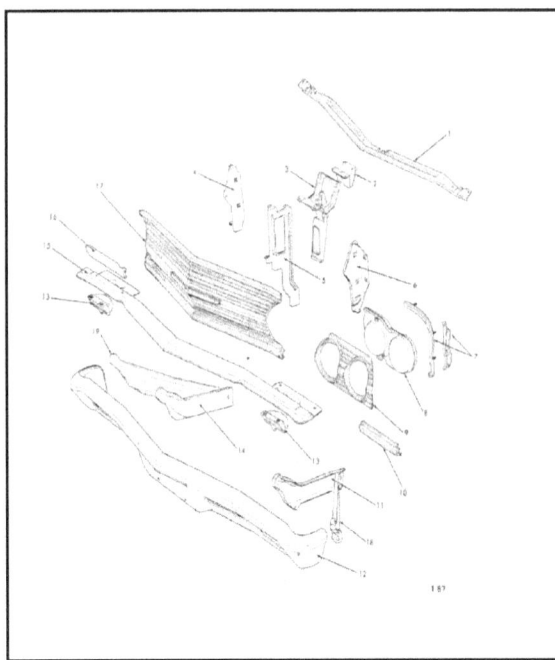

1965 Grille (Chevrolet)

Interchange Number: 1
Main Section: 3854130
Headlamp Bezels: RH, 3830724; LH, 3830723
Usage: 1964 Chevelle, all models and body styles.

Interchange Number: 2
Main Section: 3875756
Headlamp Bezels: RH, 3856900; LH, 3856899
Usage: 1965 Chevelle, all models and body styles

Interchange Number: 3
Main Section: 3873795
Extensions: RH, 3876424; LH, 3876423
Usage: 1966 Chevelle, all models and body styles
Notes: Regular Chevelle grille can be painted with black enamel to fit SS 396.

Interchange Number: 4
Main Section: 3885980
Extensions: RH, 3893976; LH, 3893975
Usage: 1967 Chevelle, all models and body styles except SS 396 or Concours

Interchange Number: 5
Main Section: 3892182
Extensions: RH, 3893976; 3893975
Usage: 1967 Chevelle SS 396
Notes: Extension same on all 1967 Chevelles.

Interchange Number: 6
Main Section: 3915400
Extensions: RH, 3926808; LH3926809
Usage: 1968 Chevelle all models and body styles except SS 396

Interchange Number: 7
Main Section: 3942789
Extensions: RH, 3938112; LH, 3938111
Usage: 1969 Chevelle, except Malibu SS 396 or Concours

Interchange Number: 8
Main Section: 3938180
Extensions: RH, 3893976; 3893975
Usage: 1969 SS 396, Malibu or Concours
Notes: Paint black with SS 396 package

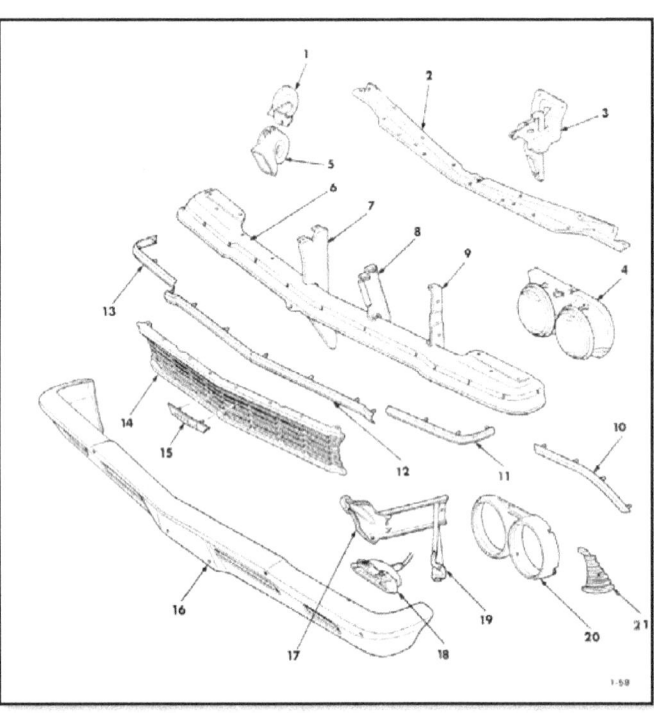

1966 grille. (Chevrolet)

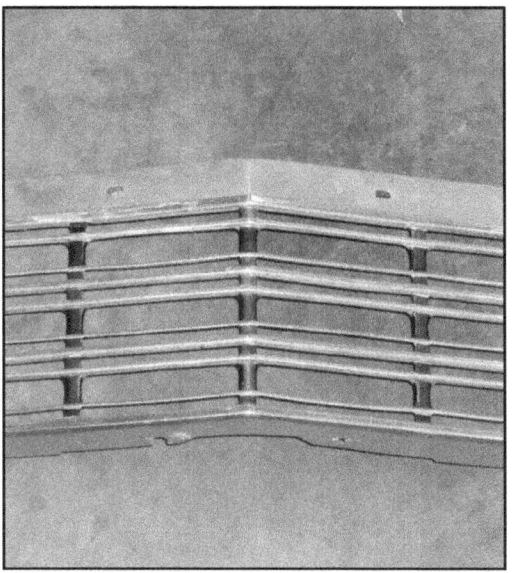

1967 Chevelle grille. Note the two holes at the top this means it is incorrect for SS or concours models

1967 SS 396 grille note no holes in the upper frame. This is the reason no SS grille cannot be used.

The grille extensions were the same on all 1967 Chevelles

Interchange Number: 9
Main Section: 3956117
Usage: 1970 Chevelle, all models and body style.
Paint to fit model application: black SS silver others

Interchange Number: 10
Main Section: 3982409
Usage: 1971 Chevelle, all models and body style.
Paint to fit model application: black SS silver others

Interchange Number: 11
Main Section: 329000
Usage: 1972 Chevelle, all models and body style.
Paint to fit model application: black SS silver others

Interchange Number: 12
Main Section: 3915400
Extensions: RH, 3926802; LH 3926803
Usage: 1968 SS 396
Notes: Main section used in interchange number 6 is the same.

Interchange Number: 14
Usage: 1967 Chevelle Concours
Main Section: 3907432
Extensions: RH, 3893976; 3893975
Notes: Extension same on all 1967 Chevelles.

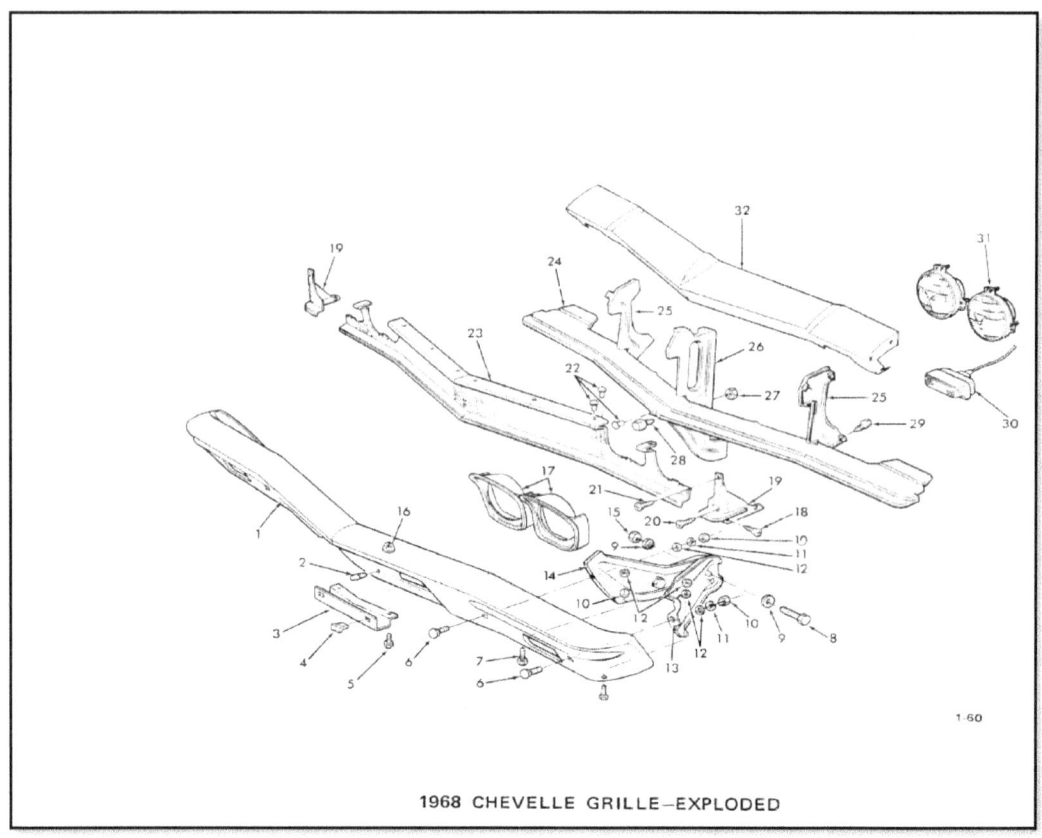

1968 grille (Chevrolet)

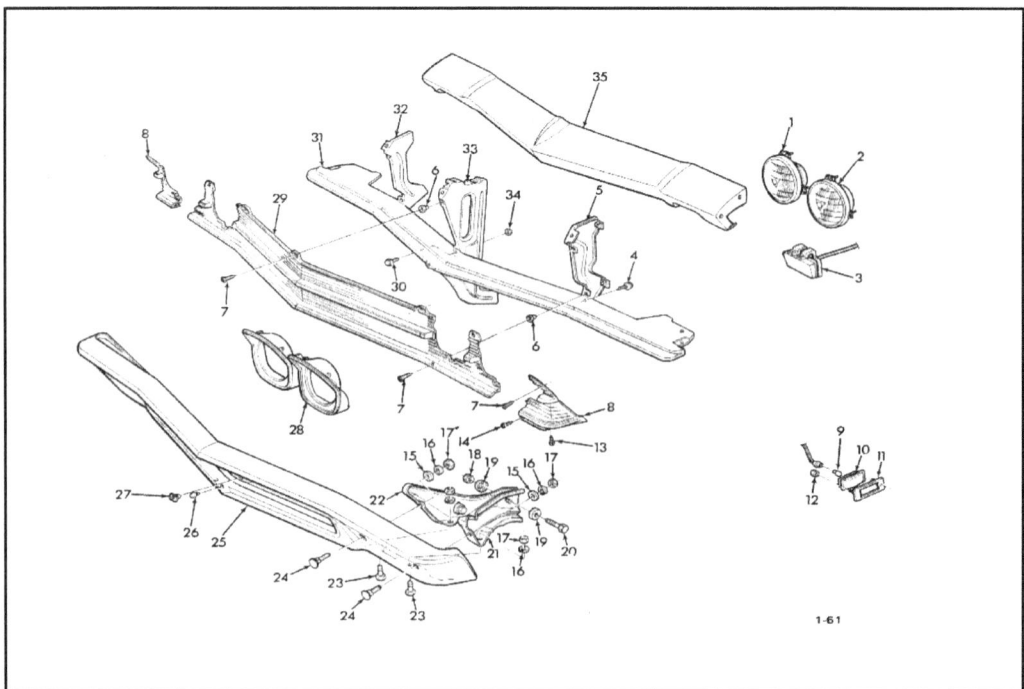

1969 Grille explode view. (Chevrolet)

Chevelle 1964-1972

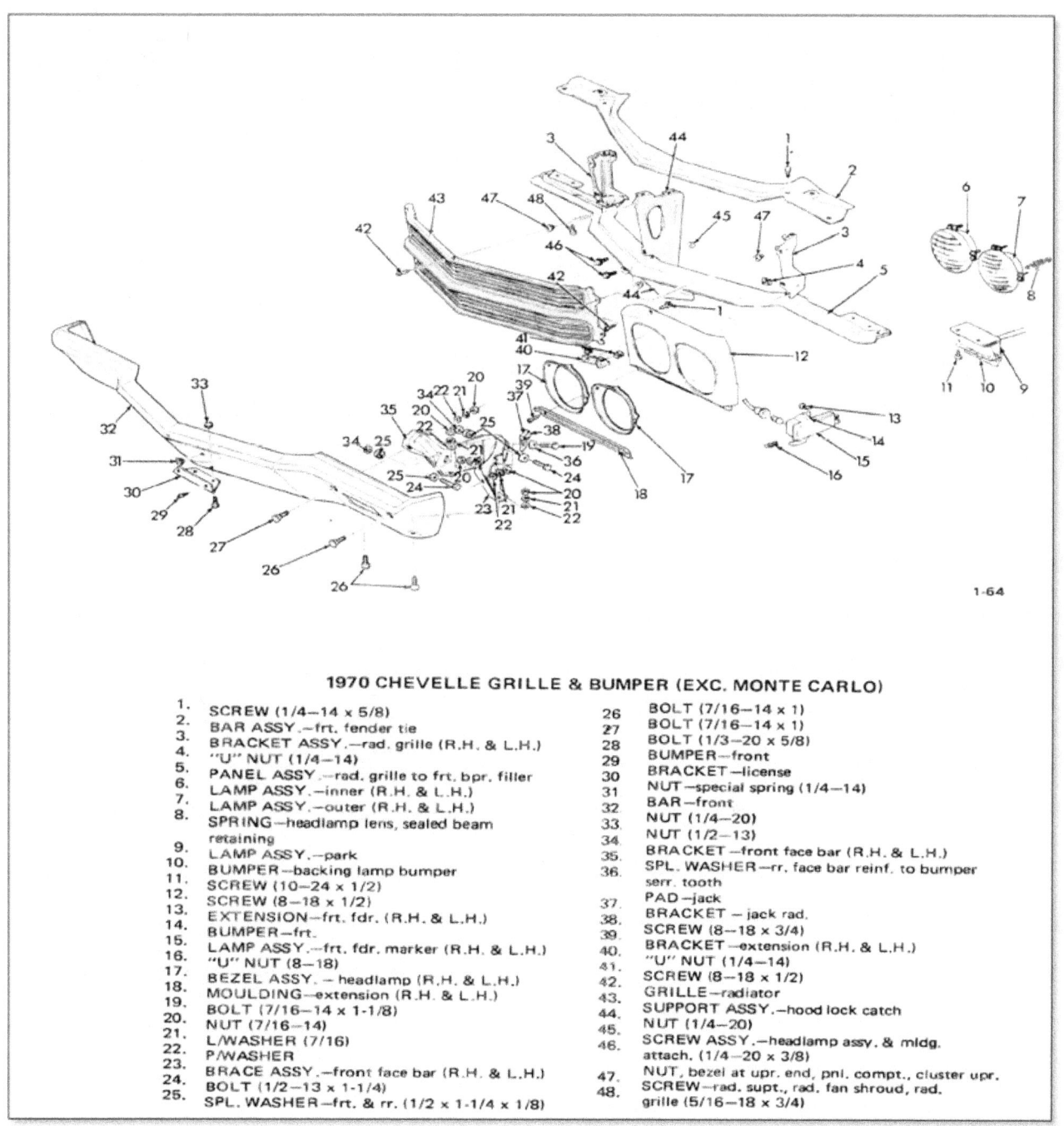

1970 CHEVELLE GRILLE & BUMPER (EXC. MONTE CARLO)

1. SCREW (1/4—14 x 5/8)
2. BAR ASSY.—frt. fender tie
3. BRACKET ASSY.—rad. grille (R.H. & L.H.)
4. "U" NUT (1/4—14)
5. PANEL ASSY.—rad. grille to frt. bpr. filler
6. LAMP ASSY.—inner (R.H. & L.H.)
7. LAMP ASSY.—outer (R.H. & L.H.)
8. SPRING—headlamp lens, sealed beam retaining
9. LAMP ASSY.—park
10. BUMPER—backing lamp bumper
11. SCREW (10—24 x 1/2)
12. SCREW (8—18 x 1/2)
13. EXTENSION—frt. fdr. (R.H. & L.H.)
14. BUMPER—frt.
15. LAMP ASSY.—frt. fdr. marker (R.H. & L.H.)
16. "U" NUT (8—18)
17. BEZEL ASSY.—headlamp (R.H. & L.H.)
18. MOULDING—extension (R.H. & L.H.)
19. BOLT (7/16—14 x 1-1/8)
20. NUT (7/16—14)
21. L/WASHER (7/16)
22. P/WASHER
23. BRACE ASSY.—front face bar (R.H. & L.H.)
24. BOLT (1/2—13 x 1-1/4)
25. SPL. WASHER—frt. & rr. (1/2 x 1-1/4 x 1/8)
26. BOLT (7/16—14 x 1)
27. BOLT (7/16—14 x 1)
28. BOLT (1/3—20 x 5/8)
29. BUMPER—front
30. BRACKET—license
31. NUT—special spring (1/4—14)
32. BAR—front
33. NUT (1/4—20)
34. NUT (1/2—13)
35. BRACKET—front face bar (R.H. & L.H.)
36. SPL. WASHER—rr. face bar reinf. to bumper serr. tooth
37. PAD—jack
38. BRACKET—jack rad.
39. SCREW (8—18 x 3/4)
40. BRACKET—extension (R.H. & L.H.)
41. "U" NUT (1/4—14)
42. SCREW (8—18 x 1/2)
43. GRILLE—radiator
44. SUPPORT ASSY.—hood lock catch
45. NUT (1/4—20)
46. SCREW ASSY.—headlamp assy. & mldg. attach. (1/4—20 x 3/8)
47. NUT, bezel at upr. end, pnl. compt., cluster upr.
48. SCREW—rad. supt., rad. fan shroud, rad. grille (5/16—18 x 3/4)

(Chevrolet)

When swapping a grille from a non 1971 SS model the grille will have to be painted black, and the Chevelle name plate discarded.

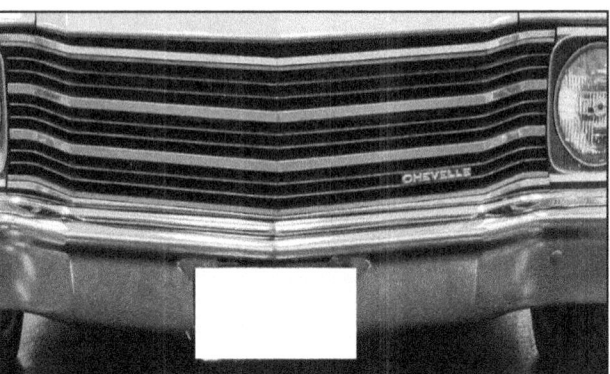

1972 grille. When swapping front Chevelle to those with SS package discard chrome trim.

Bumper, Front

Chevelle

Model	Interchange Number
1964	
All	1
1965	
All	2
1966	
All	3
1967	
All	4
1968	
All	5
1969	
All	6
1970	
All	7
1971-1972	
All	8

Interchanges

Interchange Number: 1
Part Number(s):3830727
Usage: 1964 Chevelle, all models and body styles

Interchange Number: 2
Part Number(s): 3856906
Usage: 1965 Chevelle, all models and body styles

Interchange Number: 3
Part Number(s):3869723
Usage: 1966 Chevelle, all models and body styles

Interchange Number: 4
Part Number(s):3884920
Usage: 1967 Chevelle, all models and body styles

Interchange Number: 5
Part Number(s): 3907620
Usage: 1968 Chevelle, all models and body styles

Interchange Number: 6
Part Number(s): 3926850
Usage: 1969 Chevelle, all models and body styles
Notes: due to differences in front turn lamps interchange without lamps

Interchange Number: 7
Part Number(s): 3954592
Usage: 1970 Chevelle, all models and body styles

Interchange Number: 8
Part Number(s): 3982398
Usage: 1970-1971 Chevelle, all models and body styles

Bumper, Rear

Chevelle

Model	Interchange Number
1964	
All	1
1965	
All	2
1966	
Except El Camino	3
El Camino	4
1967	
Except El Camino	5
El Camino	6
1968	
Except El Camino	7
El Camino	8
1969	
Except El Camino Deluxe	9
Malibu or SS 396	10
El Camino	8
1970	
Except El Camino or SS	11
SS	14
El Camino	8
1971-1972	
Except El Camino	12
El Camino	8

Interchanges

Interchange Number: 1
Part Number(s): 3837999
Usage: 1964 Chevelle, all models and body styles

Interchange Number: 2
Part Number(s): 3858438
Usage: 1965 Chevelle, all models and body styles

Interchange Number: 3
Part Number(s): 3869724
Usage: 1966 Chevelle wagon or El Camino

Interchange Number: 4
Part Number(s): 3869756
Usage: 1966 Chevelle, all models and body styles except wagon or El Camino

Interchange Number: 5
Part Number(s): 3895146
Usage: 1967 Chevelle, all models and body styles except El Camion or wagon

Interchange Number: 6
Part Number(s): 3895162
Usage: 1967 El Camino or wagon

Interchange Number: 7
Part Number(s): 3907622
Usage: 1968 Chevelle Deluxe except El Camino or wagon

Interchange Number: 8
Part Number(s): 3935692
Usage: 1968-1972 El Camino; 1968 Chevelle wagon

Interchange Number: 9
Part Number(s): 3907669
Usage: 1968 SS 396 or Malibu except wagon or El Camino

Interchange Number: 10
Part Number(s): 3927689
Usage: 1969 Chevelle, all models and body styles, except wagon or El Camino

Interchange Number: 11
Part Number(s): 3975450
Usage: 1970 Chevelle, all models and body styles, except wagon, El Camino, or Super Sport models

Interchange Number: 12
Part Number(s): 3982400 Upper 3982401 Lower
Usage: 1969 Chevelle, all models and body styles, except wagon or El Camino

Interchange Number: 14
Part Number(s): 3975452
Usage: 1970 Chevelle Super Sport, except El Camino

Chapter 13 Trim and Moldings

Molding

General Notes

There are many different types of molding used on cars. Thus, to help you more easily find the type of molding you need, we have grouped together the different types. They include, in this order: windshield molding, drip rail molding, rear quarter window molding, wheel lip molding, rocker panel molding, and hood molding.

When interchanging a molding, it is always a good idea to include all holding clips. Also, note that the range of molding available for interchange varies and that body style may affect some interchange situations.

When interchanging used molding, inspect it carefully for signs of pitting, scratches, or general abuse. Perhaps the molding was removed and then not replaced correctly. Molding is easily bent, so remove it carefully.

Windshield Molding

Chevelle

Model	Interchange Number
1964-1965	
All	
Upper	1
Side	5
Lower	10
1966-1967	
2-door Sedan or El Camino	
Upper	1
Side	5
Lower	10
2 door Hardtop	
Upper	2
Side	6
Lower	10

Convertible
Upper 2
Side 6
Finish 13
Lower 10
1968-1972
2-door sedan or El Camino
Upper 4
Side 8
Lower
Without Hidden Wipers 11
With Hidden Wipers 12
2-door Hardtop
Upper 3
Side 9
Lower
Without Hidden Wipers 11
With Hidden Wipers 12
Convertible
Upper 7
Side 15
Lower
Without Hidden Wipers 11
With Hidden Wipers 12

Interchanges

Interchange Number: 1
Part Number(s): RH 4430502 4430503
Part: Upper
Usage: 1964-1965 Chevelle, LeMans, Cutlass Skylark all body styles; 1966-1967 Chevelle, Cutlass, Lemans, Skylark 2 or 4-door sedans; 1964-1967 El Camino

Interchange Number: 2
Part Number(s): RH, 4541648; LH, 4541649
Part: Upper
Usage: 1966-1967 Chevelle, Cutlass, Skylark, Lemans two-door hardtop or convertible

Interchange Number: 3
Part Number(s): 7726034
Part: Upper
Usage: 1968-1972 Chevelle, Cutlass, Skylark, Lemans two-door except convertible

Interchange Number: 4
Part Number(s): 7726032
Part: Upper
Usage: 1968-1972 El Camino; 1968-1972 Chevelle, Cutlass, Skylark, Lemans four-door

Interchange Number: 5
Part Number(s): RH 4430500 LH 4430501
Part: Side
Usage: 1964-1965 Chevelle, LeMans, Cutlass Skylark all body styles; 1966-1967 Chevelle, Cutlass, Lemans, Skylark 4-door sedans

Interchange Number: 6
Part Number(s): RH, 4541650; LH, 4541651
Part: Side
Usage: 1966-1967 Chevelle, Cutlass, Skylark, Lemans two-door hardtop or convertible

Interchange Number: 7
Part Number(s): 7726036
Part: Upper
Usage: 1968-1972 Chevelle, Cutlass, Skylark, Lemans convertible

Interchange Number: 8
Part Number(s): RH 7725632 LH 7725633
Part: Side
Usage: 1968-1972 El Camino; 1968-1972 Chevelle, Cutlass, Skylark, Lemans four-door

Interchange Number: 9
Part Number(s): RH 7725634 LH 7725635
Part: Side
Usage: 1968-1972 Chevelle, Cutlass, Skylark, Lemans 2-door except convertible

Interchange Number: 10
Part Number(s): 4430558
Part: Lower
Usage: 1964-1965 Chevelle, LeMans, Cutlass Skylark all body styles; early 1966, 1967 Chevelle, Cutlass, Lemans, Skylark

Interchange Number: 11
Part Number(s): 7737629
Part: lower
Usage: 1968-1972 Chevelle, LeMans, Cutlass Skylark all body styles without hidden wipers

Interchange Number: 12
Part Number(s): 7731088
Part: lower
Usage: 1968-1972 Chevelle, LeMans, Cutlass Skylark all body styles with hidden wipers

Interchange Number: 13
Part Number(s): RH, 4543092; LH, 4543093
Part: Side (finish molding)
Usage: 1966-1967 Chevelle, Cutlass, Skylark, Lemans convertible

Interchange Number: 14
Part Number(s): RH, 7626294; LH, 7626295
Part: Side (finish molding)
Usage: 1964-1967 El Camino custom

Interchange Number: 15
Part Number(s): RH, 7728954; LH, 7728955
Part: Side
Usage: 1968-1972 Chevelle, Cutlass, Skylark, Lemans convertible

Quarter belt moldings were used with vinyl tops

Drip Rail Molding

Chevelle

Model	Interchange Number
1964-1965	
2-door sedan	1
2 door hardtop	2
El Camino	3
1966-1967	
2-door sedan	4
2 door hardtop	5
El Camino	3
1968-1972	
2-door sedan	6
2 door hardtop	7
El Camino	8

Interchanges

Interchange Number: 1
Part Number(s): RH, 4407700; LH, 4407701
Usage: 1964-1965 Chevelle two-door sedan

Interchange Number: 2
Part Number(s): Front: RH, 4456072, LH, 4456073; Rear: RH, 44056076, LH, 44056077
Usage: 1964-1965 Chevelle, LeMans, Cutlass, Skylark; all are two-door hardtop models

Interchange Number: 3
Part Number(s): RH, 7643206; LH, 7643205
Usage: 1964-1967 El Camino

Interchange Number: 4
Part Number(s): RH, 4541586; LH, 4541587
Usage: 1966-1967 Chevelle two-door sedan

Interchange Number: 5
Part Number(s): RH, 4547733; LH, 4547734
Usage: 1966-1967 Chevelle, Cutlass, Lemans, Skylark, all are two-door hardtop models

Interchange Number: 6
Part Number(s): RH, 7723584; LH, 7723585
Usage: 1968-1969 Chevelle two-door sedan or two-door hardtop without vinyl top

Interchange Number: 7
Part Number(s): RH, 7753596; LH, 7753597
Usage: 1968-1970 Chevelle two-door hardtop with vinyl top

Interchange Number: 8
Part Number(s): RH, 7734898; LH, 7734897
Usage: 1968-1972 El Camino

Quarter Belt Molding

Chevelle

Model	Interchange Number
1964-1965	
2-door sedan	1
2-door hardtop	3
Convertible	2
El Camino	7
1966-1967	
2-door sedan	4
2-door hardtop	5
Convertible	6
El Camino	7
1968-1969	
2-door sedan	8
2-door hardtop	9
Convertible	
1968	10
1969	12
El Camino	11
1970	
2-door sedan	13
2-door hardtop	
Standard Chevelle	13
Malibu	14
Convertible	15
El Camino	11
1971-1972	
2-door hardtop	13
Convertible	15
El Camino	11

Interchanges

Interchange Number: 1
Part Number(s): RH, 4430538; LH, 4430539
Usage: 1964-1965 Chevelle 2-door sedan with vinyl top or two-tone paint

Interchange Number: 2
Part Number(s): RH, 3871676; LH, 3871677
Usage: 1964-1965 Chevelle convertible

Interchange Number: 3
Part Number(s): RH, 3853108; LH, 3853107
Usage: 1964-1965 Chevelle 2-door hardtop with vinyl top or two-tone paint.

Interchange Number: 4
Part Number(s): RH, 3890188; LH, 3890189
Usage: 1966-1967 Chevelle 2-door sedan with vinyl top or two-tone paint

Interchange Number: 5
Part Number(s): RH, 3890184; LH, 3890183
Usage: 1966-1967 Chevelle 2-door hardtop with vinyl top or two-tone paint.

Interchange Number: 6
Part Number(s): RH, 3890806; LH, 3890805
Usage: 1966-1967 Chevelle convertible

Interchange Number: 7
Part Number(s): RH, 3914088; LH, 3914087
Usage: 1964-1967 El Camino with two tone paint or vinyl top

Interchange Number: 8
Part Number(s): RH, 3940514; LH, 3940513
Usage: 1968-1969 Chevelle 2-door sedan with vinyl top or two-tone paint

Interchange Number: 9
Part Number(s): RH, 3940514; LH, 3940513
Usage: 1968-1969 Chevelle 2-door hardtop with vinyl top or two-tone paint.

Interchange Number: 10
Part Number(s): RH, 3940526; LH, 3940525
Usage: 1968 Chevelle convertible

Interchange Number: 11
Part Number(s): RH, 3940504; LH, 3940503
Usage: 1968-1972 El Camino with two tone paint or vinyl top

Interchange Number: 12
Part Number(s): RH, 3962893; LH, 3962892
Usage: 1969 Chevelle convertible

Interchange Number: 13
Part Number(s): RH, 9811346; LH, 9811345
Usage: 1970 Chevelle 2-door sedan; 1970 Standard Chevelle 2-door hardtop (not correct for 1970 Malibu); 1971-1972 Chevelle two-door hardtop

Interchange Number: 14
Part Number(s): RH, 8789272; LH, 8789273
Usage: 1970 Malibu standard 2-door hardtop
Notes: Will not fit standard Chevelle

Interchange Number: 15
Part Number(s): RH, 8726848; LH, 8726849
Usage: 1970-1972 Chevelle convertible

Rocker Molding

Chevelle

Model	Interchange Number
1964	
Except Super Sport	1
Super Sport	2
1965	
Super Sport	3
1966	
Super Sport	4
1967	
2-door sedan	6
2-door hardtop	5
Convertible	5
El Camino	6
1968	
All	7
1969	
Except El Camino	8
El Camino	9
1970-1972	
Standard Chevelle	8
Malibu	10

Interchanges

Interchange Number: 1
Part Number(s): 3843904 RH 3843903 LH
Usage: 1964 Chevelle all models and body styles except Super Sport or El Camino

Interchange Number: 2
Part Number(s):
Main Section: 3846278 RH 3846277 LH
Extensions: Front: 3845630 RH 3845629 LH
             Rear: 3848348 RH 3848347 LH
Rear Quarter: 3852962 RH 3852961 LH
Usage: 1964 Chevelle Super Sport, all body styles; 1964 El Camino

Interchange Number: 3
Part Number(s): 3865362 RH 3865361 LH
Usage: 1965 Chevelle 300 all body styles; 1965 Malibu Super Sport all body styles.

Interchange Number: 4
Part Number(s): 3886232 RH 3886231 LH
Usage: 1966 Chevelle all models and body styles

Interchange Number: 5
Part Number(s): 3904584 RH 3904583 LH
Usage: 1967 Chevelle 2-door hardtop or convertible; 1967 Chevelle Concours station wagon

Interchange Number: 6
Part Number(s): 3904586 RH 3904585 LH
Usage: 1967 Chevelle 2 or 4-door sedan; 1967 El Camino

Interchange Number: 7
Part Number(s): 3928426 RH 3928425 LH
Usage: 1968 Chevelle 2-door hardtop, 2-door sedan or convertible

Interchange Number: 8
Part Number(s): 3952495
Usage: 1969 Chevelle 2-door hardtop, 2-door sedan or convertible; 1970 Standard Chevelle 2-door sedan, 2-door hardtop

Interchange Number: 9
Part Number(s): 3952496
Usage: 1969 El Camino; 1969 Chevelle 4-door -sedan or wagon

Interchange Number: 10
Part Number(s): 3980807
Usage: 1970-1972 Malibu 2-door hardtop or convertible

Wheel Lip Moldings

Chevelle

Model	Interchange Number
1964	
Front	13
Rear	
Except El Camino	10
El Camino	9
1965	
Front	14
Rear	
Except El Camino	7
El Camino	8
1966	
Front	15
Rear	
Except El Camino	5
El Camino	6
1967	
Front	16
Rear	4
1968	
Front	
Malibu	18
Concours	17
Rear	11
1969	
Front	19
Rear	3
1970-1972	
Front	20
Rear	
Except El Camino	2
El Camino	1

Interchanges

Interchange Number: 1
Part Number(s): RH 8703000 LH 87032999
Part: Rear
Usage: 1970-1972 El Camino

Interchange Number: 2
Part Number(s): RH 8702560 LH 8702561
Part: Rear
Usage: 1970-1972 Chevelle all body styles except wagon or El Camino

Interchange Number: 3
Part Number(s): RH 8700946 LH 8700947
Part: Rear
Usage: 1969 Chevelle, all body styles, including El Camino, except 4-door sedan

Interchange Number: 4
Part Number(s): RH 4229720 LH 4229721
Part: Rear
Usage: 1967 Chevelle SS 396, or Concours all body styles

Interchange Number: 5
Part Number(s): RH 3884034 LH 3884033
Part: Rear
Usage: 1966 Chevelle all body styles, except El Camino or wagon

Interchange Number: 6
Part Number(s): RH 3884036 LH 3884035
Part: Rear
Usage: 1966 El Camino or 1966 Chevelle wagon

Interchange Number: 7
Part Number(s): RH 3865362 LH 3865361
Part: Rear
Usage: 1965 Chevelle all body styles, except El Camino or wagon

Interchange Number: 8
Part Number(s): RH 3884036 LH 3884035
Part: Rear
Usage: 1965 El Camino or 1965 Chevelle wagon

Interchange Number: 9
Part Number(s): RH 3852956 LH 3852955
Part: Rear
Usage: 1964 El Camino or 1965 Chevelle wagon

Interchange Number: 10
Part Number(s): RH 3852958 LH 3852957
Part: Rear
Usage: 1964 Chevelle, all body styles except El Camino or wagon

Interchange Number: 11
Part Number(s): RH 7795076 LH 7795077
Part: Rear
Usage: 1968 Chevelle, 4-door hardtop; 1968 Malibu

Interchange Number: 12
Part Number(s): RH 3937274 LH 3937273
Part: Front
Usage: 1968 Chevelle, 4-door hardtop; 1968 Malibu

Interchange Number: 13
Part Number(s): RH 3845628 LH 3845629
Part: Front
Usage: 1964 Chevelle all body styles including El Camino

Interchange Number: 14
Part Number(s): RH 3865324 LH 3865323
Part: Front
Usage: 1965 Chevelle all body styles including El Camino

Interchange Number: 15
Part Number(s): RH 3884032 LH 3884031
Part: Front
Usage: 1966 Chevelle all body styles including El Camino

Interchange Number: 16
Part Number(s): RH 3904592 LH 3904591
Part: Front
Usage: 1967 Chevelle SS 396, or Concours all body styles

Interchange Number: 17
Part Number(s): RH 3928436 LH 3928435
Part: Front
Usage: 1968 Chevelle Concours

Interchange Number: 18
Part Number(s): RH 3955684 LH 3955683
Part: Front
Usage: 1968 Malibu

Interchange Number: 19
Part Number(s): RH 3952498 LH 3952497
Part: Front
Usage: 1969 Chevelle, all models and body styles including El Camino

Interchange Number: 20
Part Number(s): RH 3970592 LH 3970591
Part: Front
Usage: 1970-1972 Chevelle, all models and body styles including El Camino

Rear Window Molding

Chevelle

Model	Interchange Number
1964-1965	
Except El Camino	
Upper	1
Lower	2
El Camino	
Upper	3
Lower	4

1966
Upper...5
Lower...6
El Camino
Upper...3
Lower...4

1967
Upper...7
Lower...8
El Camino
Upper...3
Lower...4

1968-1972
Upper...9
Lower...12
El Camino
Upper...10
Lower...11

Interchanges

Interchange Number: 1
Part Number(s): RH 4430550 LH 4430551
Part: Upper/Side
Usage: 1964-1965 Chevelle all models and body styles except El Camino, wagon or convertible

Interchange Number: 2
Part Number(s): RH 4430538 LH 4430539
Part: Lower
Usage: 1964-1965 Chevelle all models and body styles except El Camino, wagon or convertible

Interchange Number: 3
Part Number(s): RH 4408580 LH 4408581
Part: Upper/Side
Usage: 1964-1967 El Camino

Interchange Number: 4
Part Number(s): RH 4408576 LH 4408577
Part: Lower
Usage: 1964-1967 El Camino

Interchange Number: 5
Part Number(s): RH 4542512 LH 4542513
Part: Upper/Side
Usage: 1966 Chevelle all models and body styles except El Camino, wagon or convertible

Interchange Number: 6
Part Number(s): RH 4542514 LH 4542515
Part: Lower/side
Usage: 1966 Chevelle all models and body styles except El Camino, wagon or convertible

Interchange Number: 7
Part Number(s): RH 7580180 LH 7580181
Part: Upper/Side
Usage: 1967 Chevelle all models and body styles except El Camino, wagon or convertible

Interchange Number: 8
Part Number(s): RH 7581670 LH 7581671
Part: Lower/Side
Usage: 1967 Chevelle all models and body styles except El Camino, wagon or convertible

Interchange Number: 9
Part Number(s): RH 8775846 LH 8775847
Part: Side/Upper
Usage: 1968-1972 Chevelle 2-doors; 1970-1972 Monte Carlo

Bed moldings were the same from 1964-1967 part number 3853668 for either side.

The upper Bed roof moldings are listed as part numbers 7695648 and 7695647 RH/LH and are stamped 4410028 and 4410029 1964-1965 and 4507176 and 4057177 for 1966-1967. Both will fit any 1964-1967 El Camino

Interchange Number: 10
Part Number(s): RH 8775862 LH 8775863
Part: Side/Upper
Usage: 1968-1972 El Camino

Interchange Number: 11
Part Number(s): 8775839
Part: Lower
Usage: 1968-1972 El Camino

Bed molding for 1968-1972 were listed as part number 3940523 LH and 3940524 RH Upper molding of the bed are part numbers 7741958 and 7741959 and are stamped with part numbers.

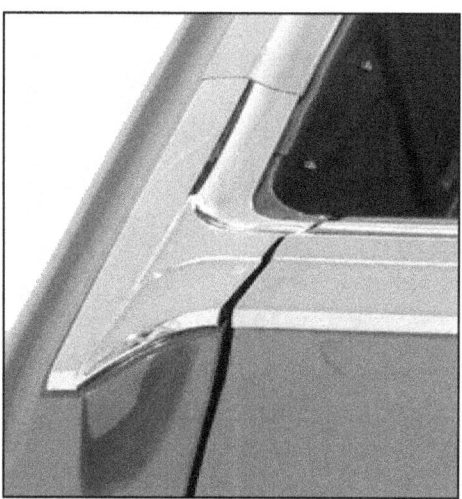

1964-1967 bed corner molding part numbers 3869283 LH and 3869284 RH stamped 4518967 and 4518968

Interchange Number: 12
Part Number(s): RH 7725808 LH 7725807
Part: Lower
Usage: 1968-1970 Chevelle 2-doors; 1970-1972 Monte Carlo

End cap bed molding from 1968-1972 listed as part numbers 7795037 LH and 7795038 RH and are stamped 7734170-RH and 7734171-LH

Chapter 14 Glass and Mirrors

Glass

The major factors in interchanging glass are fit and body style. Body style can affect the usage of glass, particularly door glass, windshield, and even back window glass. Also, because door and quarter window glass are unique to each side on some models, you will need to avoid swapping sides when replacing.

Another factor that differentiates glass is whether it is tinted. Around 80 percent of cars from this era came with some sort of tinted glass. However, note that tint does not affect interchange.

Basically, there were two manufactures of GM glass Libbey Owens Ford, stamped LOF and Pittsburgh Glass stamped PPG. Most were LOF.

You will notice several marks in white ink on the glass especially on models after 1968. Federal mark includes American Standard (AS) the Model number (M) and in later years the DOT (Department of Transportation) number for the manufacturer. In addition to this there is also the glass type: Plate, Float, Solid Tempered and Laminated.

There were also GM trademarks that you will not finds on other makers glass. Such as Soft-Ray (for tinted glass) and Flo-Lite (for float glass), plus Plate - for plate glass.

Typical glass code: Photo has bene flipped so it can be read.

These marking are sometimes printed on the inside of the glass and when read from the outside are backwards. There is no code that identify the glass as fitting a certain model. Though there is a date code, date codes have little effect on the interchange.

Tinted glass was standard on-air conditioned cars—unless the customer specifically requested that it not be. There were two types of tinted glass: Option A01, where all windows were tinted, and Option A02, where only the windshield was tinted.

Unless all the glass in a vehicle is changed, tinted glass should not be used to replace Clear glass, or vice versa. The one exception is that a tinted windshield can be used in place of a Clear windshield, thus matching the A02 option.

LOF Glass Markings

Style	AS Rating	Thickness	Type	Application
Clear				
M3	AS1		Laminated	Windshield
M51	AS2	1/4	Solid Tempered	Door
M52	AS2	3/16	Solid Tempered	Vent, Quarter, Back glass
M71	AS2	1/4	Flo-Lite	Door
M72	AS2	3/16	Flo-Lite	Vent, Quarter, Back glass
Tinted				
M4	AS1		Laminated	Windshield
M54	AS2	1/4	Solid Tempered	Door
M55	AS2	3/16	Solid Tempered	Vent, Quarter, Back glass
M74	AS2	1/4	Flo-Lite	Door
M75	AS2	3/16	Flo-Lite	Vent, Quarter, Back glass

PPG Glass Markings

Style	AS Rating	Thickness	Type	Application
Clear				
M20 8	AS2	1/4	Solid Tempered	Door
M20 6	AS2	3/16	Solid Tempered	Vent, Quarter, Back glass
Tinted				
M25 8	AS1		Laminated	Windshield
M27 8	AS2	1/4	Solid Tempered	Door
M27 6	AS2	3/16	Solid Tempered	Vent, Quarter, Back glass

Glass Code

Month Code					
A	Sept	Y	Oct.	V	Dec
N	Jan	X	Feb.	L	March
G	April	J	May	I	Jun
U	July	T	Aug		

Year Code					
A	Z	X	V	T	N
1966	1967	1968	1969	1970	1971
1979	1980	1981			
Y	G	J			
1972	1964	1965			

Windshield

Chevelle

Model   *Interchange Number*

1964-1965
All
Tinted..2
Clear...1

1966-1967
Except El Camino
Tinted..4
Clear...3
El Camino
Tinted..2
Clear...1

1968-1969
Except Convertible
Tinted..5
Clear...7
Convertible
Tinted..6
Clear...8

1968-1969
Without Radio
Except Convertible
Tinted..5
Clear...7
Convertible
Tinted..6
Clear...8
With Radio
Except Convertible
Tinted..11
Clear...10
Convertible
Tinted..12
Clear...9

Interchanges

Interchange Number: 1
Part Number(s): 7584394
Type: Clear
Usage: 1964-1967 Chevelle, Cutlass, Lemans, Skylark all models and body styles. 1966-1967 Chevelle, Cutlass, Lemans, Skylark two door or 4-door sedan or wagon; 1964-1967 El Camino

Interchange Number: 2
Part Number(s): 7584395
Type: Tinted
Usage: 1964-1967 Chevelle, Cutlass, Lemans, Skylark all models and body styles. 1966-1967 Chevelle, Cutlass, Lemans, Skylark two door or 4-door sedan or wagon; 1964-1967 El Camino

Interchange Number: 3
Part Number(s): 4539495
Type: Clear
Usage: 1966-1967 Chevelle, Cutlass, Lemans, Skylark. Two door hardtop or convertible

Interchange Number: 4
Part Number(s): 4539496
Type: Tinted
Usage: 1966-1967 Chevelle, Cutlass, Lemans, Skylark. Two door hardtop or convertible

Interchange Number: 5
Part Number(s): 7711316
Type: Tinted
Usage: 1968-1969 Chevelle, Cutlass, Lemans, Skylark 2-door sedan or 2-door hardtop; 1968-1969 El Camino; 1970-1972 El Camino without radio

Interchange Number: 6
Part Number(s): 7711318
Type: Tinted
Usage: 1968-1969 Chevelle, Cutlass, Lemans, Skylark convertible; 1970-1972 Chevelle, Cutlass, Lemans, Skylark convertible without radio

Interchange Number: 7
Part Number(s): 9869856
Type: Clear
Usage: 1968-1969 Chevelle, Cutlass, Lemans, Skylark 2-door sedan or 2-door hardtop; 1970-1972 Chevelle, Cutlass, Lemans, Skylark 2-door sedan or 2-door hardtop without radio; 1968-1969 El Camino; 1970-1972 El Camino without radio

Interchange Number: 8
Part Number(s): 9869858
Type: Clear
Usage: 1968-1969 Chevelle, Cutlass, Lemans, Skylark convertible; 1970-1972 Chevelle, Cutlass, Lemans, Skylark convertible without radio

Interchange Number: 9
Part Number(s): 9869855
Type: Clear
Usage: 1970-1972 Chevelle, Cutlass, Lemans, Skylark convertible with radio

Interchange Number: 10
Part Number(s): 9864151
Type: Clear
Usage: 1970-1972 Chevelle, Cutlass, Lemans, Skylark 2-door hardtop with radio; 1970 Chevelle, Cutlass, Lemans, Skylark 2-door sedan with radio; 1970-1972 El Camino with radio

Interchange Number: 11
Part Number(s): 9864152
Type: Tinted
Usage: 1970-1972 Chevelle, Cutlass, Lemans, Skylark 2-door hardtop with radio; 1970 Chevelle, Cutlass, Lemans, Skylark 2-door sedan with radio; 1970-1972 El Camino with radio

Interchange Number: 12
Part Number(s): 9869854
Type: Clear
Usage: 1970-1972 Chevelle, Cutlass, Lemans, Skylark convertible

Vent Window, Glass
Chevelle
Model   *Interchange Number*
1964-1965
All
Tinted..2
Clear..1
1964-1965
Except El Camino/2door sedan
Tinted..3
Clear..4
El Camino/2 Door sedan
Tinted..2
Clear..1
1968-1972
Except El Camino or 2-door sedan (1968 only)
Tinted..5
Clear..6
El Camino/2-door sedan
Tinted..7
Clear..8

Interchanges

Interchange Number: 1
Part Number(s): RH 4409664 LH 4409665
Type: Clear
Usage: 1964-1967 Chevelle, Cutlass, Lemans, Skylark all models and body styles. 1966-1967 Chevelle, Cutlass, Lemans, Skylark two door or 4-door sedan or wagon; 1964-1967 El Camino

Interchange Number: 2
Part Number(s): RH 4409666 LH 4409667
Type: Tinted
Usage: 1964-1967 Chevelle, Cutlass, Lemans, Skylark all models and body styles. 1966-1967 Chevelle, Cutlass, Lemans, Skylark two door or 4-door sedan or wagon; 1964-1967 El Camino

Interchange Number: 3
Part Number(s): RH 4537088 LH 4537089
Type: Clear
Usage: 1966-1967 Chevelle, Cutlass, Lemans, Skylark 2-door hardtop, convertible

Interchange Number: 4
Part Number(s): RH 4537090 LH 4537091
Type: Tinted
Usage: 1966-1967 Chevelle, Cutlass, Lemans, Skylark 2-door hardtop, convertible

Interchange Number: 5
Part Number(s): RH 9712540 LH 9712541
Type: Clear
Usage: 1968 Chevelle, Cutlass, Lemans, Skylark 2-door hardtop, convertible

Interchange Number: 6
Part Number(s): RH 9712542 LH 9712543
Type: Tinted
Usage: 1968 Chevelle, Cutlass, Lemans, Skylark 2-door hardtop, convertible

Interchange Number: 7
Part Number(s): RH 9712586 LH 9712587
Type: Clear
Usage: 1968-1970 Chevelle, Cutlass, Lemans, Skylark 2-door sedan; 1968-1972 El Camino

Interchange Number: 8
Part Number(s): RH 9712588 LH 9712589
Type: Tinted
Usage: 1968-1970 Chevelle, Cutlass, Lemans, Skylark 2-door sedan; 1968-1972 El Camino

Door Window, Glass

Chevelle

Model	Interchange Number
1964	
2-door sedan	
Tinted	2
Clear	1
2-door Hardtop	
Tinted	6
Clear	5
Convertible	
Tinted	8
Clear	7
El Camino	
Tinted	4
Clear	3
1965	
2-door sedan	
Tinted	2
Clear	1
2-door Hardtop	
Tinted	10
Clear	9
Convertible	
Tinted	12
Clear	11
El Camino	
Tinted	4
Clear	3
1966-1967	
2-door sedan	
Tinted	2
Clear	1
2-door Hardtop	
Tinted	14
Clear	13
Convertible	
Tinted	14
Clear	13
El Camino	
Tinted	4
Clear	3
1968	
2-door sedan	
Tinted	17
Clear	18
2-door Hardtop	
Tinted	16
Clear	15
Convertible	
Tinted	16

Clear...15
El Camino
Tinted...20
Clear...19
1969
2-door sedan
Tinted...17
Clear...18
2-door Hardtop
Tinted...22
Clear...21
Convertible
Tinted...22
Clear...21
El Camino
Tinted...20
Clear...19
1970-1972
2-door sedan (1970 only)
Tinted...17
Clear...18
2-door Hardtop
Tinted...24
Clear...23
Convertible
Tinted...24
Clear...23
El Camino
Tinted...20
Clear...19

Interchanges

Interchange Number: 1
Part Number(s): RH 4405115 LH 4405116
Type: Clear
Usage: 1964-1967 Chevelle, Cutlass, Lemans, Skylark 2-door sedan

Interchange Number: 2
Part Number(s): RH 4405117 LH 4405118
Type: Tinted
Usage: 1964-1967 Chevelle, Cutlass, Lemans, Skylark 2-door sedan

Interchange Number: 3
Part Number(s): RH 4405184 LH 4405185
Type: Clear
Usage: 1964-1967 El Camino

Interchange Number: 4
Part Number(s): RH 4405186 LH 4405187
Type: Tinted
Usage: 1964-1967 El Camino

Interchange Number: 5
Part Number(s): RH 4405119 LH 4405120
Type: Clear
Usage: 1964 Chevelle, Cutlass, Lemans, Skylark 2-door hardtop

Interchange Number: 6
Part Number(s): RH 4405121 LH 4405122
Type: Tinted
Usage: 1964 Chevelle, Cutlass, Lemans, Skylark 2-door hardtop

Interchange Number: 7
Part Number(s): RH 4405123 LH 4405124
Type: Clear
Usage: 1964 Chevelle, Cutlass, Lemans, Skylark convertible

Interchange Number: 8
Part Number(s): RH 4405125 LH 4405126
Type: Tinted
Usage: 1964 Chevelle, Cutlass, Lemans, Skylark convertible

Interchange Number: 9
Part Number(s): RH 44051128 LH 4405129
Type: Clear
Usage: 1965 Chevelle, Cutlass, Lemans, Skylark 2-door hardtop

Interchange Number: 10
Part Number(s): RH 4405130 LH 4405131
Type: Tinted
Usage: 1965 Chevelle, Cutlass, Lemans, Skylark 2-door hardtop

Interchange Number: 11
Part Number(s): RH 4405132 LH 4405133
Type: Clear
Usage: 1965 Chevelle, Cutlass, Lemans, Skylark convertible

Interchange Number: 12
Part Number(s): RH 4405134 LH 4405135
Type: Tinted
Usage: 1965 Chevelle, Cutlass, Lemans, Skylark convertible

Interchange Number: 13
Part Number(s): RH 4541588 LH 4541589
Type: Clear
Usage: 1966-1967 Chevelle, Cutlass, Lemans, Skylark 2-door hardtop or convertible

Interchange Number: 14
Part Number(s): RH 4541590 LH 4541591
Type: Tinted
Usage: 1966-1967 Chevelle, Cutlass, Lemans, Skylark 2-door hardtop or convertible

Interchange Number: 15
Part Number(s): RH 7723063 LH 7723064
Type: Clear
Usage: 1968 Chevelle, Cutlass, Lemans, Skylark 2-door hardtop or convertible

Interchange Number: 16
Part Number(s): RH 7723065 LH 7723066
Type: Tinted
Usage: 1968 Chevelle, Cutlass, Lemans, Skylark 2-door hardtop or convertible

Interchange Number: 17
Part Number(s): RH 7723056 LH 7723057
Type: Clear
Usage: 1968-1970 Chevelle, Cutlass, Lemans, Skylark 2-door sedan

Interchange Number: 18
Part Number(s): RH 7723058 LH 7723059
Type: Tinted
Usage: 1968-1970 Chevelle, Cutlass, Lemans, Skylark 2-door sedan

Interchange Number: 19
Part Number(s): RH 7723061 LH 7723062
Type: Clear
Usage: 1968-1972 El Camino

Interchange Number: 20
Part Number(s): RH 7723067 LH 7723068
Type: Tinted
Usage: 1968-1972 El Camino

Interchange Number: 21
Part Number(s): RH 8713451 LH 8713452
Type: Clear
Usage: 1969 Chevelle, Cutlass, Lemans, Skylark 2-door hardtop or convertible

Interchange Number: 22
Part Number(s): RH 8713453 LH 8713454
Type: Tinted
Usage: 1969 Chevelle, Cutlass, Lemans, Skylark 2-door hardtop or convertible

Interchange Number: 23
Part Number(s): RH 9822328 LH 9822329
Type: Tinted
Usage: 1970-1972 Chevelle, Cutlass, Lemans, Skylark 2-door hardtop or convertible; 1970-1972 Monte Carlo; 1970-1972 Grand Prix

Interchange Number: 24
Part Number(s): RH 9822326 LH 9822327
Type: Clear
Usage: 1970-1972 Chevelle, Cutlass, Lemans, Skylark 2-door hardtop or convertible; 1970-1972 Monte Carlo; 1970-1972 Grand Prix

Quarter Window, Glass
Chevelle

Model	Interchange Number
1964-1965	
2-door sedan	
Tinted	2
Clear	1
2-door Hardtop	
Tinted	4
Clear	3
Convertible	
Tinted	6
Clear	5
1966-1967	
2-door sedan	
Tinted	8
Clear	7
2-door Hardtop	
Tinted	10
Clear	9
Convertible	
Tinted	12
Clear	11
1968-1969	
2-door sedan	
Tinted	14
Clear	13
2-door Hardtop	
Tinted	16
Clear	15

Convertible
Tinted..18
Clear...17
1970-1972
2-door sedan (1970 only)
Tinted..20
Clear...19
2-door Hardtop
Tinted..22
Clear...21
Convertible
Tinted..18
Clear...17

Interchanges

Interchange Number: 1
Part Number(s): RH 4409848 LH 4409849
Type: Clear
Usage: 1964-1965 Chevelle, Cutlass, Lemans, Skylark 2-door sedan

Interchange Number: 2
Part Number(s): RH 4409850 LH 4409851
Type: Tinted
Usage: 1964-1965 Chevelle, Cutlass, Lemans, Skylark 2-door sedan

Interchange Number: 3
Part Number(s): RH 4409852 LH 4409853
Type: Clear
Usage: 1964-1965 Chevelle, Cutlass, Lemans, Skylark 2-door hardtop

Interchange Number: 4
Part Number(s): RH 4409854 LH 4409855
Type: Tinted
Usage: 1964-1965 Chevelle, Cutlass, Lemans, Skylark 2-door hardtop

Interchange Number: 5
Part Number(s): RH 4405440 LH 44054441
Type: Clear
Usage: 1964-1965 Chevelle, Cutlass, Lemans, Skylark convertible

Interchange Number: 6
Part Number(s): RH 4405442 LH 44054443
Type: Tinted
Usage: 1964-1965 Chevelle, Cutlass, Lemans, Skylark convertible

Interchange Number: 7
Part Number(s): RH 4538100 LH 4538101
Type: Clear
Usage: 1966-1967 Chevelle, Cutlass, Lemans, Skylark 2-door sedan

Interchange Number: 8
Part Number(s): RH 4538102 LH 4538103
Type: Tinted
Usage: 1966-1967 Chevelle, Cutlass, Lemans, Skylark 2-door sedan

Interchange Number: 9
Part Number(s): RH 4540580 LH 4540581
Type: Clear
Usage: 1966-1967 Chevelle, Cutlass, Lemans, Skylark 2-door hardtop

Interchange Number: 10
Part Number(s): RH 4540582 LH 4540583
Type: Tinted
Usage: 1966-1967 Chevelle, Cutlass, Lemans, Skylark 2-door hardtop

Interchange Number: 11
Part Number(s): RH 4539476 LH 4539477
Type: Clear
Usage: 1966-1967 Chevelle, Cutlass, Lemans, Skylark convertible

Interchange Number: 12
Part Number(s): RH 4539478 LH 4539479
Type: Tinted
Usage: 1966-1967 Chevelle, Cutlass, Lemans, Skylark convertible

Interchange Number: 13
Part Number(s): RH 7719706 LH 7719707
Type: Clear
Usage: 1968-1969 Chevelle, Cutlass, Lemans, Skylark 2-door sedan

Interchange Number: 14
Part Number(s): RH 7719708 LH 7719709
Type: Tinted
Usage: 1968-1969 Chevelle, Cutlass, Lemans, Skylark 2-door sedan

Interchange Number: 15
Part Number(s): RH 7763308 LH 7763309
Type: Clear
Usage: 1968-1969 Chevelle, Cutlass, Lemans, Skylark 2-door hardtop

Interchange Number: 16
Part Number(s): RH 7763310 LH 7763311
Type: Tinted
Usage: 1968-1969 Chevelle, Cutlass, Lemans, Skylark 2-door hardtop

Interchange Number: 17
Part Number(s): RH 7763324 LH 7763325
Type: Clear
Usage: 1968-1972 Chevelle, Cutlass, Lemans, Skylark convertible

Interchange Number: 18
Part Number(s): RH 7763326 LH 7763327
Type: Tinted
Usage: 1968-1972 Chevelle, Cutlass, Lemans, Skylark convertible

Interchange Number: 19
Part Number(s): RH 8780418 LH 8780419
Type: Clear
Usage: 1970 Chevelle, Cutlass, Lemans, Skylark 2-door sedan

Interchange Number: 20
Part Number(s): RH 8780420 LH 8780421
Type: Tinted
Usage: 1970 Chevelle, Cutlass, Lemans, Skylark 2-door sedan

Interchange Number: 21
Part Number(s): RH 8781140 LH 8781141
Type: Clear
Usage: 1970-1972 Chevelle, Cutlass, Lemans, Skylark 2-door hardtop

Interchange Number: 22
Part Number(s): RH 8781142 LH 8781143
Type: Tinted
Usage: 1970-1972 Chevelle, Cutlass, Lemans, Skylark 2-door hardtop

1964-1965 optional standard mirror. Another mirror without a bow-tie symbol mirror was also available.

Back Window, Glass
Chevelle

Model	Interchange Number
1964-1965	
Except El Camino	
Tinted	2
Clear	1
El Camino	
Tinted	8
Clear	7
1966-1967	
Except El Camino	
Tinted	4
Clear	3
El Camino	
Tinted	8
Clear	7
1968-1972	
Except El Camino	
Tinted	6
Clear	5
El Camino	
Tinted	10
Clear	9

1966-1967 Mirror

Interchanges

Interchange Number: 1
Part Number(s): 4490620
Type: Clear
Usage: 1964-1965 Chevelle, Cutlass, Lemans, Skylark 2-door sedan or 2-door hardtop

Interchange Number: 2
Part Number(s): 4408428
Type: Tinted
Usage: 1964-1965 Chevelle, Cutlass, Lemans, Skylark 2-door sedan or 2-door hardtop

Interchange Number: 3
Part Number(s): 4535459
Type: Clear
Usage: 1966-1967 Chevelle, Cutlass, Lemans, Skylark 2-door sedan or 2-door hardtop

Interchange Number: 4
Part Number(s): 4535460
Type: Tinted
Usage: 1966-1967 Chevelle, Cutlass, Lemans, Skylark 2-door sedan or 2-door hardtop

Interchange Number: 5
Part Number(s): 7695842
Type: Clear
Usage: 1968-1972 Chevelle, Cutlass, Lemans, Skylark 2-door sedan or 2-door hardtop

Interchange Number: 6
Part Number(s): 7695843
Type: Tinted
Usage: 1968-1972 Chevelle, Cutlass, Lemans, Skylark 2-door sedan or 2-door hardtop

Interchange Number: 7
Part Number(s): 7620312
Type: Clear
Usage: 1964-1967 El Camino

Interchange Number: 8
Part Number(s): 7620313
Type: Tinted
Usage: 1964-1967 El Camino

Interchange Number: 9
Part Number(s): 7715573
Type: Clear
Usage: 1968-1972 El Camino

Interchange Number: 10
Part Number(s): 7715574
Type: Tinted
Usage: 1968-1972 El Camino

Mirror, Outside
Chevelle

Model	Interchange Number
1964-1965	
Standard	1
Remote	2
Passenger	5
1966	
Standard	3
Remote	4
Passenger	6
1967	
Standard	
Early	1
Late	7
Remote	4
Passenger	
Early	6
Late	8
1968	
Standard	7
Remote	2
Passenger	8
1969	
Standard	9
Remote	14

Passenger..10
1970-1972
Standard
Except El Camino...11
El Camino..9
Remote
Sport...12
El Camino..14
Passenger
Except El Camino...11
El Camino..10
Sport...13

Interchanges

Interchange Number: 1
Part Number(s): 3821956
Type: Standard
Usage: 1963-1965 full-size Chevrolet; 1963-1965 Nova; 1964-1965 Chevelle
Notes: Part of the RPO Z01 Comfort and Convenience group

Interchange Number: 2
Part Number(s): 910791
Type: Remote
Usage: 1964-1965 Chevelle; 1964-1965 full-size Chevrolet; 1964-1965 Nova

1964-1965 Remote control mirror

Early 1967 Bow-tie mirror

Interchange Number: 3
Part Number(s): 3874240
Type: Standard
Usage: 1966-early 1967 Chevelle; 1966-1967 Nova; 1967 Camaro
Notes: Up to Feb 1967

Interchange Number: 4
Part Number(s): 3899857
Type: Remote
Usage: 1966- early 1967 Chevelle; 1966-1967 Nova; 1967 Camaro
Notes: Up to Feb 1967

Interchange Number: 5
Part Number(s): 3821957
Type: Standard Passenger side
Usage: 1963-1965 full-size Chevrolet; 1963-1965 Nova; 1964-1965 Chevelle
Notes: Dealer installed

Interchange Number: 6
Part Number(s): 3874241
Type: Standard/passenger
Usage: 1966-1967 Chevelle; 1966-1967 Nova; 1967 Camaro
Notes: Dealer installed Up to Feb 1967

Interchange Number: 7
Part Number(s): 3909197
Type: Standard
Usage: Late 1967-1968 Chevelle; 1968-1969 Nova; 1968 Biscayne, Bel air
Notes: After March 1 1967

Interchange Number: 8
Part Number(s): 3909198
Type: Standard/Passenger
Usage: Late 1967-1968 Chevelle; 1968-1969 Nova; 1968 Biscayne, Bel air
Notes: After March 1, 1967

Interchange Number: 9
Part Number(s): 3914753
Type: Standard
Usage: 1969 Chevelle, all models and body styles; 1970-1972 Chevelle wagon and El Camino; 1968-1969 Camaro; 1969-1970 full-size Chevrolet.

Interchange Number: 10
Part Number(s): 3914754
Type: Standard/Passenger
Usage: 1969 Chevelle, all models and body styles; 1970-1972 Chevelle wagon and El Camino; 1968-1969 Camaro; 1969-1970 full-size Chevrolet.

Interchange Number: 11
Part Number(s): 3965921
Type: Standard
Usage: 1970-1972 Chevelle, all models and body styles except wagon and El Camino
Notes: Fits either driver's or passenger side

Interchange Number: 12
Part Number(s): 9878201
Type: Remote (Bullet/Sport)
Usage: 1970-1972 Chevelle, all models and body styles

Interchange Number: 13
Part Number(s): 9878202
Type: Standard (Bullet/Sport)
Usage: 1970-1972 Chevelle, all models and body styles
Notes: Passenger side

Interchange Number: 14
Part Number(s): 3957200
Type: Remote
Usage: 1969 Chevelle, all models and body styles; 1970-1972 Chevelle wagon or El Camino

Late 1967-1968 Mirror

Mirror, Inside
Chevelle

Model	Interchange Number
1964-1965	
All	1
1966	
All	2
1967-1968	
All	3
1969-1972	
Without lamp	4
With lamp	5

Interchanges

Interchange Number: 1
Part Number(s): 910480
Usage: 1964-1965 Chevelle
Note: Part of RPO Z01 or Z13 package

Interchange Number: 2
Part Number(s): 898821
Usage: 1966 Nova, Chevelle

Interchange Number: 3
Part Number(s): 911366
Usage: 1967-1968 full-size Chevrolet, Chevelle, Camaro; 1967 Nova; 1969-early 1970 Nova
Notes: Changed April 1970 in Novas

Interchange Number: 5
Part Number(s): 911581
Usage: 1969-1972 Chevelle; 1969-1970 full-size Chevrolet without lamp

Interchange Number: 6
Part Number(s): 911712
Usage: 1969-1972 Chevelle; 1969-1970, 1972 full-size Chevrolet with lamp

1969 mirror also used on 1969-1972 El Caminos. Passenger side shown.

1970-1972 standard mirror

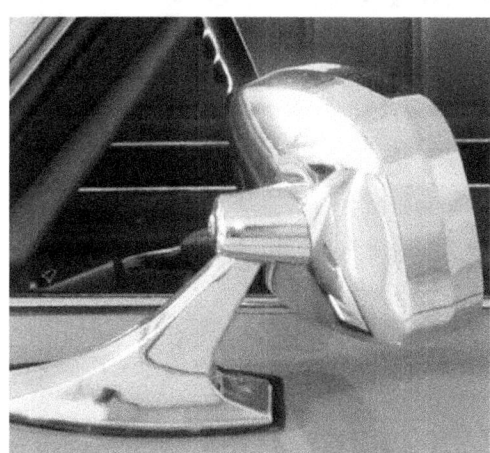

1970-1972 remote std. mirror

1970-1972 Sport mirror

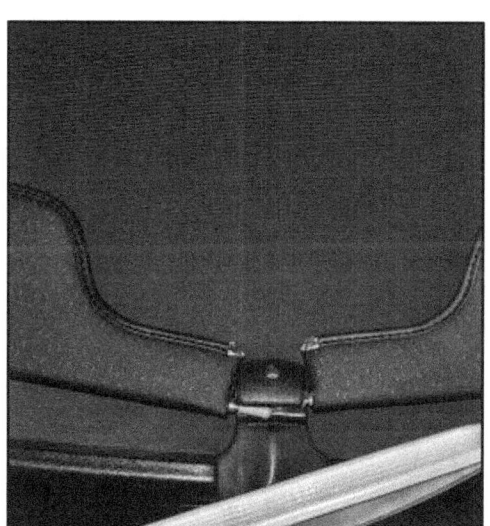

1968-1972 Inside mirror

Chapter 15 Emblems and Nameplate

General

This section covers the various emblems and name plates that were used on 1964-1972 Chevelles. Interchange is broken down by location i.e grille, hood, header, fender etc. This makes it easier to find the interchange you are looking for. Because some emblems were stamped with a part number the original part numbers based on assembly manuals are given. There may be cases were these parts were grouped under a single replacement part number giving more interchanges available if this is the case it is listed under the notes section of the interchange.

Note that certain medallions like engine call outs were used on several different models so you may find one for your Chevelle on other Chevrolet models.

Emblem, Grille

Chevelle

Model	Interchange Number
1965	
All	1
1966	
Chevelle	2
El Camino	3
SS 396	4
1967	
Except SS 396	15
SS 396	5
1968	
Except SS 396	6
SS 396	7
1969	
SS 396	8
Bow tie	18
1970	
Bow tie	13
Chevelle	
Early	11
Late	10
Chevrolet	
Early	12
Late	17
SS	9

1965 Grille emblem was red and white with a blue bow tie in the middle.

1971	
Bow tie	14
Chevelle	10
Chevrolet	17
SS	9
1972	
Bow tie	14
Chevelle	10
Chevrolet	17
SS	16

The grille emblem was used on all 1966 models except El Camino or SS 396 models

Interchanges

Interchange Number: 1
Part Number(s): 3875758
Type: Medallion
Usage: 1965 Chevelle

Interchange Number: 2
Part Number(s): 3876137
Type: "Chevelle"
Usage: 1966 Chevelle, all models and body styles except SS 396 or El Camino

Interchange Number: 3
Part Number(s): 3880624
Type: "El Camino"
Usage: 1966 El Camino

Interchange Number: 4
Part Number(s): 3891434
Type: "SS 396"
Usage: 1966 Chevelle SS 396

Interchange Number: 5
Part Number(s): 3904590
Type: "SS 396"
Usage: 1967 Chevelle SS 396

Interchange Number: 6
Part Number(s): 3920850
Type: Red and blue medallion with bow tie and stars
Usage: Early 1968 Malibu and el Camino except SS 396
Notes: Used up until Oct 1967

Interchange Number: 7
Part Number(s): 3920802
Type: "SS 396"
Usage: 1968 Chevelle SS 396, or El Camino SS 396
Notes: Stamped 3920802

Interchange Number: 8
Part Number(s): 3942781
Type: "SS 396"
Usage: 1969 Chevelle SS 396, or El Camino SS 396
Notes: Stamped 3942781

Interchange Number: 9
Part Number(s): 3968564
Type: "SS"
Usage; 1970-1971 Chevelle SS, or El Camino SS
Notes: Stamped 3968564

1966 SS 396 grille emblem

1966 Grille emblem used on El Caminos

Interchange Number: 10
Part Number(s): 3987072
Type: "Chevelle"
Usage; Late 1970-1972 Chevelle except El Camino or wagon
Notes: Stamped 3987072 Used after May 1970

Interchange Number: 11
Part Number(s): 3975396
Type: "Chevelle"
Usage; Early 1970 Chevelle except El Camino, or wagon
Notes: Stamped 3975396 Used up until May 1970

Interchange Number: 12
Part Number(s): 3979918
Type: "Chevrolet"
Usage; Early 1970 Chevelle wagon or El Camino
Notes: Stamped 5979918 Used up to May 1970

Interchange Number: 13
Part Number(s): 3972987
Type: Bow tie
Usage; 1970 Chevelle except SS
Notes: Stamped 3987072

Interchange Number: 14
Part Number(s): 3982495
Type: Bow tie
Usage; 1971-1972 Chevelle except SS
Notes: Stamped 3987072

Interchange Number: 15
Part Number(s): 3907069
Type: Red and blue medallion with bow tie and stars
Usage: 1967 Chevelle all models except SS 396

Interchange Number: 16
Part Number(s): 6264838
Type: "SS"
Usage; 1972 Chevelle SS, or El Camino SS
Notes: Stamped 6264838

Interchange Number: 17
Part Number(s): 3987056
Type: "Chevrolet"
Usage; Late 1970-1972 Chevelle wagon or El Camino
Notes: Stamped 3987056 Used after May 1970

Interchange Number: 18
Part Number(s):3952427
Type: Blue bow tie
Usage; 1969 Chevelle, except SS 396

1967 Chevelle grille header emblem, used with all but SS 396 models

1967 SS396 grille emblem

1968 Chevelle grille emblem except SS 396

1968 SS 396 grille emblem

1969 bow tie emblem used on 1969 Malibu's

1969 SS 396 grille emblem

1970 bow tie emblem used on all those except SS

1970-1971 SS grille emblem. 1972 similar.

1970 Chevelle nameplate on grille 1971-1972 similar

1970-1972 El Camino's used this nameplate on the grille

1971 bow tie.

1967 Hood nameplate was used on the front left-hand corner of the hood

1967 el Camino header emblem

1968 header emblem.

1969 Chevelle header

1968-1969 El Camino header

1964 Front fender nameplate

1964 fender marker that represented a 283-ci V-8 engine

1965 Flying V emblem was used on many different Chevrolet models

Late 1968 Callout for the 396-ci engine

1966 396 call out used on the front fenders

1968 327 Callout lamp bezels was used many Chevrolet models

Early 1968 Callout bezels

1969-1970 SS 396 nameplate used on front fenders

Emblem, Front Header or Hood

Chevelle

Model	Interchange Number
1964	
CHEVROLET	1
1965	
CHEVROLET	2
1967	
CHEVELLE	3
El Camino	4
1968	
Chevelle (script)	5
El Camino (script)	6
1969	
Chevelle (script)	5
By Chevrolet	7
El Camino (script)	6
1970-1972	
Cowl Induction	8

Interchanges

Interchange Number: 1
Part Number(s): 3844091
Type: C-H-E-V-R-O-L-E-T
Usage: 1964 Chevelle, all models and body styles. Across front edge of hood.
Notes: individual letters

Interchange Number: 2
Part Number(s): 3862174
Type: C-H-E-V-R-O-L-E-T
Usage: 1965 Chevelle, all models and body styles. Across front edge of hood.
Notes: individual letters

Interchange Number: 3
Part Number(s): 3893924
Type: "Chevelle"
Usage: 1967 Chevelle, all models and body styles, except wagon or El Camino

Interchange Number: 4
Part Number(s): 3893923
Type: "El Camino"
Usage: 1967 El Camino

Interchange Number: 5
Part Number(s): 3920825
Type: "Chevelle"
Usage: 1968-1969 Chevelle, all models and body styles, except El Camino

Notes: used with by Chevrolet block in 1969 Two different nameplates were used in 1969 and mount differently so interchange with mounting nuts. See Front fenders emblems

Interchange Number: 6
Part Number(s): 3920867
Type: "el Camino"
Usage: 1968-1969 El Camino

Interchange Number: 7
Part Number(s): 3942788
Type: "by Chevrolet"
Usage: 1969 Chevelle, all models and body styles, except El Camino

Interchange Number: 8
Part Number(s): Cowl- 3968567
Induction- 3968568
Type: "Cowl Induction"
Usage: 1970-1972 Chevelle SS or El Camino SS with RPO ZL2 hood option

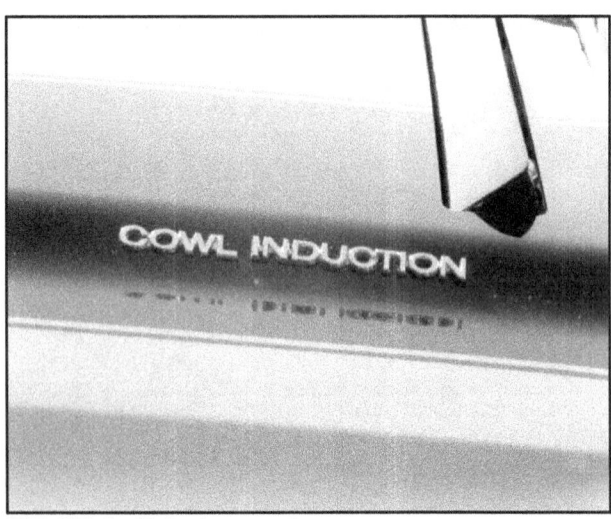

1970-1972 Cowl induction nameplates

Emblem, Fender

Chevelle

Model	Interchange Number

1964
CHEVELLE..1
V-..2

1965-1967
Flying V..3
283..5
327..6
396..4

1968
Chevelle..7
Malibu...26
307
  Early...27
  Late..8
327...11
396
  Early...9
  Late..10

1969
300...24
SS...12
307...14
350...15
396...13

1970
300 Deluxe..18
Malibu...16
El Camino..19
SS...12
307
  Except El Camino..17
  El Camino..20
350...29
396...13
454...28

1971-1972
Malibu...21
El Camino..19
SS...12
307
  Except El Camino..17
  El Camino..20
350...22

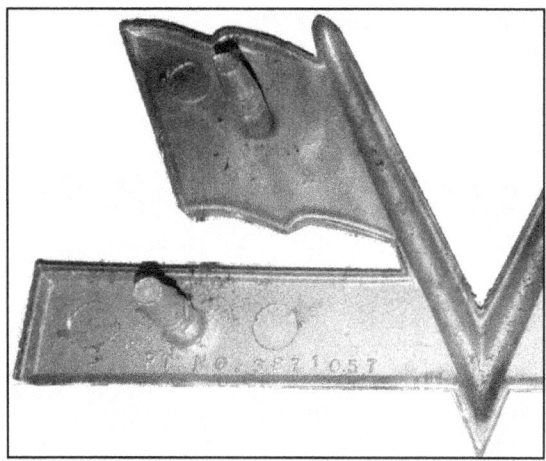

Some emblems can be identified by a part number cast into them; this one is for the 1965-1967 396 callouts.

1970-1972 SS 454 call out.

Interchanges

Interchange Number: 1
Part Number(s): 3840317
Type: "V"
Usage: 1964 Chevelle or full-size Chevrolet with a 283-ci V-8

Interchange Number: 2
Part Number(s): 3849498
Type: "Chevelle"
Usage: 1964 Chevelle all models and body styles

Interchange Number: 3
Part Number(s): 3840318
Type/Location: Flying "V" emblem used in correlation with engine displacement badge; location varies according to model
Usage: 1965-1967 Chevelle; 1965-1967 Nova 1965-1967 full-size Chevrolet; 1967 Camaro
Notes: Used with all V-8 engines except 396-ci or 427-ci versions. Stamped with part number

Interchange Number: 4
Part Number(s): 3871057
Type/Location: "396 Turbo-jet cross flags"
Usage: 1965-1967 Chevelle, full-size Chevrolet with 396-ci V-8; 1967 Camaro with 396-ci V-8

Interchange Number: 5
Part Number(s): 3863852
Type/Location: "283" emblem used in correlation with flying V above
Usage: 1965-1967 Chevelle; 1965-1967 Nova 1965-1967 full-size Chevrolet all with 283-ci V-8

Interchange Number: 6
Part Number(s): 3863853
Type/Location: "327" emblem used in correlation with flying V above
Usage: 1965-1967 Chevelle; 1965-1967 Nova 1965-1967 full-size Chevrolet; 1967 Camaro all with 327-ci V-8

Interchange Number: 7
Part Number(s): 3920825
Type/Location: "Chevelle" Script
Usage: 1968 Chevelle all models and body styles except Malibu, SS 396 or wagons see header emblem section

Interchange Number: 8
Part Number(s): 3935903-LH 3935904-RH
Type/Location: "307" lamp bezel
Usage: Late 1968 Chevelle with 307-ci all models but SS 396
Notes: Stamped with part number

Interchange Number: 9
Part Number(s): 3920877-LH 3920878-RH
Type/Location: "SS 396" lamp bezel
Usage: Early 1968 SS 396

Interchange Number: 10
Part Number(s): 3935901 LH 3935902-RH
Type/Location: "396" lamp bezel
Usage: Late 1968 Chevelle SS 396; 1968 Full-size Chevrolet with 396-ci V-8
Notes: Stamped 3935901 and 3935902

Interchange Number: 11
Part Number(s): 3935907-LH 3935908-RH
Type/Location: "327" lamp bezel
Usage: 1968 Chevelle, full-size Chevrolet with 327-ci V-8
Notes: Stamped 3920873 and 3920874

Interchange Number: 12
Part Number(s): 3949238
Type/Location: "SS"
Usage: 1969-1972 Chevelle with Super Sport package; 1969 Impala with SS 427 package
Notes: stamped with part number

Interchange Number: 13
Part Number(s): 3948030
Type/Location: "396"
Usage: 1969-1970 Chevelle with Super Sport 396 package
Notes: Stamped 3848030

1970-1972 El Camino front fender nameplate. Note engine callouts are under the name plate and special this this model.

1970 Malibu nameplate on front fenders is 10.88 inches long between studs.

Interchange Number: 14
Part Number(s): 3945291 LH 3945292- RH
Type/Location: "307"
Usage: 1969 Chevelle with 307-ci V-8
Notes: stamped with part number and part number for 350

Interchange Number: 15
Part Number(s): 3945293 LH 3945294- RH
Type/Location: "350"
Usage: 1969 Chevelle with 350-ci V-8
Notes: stamped with part number and part number for 307

Interchange Number: 16
Part Number(s): 3972917
Type/Location: "MALIBU"
Usage: 1970 Malibu except with SS package or El Camino

Interchange Number: 17
Part Number(s): 3968537-LH 3968538-LH
Type/Location: "307"
Usage: 1970 Chevelle with 307-ci except SS or El Camino
Notes: 2.70 inches between mounting studs center locating stud is at top.

Interchange Number: 18
Part Number(s): 3975411
Type/Location: "300 deluxe"
Usage: 1970 Chevelle 300 Deluxe series

Interchange Number: 19
Part Number(s): 3972937
Type/Location: "El Camino"
Usage: 1970-1972 El Camino

Interchange Number: 20
Part Number(s): 3972932
Type/Location: "307" below El Camino nameplate
Usage: 1970-1972 El Camino with 307-ci V-8

Interchange Number: 21
Part Number(s): 3982414
Type/Location: "MALIBU"
Usage: 1971-1972 Malibu, all body styles, except with SS package or El Camino

Interchange Number: 22
Part Number(s): 3963234-LH 3975454-RH
Type/Location: "350"
Usage: 1971-1972 Chevelle with 350-ci except SS
Notes: 2.70 between outer studs

Interchange Number: 24
Part Number(s): 3952499
Type/Location: "300"
Usage: 1969 Chevelle 300

Although it looks similar the 1971-1972 Malibu name plate was given a different part number and is slightly shorter. And is 7-1/2 inches between outer studs.

1971-1972 350 engine call out

Interchange Number: 25
Part Number(s): 3974354
Type/Location: "350"
Usage: 1970-1972 El Camino
Notes: Mounted below El Camino nameplate

Interchange Number: 26
Part Number(s): 3920864
Type/Location: "Malibu" script
Usage: 1968 Malibu models, all body styles except wagons or SS 396

Interchange Number: 27
Part Number(s): 3920871-LH 3920872-RH
Type/Location: "307" lamp bezel
Usage: Early 1968 Chevelle with 307-ci all models but SS 396; 1968 full-size Chevrolet with 307-ci V-8
Notes: No ribbed background

Interchange Number: 28
Part Number(s): 3975410
Type/Location: "454"
Usage: 1970 Chevelle or El Camino with SS 454 package
Notes: Stamped 3975410

Interchange Number: 29
Part Number(s): 3974223-LH 3974224-LH
Type/Location: "350"
Usage: 1970 Chevelle with 307-ci except SS or El Camino
Notes: 2.70 inches between mounting studs center locating stud is at top.

Interchange Number: 30

Part Number(s): 3975413
Type/Location: "400"
Usage: 1971-1972 El Camino with 400 ci BIG BLOCK V-8

Emblem, Rear Quarter

Chevelle

Model	Interchange Number
1964	
300	1
Malibu	2
Malibu SS	3
El Camino	7
1965	
300	4
300 Deluxe	5
Malibu	6
Malibu SS	14
El Camino	8
1966	
300	13
300 Deluxe	12
Malibu	10
Super Sport	9
El Camino	11
1967	
300	13
300 Deluxe	12
Malibu	10
Super Sport	15
El Camino	16
1968	
El Camino	17
1969	
Malibu	18
El Camino	17

Interchanges

Interchange Number: 1
Part Number(s): 4252500
Type/Location: "300"
Usage: 1964 Chevelle 300, all body styles
Notes: stamped part number

Interchange Number: 2
Part Number(s): 4252496
Type/Location: "Malibu"
Usage: 1964 Chevelle Malibu, all body styles
Stamped: 4252496

Interchange Number: 3

Part Number(s): 4252497
Type/Location: "Malibu SS"
Usage: 1964 Malibu SS all body styles
Notes: stamped 4252497

Interchange Number: 4
Part Number(s): 4477684
Type/Location: "300"
Usage: 1965 Chevelle 300, all body styles
Notes: Stamped 4477684

Interchange Number: 5
Part Number(s): 4492953
Type/Location: "300 Deluxe"
Usage: 1965 Chevelle 300 Deluxe, all body styles
Notes: stamped 4492953

Interchange Number: 6
Part Number(s): 3871638
Type/Location: "Malibu- Chevelle"
Usage: 1965 Malibu, all body styles, except wagon
Notes Stamped 4477686

Interchange Number: 7
Part Number(s): 4412514
Type/Location: "El Camino bow tie"
Usage: 1964 El Camino
Notes: Stamped 4412514

Interchange Number: 8
Part Number(s): 4493442
Type/Location: "Bow tie El Camino"
Usage: 1965 El Camino
Notes: Stamped 4496442

Interchange Number: 9
Part Number(s): 4227377
Type/Location: "Super Sport"
Usage: 1966 Chevelle Super Sport, all body styles
Notes Stamped 4227377 or 7635748

Interchange Number: 10
Part Number(s): 4429716
Type/Location: "Malibu" Script
Usage: 1966-1967 Malibu all body styles

Interchange Number: 11
Part Number(s): 4227313
Type/Location: "Bow-tie El Camino"
Usage: 1966 El Camino
Notes: Stamped 7584559

Interchange Number: 12
Part Number(s): 4226979
Type/Location: "300 deluxe"
Usage: 1966 Chevelle 300 Deluxe all body styles
Notes: Stamped 7584849

Interchange Number: 13
Part Number(s): 4226980
Type/Location: "300"
Usage: 1966-1967 Chevelle 300 all body styles
Notes: Stamped 4226980

Interchange Number: 14
Part Number(s): 4477685
Type/Location: "Malibu SS"
Usage: 1965 Malibu SS all body styles

Interchange Number: 15
Part Number(s): 4229717
Type/Location: "Super Sport"
Usage: 1967 Chevelle Super Sport, all body styles

Interchange Number: 16
Part Number(s): 4229728
Type/Location: "El Camino"
Usage: 1967 Chevelle Super Sport, all body styles

Interchange Number: 17
Part Number(s): 7795052
Type/Location: "el Camino"
Usage: 1968-1969 El Camino
Notes Stamped 7739425

Interchange Number: 18
Part Number(s): 8701037
Type/Location: "Malibu"
Usage: 1969 Malibu, all body styles
Notes Stamped 8723146

1965 300 Deluxe rear quarter panel emblem

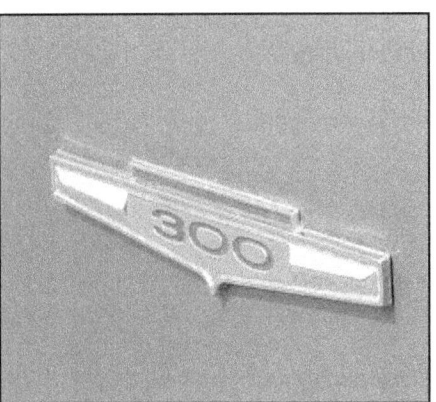
1966-1967 300 rear quarter panel emblem

1965 Malibu SS rear quarter panel emblem, the 1964 emblem is similar

1965 Malibu rear quarter emblem, features an attached Chevelle name plate, the 1964 version used only the Malibu script

1965 El Camino rear quarter panel emblem, 1964 is similar in design.

1966 Super Sport rear quarter name plate

1966-1967 Malibu Script used on rear quarter panels

1967 Super Sport rear quarter emblems.

1967 El Camino rear quarter emblem

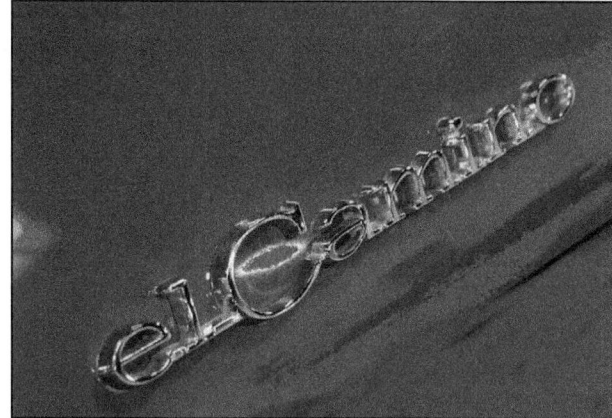
1968-1969 El Camino rear quarter emblem

1969 Malibu Rear Quarter emblem

1964-1965 Rear deck lid lettering, below is the 1964 medallion

1964 SS circle emblem

Emblem, Rear End or Tailgate
Chevelle

Model	Interchange Number
1964	
CHEVROLET	1
SS	3
Medallion	2
El Camino	4
1965	
CHEVROLET	1
Malibu SS	7
El Camino	4
1966	
Chevelle	
Except Malibu	8
Malibu	9
SS 396	29
El Camino	5
Medallion	10
1967	
Medallion	11
Chevelle	
300 Deluxe	12
Malibu	13
SS 396	14
El Camino	10
1968	
300 and Deluxe	
Medallion	20
Chevelle	15
SS 396	
Except El Camino	16
El Camino	
SS 396	17
Chevrolet	18
Bow tie	19
1969	
Chevelle by Chevrolet	21
Concours	22
SS 396	
Except El Camino	30
El Camino	
SS 396	17
Chevrolet	18
Bow tie	19
1970	
Chevelle by Chevrolet	23

Malibu..24
El Camino
SS 396..17
SS...26
Chevrolet...25
Bow tie...19

1971-1972
Chevelle by Chevrolet..............................28
SS...31
El Camino
SS 26
454...27
Chevrolet...25
Bow tie...19

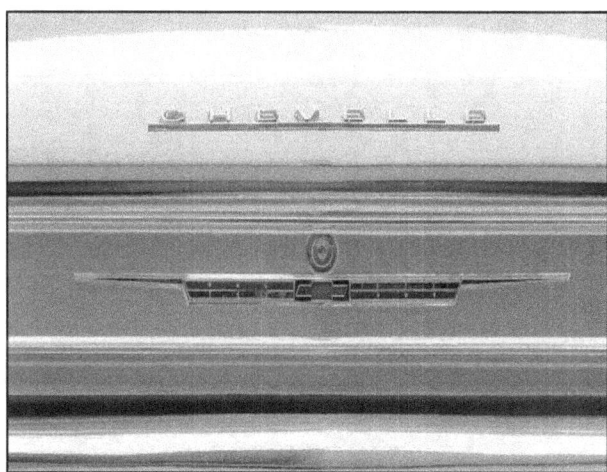

1966 Malibu used a special Chevelle nameplate on the trunk lid, it is not interchangeable with other models.

The 1966 SS 396 used a 25-1/4 inches long name plate on the rear end panel.

1966 SS 396 used this emblem in the center of the rear end panel

Interchanges

Interchange Number: 1
Part Number(s): 3853422
Type/Location: C-H-E-V-R-O-L-E-T
Usage: 1964-1965 Chevelle, all models and body styles including El Camino; 1966 El Camino

Interchange Number: 2
Part Number(s): 3853184
Type/Location: Medallion
Usage: 1964 Chevelle, all models and body styles except wagon or El Camino
Notes: Stamped 4470009

Interchange Number: 3
Part Number(s): 3853185
Type/Location: SS in circle
Usage: 1964 Malibu SS, all models and body styles

Interchange Number: 4
Part Number(s): 3871647
Type/Location: Bow-tie emblem
Usage: 1964-1965 El Camino
Notes: Stamped 4414148

Interchange Number: 5
Part Number(s): 4227115
Type/Location: Bow-tie emblem
Usage: 1966 El Camino
Notes: Stamped 4550449

Interchange Number: 6
Part Number(s): 4229508
Type/Location: Bow-tie emblem
Usage: 1967 El Camino
Notes: Stamped 7663089

Interchange Number: 7
Part Number(s): 3871645
Type/Location: "Malibu SS"
Usage: 1965 Malibu SS all body styles
Notes: Stamped 4492586

Interchange Number: 8
Part Number(s): 4229439
Type/Location: "Chevelle"
Usage: 1966 Chevelle, all models except Malibu or wagons.
Notes: Stamped 7883365

Interchange Number: 9
Part Number(s): 4227111
Type/Location: "Chevelle"
Usage: 1965 Malibu all body styles, except wagon or El Camino
Notes: Stamped 7582450

Interchange Number: 10
Part Number(s): 4227109
Type/Location: Medallion red with blue bow tie
Usage: 1966 Malibu all body styles, except wagon or El Camino

Interchange Number: 11
Part Number(s): 4229433
Type/Location: Red and blue medallion
Usage: 1967 Chevelle 300 deluxe, all body styles except wagon or El Camino

Interchange Number: 12
Part Number(s): 4229439
Type/Location: "Chevelle"
Usage: 1967 Chevelle 300 all body styles except wagon or El Camino

Interchange Number: 13
Part Number(s): 4229502
Type/Location: "Chevelle"
Usage: 1967 Malibu all body styles except wagon or El Camino
Notes: stamped 7656571

Interchange Number: 14
Part Number(s): 4229992
Type/Location: "SS 396"
Usage: 1967 Chevelle SS 396 all body styles except El Camino

1967 Chevelle 300's used a Chevelle nameplate that is similar but is not the same as the one in 1966

The 1967 Malibu's used this Chevelle name plate.

1967 SS 396 rear panel emblem

1967 Chevelle 300 Deluxe used this rear medallion

1968 SS 396 rear end panel emblem

The script used on the rear of 1968 Chevelles, except Concours and SS 396

1968-1972 Bow tie tail gate emblem

Emblem used on the tailgates of 1968-1969 El Camino's except SS 396 models.

Interchange Number: 15
Part Number(s): 7740129
Type/Location: "Chevelle"
Usage: 1968 Chevelle all models and body styles except El Camino, SS 396 or Concours
Notes: Stamped 7740129

Interchange Number: 16
Part Number(s): 7745748
Type/Location: "SS 396"
Usage: 1968 Chevelle SS 396 all body styles except El Camino

Interchange Number: 17
Part Number(s): 7795093
Type/Location: "SS 396"
Usage: 1968-1970 El Camino SS 396
Notes: Stamped 7755832

Interchange Number: 18
Part Number(s): 7795089
Type/Location: "Chevrolet"
Usage: 1968-1969 El Camino

Interchange Number: 19
Part Number(s): 8701343
Type/Location: Bow-tie emblem
Usage: 1968-1972 El Camino
Notes 7745209

Interchange Number: 20
Part Number(s): 7726922
Type/Location: Red and blue medallion
Usage: 1968 Chevelle 300 and deluxe

Interchange Number: 21
Part Number(s): 8701218
Type/Location: "Chevelle by Chevrolet"
Usage: 1969 Chevelle all models and body styles, except Wagon, Concours or El Camino

Interchange Number: 22
Part Number(s): 7795101
Type/Location: "Concours by Chevrolet"
Usage: 1969 Chevelle Concours

Interchange Number: 23
Part Number(s): 8791686
Type/Location: "Chevelle by Chevrolet"
Usage: 1970 Chevelle all models and body styles except El Camino, wagon or Malibu
Notes: Stamped

Interchange Number: 24
Part Number(s): 8791687
Type/Location: "Malibu"
Usage: 1970 Malibu all body styles except wagon or El Camino

Interchange Number: 25
Part Number(s): 8700891
Type/Location: "Chevrolet"
Usage: 1970-1972 El Camino
Notes: Stamped 3970884

Interchange Number: 26
Part Number(s): 8704030
Type/Location: "SS"
Usage: 1970-1972 El Camino SS
Notes: Stamped 8798868

Interchange Number: 27
Part Number(s): 8704040
Type/Location: "454"
Usage: 1970-1972 El Camino SS 454
Notes: Stamped

Interchange Number: 28
Part Number(s): 9834999
Type/Location: "Chevelle by Chevrolet"
Usage: 197-1972 Chevelle all models and body styles except El Camino, wagon or Malibu
Notes: Stamped

Interchange Number: 29
Part Number(s): 4227376
Type/Location: "SS 396"
Usage: 1966 Chevelle SS 396

Interchange Number: 30
Part Number(s): 8701346
Type/Location: "SS 396"
Usage: 1969 Chevelle SS396 all body styles, except El Camino or Concours or wagons
Notes: Stamped 8743772

Interchange Number: 31
Part Number(s): 3975497
Type/Location: "SS"
Usage: 1971-1972 Chevelle SS except El Camino

1970 Chevelle Name plate on decklid

1971-1972 Chevelle name plate on decklid.

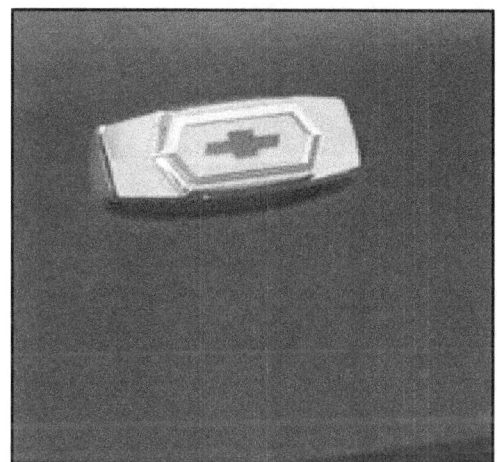
Tail gate emblems for 1964-1966 El Caminos

1967 El Camino bow tie emblem

1968-1970 El Camino tailgate with SS 396 package

Nameplate used on the tailgate of 1970-1972 El Camino's

1971-1972 Letters used on the tailgate. Except with 454

Chapter 16 Interior

Instrument Panel

Interchange here is the bare dash panel, stripped of all gauges, pads and controls.

Chevelle
Model   *Interchange Number*
1964
All..1
1965
Without Air Conditioning..2
With Air Conditioning...3
1966-1967
Chevelle 300
Without Air Conditioning..4
With Air Conditioning...5
Chevelle 300 Deluxe
Without Air Conditioning..6
With Air Conditioning...7
Malibu, SS 396 or Concours
Without Air Conditioning..8
With Air Conditioning...9
1968
Without Air Conditioning..10
With Air Conditioning...11
1969
All..11
1970-1972
Without Gauges..12
With Gauges..14

Interchanges

Interchange Number: 1
Part Number(s): 3873447
Usage: 1964 Chevelle, all models and body styles

Interchange Number: 2
Part Number(s): 3872967
Usage: 1965 Chevelle, all models and body styles, except with air conditioning

1968 Models used two instrument panels, those with air conditioning have cut outs, while those without (shown) do not.

Interchange Number: 3
Part Number(s): 3872968
Usage: 1965 Chevelle, all models and body styles, with air conditioning

Interchange Number: 4
Part Number(s): 3897575
Usage: 1966-1967 Chevelle, all models and body styles, without air conditioning. Except Deluxe, Malibu or SS 396

Interchange Number: 5
Part Number(s): 3897576
Usage: 1966-1967 Chevelle, all models and body styles, with air conditioning. Except Deluxe, Malibu or SS 396

Interchange Number: 6
Part Number(s): 3897577
Usage: 1966-1967 Chevelle Deluxe, all models and body styles, without air conditioning.

1964-1965 Glovebox door

Interchange Number: 7
Part Number(s): 3897578
Usage: 1966-1967 Chevelle Deluxe, all models and body styles, with air conditioning.

Interchange Number: 8
Part Number(s): 3897579
Usage: 1966-1967 Chevelle Malibu, Concours or SS 396 all models and body styles, without air conditioning.

Interchange Number: 9
Part Number(s): 3897580
Usage: 1966-1967 Chevelle Malibu Concours or SS 396 all models and body styles, with air conditioning.

Interchange Number: 10
Part Number(s): 8716960
Usage: 1968 Chevelle all models and body styles, without air conditioning; 1969 Chevelle 4-door sedan, 4-door hardtop, El Camino without air conditioning

Interchange Number: 11
Part Number(s): 8716960
Usage: 1968-1969 Chevelle all models and body styles, with air conditioning; 1969 Chevelle 2-door hardtop or convertible without air conditioning

Interchange Number: 12
Part Number(s): 3965419
Usage: 1970-1972 Chevelle all models and body styles, except Super Sport models or those with the optional gauge package

Interchange Number: 14
Part Number(s): 3999456
Usage: 1970-1972 Chevelle Super Sport or with the optional gauge package; 1970-1972 Monte Carlo

Compartment, Glovebox

Chevelle
Model	Interchange Number
1964-1965	
All	1
1966-1967	
Without Air Conditioning	2
With Air Conditioning	3
1968-1969	
Without Air Conditioning	4
With Air Conditioning	5

1966-1967 Glovebox door

A special door is used on 1968-1969 models with air conditioning as the glovebox compartment was attached to door.

Interchange Number: 1
Part Number(s): 3386294
Usage: 1964-1965 Chevelle, all models and body styles

Interchange Number: 2
Part Number(s): 3878159
Usage: 1966-1967 Chevelle, all models and body styles without air conditioning

Interchange Number: 3
Part Number(s): 3885196
Usage: 1966-1967 Chevelle, all models and body styles with air conditioning

Interchange Number: 4
Part Number(s): 3939635
Usage: 1968-1969 Chevelle, all models and body styles without air conditioning

Interchange Number: 5
Part Number(s): 3930197
Usage: 1968-1969 Chevelle, all models and body styles with air conditioning
Notes: One-piece plastic unit stamped to part number attached to door

Door, Glovebox
Chevelle
Model   *Interchange Number*
1964-1965
All..5
1966-1967
All..1
1968-1969
Without Air Conditioning............................2
With Air Conditioning..................................3
1970-1972
All..4

Interchanges

Interchange Number: 1
Part Number(s): 3871013
Usage: 1966-1967 Chevelle, all models and body styles
Notes: Stamped with part number

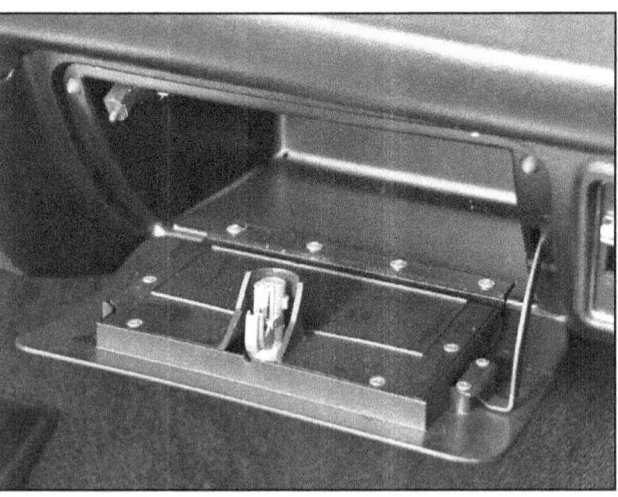
The 1970-1972 Glovebox door is a two-part design

Interchange Number: 2
Part Number(s): 3927641
Usage: 1968-1969 Chevelle, all models and body styles without air conditioning

Interchange Number: 3
Part Number(s): 3930193
Usage: 1968-1969 Chevelle, all models and body styles with air conditioning

Interchange Number: 4
Part Number(s): 3991762-Outer 3957090-Inner
Usage: 1970-1972 Chevelle, all models and body styles

Interchange Number: 5
Part Number(s): 3782091
Usage: 1964-1965 Chevelle, all models and body styles

Sun Visor

Sun visors were covered in vinyl that matched or corresponded to the color of the interior trim and usually matched the headliner in color. However, there is no mention of color or the interchange is based on this. Instead it is based on the part number for black or white to allow a larger interchange. Sun visors can be re-dyed to match your interior trim.

Chevelle
Model   *Interchange Number*
1964
Except Convertible......................................1
Convertible...2

1965
Except Convertible..3
Convertible..4

1966
Except Convertible..5
Convertible..6

1967
Except Convertible or El Camino...........................7
Convertible..6
El Camino...9

1968
Except Convertible or El Camino
Except Malibu...8
Malibu...10
Convertible..20
El Camino...12

1969
Except Convertible or El Camino
Except Malibu...13
Malibu...14
Convertible..11
El Camino...12

1970
Except Convertible or El Camino
Except Malibu...16
Malibu...15
Convertible..20
El Camino
Except Custom..17
Custom...15

1971
Except Convertible or El Camino
Early..18
Late...19
Convertible..21
El Camino
Early..18
Late...19

1972
Except Convertible or El Camino......................19
Convertible..21
El Camino...19

Interchanges

Interchange Number: 1
Part Number(s): 4442047
Usage: 1964 Chevelle, Cutlass, Skylark, Lemans all models and body styles except convertible

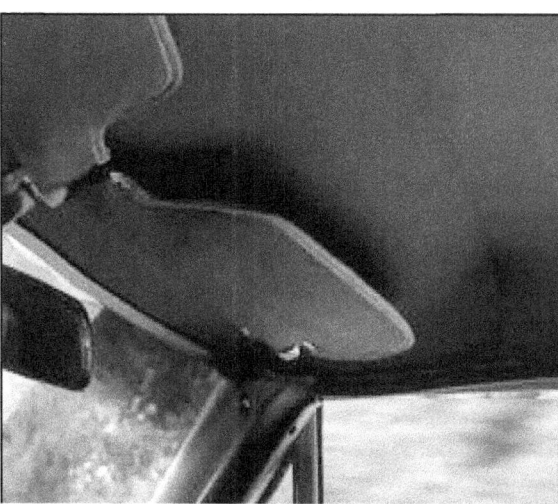
The 1967-1969 El Camino's used special visors, but they are also used on the wagons.

Interchange Number: 2
Part Number(s): 4497471
Usage: 1964 Chevelle, Cutlass, Lemans, Skylark convertible

Interchange Number: 3
Part Number(s): 4481246
Usage: 1965 Chevelle, Cutlass, Skylark, Lemans all models and body styles except convertible

Interchange Number: 4
Part Number(s): 4480644
Usage: 1965 Chevelle, Cutlass, Lemans, Skylark convertible

Interchange Number: 5
Part Number(s): 7631361
Usage: 1966 Chevelle, Cutlass, Lemans, Skylark except convertible

Interchange Number: 6
Part Number(s): 7630473
Usage: 1966-1967 Chevelle, Cutlass, Lemans, Skylark convertible

Interchange Number: 7
Part Number(s): 7666339
Usage: 1967 Chevelle, Cutlass, Lemans, Skylark except convertible or El Camino or wagon

Interchange Number: 8
Part Number(s): 7769004
Usage: 1968 Chevelle, Oldsmobile F-85, Buick Special, Tempest all body style except convertible, El Camino or wagon

Interchange Number: 9
Part Number(s): 7683442
Usage: 1967 El Camino; 1967 Chevelle Wagon 1967 Lemans Wagon; 1967 Cutlass Wagon; Skylark wagon

Interchange Number: 10
Part Number(s): 7769010
Usage: 1968 Malibu; Oldsmobile Cutlass, Buick Skylark, Lemans all body style except convertible, el Camino or wagon. Not for base models

Interchange Number: 11
Part Number(s): 7772866
Usage: 1968 Chevelle, Cutlass, Skylark, Lemans convertible

Interchange Number: 12
Part Number(s): 8765304
Usage: 1968-1969 El Camino; 1968-1969 Chevelle wagon; 1968-1969 Cutlass, Lemans, Skylark wagon

Interchange Number: 13
Part Number(s): 8743228
Usage: 1969 Chevelle, Oldsmobile F-85, Buick Special, Tempest all body style except convertible wagon or El Camino; 1969 Nova

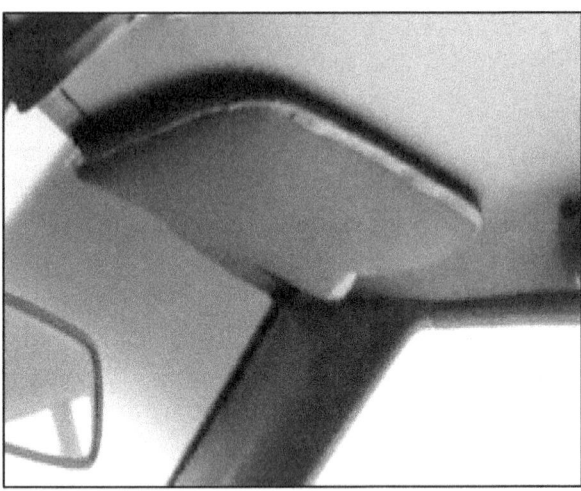
Late 1971 Chevelles used the short type of sun visor. All 1972 Chevelles used this type.

Interchange Number: 14
Part Number(s): 8765321
Usage: 1969 Malibu; Oldsmobile Cutlass, Buick Skylark, Lemans all body style except convertible, El Camino or wagon. Not for base models

Interchange Number: 15
Part Number(s): 8802658
Usage: 1970 Malibu except convertible; 1970 El Camino custom

Interchange Number: 16
Part Number(s): 8802667
Usage: 1970 Chevelle, all models and body styles except Malibu or El Camino or wagon

Interchange Number: 17
Part Number(s): 9812146
Usage: El Camino, except Custom

Interchange Number: 18
Part Number(s): 9868658
Usage: Late 1971-1972 Malibu except convertible; Late 1971-1972 El Camino custom; 1971-1972 Nova; 1971-1972 Ventura II
Notes: Short time

Interchange Number: 19
Part Number(s): 9868687
Usage: Early 1971 Malibu except convertible; Early 1971 El Camino custom
Notes: Long type

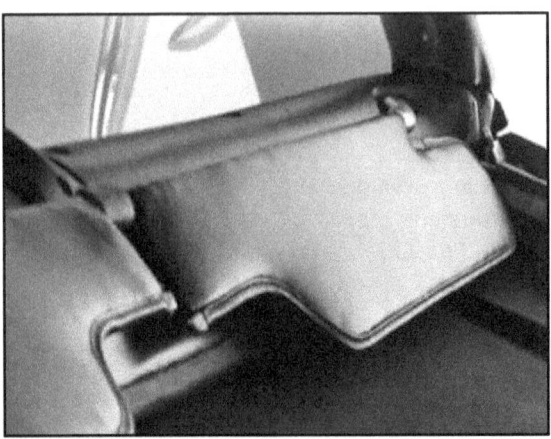
Early 1971 Chevelle hardtops used a long type visor. The convertible (shown) used the long type all year long and again in 1972

Interchange Number: 20
Part Number(s): 8765296
Usage: 1969-1970 Chevelle, Cutlass, Skylark, Lemans convertible

Interchange Number: 21
Part Number(s): 9868688
Usage: 1971-1972 Chevelle, Cutlass, Skylark, Lemans convertible

Handle, Inside Door

Chevelle
Model   *Interchange Number*
1964-1965
Except Malibu or Malibu SS..................................1
Malibu...2
1965
All..1
1966-1967
All..3
1968-1972
All..4

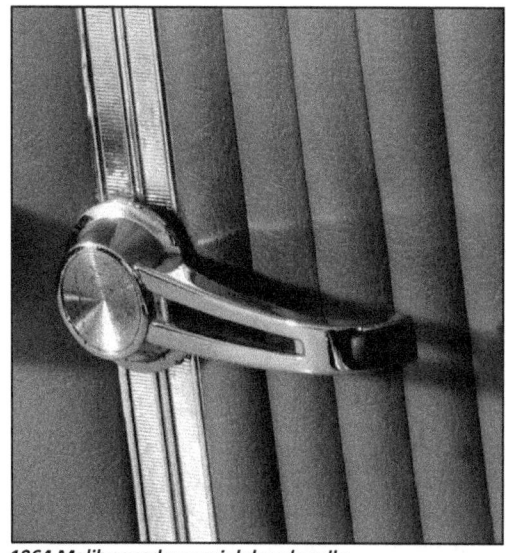
1964 Malibu used a special door handle

1964-1965 inside door handle

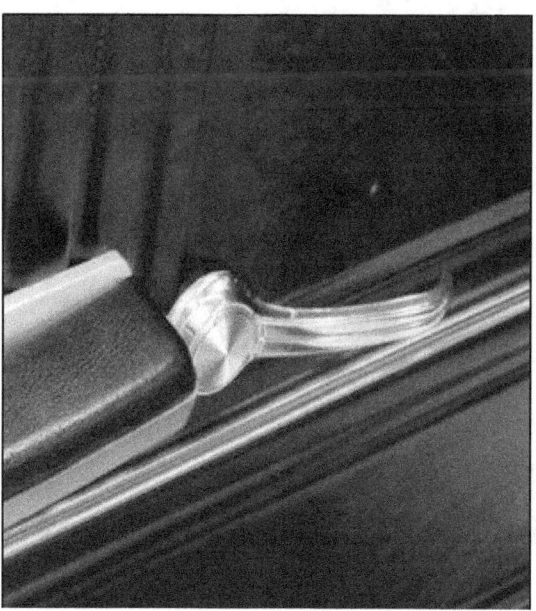
1966-1967 Door handle

Interchange Number: 1
Part Number(s): 3764017
Usage: 1959-1964 full-size Chevrolet, except Impala; 1964 Chevelle except Malibu or Malibu SS; 1962-1965 Chevy II except Nova; 1964-1965 El Camino; 1965 Chevelle all models.

Interchange Number: 2
Part Number(s): 4753532
Usage: 1960-1961 full-size Pontiac S-88; 1961-64 Oldsmobile F-85 (four-door only); 1962-1964 Chevy ii (Nova only); 1964 Chevelle Malibu only

Interchange Number: 3
Part Number(s): 4468414
Usage: 1965-1967 Chevelle; 1965-1967 Bel Air; 1965-1967 Biscayne; 1965-1967 Pontiac LeMans; 1965-1967 GTO; 1965-1967 full-size Pontiac, all except Grand Prix; 1965-1967 LeSabre; 1965-1967 Wildcat, all except Convertible; 1966-1967 Skylark; 1966-1967 Nova; 1967 Camaro (with Standard interior); 1967 Pontiac Firebird (with standard interior

1968-1972 used this handle

Interchange Number: 4
Part Number(s): 7743520
Usage: 1968-1969 Camaro; 1968-1969 Pontiac Firebird; 1968-1972 Chevelle; 1968-1972 Skylark; 1968-1972 LeMans; 1968-1972 GTO; 1968-1972 Nova; 1968-1972 Cutlass; 1968-1970 full-size Chevrolet; 1968-1972 El Camino; 1971-1972 CMC Sprint; 1971-1972 Pontiac Ventura II. All with standard trim

Handle, Window Regulator

Chevelle

Model	Interchange Number
1964	
Except Malibu	5
Malibu	6
1965-1966	
All	1
1967	
Except 300	7
300	1
1968	
All	4
1969-1972	
All	2

Interchanges

Interchange Number: 1
Part Number(s): 4472076
Usage: 1965-1966 Biscayne; 1965-1966 Bel-Air; 1965-1967 Nova; 1965-1966 Chevelle; 1967 Chevelle 300; 1967 Camaro with standard trim
Notes: Front doors only

Interchange Number: 2
Part Number(s): 7752485
Usage: 1969-1981 Camaro; 1969-1981 Firebird; 1969-1977 Chevelle, full-size Chevrolet, full-size Pontiac, full-size Oldsmobile or full-size Buick; 1969-1981 Lemans, Cutlass, Skylark, Chevelle, El Camino; 1969-1979 Nova; 1971-1976 Ventura II; 1973-1975 Omega, Apollo; 1977-1979 Phoenix; 1976-1979 Skylark

Interchange Number: 3
Part Number(s): 7752485
Usage: 1968 Camaro, Chevelle, full-size Chevrolet, full-size Pontiac, full-size Oldsmobile or full-size Buick; 1968 Lemans, Cutlass, Skylark, Chevelle, El Camino; 1968 Nova; 1968 Firebird

Interchange Number: 4
Part Number(s): 7752485
Usage: 1968 Camaro, Chevelle, full-size Chevrolet, full-size Pontiac, full-size Oldsmobile or full-size Buick; 1968 Lemans, Cutlass, Skylark, Chevelle, El Camino; 1968 Nova; 1968 Firebird

Interchange Number: 5
Part Number(s): 4619388
Usage: 1959-1960 Full-size Chevrolet except Impala; 1961-1964 Biscayne; 1963-1964 Chevy II except Nova; 1964 Chevelle except Malibu

Interchange Number: 6
Part Number(s): 4807923
Usage: 1962-1964 Nova; 1963-1964 Nova SS; 1964 Malibu

Interchange Number: 7
Part Number(s): 7680653
Usage: 1967 full-size Chevrolet, except Impala; 1967 Chevelle-except 300 models; 1967 Corvair; 1967 Cutlass; 1967 Full-size Oldsmobile, except Toronado

1964 Malibu used special window handles

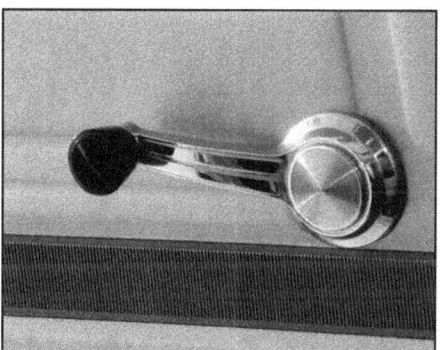
1965-1966 window handles

1964 standard Chevelles used this window handle which is more commonly found on the lower trimmed Biscayne's

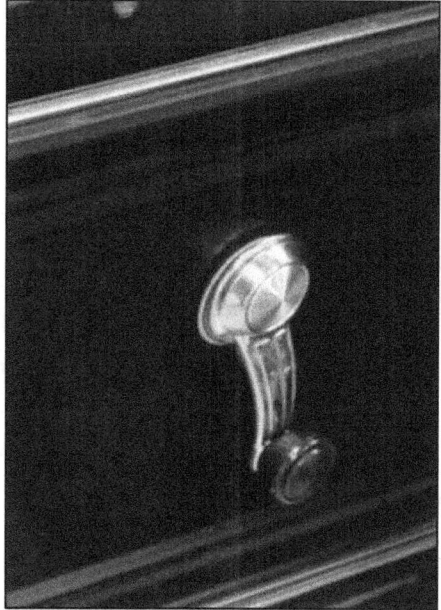
1967 Chevelle 300 models used this window regulator handle

Console

Chevelle

Model	Interchange Number
1964-1965	
Manual	1
Automatic	2
1966-1967	
Manual	3
Automatic	4
1968-1969	
All	5
1970-1972	
All	6

Interchanges

Interchange Number: 1
Part Number(s): Upper: 3844083 Rear 3844085
Usage: 1964-1965 Malibu SS; 1964-965 El Camino with 4-speed
Notes: Rear is used in interchange number 2

Interchange Number: 2
Part Number(s): Upper: 3844084 Rear 3844085
Usage: 1964-1965 Malibu SS; 1964-1965 El Camino with Powerglide
Notes: Rear is used in interchange number 1

Many times, the rear window handles will also interchange. Shown is the 1967 handle for all Chevelles except the 300 series

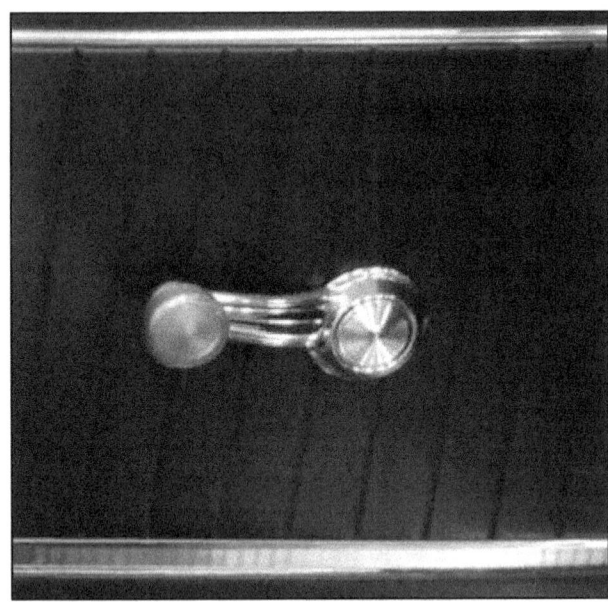

The 1969-1972 window handles were used on many GM models up to the 1980's

Interchange Number: 3
Part Number(s): Upper: Front 3878467 Rear 387156
Lower: 3876407
Usage: 1966-1967 Chevelle with 4-speed
Notes: Rear is used in interchange number 4

Interchange Number: 4
Part Number(s): Upper: Front 3878468 Rear 387157
Lower: 3876408
Usage: 1966-1967 Chevelle with automatic
Notes: Rear is used in interchange number 3

Interchange Number: 5
Part Number(s): 3919941
Usage: 1968-1969 Chevelle with all transmissions
Notes: there is a slight difference in the console doors between the years. The 1969 Door is a two-part design. But they will fit.

Interchange Number: 6
Part Number(s): 3968566
Usage: 1970-1972 Chevelle with all transmissions

1968 Window handle

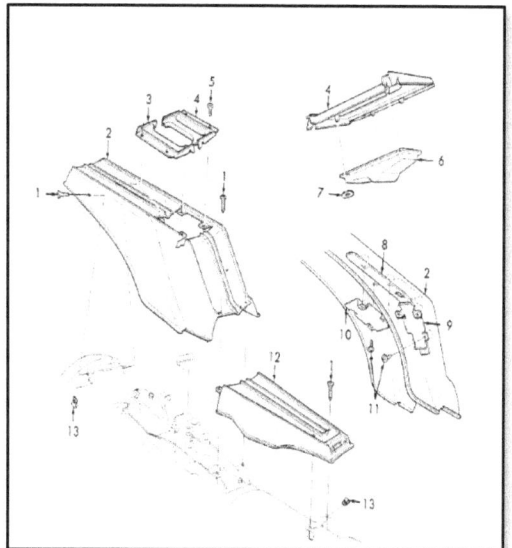
1964-1965 Console (Chevrolet)

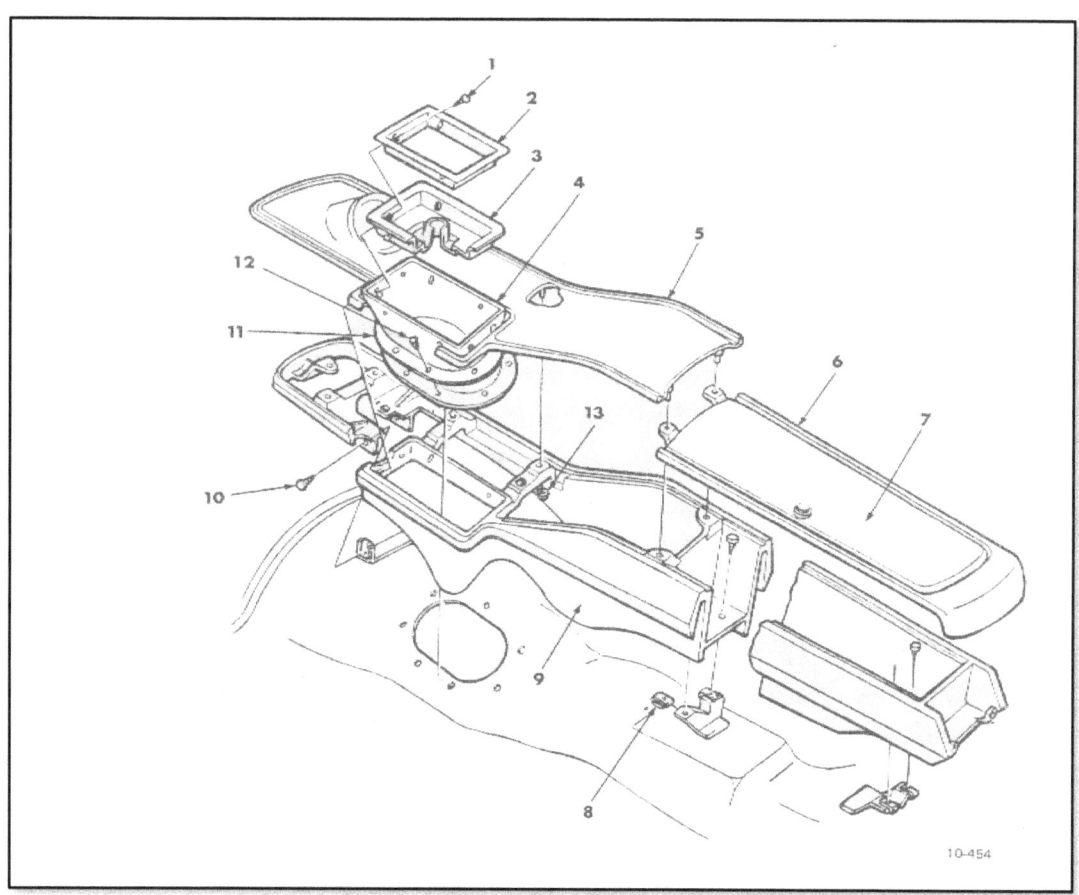
1966-1967 Console with manual transmission. (Chevrolet)

265

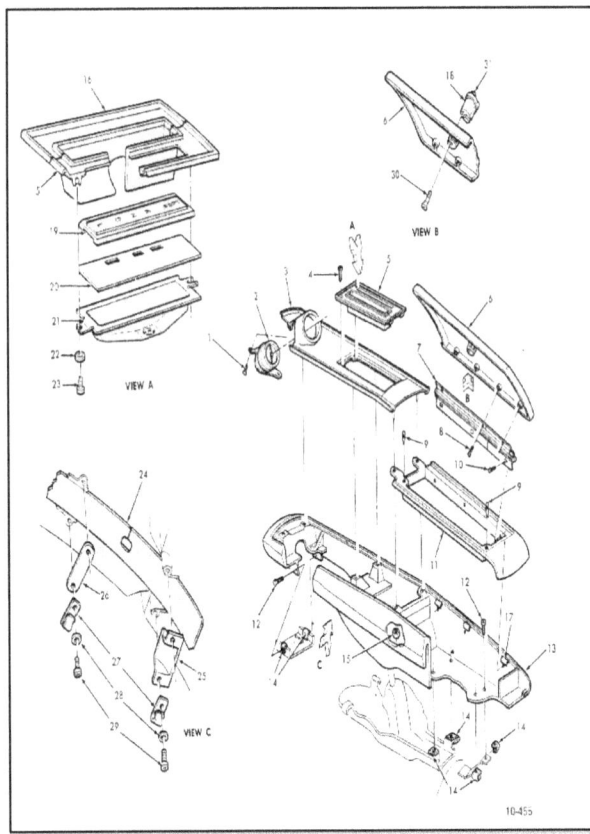

1966-1967 Console with automatic transmission. (Chevrolet)

Door Panels

All Door panels are based on either the white or black door panels. Door panels can be re-dyed to match your interior. The actual interchange will depend on the body style for example a panel from a four-door sedan or wagon will not fit your 2-door hardtop. However, in most cases a panel from 2-door will fit your convertible. Note the panels from an El Camino are a unique item and other body styles will not fit.

Another item to watch for is the trim level. Thus, entry levels like the 300 series or Deluxe models usually used a different panel than the higher trimmed Malibu or Super Sport models (which usually used the higher trimmed Malibu panels).

Each year was different in design except for the 1970-1972 model years where the general design was kept. We have included photos to help you identify the panels.

Arm Rests

Chevelle

Model	Interchange Number
1964	
Front	1
Rear	4
1965-1967	
Front	2
Rear	4
1968-1972	
Front	3
Rear	
Except Convertible	7
Convertible	6

Interchanges

Interchange Number: 1
Part Number(s): 6281544
Position: Front
Usage: 1963-1964 Nova 2 door hardtop or convertible; 1963-1964 Malibu 2 door hardtop or convertible

Interchange Number: 2
Part Number(s): 4473130
Position: Front
Usage: 1965 Malibu SS; 1966-1967 Chevelle 2 door hardtop or convertible; 1966-1967 El Camino Custom
1967 Nova four-door

Interchange Number: 3
Part Number(s): RH 7766490 LH 7766491
Position: Front
Usage: 1968-1972 Chevelle all body styles except wagon

Interchange Number: 4
Part Number(s): RH 4473160 LH 4473161
Position: Rear
Usage: 1964-1967 Chevelle 2-door hardtop

Interchange Number: 5
Part Number(s): RH 7755738 LH 7755739
Position: Rear
Usage: 1968-1972 Chevelle Convertible

Interchange Number: 7
Part Number(s): RH 7759636 LH 7759637
Position: Rear
Usage: 1968-1972 Chevelle 2 door hardtop

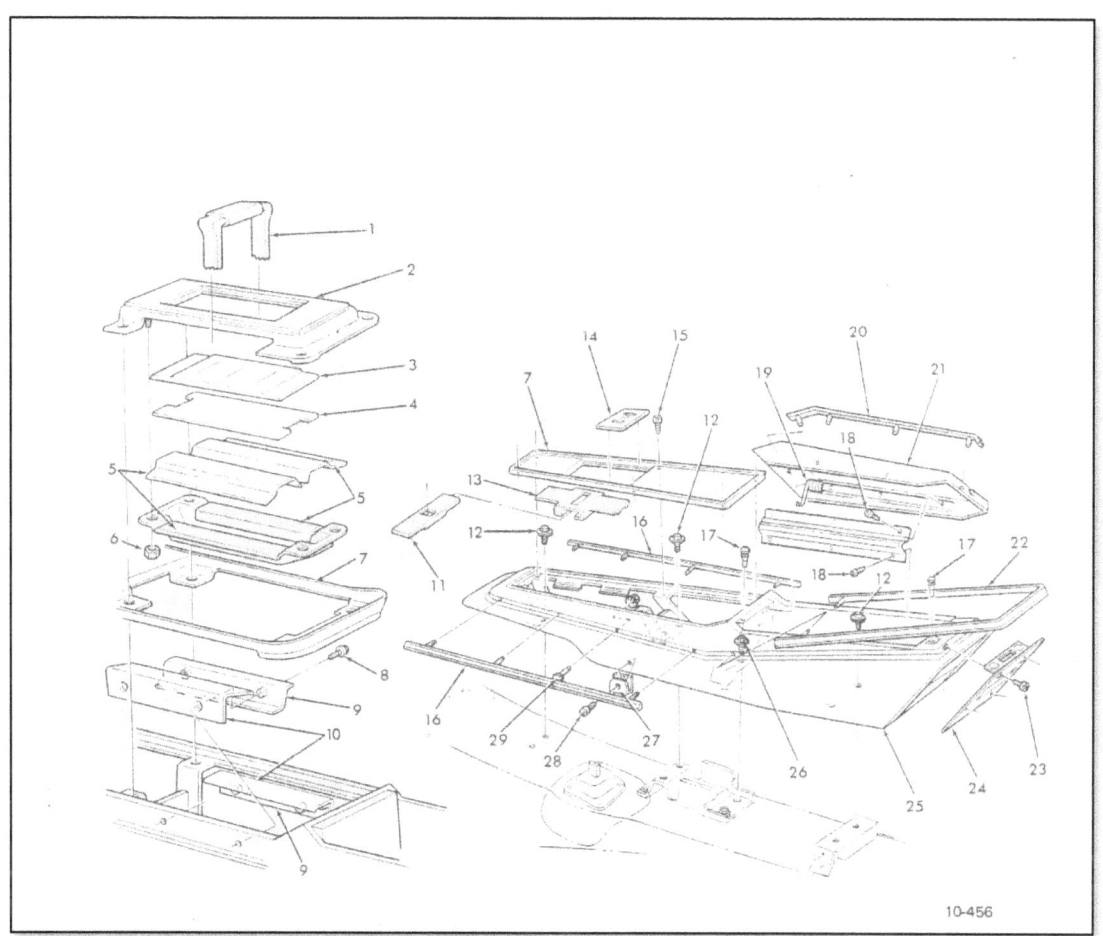

1968 Console the 1969-1972 console is similar (Chevrolet)

1964 300 series door panels

1964 Door Panels for Malibu and Super Sport models

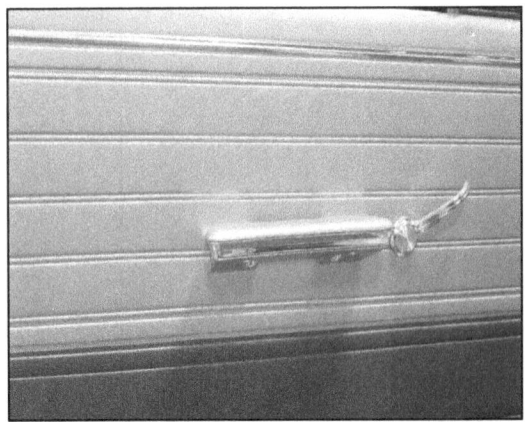

The lesser trimmed models like this 1965 300 used different panels than the Malibu and they can be hard to find now.

1967 door panel for Malibu line, includes SS 396

The 1965 Malibu door panels included a bow tie symbol

1968 Door panel for SS models

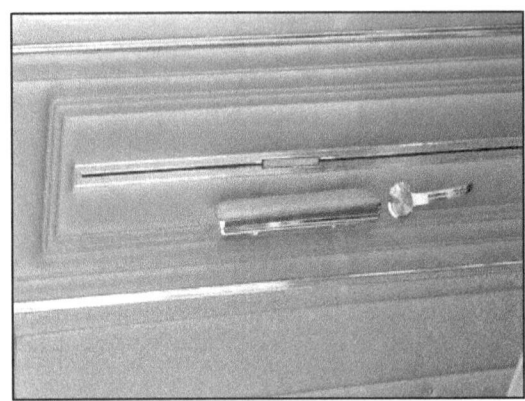

1966 Chevelle 300 door panels

1969 door panel for SS 396

1970-1972 door panel

Seat Adjustment Rails

Chevelle
Model	Interchange Number
1964-1965	
Except El Camino	
Bench	1
Bucket	
Drivers	2
Passengers	3
El Camino	
Bench	4
Bucket	
Drivers	5
Passengers	6
1966	
Except El Camino	
Bench	1
Bucket	
Drivers	9
Passengers	10
El Camino	
Bench	4
Bucket	
Drivers	5
Passengers	6
1967	
Except El Camino	
Bench	
Early	7
Late	8
Bucket	
Drivers	9
Passengers	10
El Camino	
Bench	4
Bucket	
Drivers	5
Passengers	6
1968-1972	
Bench	8
Bucket	
Drivers	9
Passengers	10

Interchange

Interchange Number: 1
Seat Type: Bench
Part Number(s): RH, 4411994; LH, 4411995
Usage: 1964-1966 Chevelle, except El Camino; 1964-1966 Skylark;1964-1966 Cutlass; 1964-1966 LeMans

Interchange Number: 2
Seat Type: Bucket (driver's)
Part Number(s): Inner, 4417896; outer, 7628330
Usage: 1964-1965 Chevelle, except El Camino); 1964-1965 Skylark; 1964-1965 Cutlass; 1964-1965 LeMans
Notes: Inner rail also used in interchange number 3

Interchange Number: 3
Seat Type: Bucket (passenger's)
Part Number(s): Inner, 4417896; outer, 7628329
Part Number(s): Inner, 4417896; outer, 7628330
Usage: 1964-1965 Chevelle, except El Camino); 1964-1965 Skylark; 1964-1965 Cutlass; 1964-1965 LeMans
Notes: Inner rail also used in interchange number 2

Interchange Number: 4
Seat Type: Bench
Part Number(s): RH, 4459308; LH, 7628331
Usage: 1964-1966 El Camino
Notes: Left-hand rail is also used in interchange 5

Interchange Number: 5
Seat Type: Bucket (driver's)
Part Number(s): Inner, 4459311; outer, 7628331
Usage: 1964-1966 El Camino
Notes: Outer rail also used in interchange number 4
Inner rail also used in interchange number 6

Interchange Number: 6
Seat Type: Bucket (passengers)
Part Number(s): Inner, 4459311; outer, 4459310
Usage: 1964-66 El Camino
Notes: Inner rail also used in interchange number 5

Interchange Number: 7
Seat Type: Bench
Part Numbers: RH, 7659761; LH, 7659762.
Usage: Early 1967 Chevelle ,except El Camino
Early 1967 Skylark, Cutlass, LeMans
Notes: Has a stop set screw in the upper channel

Interchange Number: 8
Seat Type: Bench
Part Numbers: RH, 7712007; and LH 7779428.
Usage: Late 1967-1972 Chevelle, Skylark, Cutlass, LeMans

Interchange Number: 9
Seat Type: Bucket (driver's)
Part Number(s): 4547730 Inner 7779417 Outer
Usage: 1966-1972 Chevelle (except 1967 El Camino) 1967-1972 Skylark, Cutlass, LeMans; 1968-1972 El Camino.
Notes: Inner rail also used in Interchange Number 10

Interchange Number: 10
Seat Type: Bucket (passenger's)
Part Number(s): Inner, 4547730; outer, 8768007
Usage: 1967-1971 Chevelle, except 1967 El Camino; 1967-1971 Skylark, Cutlass, LeMans; 1968-1972 El Camino
Notes: Inner rail used in interchange 9

Interchange Number: 11
Seat Type: Bench
Part Number(s): 7659759 RH 7659760 RH
Usage: 1967 El Camino

Interchange Number: 12
Seat Type: Bucket (driver's)
Part Number(s): 7584996 RH 7659788 LH
Usage: 1967 El Camino

Interchange Number: 14
Seat Type: Bucket (passengers)
Part Number(s): 7659789 RH 7584996 LH
Usage: 1967 El Camino

Seat Frame

Note this is the bare seat frame, stripped of all trim and padding. In doing so the interchange becomes much wider and allows other GM makes to be used.

Chevelle

Model	Interchange Number
1964-1965	
Bench	1
Buckets	
Drivers	7
Passengers	8
1966	
Bench	
Without Headrests	1
With Headrests	2
Buckets	
Drivers	9
Passengers	10
1967	
Bench	
Without Headrests	3
With Headrests	4
Buckets	
Drivers	11
Passengers	12
1968	
Bench	
Without Headrests	5
With Headrests	6
Buckets	
Drivers	
Without Headrest	13
With Headrests	14
Passengers	
Without Headrest	15
With Headrests	16
1969-1970	
Bench	17
Buckets	
Drivers	18
Passengers	18
1971-1972	
Bench	17
Buckets	
Drivers	19
Passengers	20

Interchanges

Interchange Number: 1
Seat Type: Bench
Part Number(s): Back: 7583032 RH 7583033
Cushion: 4526462
Usage: 1964-1965 Chevelle, Lemans, Cutlass, Skylark 2-door hardtop or convertible; 1966 Chevelle, Lemans, Cutlass, Skylark 2-door or convertible without headrest

Interchange Number: 2
Seat Type: Bench
Part Number(s): Back: 7590340 RH 7590341
Cushion: 7589832
Usage: 1966 Chevelle, Lemans, Cutlass, Skylark 2-door or convertible with headrests

Interchange Number: 3
Seat Type: Bench
Part Number(s): Back: 766819 RH 7668193
Cushion: 7668338
Usage: 1967 Chevelle, Lemans, Cutlass, Skylark 2-doo or convertible without headrests

Interchange Number: 4
Seat Type: Bench
Part Number(s): Back: 7668196 RH 7668197
Cushion: 7668338
Usage: 1967 Chevelle, Lemans, Cutlass, Skylark 2-door or convertible with headrests

Interchange Number: 5
Seat Type: Bench
Part Number(s): Back: 7720122 RH 7720123
Cushion: 7668338
Usage: 1968 Chevelle, Lemans, Cutlass, Skylark 2-door or convertible without headrests

Interchange Number: 6
Seat Type: Bench
Part Number(s): Back: 7771257 RH 7771258
Cushion: 7668338
Usage: 1968 Chevelle, Lemans, Cutlass, Skylark 2-door or convertible with headrests

Interchange Number: 7
Seat Type: Bucket Drivers
Part Number(s): Back: 4526447
Cushion: 4526460
Usage: 1964-1965 Chevelle, Lemans, Cutlass, Skylark 2-door hardtop or convertible with bucket seats

Interchange Number: 8
Seat Type: Bucket Passengers
Part Number(s): Back: 4526448
Cushion: 4526460
Usage: 1964-1965 Chevelle, Lemans, Cutlass, Skylark 2-door hardtop or convertible with bucket seats

Interchange Number: 9
Seat Type: Bucket Drivers
Part Number(s): Back: 4539540
Cushion: 4538222
Usage: 1966 Chevelle, Lemans, Cutlass, Skylark 2-door hardtop or convertible with bucket seats, except recline back

Interchange Number: 10
Seat Type: Bucket Passengers
Part Number(s): Back: 4539541
Cushion: 4538222
Usage: 1966 Chevelle, Lemans, Cutlass, Skylark 2-door hardtop or convertible with bucket seats, except recline back

Interchange Number: 11
Seat Type: Bucket Drivers
Part Number(s): Back: 7686200
Cushion: 7668315
Usage: 1967 Chevelle, Lemans, Cutlass, Skylark 2-door hardtop or convertible with bucket seats, except recline back

Interchange Number: 12
Seat Type: Bucket Passengers
Part Number(s): Back: 7668160
Cushion: 7668315
Usage: 1967 Chevelle, Lemans, Cutlass, Skylark 2-door hardtop or convertible with bucket seats, except recline back

Interchange Number: 13
Seat Type: Bucket Drivers
Part Number(s): Back: 730127
Cushion: 7768627
Usage: 1968 Chevelle, Lemans, Cutlass, Skylark 2-door hardtop or convertible with bucket seats, except recline back or with headrests

Interchange Number: 14
Seat Type: Bucket Passengers
Part Number(s): Back: 730128
Cushion: 7768627
Usage: 1968 Chevelle, Lemans, Cutlass, Skylark 2-door hardtop or convertible with bucket seats, except recline back or with headrests

Interchange Number: 15
Seat Type: Bucket Drivers
Part Number(s): Back: 730970
Cushion: 7768627
Usage: 1968 Chevelle, Lemans, Cutlass, Skylark 2-door hardtop or convertible with bucket seats with headrests, except recline back; 1968 Nova

Interchange Number: 16
Seat Type: Bucket Passengers
Part Number(s): Back: 730969
Cushion: 7768627
Usage: 1968 Chevelle, Lemans, Cutlass, Skylark 2-door hardtop or convertible with bucket seats with headrests, except recline back; 1968 Nova

Interchange Number: 17
Seat Type: Bench
Part Number(s): Back: 9812322
Cushion: 9865955
Usage: 1969-1972 Chevelle, Lemans, Cutlass, Skylark 2-door hardtop or convertible

Interchange Number: 18
Seat Type: Bucket Drivers/Passengers
Part Number(s): Back: 9865958
Cushion: 9865953
Usage: 1969-1970 Chevelle, Lemans, Cutlass, Skylark 2-door hardtop or convertible; 1969 Full-size Chevrolet, Oldsmobile, Pontiac or Buick with bucket seats; 1969-1970 El Camino; 1969-1970 Nova

Interchange Number: 19
Seat Type: Bucket Drivers
Part Number(s): Back: 9816999
Cushion: 9865953
Usage: 1971-1972 Chevelle, Lemans, Cutlass, Skylark 2-door hardtop or convertible.

Interchange Number: 20
Seat Type: Bucket Passengers
Part Number(s): Back: 9816998
Cushion: 9865953
Usage: 1971-1972 Chevelle, Lemans, Cutlass, Skylark 2-door hardtop or convertible.

Seat Belts, Front

Chevelle

Model	Interchange Number
1964-1965	
Standard	1
Deluxe	2
Custom Deluxe	3
1966	
Standard	1
Deluxe	4
Custom Deluxe	5
Shoulder straps	
Standard	
Except Convertible	6
Convertible	7
Deluxe	
Except Convertible	8
Convertible	9
1967	
Standard	10
Deluxe	11
Shoulder straps	
Standard	
Except Convertible	12
Convertible	13
Deluxe	
Except Convertible	14
1968	
Standard	15
Deluxe	16
Shoulder straps	
Standard	
Except Convertible	
Early	18
Late	17
Convertible	20
El Camino	51
Deluxe	
Except Convertible	
Early	18
Late	17
Convertible	53
El Camino	52
1969	
Standard	20
Deluxe	21
Shoulder straps	
Standard	
Except Convertible or El Camino	22
Convertible	24
El Camino	23

Deluxe
Except Convertible or El Camino..............................27
Convertible..............................25
El Camino..............................26
1970
Standard..............................28
Deluxe..............................29
Shoulder straps
Standard
Except Convertible or El Camino..............................30
Convertible..............................32
El Camino..............................31
Deluxe
Except Convertible or El Camino..............................33
Convertible..............................35
El Camino..............................34
1971
Standard..............................36
Deluxe..............................37
Shoulder straps
Standard
Except Convertible or El Camino..............................38
El Camino..............................39
Deluxe
Except Convertible or El Camino..............................41
Convertible..............................40
El Camino..............................54
1972
Early 4-point style
Standard..............................36
Deluxe..............................37
Shoulder straps
Standard
Except Convertible or El Camino..............................38
El Camino..............................39
Deluxe
Except Convertible or El Camino..............................41
Convertible..............................40
El Camino..............................54
Late 3-point style
Standard
Bench Seat
Except Convertible or El Camino
Plastic Buckle..............................45
Cast Buckle..............................46
Convertible
Plastic Buckle..............................47
Cast Buckle..............................46
El Camino
Plastic Buckle..............................55
Cast Buckle..............................56
Bucket seats
Plastic Buckle..............................42

Cast Buckle..............................44
Deluxe
Bench Seat
Except Convertible or El Camino..............................47
Convertible..............................50
El Camino..............................55
Bucket
Except Convertible..............................43
Convertible..............................49

Interchanges

Interchange Number: 1
Type: Standard
Part Number(s): 3955366
Usage: 1964-1966 Chevelle, Nova; 1965 full-size Chevrolet.

Interchange Number: 2
Type: Custom
Part Number(s): 3957858
Usage: 1964-1965 Chevelle, Nova; 1965 full-size Chevrolet.

Interchange Number: 3
Type: Custom Deluxe
Part Number(s): 3957807
Usage: 1964-1965 Chevelle, Nova; 1965 full-size Chevrolet.

Interchange Number: 4
Type: Custom
Part Number(s): 3955378
Usage: 1966 Chevelle, Nova, full-size Chevrolet

Standard 1964-1966 seat belts.

Interchange Number: 5
Type: Custom Deluxe
Part Number(s): 3955370
Usage: 1966 Chevelle, Nova full-size Chevrolet

Interchange Number: 6
Type: Standard Shoulder strap
Part Number(s): 4228421
Usage: 1966 Chevelle, Nova, full-size Chevrolet except convertible

Interchange Number: 7
Type: Standard Shoulder strap
Part Number(s): 4228425
Usage: 1966 Chevelle, full-size Chevrolet convertible

Interchange Number: 8
Type: Deluxe Shoulder strap
Part Number(s): 4228365
Usage: 1966 Chevelle, Nova, full-size Chevrolet except convertible

Interchange Number: 9
Type: Deluxe Shoulder strap
Part Number(s): 4228380
Usage: 1966 Chevelle, full-size Chevrolet convertible

Deluxe belts usually had a bright buckle. Shown is the 1967 Fisher coach buckle

Interchange Number: 10
Type: Standard
Part Number(s): 8700637 LH 8701648 RH
Usage: 1967 Chevelle, Nova, full-size Chevrolet

Interchange Number: 11
Type: Deluxe
Part Number(s): 8700479 LH 8700478 RH
Usage: 1967 Chevelle, Nova, full-size Chevrolet

Interchange Number: 12
Type: Standard Shoulder
Part Number(s): 7792095
Usage: 1967 Chevelle, Nova, full-size Chevrolet except convertible

Interchange Number: 13
Type: Standard Shoulder
Part Number(s): 7792108
Usage: 1967 Chevelle, full-size Chevrolet convertible

Interchange Number: 14
Type: Deluxe Shoulder
Part Number(s): 7792076
Usage: 1967 Chevelle, Nova, full-size Chevrolet except convertible

Two types seat belts were used in 1967 models one had the Fisher coach logo and the other (shown) was the GM Mark of Excellent.

1967 Fisher coach standard belt.

Interchange Number: 15
Type: Standard
Part Number(s): 8700759 LH 8700758 RH
Usage: 1968 Chevelle, Nova, full-size Chevrolet, Except Nova sedan; 1968 Lemans, Skylark, Cutlass, Full-size Pontiac, Buick, Oldsmobile

Interchange Number: 16
Type: Deluxe
Part Number(s): 8700722 LH 8700723 RH
Usage: 1968 Chevelle, Nova, full-size Chevrolet, except Nova sedan; 1968 Lemans, Skylark, Cutlass, Full-size Pontiac, Buick, Oldsmobile

Interchange Number: 17
Type: Standard Shoulder
Part Number(s): 8700192
Usage: Late 1968 Chevelle, Nova, Camaro except convertible or El Camino; 1968 Lemans, Skylark, Cutlass, Full-size Pontiac, Buick, Oldsmobile 4-door sedan only

Interchange Number: 18
Type: Standard Shoulder
Part Number(s): 8700013
Usage: Early 1968 Chevelle, Nova, Camaro except convertible or El Camino; 1968 Lemans, Skylark, Cutlass, Full-size Pontiac, Buick, Oldsmobile 4-door sedan only

Interchange Number: 19
Type: Deluxe Shoulder
Part Number(s): 8702435 LH 8702434 RH
Usage: 1968 Chevelle, Lemans, Skylark, Cutlass convertible

Interchange Number: 20
Type: Standard
Part Number(s): 8701649 LH 8701648 RH
1969 Chevelle, Cutlass, Skylark, Lemans; 1969 full-size Chevrolet, Buick, Pontiac, Buick

Interchange Number: 21
Type: Deluxe
Part Number(s): 8702435 LH 8702434 RH
Usage: 1969 Chevelle, Cutlass, Skylark, Lemans; 1969 full-size Chevrolet, Buick, Pontiac, Buick

Interchange Number: 22
Type: Standard Shoulder
Part Number(s): 8701690
Usage: 1969 Chevelle, Cutlass, Skylark, Lemans except convertible or El Camino; 1969 full-size Chevrolet, Buick, Oldsmobile, Pontiac 4-door sedan only; 1969 Nova; 1969 Camaro

Interchange Number: 23
Type: Standard Shoulder
Part Number(s): 8701694
Usage: 1969 El Camino

Interchange Number: 24
Type: Standard Shoulder
Part Number(s): 8701681
Usage: 1969 Chevelle, Skylark, Lemans, Cutlass convertible

Interchange Number: 25
Type: Deluxe Shoulder
Part Number(s): 8701532
Usage: 1969 Chevelle, Skylark, Lemans, Cutlass convertible

Interchange Number: 26
Type: Deluxe Shoulder
Part Number(s): 8701551
Usage: 1969 El Camino

1968 Custom seat belt

Interchange Number: 27
Type: Deluxe Shoulder
Part Number(s): 8701532
Usage: 1969 Chevelle, Cutlass, Skylark, Lemans except convertible or El Camino; 1969 full-size Chevrolet, Buick, Oldsmobile, Pontiac 4-door sedan only

Interchange Number: 28
Type: Standard
Part Number(s): 8703373 LH 8703372 RH
Usage: 1970 Chevelle, Cutlass, Skylark, Lemans; 1970 full-size Chevrolet, Oldsmobile, Buick, Pontiac

Interchange Number: 29
Type: Deluxe
Part Number(s): 8703385 LH 8703384 RH
Usage: 1970 Chevelle, Cutlass, Skylark, Lemans; 1970 full-size Chevrolet, Oldsmobile, Buick, Pontiac

Interchange Number: 30
Type: Standard Shoulder
Part Number(s): 8703491
Usage: 1970 Chevelle, Cutlass, Skylark, Lemans except convertible or El Camino; 1970 Nova; 1970 Full-size Chevrolet, Oldsmobile, Pontiac, Buick except convertible

Interchange Number: 31
Type: Standard Shoulder
Part Number(s): 8703541
Usage: 1970 El Camino

Interchange Number: 32
Type: Standard Shoulder
Part Number(s): 8703493
Usage: 1970 Chevelle, Cutlass, Skylark, Lemans convertible

Interchange Number: 33
Type: Deluxe Shoulder
Part Number(s): 8703497
Usage: 1970 Chevelle, Cutlass, Skylark, Lemans except convertible or El Camino; 1970 Nova; 1970 Full-size Chevrolet, Oldsmobile, Pontiac, Buick

Interchange Number: 34
Type: Deluxe Shoulder
Part Number(s): 8703542
Usage: 1970 El Camino

Interchange Number: 35
Type: Deluxe Shoulder
Part Number(s): 8703583
Usage: 1970 Chevelle, Cutlass, Skylark, Lemans convertible
Notes: Fits front or rear seats

1969 Standard belt, the 1968 is similar

Interchange Number: 36
Type: Standard
Part Number(s): 8705858 LH 8705857 RH
Usage: 1971-early 1972 Chevelle, Cutlass, Skylark, Lemans; 1971 full-size Chevrolet, Pontiac, Buick, Oldsmobile

Interchange Number: 37
Type: Deluxe
Part Number(s): 8704587 LH 8704586 RH
Usage: 1971-early 1972 Chevelle, Cutlass, Skylark, Lemans; 1971 full-size Chevrolet, Pontiac, Buick, Oldsmobile

Interchange Number: 38
Type: Standard Shoulder
Part Number(s): 8794576
Usage: 1971-early 1972 Chevelle, Cutlass, Skylark, Lemans except convertible or El Camino; 1968 full-size Chevrolet, Buick, Oldsmobile, Pontiac 4-door sedan

Interchange Number: 39
Type: Standard Shoulder
Part Number(s): 8704577
Usage: 1971 El Camino

Interchange Number: 40
Type: Deluxe Shoulder
Part Number(s): 8705522
Usage: 1971-early 1972 Chevelle, Cutlass, Skylark, Lemans convertible

1970 Standard belt

1970 Custom belt.

Interchange Number: 41
Type: Deluxe Shoulder
Part Number(s): 8704848
Usage: 1971-early 1972 Chevelle, Cutlass, Skylark, Lemans except convertible or El Camino

Interchange Number: 42
Type: Standard
Part Number(s): 8706605 LH 8706604 RH
Usage: Late 1972 Chevelle, Cutlass, Skylark, Lemans; Late 1972 El Camino with bucket seats
Notes: three-point hitch with plastic buckle

Interchange Number: 43
Type: Deluxe
Part Number(s): 8706607 LH 8706606 RH
Usage: Late 1972 Chevelle, Cutlass, Skylark, Lemans; Late 1972 El Camino with bucket seats
Notes: three-point hitch

Interchange Number: 44
Type: Standard
Part Number(s): 8707215 LH 8707216 RH
Usage: Late 1972 Chevelle, Cutlass, Skylark, Lemans; with bucket seats; Late 1972 El Camino with bucket seats
Notes: three-point hitch with cast buckle

Interchange Number: 45
Type: Standard
Part Number(s): 8706595 LH 8706594 RH
Usage: Late 1972 Chevelle, Cutlass, Skylark, Lemans with bench seat except convertible or El Camino
Notes: three-point hitch with plastic buckle

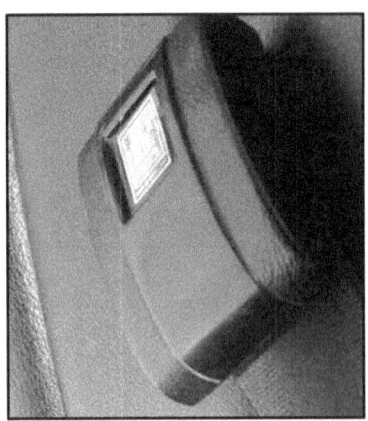
1971-early 1972 standard seat belt.

Interchange Number: 46
Type: Standard
Part Number(s): 8707213 LH 8707212 RH
Usage: Late 1972 Chevelle, Cutlass, Skylark, Lemans with bench seat
Notes: three-point hitch with cast buckle

Interchange Number: 47
Type: Deluxe
Part Number(s): 8706579 LH 8706578 RH
Usage: Late 1972 Chevelle, Cutlass, Skylark, Lemans coupe with bench seat except convertible
Notes: three-point hitch

Interchange Number: 48
Type: Deluxe
Part Number(s): 8706599 LH 8706578 RH
Usage: Late 1972 El Camino with bench seat

With the 4-point hitch the shoulder belt was tucked up to the roof.

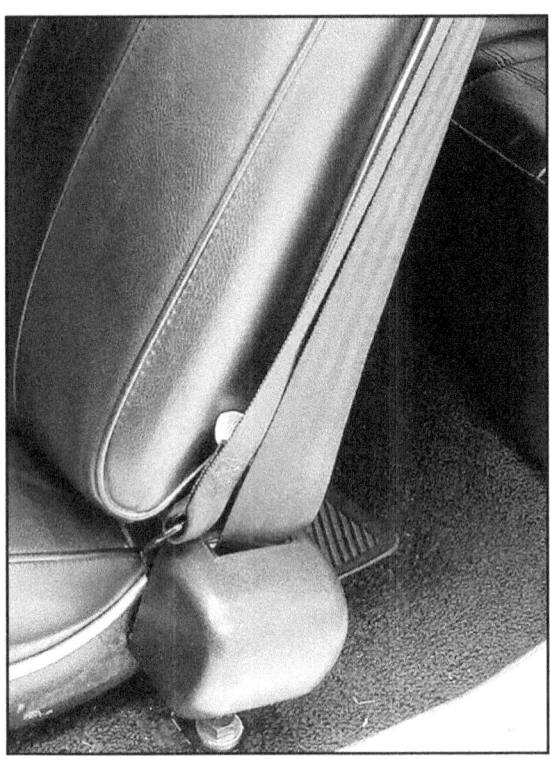
Late 1972 Models switched to a three-point hitch

Interchange Number: 49
Type: Deluxe
Part Number(s): 8706621 LH 8706620 RH
Usage: Late 1972 Chevelle, Cutlass, Skylark, Lemans convertible with bucket seats

Interchange Number: 50
Type: Deluxe
Part Number(s): 8706631 LH 8706631 RH
Usage: Late 1972 Chevelle, Cutlass, Skylark, Lemans convertible with beach seats

Interchange Number: 51
Type: Standard Shoulder
Part Number(s): 8700232
Usage: 1968 El Camino

Interchange Number: 52
Type: Deluxe Shoulder
Part Number(s): 8700234
Usage: 1968 El Camino

Interchange Number: 53
Type: Standard Shoulder
Part Number(s): 8701532
Usage: 1968 Chevelle, Cutlass, Skylark, Lemans convertible

Interchange Number: 54
Type: Deluxe Shoulder
Part Number(s): 8705488
Usage: 1971-early 1972 El Camino

Interchange Number: 55
Type: Standard
Part Number(s): 8706597 LH 8706598 RH
Usage: Late 1972 El Camino with bench seat
Notes: Plastic buckle

Interchange Number: 56
Type: Standard
Part Number(s): 8707215 LH 8707214 RH
Usage: Late 1972 El Camino with bench seat
Notes: 3-point hitch with cast buckle

Interchange Number: 57
Type: Standard
Part Number(s): 8706637 LH 8706636 RH
Usage: Late 1972 Chevelle, Cutlass, Skylark, Lemans convertible with bench seat
Notes: 3-point hitch with plastic buckle

Several different Belt manufacturers were used. Model# is the model of the belt at that manufacture. The date refers to the manufacture date This would be Jan 11, 1967. Date has little effect on the interchange. Make sure the buckle and the receiving belt are from the same manufacturer, or it may not attach properly.

A

Air Cleaner	48
Alternator	140
Ammeter	158
Arm Rests	266
Automatic Transmissions	75

B

Back Window, Glass	231
Battery Tray	142
Booster Chamber	124
Brake Drum	126
Brake Pedal Pad	130
Brake, Parking	131
Brake, Pedal	129
Bumper, Front	214
Bumper, Rear	215

C

Calipers	129
Caps, Styled Wheels	187
Carburetor	37
Carburetor, Carter	38
Carburetor, Holley	38
Carburetor, Rochester	37
Clock	163
Coil	138
Compartment, Glovebox	257
Compressor	149
Condenser	150
Connecting Rods	20
Console	264
Control Arms, Front	88
Convertible Top Switch	151
Crankshaft	17
Cylinder Block	11
cylinder heads	16
Cylinder Heads	24

D

Differential Case	118
Distributor Housing	134
Door Handle, Outside	202
Door Panels	266
Door Window, Glass	227
Door, Glovebox	258

Drive Shafts	112
Drum, brake	126

E

Emblem, Fender	243
Emblem, Front Header	242
Emblem, Grille	236
Emblem, Hood	242
Emblem, Rear End	250
Emblem, Rear Quarter	246
Emblem, Tailgate	250
Engine	11
Exhaust Manifolds	65

F

Flywheels	21
Frame	85
Frame, inspecting	86
Front Doors	197
Front Fenders	193
Front Springs, Coil	89
Fuel Gauge	159
Fuel Pump	30
Fuel Tank	30
Fuel Tanks	30

G

Gauge, gas	159
Gauges, Ammeter	158
Gauges, Oil Pressure	161
Gauges, Tachometer	155
Gauges, Temperature	162
Gearshift	78
Glass	224
Glass, Back Window	231
Glass, Door Window,	227
Glass, Quarter Window	229
Glass, Vent Window	226
Glass, Windshield	225
Glovebox, Door	258
Grille	209
Guages, Speedometer	153

H

Handle, Inside Door	261
Handle, Outside Door	202
Handle, Window Regulator	262

Headlamp, Switch	164
Heater Core	149
Heater Motor	148
Hinges, Front Door	202
Hinges, Hood	192
Hinges, Tailgate	208
Hinges, Trunk Lid	207
Hood	189
Horns	150

I

Ignition Coil	138
Instrument Panel	256
Intake Manifold	33

L

Lamps, Back Up	175
Lamps, Dome	177
Lamps, Front Parking	165
Lamps, Side Marker	169
Lamps, Taillights	171

M

Manifolds, Exhaust	65
Master Cylinder	121
Mirror, Inside	234
Mirror, Outside	232
Molding, Drip Rail	218
Molding, Quarter Belt	218
Molding, Rear Window	221
Molding, rocker	219
Molding, Wheel Lip	220
Molding, Windshield	216
Moldings	216
Motor, Power Window	152
Motor, starter	132
Motor, Windshield Wiper	143
Motor. Heater	148

O

Oil Pan	56
Oil Pressure, gauge	161
Oil Pump	55

P

Pad, Brake Pedal	130
Parking Brake	131
Pedal, Brake	129
Power Steering Pump	102
Power Window Motor	152
Pump, oil	55
Pump, Power Steering	102

Q

Quarter Belt Molding	218
Quarter Panel	204
Quarter Window, Glass	229

R

Radiator	56
Rear Axle, Axle Shafts	120
Rear Axle, Identification	114
REAR AXLE, INTERCHANGE	118
Rear Springs, Coil	95
Rear Window Molding	221
Rocker Arm	27
Rocker Molding	219
Rocker Panel	203
Roof	203
Roof, Folding	204

S

Seat Adjustment Rails	269
Seat Belts, Front	272
Seat Frame	270
Shift Patterns and Indicators	82
Short Block	13
Short Block Testing	16
Signal Lever	151
Skirts, Front Fenders	196
Sorings, front	89
Speedometer	153
Springs, Hood Hinge	192
springs, rear	95
Starter	132
Steering Column	108
Steering Gearbox	99
Steering Knuckle	97
Steering Wheel	103
Sun Visor	258
Support Wall, Radiator	196
Sway Bar, Front	97
Switch, Convertible Top	151
Switch, headlamp	164
Switch, Windshield Wiper	146

T

Tachometer 155
Tailgate 206
Temperature Gauge 162
Transmission 69
Transmission, Casting Numbers 71
Transmission, manual interchange 72
Transmissions, Automatic intechanges 75
Transmissions, manual 69
Trim Rings 188
Trunk, Lid 206

V

Valve Covers 28
Vent Window, Glass 226
VIN Tag 6

W

Wheel Lip Moldings 220
Wheel, steering 103
Wheels 179
Wheels Covers 183
Wheels, Five Spoke 179
Wheels, Rally 179
Wheels, SS 179
Wheels, Stamped Steel 179
Windshield 225
Windshield Molding 216
Windshield Washer Jar 145
Windshield Wiper Motor 143
Windshield Wiper, Linkage 146
Windshield Wiper, Switch 146

www.ingramcontent.com/pod-product-compliance
Lightning Source LLC
Chambersburg PA
CBHW081347230426
43667CB00017B/2753